The Return of the God of Wealth

The Transition to a Market Economy
in Urban China

The Return
of the God
# of Wealth

The Transition to a Market
Economy in Urban China

Charlotte Ikels

Stanford University Press
STANFORD, CALIFORNIA

Stanford University Press, Stanford, California

© 1996 by the Board of Trustees of the Leland Stanford Junior University

Printed in the United States of America

CIP data appear at the end of the book

Stanford University Press publications are distributed exclusively by Stanford University Press within the United States, Canada, Mexico, and Central America; they are distributed exclusively by Cambridge University Press throughout the rest of the world.

For Ezra

| *Acknowledgments*

The research on which this book is based could not have been undertaken and sustained without the moral, logistical, and financial support of numerous individuals, institutions, and organizations. As indicated in the Introduction, three lengthy and several shorter field trips to Guangzhou provided the necessary opportunities for data collection. In 1980 my husband, Ezra F. Vogel, received a research scholar grant from the Committee for Scholarly Communication with the People's Republic of China (CSCPRC) to conduct research in Guangzhou, where his sponsoring unit at the time was Zhongshan University. I went along as a humble spouse but was nevertheless treated as a genuine scholar by the university administration, which attempted to facilitate my own work on residents committees and the elderly. Unfortunately, there was little local interest in the topic of aging at the time, and the fruits of my research were limited and disappointing.

In the mid-1980s two fortuitous events occurred. The first was the establishment of a sister province relationship between Massachusetts and Guangdong that resulted in several opportunities to host visiting delegations from Guangdong. Provincial officials were amazed to learn that my husband spoke *putonghua*, the official national language, while I spoke Cantonese, the provincial (unofficial) language. They thought we had chosen this division of labor on purpose. The second fortuitous event was the arrival at the Fairbank Center (Harvard University) of Zhang Lei, the Director of the Guangdong Academy of Social Sciences (GASS). In a chat with him I happened to mention that I was especially interested in gerontology. His face lit up. China, it turned out, had become very interested in aging since our 1980 stay. The 1982 national census had revealed that China's population was rapidly aging, and many officials and scholars were charged with considering the impact of this fact on China's economic development. Zhang Lei urged me to come to Guangzhou under the sponsorship of the provincial academy's Population Research Institute, directed by Liu Xiaotong. Eventually these good personal relationships resulted in our second lengthy stay in Guangzhou, in 1987, when my husband was hosted by the Provincial Economic Commission and I by GASS, though I too was taken under the wing of Yang Mai, the Deputy Director of the Economic Commission.

My research in 1987 was very successful; the Guangzhou city government gave its official approval to my project so that the lower administrative echelons did not have to worry about the propriety or the consequences of letting a foreigner spend weeks trooping the lanes of their jurisdictions and interviewing a random sample of their households. The staff of the two street committees and of their six residents committees gave me assistance above and beyond the call of duty, tolerating my peculiar interviewing hours, which did not acknowledge the Chinese long lunch hour and frequently extended well beyond the official end of the workday. In addition, they as well as my colleagues from GASS voluntarily took over the interviews when my voice faltered or, unbelievably, a non-Cantonese speaker turned up in the sample.

In 1991 I returned to the two neighborhoods, this time as a CSCPRC research scholar myself, to reinterview the original 200 households. The success of the residents committees staff in accounting for all 200 of the original households is mute testimony to both their diligence and the close-knit nature of old Chinese urban neighborhoods. Besides accompanying me daily on the interviews, my colleagues at GASS in both 1987 and 1991 not only arranged many interviews with officials in various city and provincial government offices, as well as tours of homes for the aged and hospitals, but also welcomed me into their lives. For this I am especially grateful to Guan Xiufang, Zheng Zizhen, Deng Ying, and Xiao Tsang.

Additional support, both logistical and moral, was amply provided during all three of my lengthy fieldwork stays by the officers and staff of the U.S. Consulate in Guangzhou under the direction of Consuls General Richard Williams, Mark Pratt, and Dennis Harter. In the United States many thanks go to Nancy Hearst of the Fairbank Center library at Harvard, whose collection of city and provincial yearbooks helped fill in the gaps in my data, and to Gong Xiaoxia for her help in translating "Li Dongdong's" advice column in *Nanfang Ribao*. For editorial assistance I am grateful to Ellen F. Smith and Stephanie Fay. And, finally, special thanks go to my husband, Ezra F. Vogel, to whom this book is dedicated, for his willingness to share Guangzhou.

C.I.

Contents

A Note on Language   xiii

Introduction   1
1 | The City of Guangzhou   7
2 | Living Standards   54
3 | Family and Household   97
4 | Education   140
5 | Employment   177
6 | Leisure Activities   222
Conclusion   263

Notes   273
References   297
Index   305

Photo sections follow pages 96 and 176.

| Maps, Tables, and Figures

| Maps

1. The Inner Pearl River Delta, Guangdong Province   xiv
2. Guangzhou City, 1995   xv

| Tables

1.1. Population, Area, and Density of Guangzhou Administrative Divisions, 1993   25
2.1. Urban Monthly Per Capita Living Expenditures for Guangzhou, 1980–92, and for China, 1987   75
2.2. Urban Monthly Per Capita Living Expenditures, by Percentages, in China, 1987, and Guangzhou, 1987 and 1990   76
2.3. Number of Durable Goods per 100 Urban Households in Guangzhou, 1980–93, and in China, 1987   77
2.4. Circumstances of Household Moves in Guangzhou, January 1988 to January 1991   91
3.1. Living Arrangement of Elderly by Sex, in Percentage, in Guangzhou, 1987   130
3.2. Living Arrangement of Elderly by Sex of Child, in Percentage, in Guangzhou, 1987   131
5.1. New Workers in State Work Units in Urban Districts of Guangzhou, 1990   191
5.2. Average Monthly Wages by Ownership System in Urban Areas of Guangdong, 1990   196
5.3. Reasons for Leaving State Work Units in Urban Districts of Guangzhou, 1990   216
5.4. Work Force Entries and Exits, by Sector, for Households in Guangzhou, January 1988 to January 1991   217

| Figures

1. A Housing Management Bureau unit of 7.5 square meters   80
2. Two floors of an overseas Chinese house   81
3. An apartment in new housing constructed by a real estate development corporation   82

A Note on Language

Standard Chinese (*putonghua*) terms are romanized in pinyin. Cantonese terms (used when I know no *putonghua* equivalent) are romanized using the Yale system and are identified as Cantonese by a *C.* in parentheses. All translations from *putonghua* and Cantonese are my own unless otherwise noted.

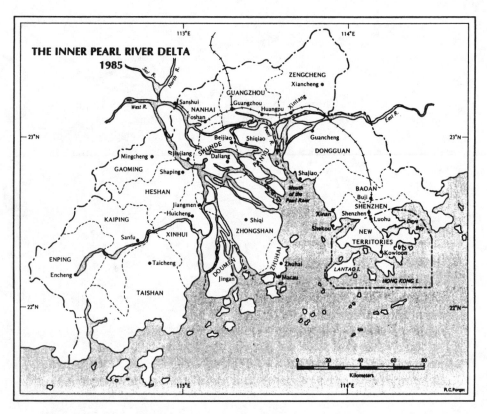

Map 1. The Inner Pearl River Delta, Guangdong province. From Ezra Vogel, *One Step Ahead in China: Guangdong Under Reform* (Cambridge, Mass.: Harvard University Press, 1989), p. 130; reproduced by permission.

Map 2. Guangzhou City, 1995. Adapted from Ezra Vogel, *One Step Ahead in China: Guangdong Under Reform* (Cambridge, Mass.: Harvard University Press, 1989), p. 199.

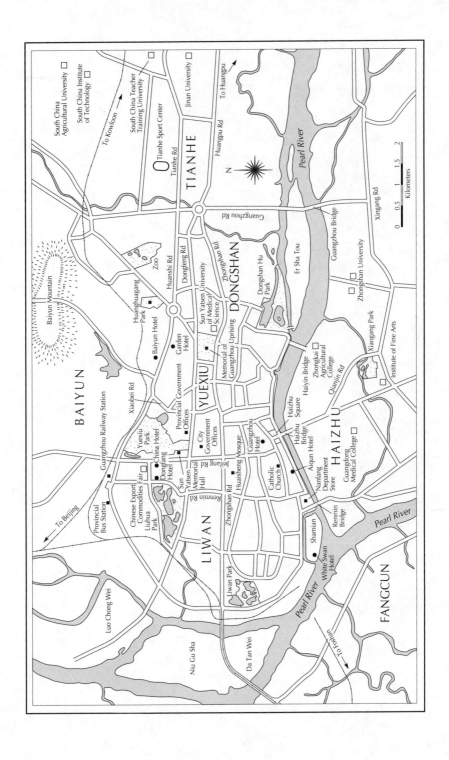

The Return of the God of Wealth

The Transition to a Market Economy
in Urban China

Introduction

Nowadays, when people who have not been in China for ten or more years return to visit family and friends, they are usually astounded by the wealth, liveliness, and even chaos that characterize contemporary urban life. Scholars brought up on Martin Whyte and William Parish's 1984 work, *Urban Life in Contemporary China*, which describes life during the Maoist era, cannot believe their eyes. Where, they ask, did those ration shops and long lines go? Where did all these bright clothes and motor vehicles come from? Do ordinary folk really live in these ten-story apartment buildings? Can those be girlie magazines at the same streetside stall as *Renmin Ribao* (People's Daily)? Such startling changes are only the most visible of the remarkable transformations China's cities have been undergoing for at least a decade and a half since China began to reform its national economy. The purpose of this work is to introduce the reader to contemporary urban life and to examine how the many reforms have brought about changes not only in the material circumstances of life but also in the overall well-being of urban residents, their family life, education, experience of the workplace, and leisure pursuits.

When the Chinese government officially embarked on the reform of its economic system in 1978, two years after the death of Mao Zedong, it lacked a strong theoretical basis to justify shifting from a strictly centrally planned economy to a "commodity" economy. The government maintained that the anticipated reforms would not contravene Marxist theory but rather would help to adapt socialism to the special circumstances found in China; that is, ideologically speaking, the reforms would allow the development of "socialism with Chinese characteristics." The thorough disenchantment of most party members—to say nothing of virtually the entire

Chinese public—with the highly politicized atmosphere of the Cultural Revolution (1966–76) played no small role in this temporary willingness to downplay ideology. Thus, instead of justifying its actions ideologically, the central government focused first on resolving concrete economic problems (e.g., rural underemployment, urban unemployment, shortages of consumer goods, and inefficiency in state enterprises), tackling these problems with whatever methods seemed likely to work. Using such dicta as "Practice is the only criterion of truth" and "It doesn't matter whether the cat is black or white so long as it catches mice," the Communist Party leaders in Beijing put ideology on the sidelines and concentrated on "enlivening" the economy.

As reform "deepened" and as private markets flourished, "individual households" (private entrepreneurs) became wealthy, and foreign investment flowed into the country, however, those worried about the direction China was taking began to ask awkward questions. These questions (Isn't this leading to a restoration of capitalism? Wasn't the Communist revolution fought to free China of foreign influence?) required answers, and at the Thirteenth Party Congress in late 1987, the reformers came up with an innovative reinterpretation of Marxist theory. China was said to be in the "initial stage of socialism," when it was neither necessary nor desirable for all productive forces to be under state control. Although it is true, they argued, that socialism will inevitably succeed capitalism, China had made a mistake by leaping prematurely into the later stages of socialism (characterized by state and collective, but excluding private, ownership of the means of production) before capitalism itself had been adequately developed. Permitting the private sector to develop more fully now was merely a corrective. As to the question of foreign influence, the situation prior to 1949 was said to be totally different from the current situation. Then imperialists had imposed themselves on China and dictated how its economy would develop; now foreigners are invited to China by the people themselves and invest their funds under guidelines developed by a sovereign Chinese government.

Whether anyone was convinced by these arguments is difficult to know. In any case, despite occasional stalls and even temporary reversals, as in the late 1980s when inflation got out of hand and political stability seemed threatened, China's move away from a centrally planned economy has continued. State enterprises have struggled to become more efficient: by requiring newcomers to the urban labor force to sign time-limited contracts; by attempting to shed their many social welfare roles; by easing excess employees into off-plan subsidiary factories, shops, and restaurants; and by contracting out to independent managers almost complete responsibility and power for making decisions. In fact, under this contract system so much power was transferred to managers that many questioned whether these enterprises could any longer be considered state enterprises at all.

To deal with such questions the party in the winter of 1992–93 reformulated its rationale for the various economic reforms. It stated forthrightly that its objective was to create a "socialist market economy." Theorists carefully explained away the seeming oxymoron of a market economy that is socialist at the same time. The essence of a socialist economy, they pointed out, is ownership of the means of production, not management of the means of production. So long as the state remains the owner of the means of production, it does not really matter who is responsible for running the factories, utilities, or airlines. To make this point even clearer, state enterprises now are referred to in the media not as *guoying* (state-operated) but as *guoyou* (national) enterprises.

It is difficult to believe that the reformers set out in 1978 to create a socialist market economy in China. The theoretical justifications strike one as ad hoc and after-the-fact rationalizations of the outcomes (expected or otherwise) of various pragmatic decisions. And not all policy outcomes were especially desired or easy to justify theoretically. For example, an important element of the early reforms was the "opening up" to the outside with the objective of attracting foreign investment. But as Deng Xiaoping put it, "When you open the door, flies come in." Those opposed to the reformers' goals see these "flies" (said to include everything from pornography and "spiritual pollution" to foreign political efforts to overthrow the Communist government) as too great a threat to the country's moral fiber to accept passively. Consequently, though the masses have been left relatively undisturbed in their quest to make money, the party has launched periodic campaigns to strengthen the ideological backbone of students and intellectuals as well as party members.

Similarly, not all economic outcomes of the post-1978 reforms are viewed favorably. Increases in crime and corruption (when not blamed on external influences) are attributed directly to unequal access to the benefits of the reforms, and the growing gap in income between different segments of the urban population is feared as a source of political instability. To deal with these problems the government has relied on both a mix of deterrents (tough talk and a willingness to employ capital punishment) and the construction of a safety net for those who lose their jobs or are forced to seek employment in the less prosperous sectors of the economy.

On balance, however, the Chinese government is determined to continue its transition from a centrally planned economy to a (socialist) market economy. Even opponents of the reforms realize that the Chinese public is unlikely to accept the restoration of the controls on labor mobility that characterized the Mao era. In early 1992 paramount leader Deng Xiaoping made a tour of southern Guangdong province, where the reforms have been in effect the longest and, arguably, have changed the face of China the most, and pronounced what he saw "good." This cryptic analysis set off another round of hyperinvestment and inflation, followed in the summer of 1993 by a brief attempt to restrict the availability of bank loans to cool down the economy. Such an approach—two steps forward, one step back—seems likely to extend indefinitely into the future.

This brief account of the post-Mao economic reforms is intended merely as an overview of their impact at the national level. The chapters that follow examine specific reforms and the changes they have brought about, analyzing their impact on individuals. The most productive way to carry out this task is to concentrate on a single site and its inhabitants and to follow local developments over an extended period. Because I am an urban anthropologist and am especially interested in the impact of these reforms on daily life in urban China, I have chosen Guangzhou (Canton), the capital of Guangdong province, as the site of my research.

Guangzhou is China's sixth largest city, and it is the hub of the Pearl River Delta, the region of China that was first given permission to open to the outside. Guangzhou has taken the lead in introducing many of the urban reforms that subsequently were adopted by the central government and extended to all of China's cities. How much one can safely generalize from my findings in Guangzhou to the rest of urban China is an interesting question. Skeptics will argue that Guangzhou is exceptional, that its proximity to Hong Kong and the high proportion of its residents with relatives living abroad have so thoroughly exposed it to alternatives to socialism that what is possible in Guangzhou is not necessarily possible (or even thinkable) elsewhere in China. There is some truth to this view; it is undeniable that Guangzhou has benefited enormously from investment from Hong Kong and overseas Chinese and that other regions of China are unlikely to benefit to the same degree. It is also true that because of a common language (to say nothing of proximity) residents of Guangzhou can more readily access Hong Kong media than residents of other parts of China and can thereby acquire a different perspective on China itself.

Yet this focus on Guangzhou's uniqueness overlooks a number of other important facts. First, most cities in China have their own distinctive characteristics. Who would argue, for example, that Beijing or Shanghai or Lhasa or Huhhot, for that matter, is typical of most Chinese cities? Second, from the time the People's Republic of China was established (1949), Guangzhou has been subject to national policies as much as any other urban area. It implemented the restrictive household registration system, abolished the private sector, organized street offices and residents committees, sent its youth to the countryside, carried out the Cultural Revolution, enforced the one-child family policy, and so forth. For the last decade and a half it has been implementing Beijing's economic reform policy. Almost no cities outside China have adopted any of these policies. A third reason for focusing on Guangzhou is that we already have a valuable body of background information from Ezra Vogel (*Canton Under Communism: Programs and Politics in a Provincial Capital, 1949–1968*, 1969, and *One Step Ahead in China: Guangdong Under Reform*, 1989), detailing the evolution of economic policy in the region over nearly 40 years. No other locality in China has been scrutinized so closely. My own work departs from Vogel's in its explicit focus on individual experience of the economic reforms.

My data for this book derive from three extended research stays in Guangzhou as well as from several shorter visits over a fifteen-year period. I visited the city first in late 1979 and most recently in the summer of 1994. In 1980 I spent three months on the campus of Zhongshan University and acquired my baseline perceptions of what life in Guangzhou was like at that time. In 1987, with the Guangdong Academy of Social Sciences as my host unit, I returned for seven months of highly focused research on the elderly and their families. At that time I interviewed a random sample of 200 households (100 each in two neighborhoods) in which at least one person was 70 years of age or older, asking about a wide variety of topics. (Illustrations or findings in the text described as from the Guangzhou Family Study are based on interviews with these households.) In 1991, with a grant from the Committee for Scholarly Communication with the PRC, I returned to the same unit and the same households for another five months of interviewing. As a Cantonese speaker I also had ready access to other populations. Thus I could test out my ideas or seek clarification from local researchers, policymakers, and professional colleagues as well as from people encountered in restaurants, shops, and hotels and from taxi drivers and seatmates on the bus. Over the years I also came to know many individuals independent of the sample households who shared their personal experiences and opinions with me. Their stories too are recounted here, though details are sometimes changed to assure their anonymity.

Another major source of data for this book is the mass media, especially television. Nearly every household in Guangzhou has access to television. I regularly watched the most popular programs to understand what the authorities considered appropriate fare for the viewing audience and tried to learn what the audience thought of the various programs. Since my last long stay in 1991 I have followed events in Guangzhou through the local newspapers (as well as through three short visits, in 1992, 1993, and 1994). I have also tried to keep up with publications by American (and other) scholars working on the same general topic.

In the pages ahead I attempt to give the reader an understanding of contemporary urban life and to interpret it in relation to changes brought about by the post-Mao reforms. I begin each chapter with a brief description of life in Guangzhou before the economic reforms; next I describe the reforms, their implementation, and their outcomes; and finally I present the experiences and views of urban residents themselves as they face the transition from a planned economy to a (socialist) market economy. The sequence of the chapters is designed to introduce the reader to the particular setting of Guangzhou (Chapter 1) and then to move from the most general topic, the material circumstances of contemporary urban life (Chapter 2), to the more detailed topics of the family (Chapter 3), school (Chapter 4), workplace (Chapter 5), and leisure activities (Chapter 6). All these substantive chapters include national, local, and individual data so that the reader acquires an integrated view of the reforms and their outcomes. The Conclusion reviews the findings of the preceding chapters and evaluates their impact on the overall well-being of Guangzhou's residents.

1 | *The City of Guangzhou*

This chapter introduces the city of Guangzhou — the physical characteristics, history, and cultural features that make it distinctive. The discussion that follows begins with the China-wide features of the urban administrative hierarchy and the waning significance of the household (*hukou*) registration system that since 1958 has rigidly differentiated the urban from the rural population. It goes on to examine the most public aspects of urban life — those a resident is exposed to daily and that a visitor becomes aware of after only a few days — norms of hygiene and courtesy, the resolution of public disputes, sexual harassment, and issues of personal security. Finally, the focus shifts to the role of the smallest unit of urban administration, the street committee (or ward), and its impact on neighborhood life.

The Setting

Guangzhou's location on the southeast coast of China, far from the imperial palace and the ministries of the central government, has contributed to the development of a distinctive regional subculture. This Cantonese subculture, although Han Chinese in nature,* nevertheless shows marked vari-

---

* Historically "Han Chinese" has designated the descendants of the population that originated in the Yellow River Valley of north China, the area considered the "cradle of Chinese civilization," who eventually spread throughout the eastern half of the country, displacing or assimilating the indigenous populations. In its current official usage within China, "Han Chinese" refers to the numerically dominant nationality (ethnic group) that constitutes approximately 93 percent of the country's population. This nationality speaks standard Chinese (*putonghua*) or one of its regional variants as its native language. For a fuller discussion of regional and ethnic variation within China, especially as it affects Cantonese self-perceptions, see Friedman 1994 and Gladney 1994.

ations from the Beijing standard and manifests itself in such diverse arenas as diet, language, and the receptiveness of the local population to influences from outside China. These differences, recognized and readily remarked upon by residents of both Guangzhou and other parts of China, have played a role in the genesis of regional stereotypes.

The Physical Environment

Guangzhou sits astride the Tropic of Cancer at about the same latitude as Honolulu and Mexico City. Unlike those two cities, however, Guangzhou is protected by neither ocean waters nor high altitude from the brutal heat of the tropical sun. The mean annual temperature in the city proper is normally around 70–71° F., with daily highs regularly in the upper 80s or 90s four or five months of the year. The mean annual relative humidity is close to 80 percent, but during the hottest months it is several percentage points higher. This unrelenting combination of heat and humidity easily explains the residents' nearly insatiable demand for electric fans (and, increasingly, for air conditioners) as well as their heightened sense of anticipation when a thunderstorm or typhoon, certain to move the air around, is predicted. Because of the general lack of indoor heating (even schools and day-care centers are unheated) Guangzhou's mild winters are locally perceived as cold; a January outdoor temperature in the 40s or low 50s is usually matched indoors. A reluctance to suffocate in coal smoke while cooking forces residents of older housing to keep their windows open a good part of the day. Thus most people, especially those not engaged in physical activity—for example, schoolchildren and the elderly—wear several layers of clothing during the winter months. Residents of newer housing with superior electrical wiring are just beginning to acquire electric space heaters like those used in Hong Kong.

With the exception of Yuexiu Park in the northern part of Yuexiu district, most of the core city is flat. The highest point near the older districts of the city is White Cloud (Baiyun) Mountain, which stands 383 meters above sea level. The name derives from the clouds that frequently shroud the mountain's summit as cold winds from the north meet warmer winds coming up from the south. Because much of the land east of White Cloud Mountain is semiprotected secondary-growth forest, urban growth has been restricted to the north and channeled instead toward the east. The oldest settled parts of the city are on the north bank of the Pearl River. Over the centuries the river has deposited so much silt that its channel has narrowed substantially; sites located almost on the water's edge during the Tang Dynasty (A.D. 618–907) now sit high and dry a mile inland. Despite this silting the Pearl River and its main tributary, the West River, which is navigable well into Guangxi, have long been major transport routes into the interior of the country, and for centuries Guangzhou has been, albeit with interruptions, an important port for both domestic and foreign merchants.

Guangzhou's mild climate, abundant rainfall, and access to rivers and the sea have meant that all kinds of food are available year-round. No mounds of hardy cabbages need be trucked into the city to provide residents with vitamins in the winter, for farm-fresh vegetables can be purchased at every season. Two crops of rice per year, and in some areas even three, are commonly planted. The national perception of the quality of Cantonese cuisine is captured by the popular saying "For eating it's Guangzhou." What both locals and outsiders most appreciate is the freshness of the food, especially the seafood. Most Cantonese dislike purchasing fish or fowl that is not still breathing at the time of the sale. To enhance one's appreciation of this freshness, food tends to be lightly cooked and lightly spiced. Foreigners are frequently taken aback by the traces of still pink flesh in an order of chicken or by the firm flesh of a steamed fish. Cantonese, for their part, view American overcooking with dismay.*

Cantonese are aware that outsiders, even within China, do not eagerly embrace every item of Cantonese food. They mock the more timid eating habits of other Chinese by asserting that while "Shandong people do anything and Beijing people endure anything, Cantonese people eat anything!" The true test of manly (or womanly) courage for a visitor to Guangzhou is to have a meal at the Snake Food Restaurant. This restaurant, which dates back to the beginning of the century, is famous for such delights as deep-fried fresh snake and cat, chicken, and snake soup (euphemistically known as tiger-phoenix-dragon soup). In fact, during the winter shredded-snake soup is likely to be on the menu of almost any restaurant because snake meat, like dog meat, is regarded as especially nourishing in cold weather. The association of particular foods, both animal and vegetable, with good health has a long history in China. In 1991 I was surprised to find that one of the households in the Family Study that had kept cats in 1987 had acquired a hedgehog. I thought this a most unusual pet until I learned that

---

* This fastidiousness leads to great discomfort for Cantonese living abroad, where they must usually purchase dressed or cut-up chickens and fish from supermarkets. What many people in the United States consider "fresh" fish is considered inedible in Guangzhou. In 1991 when I invited several friends to the Western buffet at the China Hotel (one of the fanciest in the city), I inadvertently chose the night that featured seafood. My guests assured me that this was absolutely the right thing to do because seafood is considered superior to other dishes. Though they sampled dutifully, I could not help noticing the little mounds of rejects that accumulated on their plates. The reason: "Not fresh." Similarly, when the host of a provincial delegation to Boston ordered fish at a fancy seafood restaurant overlooking Boston Harbor, a member of the delegation told me, "It was truly splendid looking, but when we went to eat it, we found that it was overcooked. It was totally ruined! We didn't know what to say."

the hedgehog had been purchased for its medicinal value. An adult daughter suffered from unpredictable swings in temperature that the hedgehog was destined to remedy. The immediate problem, however, was how to kill the prickly animal.

Visitors to Guangzhou frequently tour the market at Qingping Road (in Liwan district across the river from Shamian) to observe the wide array of unusual animals intended for medicinal consumption, but one need not go to a specialty market to procure such creatures, for people from the countryside come into the city whenever they make a suitable capture. In 1992, for example, I observed a man on Xiaobei Road asking 400 yuan for a badger. Similarly, a few days earlier and just a few hundred yards away I had encountered a man squatting along Huanshi Road periodically tugging at a string attached to the legs of two small owls, which hopped and stretched their wings whenever he did so. A woman with a baby strapped to her front came along and asked the price. Despite helpful bargaining tips offered by an observer ("They're awfully thin"), the woman purchased them both without further ado.

Guangzhou has a steady supply of vegetables and fruits. In China generally fruit is considered a high-status food; it is offered to guests and completes even the fanciest meal. Litchis, or lichees, from Zengcheng county (one of Guangzhou's four constituent counties) were regularly sent as gifts to the Chinese emperor. No doubt the perishability of most fruits contributed to their reputation as a luxury food. Even as recently as 1980 there was only a limited supply of fresh fruit available in Guangzhou city proper because grain production was still being emphasized, and specialized fruit-producing communes in the suburbs were sending most of their fresh products to Hong Kong or exporting preserved fruits overseas. For rural growers to transport fresh fruit by bicycle into the city in the hot sun of a Guangzhou summer was to invite almost instant spoilage. At that time watermelons were the only local fruit found in any kind of abundance.

With the shift in agricultural production from production teams to households in the early 1980s, more and more farmers began to specialize in raising fruit. Consequently, by the mid-1980s the markets were nearly saturated with fruits: many varieties of orange, tangerine, and banana as well as mangoes, litchis, longans (dragon's eyes), carambola (star fruit), and papayas and pineapples, originally from the Americas. Watermelons remain a perennial favorite. As soon as they come into season, in June, the city tolerates a large influx of growers who simply pile a truckload of watermelons on a bed of straw directly on the sidewalk. Each grower stays for several days, sitting or sleeping — day and night, rain or shine — beside his mound of watermelons until they are sold off or beyond selling. This lengthy digression into Cantonese food does not reflect a mere quirk of the writer; rather it is a direct consequence of spending time in Guangzhou, where food is a topic of pride and, shall we say, consuming interest to the local population.

Historical Background

Two symbols, one historic and the other modern, are closely associated with the city of Guangzhou. The ancient one is the ram, which has given Guangzhou its alternative name, Yangcheng (City of Rams); the more modern one is the red flower (*hongmian*) of the kapok (a kind of cotton-wood) tree. According to legend Guangzhou has a history of over 2,800 years. In 887 B.C., during the reign of King Yi of the Zhou Dynasty, five immortals flew to Guangzhou on the backs of five rams, each ram holding a sheaf of grain in its mouth. This event, which signified that the local population would subsequently enjoy rich harvests, is commemorated by a statue of the five rams (which actually look more like goats) in Yuexiu Park in the heart of the city. The ram name and motif are widely used in Guangzhou. For example, one of the three daily newspapers is the *Ram City Evening News* (*Yangcheng Wanbao*), and a huge new housing development in the easternmost section of Dongshan district is named Five Rams New Village. During the 1987 Sixth National Games, held in Guangzhou's brand-new Olympic-class stadium in Tianhe district, a Disneyesque cartoon ram was pressed into service as the ubiquitous symbol of the games. This cute little guy could be seen in pictures all over the city, dressed in various athletic costumes as he lifted weights, ran, jumped, or carried the torch to ignite the flame that officially opened the games. Since 1987 he has served as an inspiration for civic-minded behavior; for example, on posters he is pictured cheerfully dropping litter into receptacles rather than onto the street.

The origin of the *hongmian* as the official city flower dates back only to 1983.[1] At that time it was picked to represent the city because of its brilliant red color, said to reflect Guangzhou's history of patriotic and revolutionary martyrs.[2] In the late spring kapok trees (they are not, in fact, very common in Guangzhou) are almost entirely covered with these bright red flowers. Knowledgeable local residents, mostly middle-aged or older women, who have scouted out the trees in advance, await the first heavy rain of the season and rush out early the next morning to gather the flowers that have fallen to the ground. The salvaged *hongmian* are then threaded and strung into the equivalent of a Hawaiian lei (though unlike the flowers of a lei they are not considered ornaments but medicinal plants) and are immediately hung out to dry. Later in the summer the dried blossoms become one of the ingredients in a healthful soup or tonic that protects the body against the effects of the heat. In a less traditional vein the official logo of Guangdong Television consists of a television broadcasting tower emerging from the center of a *hongmian* — an apt symbol since kapok trees are relatively conspicuous in Yuexiu Park, the site of the tower. In addition, a large stylized *hongmian* ornaments the tail of planes belonging to China Southern Airlines, the regional carrier. Finally, the city government has a stock of tiny red *hongmian* pins that its representatives carry with them on trips abroad for distribution at official and semiofficial gatherings.

Settlement of the Guangzhou area actually predates the legendary arrival of the five immortals by several millennia.[3] As early as 5000 B.C. Neolithic sites were scattered throughout the Guangdong and Fujian coastal areas and extended even to Taiwan. Prior to about the eighth century B.C. Guangdong province was inhabited by non-Han populations of Miao, Li, and Yao. Now deemed national minorities, these peoples were gradually forced out of the most desirable agricultural areas to mountainous areas in northwestern Guangdong and on Hainan Island. (Previously a part of Guangdong, Hainan was made an independent province in 1988.) In the eighth century B.C. migrants from the Yangzi River Valley are thought to have brought settled agriculture to the region. The preponderant population, however, was the Zhuang, a Thai people still found in large numbers in Guangxi. In 214 B.C. the founder of the Qin Dynasty (221–206 B.C.) unified China for the first time and established Nanhai prefecture, with its walled seat in Guangzhou. Over the centuries the city walls surrounding the prefectural government buildings were gradually extended until by the late Qing (A.D. 1644–1911) the whole of what is now Yuexiu district was enclosed. To this day both the city and the provincial government headquarters continue to be located within Yuexiu district, though the Municipal Planning Bureau envisions an eventual relocation of the city government to Tianhe district.

During the Qin and Han (206 B.C–A.D. 220) Dynasties many Han Chinese moved to Guangzhou and assimilated the Zhuang, but during most periods large migrations were relatively infrequent, for Guangzhou was separated from the north by mountains, and overland travel was by foot. But Guangzhou's location at the head of the Pearl River Delta made it easily accessible to foreign traders coming by sea. As the first Chinese city encountered by merchants arriving from the Indian Ocean, Guangzhou soon came to be known as the chief port on the Silk Road of the Sea. During the Tang Dynasty Arab traders came regularly to Guangzhou, and the vestiges of these visits are still apparent in western Yuexiu district in an area adjacent to what was, until the early years of this century, the main west gate to the city. Guangzhou's only self-consciously Muslim restaurant (i.e., serving no pork) is located here at the junction of Zhongshan and Renmin Roads. Just three blocks east stands the Huaisheng Mosque, built, it is said, by the first person to preach Islam in China. This man persuaded some Arab merchants already resident in Guangzhou to donate funds to build the mosque, which is over 1,300 years old. The original structure burned down during the Yuan Dynasty (A.D. 1279–1368) but was eventually rebuilt. Adjacent to the mosque is the so-called Guangta Pagoda, which in fact is designed more like a minaret than a pagoda. When it was constructed, the mosque was situated on the north bank of the Pearl River (which now flows a mile to the south), and for navigational safety a lamp had to be lighted at the top of the pagoda every night. This light and/or the smooth-sidedness of the structure account for its name, *guang*, meaning either "bright" or "smooth," and *ta*, meaning "tower."

The current number of Chinese Muslims (the Hui, not to be confused with Turkic or other minority Muslims such as recent migrants from Xinjiang, in far northwest China) living in Guangzhou is not high — on the order of 6,000, according to officials at the Hui Nationality elementary school. This school, located a few blocks east of Huaisheng Mosque, was founded in 1929 by the mosque and originally taught both Arabic and Chinese; it is now run by the Municipal Education Bureau and follows the standard curriculum. In 1991 only 150 out of 945 students at the school were of Hui nationality. Out of deference to Hui beliefs and practices the school cafeteria does not serve pork, and students and teachers of Hui nationality need not come to school on two Islamic holy days. This historically Muslim area is the location of one of the two neighborhoods included in the Family Study, but no Hui household appears in the sample (though there were a very few in the sampling frame).

During the Northern Song Dynasty (A.D. 960–1127) communication between Guangzhou and the interior of China was improved by the rebuilding of one road over the mountains and by the construction of a plank road along a gorge on the North River (a major tributary of the Pearl). Guangzhou's sea trade began to slacken, however, by the time of the Southern Song (A.D. 1127–1279), which established its capital at Hangzhou in Zhejiang province, when merchants found it more convenient to conduct trade through ports in Fujian province. Trade declined precipitously after the twelfth century as turmoil in the Middle East weakened the Arabs' capacity to organize long trading voyages. Despite official prohibitions against sea trade during the Ming Dynasty (A.D. 1368–1644), Chinese merchant ships from Fujian continued to trade with Southeast Asia and the East Indies, even setting up local communities of overseas Chinese merchants in the various distant ports.

Not until the sixteenth century and the arrival of the Portuguese did Guangzhou's role as an international port slowly begin to revive. Although the Portuguese were forbidden to settle in Guangzhou, beginning in 1557 they were allowed to conduct their trade from a permanent base in Macao. In 1685 the Kangxi Emperor opened China's ports to foreigners, but in 1757, by which time the British had become the dominant European trading power, the Qianlong Emperor restricted European merchants to Guangzhou. Their trade was carefully regulated and had to be carried out through official government-approved agents, or *hong*, organized into a guild known as the *cohong*. Foreigners were forbidden to enter the walled city of Guangzhou and could live at specially designated areas known as "factories" (these were not manufacturing facilities) only during the trading season.

The Chinese exported silks, tea, furniture, and ceramics ("china") in exchange for silver, arms, and, increasingly, opium. Frustrations with the nature and procedures of the trade at Guangzhou built up on both sides and culminated in the Opium War of 1839–42. As a result of both the treaty ending this war and subsequent military actions, China was forced to open up first five, and eventually more than 80, ports to foreign trade. The European communities in these treaty ports acquired their own residential areas on islands or stretches of land separated from the Chinese population by a river, creek, or other waterway. In Guangzhou the foreigners congregated on Shamian, a sandy island in the Pearl River, immediately southwest of the walled city. Here, as in the other treaty ports, they laid out streets, built European-style residences, erected churches, and lived under the rule of officials from their own countries. The European presence in Guangzhou was never very large. According to Vogel, in 1932, when the number of foreign residents was near its height, there were no more than 894 foreigners out of a total population of over a million.[4]

But foreign residents were not the only source of foreign influence in Guangzhou. The city's long history of contact with the outside had provided opportunities for local people themselves to go abroad. As a result of trade and contacts with Christian missionaries, Cantonese (broadly understood as any Chinese from Guangdong province) were already in North America decades before the California Gold Rush.[5] The vast majority, however, came to the United States only with the Gold Rush, and they came disproportionately, though not exclusively, from the single county of Taishan on the southeast coast. In the nineteenth century Taishan lacked enough land to support its population; its agricultural output could feed its inhabitants for only four months of the year. Consequently, Taishan people were forced to look beyond agriculture to make their living. Because of the county's location on the coast, not far from the mouth of the Pearl River Delta, foreign vessels reached it easily. The people of Taishan learned quickly of the opportunities on the West Coast of North America and flocked to take advantage of them.

Taishan and the surrounding counties rapidly became rich because of the remittances sent back by the men working abroad. These men spent most of their adulthood in the United States but retired in late middle or old age to their home communities to enjoy the fruits of their labor. They built Western-style houses, contributed money to schools and other worthy local projects, and along with their children promptly became the prey of bandits and kidnappers when, in the wake of the Republican Revolution, public order broke down. Both absentee and returned migrants took two steps to protect their wealth and progeny. The first was to build multistory guardhouses and walled enclosures in their home villages. The second was to abandon the villages entirely and move their families to the greater security of Guangzhou. By the late 1920s whole areas in Dongshan district, east of the old city walls, which by then had been torn down, consisted of the relocated families of overseas Chinese. These families, which anticipated sending the younger generation abroad, valued education, especially the teaching of English, and in some cases even converted to Christianity. The second of the two neighborhoods in the Family Study is located in Dongshan district and includes many such overseas Chinese households.

When the Communists took over China in 1949, the position of foreigners and of Chinese identified with them underwent a total reversal. Foreigners fled or were expelled. Families of overseas Chinese advised their relatives to delay their return and urged them to exercise restraint when writing or sending articles. The Chinese government itself was ambivalent about these Chinese.[6] On the one hand, their association with foreigners and with foreign countries that were hostile to the Communist regime made their loyalty suspect. On the other hand, the remittances they attracted from abroad constituted a valuable source of foreign exchange to which the government wanted access.

The policy compromise was to deal with the families of overseas Chinese according to their official class background (e.g., as capitalists, landlords, rich peasants, etc.) and their political affiliation (e.g., as supporters of the Guomindang, Japanese collaborators, or Communist sympathizers). Once these issues had been dealt with, the government attempted to encourage the return of Chinese from abroad. A new residential area in Dongshan district that came to be known as Overseas Chinese New Village was set aside for the erection of private villa-style housing for their families. Not coincidentally, this site was adjacent to that of the Friendship Store, a relatively upscale department store originally open only to those able to make purchases with foreign currency (actually with certificates issued by the Chinese government in exchange for foreign currency). At the time of the Cultural Revolution, particularly during the rampages of the Red Guards in 1966–68, the families of overseas Chinese along with those of intellectuals became preferred targets because of their presumed fascination with ideas and things non-Chinese. Their houses were invaded, often repeatedly, and everything from the music of European composers to Western-style furniture was subject to confiscation or destruction.

Despite this ideological abhorrence of contact with the outside, nations establishing diplomatic relations with China were encouraged to come to trade. Throughout the period Guangzhou was host to the Chinese Export Commodities Fair (the Canton Trade Fair), held twice a year, at which factories from all over China exhibited their products. When in 1979 China began actively to solicit investment (as opposed to buyers or remittances) from abroad, overseas Chinese were high on the list of expected investors; the government attempted to make amends for previous injuries and, more important perhaps, to demonstrate a respect for private property rights. For example, housing space that had been confiscated or arbitrarily assigned to others was gradually restored during the 1980s to its original owners (the difficulties involved in implementing this policy are discussed in Chapter 2).

The transformation of the economy of Guangzhou (and, indeed, of Guangdong province as a whole) in the first decade following the post-Mao economic reforms is covered in detail by Vogel.[7] Here I note only a few points. First, Guangzhou has many faces. In addition to being an industrial and commercial city, it is also the seat of the provincial government and a major cultural center. The city and the province each operate their own television stations, located a little over a mile apart on Huanshi Road. While the provincial station relays the broadcasts of the two national stations (China Central Television, or CCTV), it also produces much of its own programming, which it then makes available for sale or exchange with other Chinese stations. Guangzhou Television broadcasts a mix of national, provincial, and self-generated productions; its mission is to boost Guangzhou and to educate the local populace to the changes taking place around it. Most of the province's colleges and universities, major medical facilities, and research, science, and technical institutions are located in Guangzhou. The city is also the headquarters of the regional (multiprovince) military command.

Second, in accordance with its many faces, Guangzhou has a diverse economy that is reflected in the composition of its labor force. In 1992 industry employed 34.8 percent of the workers in the city proper and commerce (shops, restaurants, warehouses, etc.) employed 15.6 percent, but no other sector accounted for even 12 percent of the labor force. Guangzhou's political and cultural importance can be seen by the proportion of workers in education, arts, and broadcasting (5.0 percent); administrative, party, and mass organs (4.1 percent); public health and welfare (2.3 percent); and scientific, research, and technical services (1.4 percent) — together these fields account for 12.8 percent of the city's workers.[8]

Third, in 1984 Guangzhou became one of fourteen coastal cities that the central government favored for the development of ties with the international business community. This status gave city authorities substantial leeway in drawing up independent development plans. In accordance with their new freedom the municipal authorities in October 1984 promulgated a set of preferential regulations specifically intended to encourage overseas Chinese and Hong Kong, Taiwan, and Macao "compatriots" to invest in Guangzhou. Incentives included discounts on land fees, access to the domestic market for products made by the investor's enterprise, the right to select two relatives or friends to switch their official household registration from rural to urban (but only to the town where the investor's enterprise was located), facilitation of the issuance of exit visas to their relatives, and so on.[9] Not surprisingly, this policy soon bore fruit. In 1985 various joint ventures and foreign-owned enterprises accounted for only 1.9 percent of the total value of industrial goods and services; in 1991 this share had risen to 23 percent.[10] Most of the joint ventures and foreign-owned businesses involve investors from Hong Kong whose ability to speak the local language, frequent personal ties to residents of the city, and location just across the border give them cultural and strategic advantages over other foreign investors.

Finally, Guangzhou has again become an important center of international trade. In 1980 the value of goods passing through Guangzhou customs (with entry points by rail, air, and the port at Huangpu) totaled U.S. $4.4 billion; by 1991 that figure had more than quadrupled to U.S. $19.7 billion. Guangzhou's own share of that trade accounted for 27 percent of the total value.[11] Figures on domestic trade, for example, intra- or interprovincial trade, are, of course, not included in customs data. As this sketch of recent economic developments indicates, by 1990 Guangzhou was no longer "a tired old man" compared to the counties in the Pearl River Delta; instead it had become a dynamic regional center of industry and trade. Furthermore, as an administrative and cultural center open to influences from outside China, it was ideally positioned to serve as a medium for the transmission of new ideas and techniques to the inland provinces.

Population

Ethnically the population of Guangzhou is overwhelmingly Han Chinese. The Hui, estimated to number about 6,000, are believed to constitute Guangzhou's largest minority nationality. The Chinese government's concept of ethnic diversity, however, does not accommodate certain social realities. For example, neither official statistics nor official rhetoric recognizes differentiation within the Han population, though the various subpopulations forced to share the same ethnic label most certainly recognize and respond to such differences. Two major cleavages in the Han population are relevant to people in Guangzhou. The first, and most important, is regional — there is a distinct sense of us (Cantonese or people of Guangdong province) versus them ("northerners" or people from outside Guangdong province) and vice versa; the second is intraprovincial, based primarily on differences in language and native place.

Regional Differentiation

The differences between north and south have a long history, but the tensions they can generate have been exacerbated by some of the government's policies since 1949. First, Guangzhou was among the "later liberated areas" — the People's Republic of China was actually established two weeks before the city of Guangzhou was in Communist hands. To put the new provincial government firmly in place and to carry out land reform correctly and speedily, Beijing sent thousands of cadres and soldiers into the city. Basically these people never left. They continued to occupy most of the highest positions in the government and military, regardless of their technical qualifications, because for years the most important qualification for a position of responsibility was loyalty. Many of these people were ascetic revolutionaries who took a dim view of city life anywhere in China, but especially in the former treaty ports such as Guangzhou that had had a great deal of contact with foreigners.[12] Though local people were gradually promoted to positions of power, they remained under the close supervision of old revolutionaries into the early 1980s.

Second, the Communists were determined to create a new socialist culture that would truly unify China. They intended to reach into every level of society and alter the way people thought, talked, and related to one another. These were goals for all of China, but the Cantonese found particularly grating the government's decision that they would have to give up their language. It was bad enough to have to listen to northern officials using an unintelligible language (*putonghua*) and denigrating their efforts to speak it, but to be told that *putonghua* would be the only language of the schools as well was to strike at the core of their local identity. Just as the official story on ethnicity in China is that the Han Chinese are essentially a homogeneous group, the official story on language is that all Han Chinese speak standard Chinese, that is, *putonghua* (of which Mandarin, spoken in Beijing, is the most prestigious version) or a dialect of it. To linguists dialects are more or less mutually intelligible versions of the same language. In theory a native speaker of one dialect of a language might find the pronunciation and some word choices of the speaker of another dialect a little strange, but within a matter of weeks each would generally be able to understand the other's speech, not perfectly, but well enough to get along in most circumstances.

It is safe to say that the differences between Cantonese and *putonghua* go beyond those normally accounted for in the conventional definition of dialects.* Theorists outside China are divided on how to handle this discrepancy. Most, recognizing that Cantonese and *putonghua* certainly share the same roots, are content to speak of a northern dialect (Mandarin) and several southern dialects (e.g., Wu, spoken in Shanghai and Zhejiang; Xiang, spoken in Hunan; and Yue — Cantonese — spoken in Guangdong and parts of Guangxi). Some, however, recognizing that political rather than linguistic criteria are at the root of the official decision, argue that the term "dialect" should be replaced.[13]

Cantonese have successfully resisted the substitution of *putonghua* for Cantonese. In theory all elementary and secondary school classes are taught in *putonghua*, but in fact there is considerable variation. In Guangzhou teachers are allowed to use Cantonese to "explain" things; in other parts of Guangdong, including an elite secondary school just outside Guangzhou, Cantonese is almost always used except for Chinese and English classes. In government offices *putonghua* is spoken when "northern" officials are present; when they are absent, the office staff conduct their business in Cantonese. The provincial and city television stations broadcast almost all local programming (as well as any programs they purchase from Hong Kong) in Cantonese. Viewers are frequently treated to the bilingual interview: the local reporter asks questions in Cantonese of an official who replies in *putonghua*. On the street, in restaurants, on public transportation, one seldom hears anything other than Cantonese. Beijing is not happy with this state of affairs. In the spring of 1992 the central government set a new round of deadlines in its quest to replace Cantonese in the workplace. According to a report in *China Daily*, provincial officials were required to shift to *putonghua* by the end of 1992; city officials, by the end of 1993;

---

* Nonspeakers find it even more difficult to appreciate the distance between the two dialects because the written language is officially the same; thus a speaker of *putonghua* can easily read a newspaper published in Guangzhou, for the characters, the syntax, and the vocabulary are the same. Cantonese for their part can read Beijing newspapers for the same reason foreigners can — they have been taught to read in *putonghua*. The spoken language, however, is something else again. The most obvious differences are in pronunciation (phonetics and tones) and in vocabulary, though there are also differences in syntax. When writing, a Cantonese uses what to a Cantonese are literary words — in many cases the spoken word is entirely different and not expressible in characters. Sometimes Cantonese cheat and make up characters for these Cantonese words, though this is more likely to happen in Hong Kong than in Guangzhou. The convention is to put a little mouth radical on the left side of a likely phonetic — this tactic conveys the meaning "the word I'm trying to write sounds like this in Cantonese."

county officials, by the end of 1994; and township officials, by the end of 1995.[14]

Yet one suspects that Beijing will be frustrated in its efforts to replace Cantonese with *putonghua*. The major foreign investors in China are Cantonese from Hong Kong, most of whom do not speak *putonghua*. To entice these investors further north may require greater linguistic flexibility on the part of the Chinese government. Perhaps the best predictor of the future viability of Cantonese as a language, however, is that the wives and children of resident northerners now routinely speak Cantonese. There were a number of "northern" families in the Family Study. Most of them were from Hebei or Shandong province, but they had been living continuously in Guangzhou since the early 1950s. In every case the elderly husband disclaimed any competence in spoken Cantonese whereas the wife, who also came from the north, had learned to speak it, and all their children could speak it.

A third, more recent, policy affecting relations between north and south has been the opening of the country to foreign investment since 1979. This opening has been selective and incremental. As a first step, in 1979 China promulgated its law on Chinese-foreign joint ventures.[15] Though there were no formal restrictions on where joint ventures could locate, the stipulation that they market most of their products abroad inevitably meant that coastal cities with port facilities would be preferred over inland cities. Next, in 1980 the Chinese government authorized Special Economic Zones (SEZs), where joint ventures and wholly owned (foreign) investor enterprises could operate with greater administrative flexibility than was the norm elsewhere in China. Three of the four zones (Shenzhen, Zhuhai, and Shantou) are located in Guangdong, while the fourth (Xiamen) is in the adjacent coastal province of Fujian. The selection of these sites was motivated by the desire to interest overseas Chinese; all the sites are close to concentrations of overseas Chinese or are areas from which overseas Chinese went abroad. The largest of the SEZs, Shenzhen, is located just across the border from Hong Kong and a mere hour and a half train ride from Guangzhou. In 1984 the Chinese government further liberalized regulations on foreign investment in fourteen coastal cities, including, as we have seen, Guangzhou. The net result of these policies has been an influx of foreign, primarily overseas Chinese, funds into both Guangzhou and Guangdong as a whole.[16]

During the 1980s the bases of personal power in Guangzhou shifted inexorably. Whereas before the reforms one needed access to influential persons (through a network of relationships referred to as *guanxi*) to acquire scarce goods or services, now one needs money or both access and money. Entrepreneurs, a group long despised as petit bourgeois capitalists, now flaunt their wealth with official approval. Many of the most successful are Cantonese with relatives abroad. The local northerners are seeing the behavior they came to squelch suddenly back and in favor. It is a bitter pill to swallow. Cantonese, on the other hand, feel they have finally come out from under the heavy hand of Beijing. One taxi driver, for example, described with glee a trip he took to Beijing in the mid-1980s. At that time large hotels were still making efforts to protect foreign tourists from riffraff. Anyone who looked like a local and was unaccompanied by a foreigner was likely to be challenged by hotel security and denied entry. Yet Cantonese were easily able to walk right by these guards because, as soon as the guards heard them speaking Cantonese and observed their fashionable clothing, they assumed the visitors were overseas Chinese. Indeed, Cantonese see Guangzhou (and themselves) as a national trendsetter, determining popular taste in consumer goods and mass culture — vying for leadership, perhaps, with Shanghai.

This current perception has reinforced traditional stereotypes. Cantonese have long thought of themselves as adventurous, clever, willing to take risks, and open to new ideas. They have viewed northerners as stodgy and plodding, naive, incapable of thinking for themselves, and ideologically rigid. Not surprisingly, northerners' perceptions of Cantonese reflect a different set of values related at least in part to their proximity literally and figuratively to the centers of political power. Northerners view the stereotypical Cantonese as slippery, cunning, materialistic, reckless, and rebellious. In contrast, northerners view themselves as trustworthy, honest, ideologically committed, and concerned relatively more with moral than materialistic matters. What is particularly interesting is that though these stereotypes exist, they do not usually result in overtly hostile behavior. Cantonese generally believe that, as in the case of language, they have won over most of the resident northerners; for example, non-Cantonese assigned by the central government to the very highest posts in the province frequently turn around and lobby Beijing to gain special privileges for Guangdong.

Intraprovincial Differentiation

Writing in the late 1960s, Vogel distinguished four subpopulations of Han living in Guangdong: the (definitive) Cantonese, the Hakka, the Chaozhou, and the Boat People.[17] From an intraprovincial perspective the definitive Cantonese are those speaking Cantonese and living in the Pearl River Delta or the northern and western hinterlands of Guangzhou. Some of these people themselves speak a subdialect of Cantonese (Taishanese) but are nevertheless recognized as Cantonese. According to some Guangzhou residents, the purest Cantonese is not simply the version associated with the city itself but that associated with Liwan district, an old commercial and residential district west of the (formerly) walled city. This pure form of Cantonese, however, seems to be extinct. Nobody knew what was special about it or could recall having heard it spoken.

The Hakka (literally "guest people") are, as the name suggests, later migrants to Guangdong. Even though the Hakka arrived from the north as early as the twelfth century, they found the plains and valleys of Guangdong already occupied and were forced to settle in the mountains. They retained their own language (spoken also by Hakka who migrated to other provinces) and remain a distinct population. Physically they (and the other subpopulations) are indistinguishable from Cantonese. The Chaozhou, who speak Min (the southern dialect of *putonghua* spoken by most Han in Fujian and in Taiwan), live primarily in the coastal counties in the northeastern parts of Guangdong.

I learned a rough rule of thumb about the mutual intelligibility of these various languages from my first Hong Kong research assistant, who encountered elderly speakers of all these languages while accompanying me on interviews in the early and mid-1970s. Her mother was a Cantonese and her father a Hakka, so that she understood both these languages (as well as *putonghua* and English for good measure). She had problems, however, with some of the Cantonese subdialects. On encountering speakers from Shunde county, relatively close to Guangzhou but on the west side of the Pearl River Delta, she confessed to understanding about 80–90 percent of what was said. For Taishanese the rate was closer to 60–70 percent. Her comprehension of Chaozhou speech, however, was on the order of 30 percent; consequently, we had to drop the Chaozhou from the study.

With the rise of the mass media, especially radio and television, standard Cantonese has become extremely widespread. Intraprovincial differences among the subpopulations still exist, but they manifest themselves primarily in the mountain districts or on the northeast coast, where the subpopulations had their origins. Because the speakers of these languages who live in Guangzhou do not congregate in special sections of the city (in part because work units make housing assignments), they necessarily learn Cantonese. Furthermore, none of these populations makes a point of being different. They have no desire to seek recognition as distinctive national minorities; they are proud to be Han.

The Boat People are the subpopulation with the most problematic label; in Hong Kong they are known as Tanka (literally "egg people" with the connotation that they are born of reptiles). As the name suggests, historically the Boat People lived on boats and made their living by fishing (and, depending on the times, by smuggling and piracy). Both the settled village population and government officials viewed these highly mobile people with suspicion. In Guangzhou the Communists settled most of the Boat People onshore in Haizhu district in the 1950s and required them to send their children to school. Even prior to that time the Boat People of both Guangdong and Hong Kong were Cantonese speakers, but they were not accepted as Cantonese (or even sometimes as genuine Han) by the local people. By the late 1980s, however, the Boat People in Guangzhou seemed to have assimilated—at least they were no longer being mentioned as a distinctive ethnic group.

Urban Guangzhou

Attempts by sociologists and demographers to study urbanization in contemporary China have been frustrated because official Chinese government criteria for determining whether a place is urban or rural often differ from those used by the international community. Furthermore, the Chinese criteria have changed several times in response to policy decisions: to form communes, for example, or to create linkages between cities and their rural hinterlands. Moreover, outsiders attempting to determine the size of the urban population in China have sometimes misunderstood the population categories employed by the Public Security Bureau, the agency responsible for maintaining the household registration system. Some of the problems the current definitions present are discussed below insofar as they affect our understanding of the urban population of Guangzhou.[18]

Formal Administrative Divisions

Since 1988 Guangzhou city or Guangzhou municipality (*Guangzhou Shi*) has been officially divided into eight city districts (*shiqu*) and four counties (*xian*). In official statistics the data for the eight districts are often presented separately from those of the city as a whole; it is the total of the districts rather than the total of the city as a whole that provides the more meaningful measure of the "urban" population. In this book the phrase Guangzhou city proper (or simply the city proper) refers to the eight districts. At the end of 1993 the official population of the city as a whole was 6,236,647 (60 percent in the eight districts and 40 percent in the counties). In the population of the city proper, Guangzhou ranks sixth in the nation, behind Shanghai, Beijing, Tianjin, Shenyang, and Wuhan and just ahead of Chongqing and Harbin. Conceptually, however, the city proper is further divided into the "old city districts" and the former "suburban" or "new districts." The old city districts include the three districts (Liwan, Yuexiu, and Dongshan) on the north bank of the Pearl River and

Haizhu district, directly opposite them on the south bank. Of these four districts Haizhu, which still has farmland under cultivation, is the most rural. In this book I sometimes refer to the old city districts as the city core (or core of the city), and I draw most of my illustrations of daily life from this section of Guangzhou.

The former suburban areas are quite diverse and include Fangcun, with a largely old (1950s) industrial area and a rural hinterland on the south bank of the Pearl, west of Haizhu district, and Huangpu, the deepwater port of Guangzhou and the site of the Guangzhou Economic and Technological Development Zone. Huangpu, located 35 kilometers east of the city core, until 1994 could be reached only by a congested road, making recruitment of workers for the zone difficult and raising the blood pressure of foreign managers, who spent one and one-half to two hours commuting there. Tianhe district, adjacent to Dongshan district, has been targeted by the Municipal Planning Bureau as the primary area for residential and commercial expansion. When Tianhe Stadium was first sited here in the mid-1980s, it sat majestically in the middle of nowhere. Wide boulevards led to it and surrounded it, but at the time they seemed out of proportion to the need, for the immediate vicinity was still agricultural. Within a short time, however, new housing and a variety of commercial buildings, both large and small, have been erected along these boulevards, and now the ride from the center of the city to the stadium is entirely through built-up areas. Nevertheless, much of nearer Tianhe remains under construction; the full range of urban amenities is not yet in place, and dust rises from sites newly cleared of vegetation. Baiyun district is the largest by far of all the city districts, accounting for 72 percent of the city proper. Except for its southern fringe, which has been undergoing intensive development since the mid-1980s and has long been the location of Guangzhou's airport, Baiyun district has a demography more characteristic of Guangzhou's counties than of its other city districts; that is, it is large and not densely populated. Table 1.1 provides the population, size, and density of the eight districts and the four counties (of which three are administratively "cities").

The population figures in the table, derived from the annual tally of household registration figures kept by the Public Security Bureau, reflect a serious undercount of the actual population. Missing from these figures is the "floating" or migrant population in Guangzhou, estimated at about one million people.[19] Most of the floating population is made up of people from elsewhere in the province who come to Guangzhou seeking employment, primarily in the construction industry or in the low-level service jobs, such as street sweeping or domestic work, that no local person wants. Some workers, such as members of rural construction teams, come to Guangzhou with a job in hand, and it is the responsibility of their employers to provide

TABLE 1.1
*Population, Area, and Density of Guangzhou Administrative
Divisions, 1993*

	Population	Area (sq. km.)	Density (per sq. km.)
Whole City	6,236,647	7,434.4	839
City Districts	3,726,270	1,443.6	2,581
Liwan	537,544	11.8	45,555
Yuexiu	465,345	8.9	52,286
Dongshan	563,974	17.2	32,789
Haizhu	710,153	90.4	7,856
Fangcun	149,037	42.6	3,499
Huangpu	169,823	121.7	1,395
Tianhe	381,908	108.3	3,526
Baiyun	748,486	1,042.7	718
Counties	2,510,377	5,990.8	419
Hua City	529,266	961.1	551
Conghua	452,971	1,974.5	229
Zengcheng City	705,861	1,741.4	405
Panyu City	822,279	1,313.8	626

SOURCE: Guangzhou Shi Tongji Ju, *Guangzhou tongji zhaiyao 1994* (Guangzhou statistical summary 1994) (Guangzhou, 1994), pp. 1–2.

them with accommodations (usually in temporary structures on or adjacent to the construction site). Others come with just the hope of obtaining a job and if unsuccessful soon move on to other parts of the delta region. At night these people sleep in crowded hotels (or, when their money runs out, under overpasses); during the day they squat beside busy roadways with little wooden signs advertising their skills and try to catch the attention of people seeking an extra hand. When their presence becomes a public nuisance, they are summarily sent back to their home districts. Most of the migrants are found in the former suburban districts or the counties, where construction is under way, rather than in the old districts of the city. They are immediately distinguishable from ordinary residents of Guangzhou by their simple dress, unfashionable haircuts, slight stature (even by Guangdong standards), and suntanned appearance.

Official residence in Guangzhou, or elsewhere in China, is determined by one's household (*hukou*) registration. The government introduced the household registration system in 1958, and although some writers, both Chinese and foreign, argue that population registration has its origins in China's past, I find the argument of Michael Dutton, that the origins of the current household registration system lie in the Soviet Union, more persuasive.[20] The supporters of the historical argument claim that China has long utilized residence-based groupings to keep its population under surveillance. Dutton, however, points out that the primary concern behind previous residence-based groupings was the political and ethical behavior of the population, whereas that of the current system is economic; that is, the Communist government has enforced population registration to control migration and allocate labor according to the needs of the state's economic plans. (See the discussion of residence-based groupings later in this chapter, in the section "Neighborhood Organization.")

The *hukou* system divides the Chinese population into two categories of residence, usually translated as "rural" and "urban," each with different rights. These translations, although they might have been appropriate when the system was first implemented, are extremely misleading. Unfortunately, however, they are no more misleading than the accurate translations of the categories: "agricultural" (*nongye*) population and "nonagricultural" (*feinongye*) population. Before explaining how these terms are misleading, let us first look at the rights associated with each status. Originally the agricultural population was conceptualized as living in rural villages, with the right to local employment (on the production team of the village during the commune period, for example, or individually now, on land received at the time of decollectivization). The agricultural population was, and still is, responsible for meeting its own subsistence needs for grain; it lives in its own private housing. The nonagricultural population normally, but not always, lives in towns and cities. By definition it is employed outside agriculture and thus could not, prior to the reintroduction of a free market in grain, meet its own grain needs. Instead, until mid-1993 these needs were met through state-supplied grain rations. Until very recently employment of the nonagricultural population was the responsibility of the state (the central, provincial, and city authorities), and the employer had the primary responsibility of assigning housing and providing various benefits, for example, subsidies for transport, health insurance, day-care facilities.

Since the early 1980s the Chinese government has encouraged the migration of excess agricultural labor into small towns in the rural suburbs or counties. Sometimes this movement is truly migration because the workers actually live in the town; sometimes the movement is merely a daily commute. In either case, however, the workers are employed primarily outside the agricultural sector even though they are still likely to have household members living in a village and working in agriculture or village-run industries. Theoretically, those residing outside their official residence for more than a few days (merchants, petty traders, relatives visiting from afar, etc.) are supposed to obtain a temporary registration permit. The rules governing the issuance of these temporary permits are determined largely at the local level, but there are strict national guidelines: the larger the city, the more restrictive it is required to be.

As the distinctions in privileges between rural and urban dwellers are reduced, the importance of the *hukou* system in regulating migration seems to be diminishing. The abolition of grain coupons, for instance, means that urban residents, like rural residents, are responsible for supplying their own grain needs. The restoration of home ownership rights to urban landlords has opened up an alternative to workplace-based housing assignments. If a person with a rural *hukou* is able to pay the rent requested by a private home owner, the local government seldom interferes. In fact, the city government has even agreed that the children of illegal residents are entitled — for a fee — to enroll in their neighborhood school. Most telling of all, perhaps, even old-time urban residents who move within Guangzhou city proper frequently do not bother to change their *hukou* registration, that is, to register their address change with a different street committee office. Many residents settled in new housing in Baiyun and Tianhe, for example, have declined to shift their registration because they want their children to be eligible to attend superior schools in their former neighborhoods. They are able to get away with this because neighborhood organization lags behind housing construction. Some new developments are occupied for more than a year before even the rudiments of residents committees are put in place.

The gap between household registration status and employment status is easily observed. In 1991, for example, while the city proper had an official agricultural population of 22.6 percent, only 11.4 percent of its employed population was actually working in the primary sector (agriculture, forestry, animal husbandry, and fisheries).[21] No employment figures are broken down by district or county, but probably the rural character of at least some of these subdivisions is similarly misrepresented. Thus, as I indicated at the beginning of this section, the *hukou* definitions as well as the inclusion of rural counties in administrative cities (*shi*) make it difficult to talk clearly about the nature of the Chinese urban population.

The Urban Ambience

As I have already suggested, distinctions based on ethnicity or household registration status are not particularly significant in the ordinary ebb and flow of daily life. Most people living in Guangzhou face the same problems and share the same concerns whenever they venture out of their homes and into the public domain. In short, all must cope with a city in the midst of a construction boom, a dense population, an inadequate transportation system, and a high crime rate (in 1992 the crime rate of Guangdong province was estimated at almost three times that of the nation as a whole).[22] The two sections that follow look first at ordinary and next at extraordinary — immoral and criminal — public encounters.

Ordinary Public Encounters

In the core city simply going for a walk can be an ordeal, for innumerable construction projects play havoc with the sidewalks. The areas around construction sites are full of mounds of earth, pavement broken by heavy-duty equipment, uneven surfaces, and hardened lumps of concrete. It is not worthwhile for the municipal authorities to repair this damage because it is likely that as soon as they complete repairs, another project will begin and undo their work. Additional hazards are generated by people who treat the streets and sidewalks as dumps, freely throwing papers and organic material anywhere. Given the scarcity of waste containers, they have little choice. During most of the day there are few trash barrels to be seen; they are hauled out of their hiding places only briefly, just in time for the daily refuse collection. If the barrels were left in the open for any length of time, they would attract many scavengers and probably create a danger to public health. Thus, anyone walking along the sidewalk (to say nothing of walking in the gutter) constantly risks tripping over damaged pavement, slipping on orange peels, or even stepping into a pile of discarded chewed sugarcane. Daily street sweeping and refuse collection keep the situation from getting out of control, but the walker must be ever vigilant.

Hygienic practices still leave a great deal to be desired. While Guangzhou residents are generally spared the indignity of stepping into dog excrement (dogs may not be kept as pets), in crowded neighborhoods lacking indoor toilets they face the real risk of stepping into human excrement. Rather than visit the public toilets, parents and grandparents in these neighborhoods allow and even induce their infants and small children to urinate and occasionally defecate on the sidewalks outside their entryways. Despite government efforts to eliminate spitting, the practice remains common, and people spit almost anywhere except on or directly at another person. The public-spirited spit directly ahead of themselves and thoughtfully trample the coughed-up sputum on their next step. Expulsion of matter from the nose is more circumspect. In the absence of a handkerchief or tissue the person in need stands on the edge of the sidewalk and leans over the gutter before attempting to clear the nose with a forceful blow. These practices, more likely to be encountered among those newly arrived from the countryside, evoke distaste from long-term residents. But even among the urban born, noises issuing from the digestive tract, such as farting and belching (softly), are viewed as natural and inevitable and warrant neither embarrassment nor comment when they occur.

Guangzhou residents are fastidious about their eating practices, though the rules they follow differ from those in the West. The cardinal rule (not always practicable) is to avoid contaminating anything that is going into one's mouth with one's hands. Thus, foods purchased at snack stalls are on toothpicks or skewers or are wrapped in paper. The purchaser slowly removes the wrapper as the food disappears. Oranges and melons are cut into segments and eaten directly from the peel. One's hands should not touch the edible portions. Two Chinese guests were quite taken aback when I picked up a sandwich with my bare (and unwashed!) hands in a fancy coffee shop. Despite their unfamiliarity with Western eating utensils, they determinedly used them to cut their sandwiches into bite-size pieces.

Because of high rates of hepatitis (one public health official estimated that at least 20 percent of Guangzhou's population was infected with the disease), customers in establishments suspected of having low sanitation standards employ several strategies to protect themselves from contagion. One is to bring their own eating utensils — cups, chopsticks, or even a small fork — to the restaurant rather than use those provided. Another is to attempt to sterilize the teacups and chopsticks provided by pouring hot tea into the teacup and using it as a tiny washbasin for the chopsticks, swishing the hot tea around the cup, and throwing this wash-up water out the nearest window or into a dirty bowl before actually beginning the meal. Concern about hepatitis is also reflected in the home. One of the latest household appliances to gain favor with consumers is the electric sterilizer; this appliance, about the size of a microwave oven, is used to sterilize the dinner dishes after they have first been washed.

Because of the dense crowds and shortage of buses, competition for space on public transportation is keen — so keen, in fact, that many prefer to use their bicycles to get to work. Buses are frequently so overcrowded that would-be passengers surge onto the bus as quickly as possible — before everyone, and sometimes even before *anyone*, has been able to get off. People do get up, however, to give old people or people carrying small children their seats, and they usually stand so that those next to them do not feel their modesty is being compromised. When passengers bump or step on each other's feet maneuvering on crowded buses, they might not actually say "Excuse me," but if their eyes meet and one makes a small gesture of apology, the other usually responds with a small gesture of acceptance. Similarly, pedestrians try to avoid bumping into each other on the sidewalk, though to succeed they must constantly monitor those around them. People frequently amble along at a slow pace or stop in the middle of the sidewalk to adjust their child's shoe without any thought that they are blocking others. On the street bicycles flow at a steady pace, and commuters hoping to travel faster or to move against the flow risk an accident and possibly an angry encounter.

Any observer of public interaction in China's cities quickly realizes that those involved ignore or grudgingly shrug off most incidents of bumping, colliding, or other interpersonal accidents involving strangers; some, however, escalate into verbal or even physical assaults. But unlike similar disputes in the United States, these are usually resolved peacefully through the efforts of ad hoc mediators who are neither officials nor associates of the disputants. William Jankowiak carried out a systematic study of this process of public dispute mediation in Huhhot, the capital of Inner Mongolia.[23] That the same dynamic of dispute resolution can be found in two such distant parts of China speaks volumes for the argument that China's urban dwellers share a distinctive national culture that overrides regional and ethnic variations.[24] Some examples of incidents I have observed over the years in Guangzhou are presented below.

Case 1. An Unpurchased Ticket (October 1987)

Since failure to pay for bus rides is a widely practiced petty fraud, I was startled by the forceful reaction of a young female ticket seller to one such incident. Three young men, obviously from the countryside, had gotten off the bus when suddenly the ticket seller tore off after them, grabbed one of the men by his shirt, and yelled at him to buy a ticket. He offered no resistance but simply hugged his cloth bundle to his chest and looked at her, his expression blank (perhaps he did not understand Cantonese). His two companions looked on silently. When he gave no indication that he was going to pay, the ticket seller began shaking him around. The other female ticket seller jumped off the bus to help her. Together they slammed him against the side of the bus, at which point the male driver of the bus also jumped off to help. Passersby stopped to stare. Passengers on the bus became restive at the delay and began yelling for the man to hurry up and buy a ticket. Without a word of protest or self-defense, he finally bought one. End of incident.

Case 2. You Ruined My Suit (November 1987)

One day a broken water main flooded the street directly in front of the city party headquarters. As I skirted the edge of the flood, I saw a man in his 30s arguing furiously with a taxi driver. He was wearing a brand-new Western-cut blue suit that was soaked through on one side. A guard at the gate watched but showed no interest in intervening. The argument developed because the taxi had driven through the water without slowing down and had sprayed the man, who had been on his bicycle. Somehow he had managed to place himself and his bicycle in front of the taxi, blocking its passage, and was yelling at the driver, who refused to open the door and come out.

As traffic backed up behind the taxi, onlookers and other drivers urged the two to continue their argument by the side of the road. In response, the man in the blue suit moved his bicycle toward the side of the road, but in such a way that it continued to block the escape of the taxi. At first it looked as if the taxi was going to pull over. When instead it made a move to drive off, the man in the blue suit quickly jumped in front of it and placed his hands firmly on the taxi's hood. He executed this maneuver several times, eventually forcing the driver out of the taxi, whereupon he was surrounded by several men who seemed to be allies of the offended bicycle rider. Threatening gestures were made. Finally, a man in his 30s or so, with pants rolled up as he made his way through the flood, intervened to restore order. He suggested that the taxi driver admit his error and that the injured party settle for an apology. Possibly this is what happened (I could not hear), because the driver was able to get back in his cab, and the group surrounding him dispersed. The man in the blue suit, still grumbling to a companion, then walked his bike through the main gate into party headquarters. The mediator was wearing no uniform, but he might have been associated with one of the city vehicles sent to stop the flooding.

Case 3. You Had Better Pay for My Taillight (November 1992)

I encountered a small crowd surrounding a new private (presumably unit-owned) car that was stopped half in the bicycle lane and half in the motor vehicle lane of a busy street. The driver had been attempting to pull out into traffic from a driveway when he was struck on the left rear side by a bicycle-riding couple. The driver was demanding damages on the spot of 200 yuan (at the then current exchange rate, about $38). An unhappy young woman (presumably the passenger on the bicycle) was holding a bike to one side while a young man (presumably the cyclist) was trying to get the damages down to 90 yuan. The driver stomped from the driver's door to the taillight and back again several times, arguing that he had to pay not only for a new taillight bulb and its cover but also for the labor involved. The young man, perhaps a factory worker or a construction worker, seemed repentant and diffident. He exhibited no movement whatsoever but just said softly that 90 yuan seemed like enough. The motorist threatened to report the event if the offender did not pay up. Things were going nowhere. Other cyclists were being forced to dismount and maneuver their bicycles through the crowd to get to the other side. Suddenly a man in his 30s or 40s appeared and summarily told the disputants to settle and stop blocking the road. At this point the young man turned over 200 yuan (probably close to a month's income), and the driver left. The young woman blinked back tears.

Case 4. I Did Not Litter (August 1994)

While passing the Baiyun (White Cloud) Hotel, I encountered a dispute in progress between a sanitation worker in his 30s and a couple of about the same age. The cause of the dispute appeared to be the sanitation worker's demand that the man pay a fine for having disposed of his cigarette in an unauthorized place: a foot-square hollow concrete block that others had already treated as a waste receptacle—a few cigarette butts and discarded bus tickets as well as some twigs and leaves sat in the bottom. The man and the woman accompanying him argued that the demand for a fine was absurd (I have already noted the amount of trash and garbage routinely found on the street) and protested loudly. Besides calling the sanitation worker "stupid" (*sha*), the woman said abusively that the situation was no rightful concern of his anyway since the concrete block was clearly on the property of the White Cloud Hotel. (It was part of the cement border separating the grounds of the hotel from the public sidewalk.) "Do you work for the White Cloud Hotel?" she shrieked.

Both men were yelling, primarily in Cantonese, though at one point they shifted briefly into *putonghua*. A small crowd gathered, its sympathies openly with the accused, who claimed that the charges against him were ridiculous. In the first place, it was not true that he had disposed of his cigarette in the receptacle—he still had the butt in his hands and showed it to the onlookers. At most he had merely flicked ashes into it! In the second place, it was easy to assume that this structure was meant for trash—look at what was already there. In the third place, take a look around: could anything else in the vicinity be taken for a waste receptacle? The accused insisted anyone would support his position. He suggested the sanitation worker solicit opinions from the onlookers.

One woman of about 40 had been observing the scene with a scowl on her face. She burst in to say that the accused was quite right; this matter should be dropped immediately. A male in a uniform then wandered over, observed the scene briefly, said nothing, and walked away after motioning one segment of the crowd to step back a bit. A man in his twenties also tried to persuade the sanitation worker to drop his demand. He was smiling amiably, trying to calm the situation, but was called out of the fray by his girlfriend, who wanted to move on. The uniformed male returned, glanced around, and after a moment left without taking action. Next another man, perhaps in his late teens, also smiling as if this must surely be a joke, attempted to defuse the situation.

It became clear that the accused believed he had gained the upper hand (the support of the crowd), whereupon he demanded to see the identification papers of the sanitation worker, threatening to report him to a supervisor. Then—somehow—a compromise was reached in which the accused agreed to pay the fine of 10 yuan (or part of it), provided the sanitation worker removed the trash from the concrete block so that no one else would make an innocent mistake and be similarly taken advantage of. The sanitation worker accepted the 10 yuan, gave the accused a receipt, and then squatted to remove the debris. The accused and, especially, his female companion kept pointing out more items that should be picked out.

How to interpret this? First, although initially it appeared that the two men would come to blows (eyes wide, arms in motion, blood vessels standing out), in fact they never touched one another or made any overtly threatening gestures. Second, most onlookers seemed disbelieving. A few were genuinely irritated at the demand for payment, as if it added up to nothing less than official thievery. Third, the accused, despite his initial steadfast refusal to pay, seemed to think it more advisable to argue his case than to defy the sanitation worker's authority by walking away. Fourth, a person of higher rank came by and offered no support, thus presumably undermining the sanitation worker's position. Finally, perhaps the sanitation worker was from the countryside and had a difficult time defending himself once it became obvious he had no support. (His hands were trembling as he removed the cigarette butts and bus tickets from the block.)

As in the cases recounted by Jankowiak, ad hoc dispute resolution in Guangzhou focuses on the need to restore public order rather than on strict determination of guilt or innocence. The reminder that others — bus passengers, drivers, cyclists, or pedestrians — are being inconvenienced by the quarrel is usually sufficient to bring about a quick resolution. Relative status also seems to play a role in determining who wins and who loses. Motor vehicle drivers pride themselves on being aggressive and easily intimidate most cyclists and pedestrians when they storm out of their vehicles. Similarly, a person from the countryside is at a disadvantage in a public quarrel with an urban resident. Accused parties, particularly if they are in fact guilty, usually realize that the only way they are likely to win over a crowd is to appear calm, misunderstood, and contrite. In this submissive pose they might be able to persuade the crowd to suggest a lighter "sentence" to the accuser, whose ranting and raving will seem unreasonable given the diffidence of the accused. Jankowiak found the same posturing of disputants in Huhhot. In urban China an adult's loss of self-control in public is considered socially irresponsible and a serious personal failing. In this context, once the escalation of a dispute is disrupted, most participants are prepared to seek a resolution of the conflict.

Extraordinary Public Encounters

Immoral and criminal behaviors are being discussed together here primarily because in China the line between them is difficult to draw. From the authorities' point of view any behavior that threatens public morality or public safety is worthy of notice and of punishment. (For the role of the state in promoting morality, see Chapter 4.) Circulating pornographic videotapes, advocating political alternatives to the leadership of the Chinese

Communist Party, using one's official position for personal gain, or committing burglary or murder could all bring one to the attention of the authorities. Ordinarily the police (Public Security Bureau) spend most of their time dealing with obvious public safety issues, such as street crime and house break-ins, but when other special agencies call on them for assistance or they receive a command from the center, they focus their attention on other matters such as prostitution, smuggling, or corruption. Most residents of Guangzhou are aware of these latter crimes and generally disapprove of them (at least in principle), but they seldom worry about being victimized by them. In daily life people are much more concerned about crimes that affect their immediate personal safety.

For girls and women the usual worries about safety are augmented by concerns about sexual harassment, indecent assault, and rape. The official portrayals of strict socialist morality characteristic of the 1970s led some outside observers to believe that sexual offenses in China under Mao were rare, but *New York Times* reporter Fox Butterfield, who was in Beijing from 1980 to 1981, found otherwise. During Butterfield's stay prostitution was well established in Beijing, and Chinese women were complaining of being felt up on the bus and of being confronted by exhibitionists. Obscene language was in use, and engaged couples spoke frankly of premarital sex.[25] In the early and mid-1980s Jankowiak found high rates of sexual harassment in Huhhot. All of his 47 female informants reported experiencing or observing at least one such incident within the previous three years. During his own fifteen hours of observation in a public market, he witnessed an average of two cases of harassment per hour — most of it verbal but some physical. Almost all the victims were under 25.[26]

Although I did not investigate sexual harassment in Guangzhou in any scientific fashion, whenever I raised the issue, it rapidly became clear that the experience is probably as frequent in Guangzhou as in Huhhot.[27] For example, if I mentioned my own experiences, the woman listening would tell of a similar incident that had happened to her or one of her friends. One young woman related several such incidents, two of them from her childhood spent elsewhere in Guangdong. When she was only six years old, she encountered an exhibitionist on a public street. She rushed home, described the event to her father, and asked him why a grown-up would do such a thing. Thereafter her outside activities were restricted, a lesson that probably explains why she never told her parents about subsequent incidents. A few years after the encounter with the exhibitionist, while she was riding on a crowded bus and unable to move, an "old man" (from a ten-year-old's perspective) ejaculated on her. Years later, while she was walking early one morning along Beijing Road, a man crossed the street and approached her. As he did so, his hand shot out and felt her crotch. She had the presence of mind to bop him with her umbrella, a reaction he was apparently unprepared for, and she was able to run away.

Her most dangerous experience was her most recent one, which occurred in the mid-1980s. One Saturday night about midnight she was returning on her bicycle from a dance at her work unit. It was extremely dark, and there were few other bicycles about. In the distance she could just barely make out a bike rider ahead of her. She decided to peddle a little closer to that rider so that it would not be obvious to others that she was alone. As she approached, however, she sensed that the lead bike had begun to slow down, and then she noticed that the rider had somehow managed to pull his pants down to his thighs. She could see his bare backside. She dropped back and stopped. When the man became aware that she was no longer following, he stopped his bike and turned around. When he saw that she was stopped, he began to turn his bike around to peddle toward her, but she seized that opportunity to peddle right past him as rapidly as she could. She was close to home and hurried in.

Similar incidents, usually not so serious as this one, have been common enough that girls and young women in Guangzhou usually do not think it safe to go about unescorted at night. Even in pairs they fear being anywhere other than around their own doorways or on busy streets after 9:30 or 10 in the evening. People are even beginning to shun the public parks as soon as it gets dark. For example, in March 1991 a young couple was attacked around 8 P.M. in Yuexiu Park by three men from outside the province. They tied up the male at knifepoint and dragged the female off into the woods, where they raped her. Her boyfriend was able to free himself and ran to get the police, who captured two of the culprits. People shook their heads and observed that although the parks would once have been full even at night, now that almost everyone stays home and watches television, the parks are no longer safe.

For women in service work or in the sex trade the risks of harassment, injury, and even death are, of course, substantially greater than for members of the general public. (See the case of Miss Lin in Chapter 5.) In 1992 Guangzhou police were seeking a man known as the "Canton Ripper," who was believed responsible for the deaths of at least six young women between August 1991 and June 1992. All the victims were in their twenties and thought to be prostitutes from elsewhere. After raping and killing his victims by strangulation or stabbing, the Ripper dismembered the bodies, stuffed the remains into burlap rice bags, and dumped them into rubbish bins. Police blamed the killer's existence at least in part on side effects of the economic reforms that have brought about a resurgence in crime all over China, but in Guangdong in particular.[28]

In 1991 to deal with prostitution that was escalating out of control (see

Chapter 2 for a fuller description of its prevalence in Guangzhou), the central government ordered twelve cities to set up labor camps for prostitutes and their clients. As part of this nationwide campaign the police reported the arrest of 200,000 prostitutes and their clients in the first ten months of 1992.[29] Locally in Guangzhou the campaign entailed, in addition to arrests, notification of the client's work unit and spouse that he had been caught with a prostitute. To elicit the cooperation of hotels, a common venue of prostitution, one such establishment, notorious for employing Russian masseuses, was completely shut down for about two weeks. The offending hotel was located only a few minutes' walk from my own, which in the spring of 1991 had been a virtual vice den. When I returned in the fall of 1992 to the same hotel, prostitutes were no longer much in evidence, but I had a funny feeling about the true nature of the newly opened karaoke bar on the top floor.

Property crimes are by far the most common crimes experienced by the general public. Purse slashing and pickpocketing are ubiquitous; in the old city someone in just about every household has experienced one or the other.[30] Whenever I held up my own slashed purse as a stimulus to conversation, the observer would laugh ruefully and recount a similar experience. Bicycle thefts are nearly as common. One day in March 1991, while interviewing three families in the Yuexiu neighborhood, I decided to ask about the frequency of this crime. The first family reported losing four of its bicycles to thieves in 1988; the third reported losing two within the past year. The second had lost no bicycles but reported that a man with a knife had broken in on the ground floor next door the preceding night. Whereas thieves used to work by poking hooked rods or poles through barred windows, now burglars enter buildings and rob occupants who are at home. Residents of even the upper floors of new housing are now routinely installing an iron grating on their own doorway and chipping in to install one at the ground-level entrance to the main stairwell, access to which is increasingly limited to those who punch in a number and identify themselves over an intercom.

Perpetrators of street crime have become more audacious and violent. In the spring of 1991 in the Dongshan neighborhood where I was interviewing, a rash of gold necklace snatchings took place. The first case known to me involved a daughter of one of my informants. She had been visiting her mother, and on her way home at eleven in the morning, while passing a vacant building, was seized from behind by someone who pinned her arms to her body. Another person then threw an unknown liquid into her eyes, blinding her at least temporarily, and ripped a gold chain and locket worth more than 1,000 yuan right off her neck. The victim was assisted to the hospital for treatment, and though she was released the same day, she was still having trouble with her vision. When I asked two different family members whether the incident (which had occurred only a few hours earlier) had been reported to the police, I was told: "The necklace is gone. What good would it do?" Two days later two more midday blindings occurred in the same general area. About two weeks later in another district of the city two men were caught in the act and arrested. With their arrest the epidemic ended.

In addition to out-and-out crimes, scams of all sorts abound—some so trivial or pathetically obvious that you have to wonder how the perpetrators can make a dishonest living. For example, one friend recounted that while she was waiting for the bus one day, a young man showed her his cut shoulder bag and told her that someone had slashed it and taken his money. He asked whether she had any money she could give him to help with bus fare. When she showed him the 0.2 yuan note she held in her hand to indicate that was all she had, he snatched it and ran off. And I observed a young couple from the countryside who regularly stationed themselves along a busy street and simulated bargaining over a jade bracelet. When no likely prospect was visible, the man squatted on the sidewalk and the woman stood next to him, lounging against a wall with her baby strapped to her back. As soon as they spotted a possibility, the couple would spring into their bargaining pose, he still squatting and she standing directly in front of him. Holding on to opposite sides of the jade bracelet and tugging at it, they would vigorously argue over the asking price. Presumably a passerby would take interest in the negotiations and, tempted by the seller's low asking price, outbid the woman. The bracelet, however, was likely to be worth much less than the customer actually paid. I never saw anyone taken in by this routine.

My morning tea companions warned me of various other scams and swindles, such as deception in money exchange or in the purchase of smuggled goods. They also advised against any contact with members of minority nationalities, who sometimes arrive in Guangzhou by train in traditional dress and try to sell jewelry. You can never be sure of the authenticity of what they sell, and, according to local wisdom, their real goal is to steal your money. They are believed to have some kind of drug concealed in the folds of their upper garments that they blow into your face to make you dizzy and disoriented, easy prey for theft.

Perceptions of the general incidence of crime as well as Guangzhou residents' frequent experience as victims suggest that this is not a city where doors and bicycles may be left unlocked, or one where people may safely remain oblivious to their surroundings. Although the government attributes the apparent increase in crime to "side effects" of the open door, particularly to "spiritual pollution," some observers of China note increases in urban crime that predate the open-door policy. In their study of urban life in the mid-1970s, Martin K. Whyte and William L. Parish report that their informants felt that social control of all sorts of deviant behaviors (e.g., gambling, fortune telling, and crime) had broken down since the 1950s and early 1960s. In the late 1970s increased disorderly conduct and crime were officially explained as side effects of the Cultural Revolution, referred to in the post-Mao era as the "ten chaotic years" (1966–76). According to this view onetime Red Guards, who formerly had been allowed (and even encouraged) to run amok or who had grown up without adult supervision (since their parents were in labor camps), were now returning to the cities and, in the absence of both self-discipline and employment, were turning to crime.

In their own analysis of the reasons underlying the increase in disorder, Whyte and Parish consider three theoretical perspectives on social control: the solidarity, deterrence, and legitimate opportunity "schools." They found that "neighborhoods and work units in which people had more access to opportunities to purchase needed commodities and acquire secure employment and promotion opportunities seem to have remained more orderly than other areas." Thus, they argue,

what is needed to restore and maintain the high levels of urban social control that existed in earlier years is not so much to improve the devices for detecting and sanctioning offenders or for promoting social solidarity, but to repair the disrupted opportunity structure, so that urbanites will feel they have predictable chances for improving their lives and will be motivated to exert themselves and obey the official rules.[31]

In the 1990s the disruptive population is believed to consist primarily, not of returned former Red Guards, but of individuals from elsewhere who come to Guangzhou to seek their fortunes but who cannot compete equally with the city's residents because of their educational status, language differences, and *hukou* registration. In the sense that Guangzhou's higher standard of living and relatively open employment system function as magnets for the ambitious from all over the country, it can be said that the increase in the crime rate is a consequence of the economic reforms. But this link between the open door and crime is very different from the ideological one proposed by the government.

The authorities have been disturbed by increases in the urban crime rate, though the magnitude of local fluctuations over the past decade and a half is not easy to know or to interpret. Periodic official crackdowns inevitably result in reports of high numbers of the targeted crimes (and high numbers of arrests and convictions) that do not necessarily reflect a real increase (or decrease) in their incidence. Nevertheless, it has become clear that certain crimes are associated with large-scale organized gangs (*heishe*, "black [se-

cret] societies"). These criminal gangs are said to have infiltrated Guangdong from Hong Kong and Macao and also to have come down from
provinces in the north. They are most likely to be involved in smuggling (of
cars, household appliances, and drugs), counterfeiting (of renminbi [or
yuan], Hong Kong dollars, and U.S. dollars), manufacturing of false papers (passports, credit cards, identification cards), protection rackets, highway and train banditry, and so forth.[32] In any case the authorities have not
taken the advice of Whyte and Parish (to reduce crime by improving the
opportunity structure) but have chosen to focus on deterrence. Deterrence
takes two forms: prevention and punishment, both of which are believed to
be served by the liberal employment of capital punishment administered by
a pistol shot to the head.

Deng Xiaoping, in a talk on January 17, 1986, that was reprinted in a
special volume of his works published and circulated in the summer of
1987 — presumably to set the tone for the forthcoming Thirteenth Party
Congress — called for a crackdown on criminals. It is worth quoting at
length.

The death penalty cannot be abolished, and some criminals must be sentenced to
death. Recently I have read some relevant documents, from which I understand
there are a great many habitual criminals who, on being released after a few years'
remoulding through forced labour, resume their criminal activities, each time becoming more skillful and more experienced in coping with the public security and
judicial organs. Why don't we have some of them executed in accordance with the
law? Why don't we punish severely, according to law, some of those people who
traffic in women and children, who make a living playing on people's superstitions
or who organize reactionary secret societies, and some of those habitual criminals
who refuse to reform despite repeated attempts to educate them? Some of them
must be executed, but of course we have to be very careful in such matters. . . . Those
who have merely made mistakes in the political and ideological sphere but have not
violated state law should not be given any criminal sanctions, let alone the death
penalty. But some of the perpetrators of serious economic or other crimes must be
executed as required by law. Generally speaking the problem is that we are now too
soft on criminals. As a matter of fact, execution is one of the indispensable means of
education. . . . Nowadays the death penalty is reserved for murderers only, but how
about those who have committed other serious crimes? In Guangdong Province
prostitution is rampant — why don't we crack down on the worst proprietors of
brothels? The ones who refuse to reform after being jailed and released several times
should be severely punished as required by law. Some governmental functionaries
have committed economic crimes so serious that they caused the state financial
losses amounting to as much as several million, or even ten million, yuan. Why can't
they be sentenced to death in accordance with the Criminal Law?[33]

Public bulletin boards outside street committee offices regularly display
execution notices, immediately identifiable from a distance by a prominent

red checkmark that indicates the sentences have been carried out. Executions are not distributed throughout the year but instead peak immediately before dates of political significance such as National Day, on October 1, or Spring Festival, when the population is highly mobile.[34] In 1987 the weeks before the Thirteenth Party Congress were also notable for a step-up in executions. Summaries of two typical execution notices follow that detail the crimes behind twenty executions carried out in Guangzhou on September 19, 1987.

First Set of Cases

Two men, one aged 24 from Zhejiang province and one aged 26 from Jiangsu province (though both were living in Shanghai), came to Guangzhou, where they committed numerous robberies and one murder in the commission of a robbery.

A 23-year-old man from a county in Guangdong and a comrade had many robberies to their names. In their last operation they robbed and injured a taxi driver but were nabbed by public security officers. As they sat in custody in the public security vehicle, one of the men managed to set off a bomb, which killed him and injured his comrade, the 23-year-old, who was subsequently executed.

A 25-year-old man from Panyu (one of Guangzhou's constituent counties) had been involved in many robberies, including gang-style robberies.

A 31-year-old man from Liaoning province had carried out many thefts and robberies. He had already served time yet returned to robbery after his release.

A 30-year-old man from Jilin province and a 31-year-old from Jiangsu repeatedly robbed and stole. They too had already served time for these offenses yet returned to them after release.

A 22-year-old man from Shandong province and a 23-year-old from Hebei province repeatedly robbed and stole. They had already served three years but returned to their criminal ways following release.

A 24-year-old man and a 25-year-old, both from a county in Guangdong, were involved in multiple thefts from construction sites. They were cited for at least 27 such incidents.

Second Set of Cases

Three men, two aged 24 and one aged 25 (all from Guangdong, including one from Panyu county), were involved in a car-theft ring. They were cited for having stolen at least ten cars or vans as well as numerous motorcycles.

A 24-year-old man from Guangzhou specialized in breaking into houses and stole innumerable televisions, tape recorders, and the like. He was involved in over 40 thefts after having already served time. He also beat up fellow prisoners.

A 26-year-old man, a Guangdong native who had been living in Hong Kong, was involved in stealing and reselling cars in Guangzhou.

A 24-year-old man from Hua county (one of Guangzhou's constituent counties) had a record of thefts from companies, work units, and dwellings.

A 24-year-old man, a Guangdong native, was involved with a partner in selling knockoffs of wristwatches. He came to doubt his partner's honesty in the division of their take and in a public place pulled a knife on him and stabbed him. When bystanders attempted to intervene, he stabbed and killed one of them. (Such an outcome in an ad hoc mediation is extremely rare, but because this was not a dispute between strangers, it was perhaps more risky for outsiders.)

A 28-year-old man from Jiangsu became involved in a fight with two others in a Guangzhou hotel, during which he killed one and injured the other. He had a previous arrest record.

A 24-year-old man from Taishan county had a record of thefts and robberies. While in prison he severely beat up the fellow prisoner who had informed on him.

The circumstances of these crimes (with the exception of the two men with a bomb) are all fairly typical of cases involving individuals sentenced to death. Other execution notices from the same period include cases of embezzlement, rape, and forcing women into prostitution. An analysis of the demographic characteristics of 36 people sentenced to death in Guangzhou (as recorded on six of the fifteen official execution notices appearing in the fall of 1987, the first four in September and the last two in November) reveals some interesting facts.* First, and least surprising perhaps, is that all the condemned criminals were men. Second, they were almost all (78 percent) in their 20s; seven were in their 30s, and one was 45. No one was younger than 20. Third, contrary to popular perceptions, though the criminals hailed from a total of nine provinces, most (61 percent) were natives of Guangdong itself, including 25 percent who were natives of Guangzhou city proper or its four counties. These data reflect the characteristics of those who are captured and convicted of the most serious crimes. It is possible that those who commit minor crimes are opportunists from out of town rather than the hardened criminals described in the cases above.

* I left Guangzhou for over a week in October 1987, and when I returned, the notices were being replaced so rapidly that I simply could not keep up with them. Many more than 36 people were executed in Guangzhou from September to November. Their sentencing was sometimes included on the evening news, though not their actual execution.

Neighborhood Organization

Below the district level Guangzhou city proper is divided into subdistricts known as street (*jiedao*) committees (sometimes translated as "wards") that are further subdivided into residents committees. In districts that are primarily rural the corresponding lowest administrative unit is the village committee. The core city includes 73 street committees: 20 in Liwan, 19 in Yuexiu, 15 in Dongshan, and 19 in Haizhu. Each street committee in Guangzhou is usually responsible for a neighborhood with a population in excess of 20,000. In 1991 the neighborhood where I worked in Yuexiu district had 24,900 residents whereas that in Dongshan district had nearly 60,000. This is an exceptionally large population for a street committee and represents a tremendous increase over the population of 38,000 in 1987, when I began working in the area. The increase is the result of five new residents committees formed to accommodate the occupants of a big new housing development in a previously undeveloped area located a good taxi ride away from the street committee office. One suspects that this arrangement is temporary and that ultimately another street committee will be erected. All the households in the Family Study are from three of the original fourteen residents committees. Most people have few reasons to visit their street committee office, because street committee business is normally conducted through its subordinate residents committees. For example, the Yuexiu neighborhood, a relatively small one, is divided into 10 residents committees and 128 small groups that, in theory at least, have regular contact with the households under their jurisdiction.

Whereas the street committee staff includes both men and women, is salaried, and consists of people of working age, the staff of a residents committee is nearly always female, largely unsalaried, and composed mostly of those already out of the labor force. Their work activities are guided by one or two low-salaried members who might or might not be of working age and who do not necessarily live within the jurisdiction, though they usually live nearby. These salaried leaders attend weekly meetings at the street committee office to learn their assignments for the week. They then relay this information to the heads of their small groups, which consist entirely of volunteers.

Residents committees have many ongoing responsibilities, such as promoting security, resolving disputes among family members or between neighbors, monitoring selected segments of the population, and enforcing the one-child family policy. In addition, they must be prepared to respond to any new directives — national, provincial, city, or district — as they arise. Thus, for example, one of the residents committees in which I interviewed had to scour the neighborhood for standing water when an epidemic of dengue fever (spread by mosquitoes) broke out in the immediate area in 1987. Similarly, when a typhoon approaches, the street committee orders that all residents be advised to remove flowerpots from balconies and secure other exposed items to prevent injury to those below.[35]

Residents' views (positive or negative) of residents committee workers are affected by their own age and sex as well as by the general political atmosphere. During the Cultural Revolution when youth were pressured to "volunteer" to go to the countryside and the work of pressuring them fell on the residents committee workers, tensions between the two groups were high. And when these same youth returned to the cities illegally and the task of reporting them to the authorities fell on the residents committee workers, tensions were again high.[36] Young males (and females) found themselves constantly being supervised and dictated to by middle-aged and older women, a situation they found difficult, to say the least. Defenseless, disabled, or older people who benefit from services provided by the residents committee, however, understandably hold a more positive view.

One of the consequences of the economic reforms has been to make residents committee work, particularly at the level of the small group, less attractive to the kinds of people who used to volunteer. Economic, ideological, and personal factors conspire to make alternative activities more attractive. Why do unpaid work when there are so many possibilities for paid work or for assisting one's family members so that they are freer to engage in paid work? For many the concept of "serving the people" has been tossed into the dustbin of history—viewed at best as attractive primarily to the simple-hearted. Finally, whereas in the 1960s and 1970s residents committee work was one of the few outlets for the energy of the newly retired and served to alleviate their boredom, now retirees can watch television, go to dance halls, and otherwise indulge themselves. The net result of this shrinkage in the number of volunteers and in their level of participation has been to increase the burdens on the paid staff and on the leaders of the small groups, who are often run ragged by their efforts to carry out their many functions.[37] I discuss some of their more important functions below.

Political Functions

As I have indicated, the perceived high incidence of crime in Guangzhou means that public security is a major concern of most residents. In cooperation with the local police station, residents committees help organize watches at the entrances to lanes or buildings considered particularly vulnerable to crime. Occasionally they even organize three shifts of patrols that circulate through a neighborhood 24 hours a day. The households so protected contribute a small sum of money to pay the watchers, most of whom are elderly with little or no other source of income. They also set up supervised parking lots for bicycles (used by motorcycles as well), both to protect them against theft and to avoid the chaos caused when bicycles are parked anywhere and everywhere. The fees from those who use these lots pay the bicycle supervisors and provide a small income for the sponsoring residents committee. Residents committee personnel, moreover, pass on information about crimes that occur in the neighborhood so that people can take extra precautions when necessary.

The residents committee also helps maintain the accuracy of the household registration system. It must verify to the street committee the legitimate residency in the community of someone who applies at the street office for a permit of one sort or another. Members of the small groups are likely to know whether any given household is harboring someone from outside the city; they use their discretion in deciding whether to report this situation. Now that population mobility is common and legitimate, however, less attention is paid to this matter. When someone dies at home, the family must summon a member of the residents committee to verify that a death has occurred as the first step in obtaining from the local police station a death certificate, without which the body will not be picked up by the authorities.

Currently the most important and tension-generating responsibility of the residents committee is to ensure compliance of the residents with the one-child family policy. (See further discussion in Chapter 3.) This is a joint responsibility of work units and neighborhood committees, which work closely together, particularly when a violation of the policy is suspected. A woman with an unauthorized pregnancy will be urged all day long at her workplace and all evening long in her neighborhood to submit to an abortion. Such pressure is difficult to resist. The person in charge of women's affairs, or birth control, knows the mode employed by each couple of reproductive age in the neighborhood and knows each year exactly how many women in the jurisdiction are authorized to become pregnant. Those required to practice birth control are married couples who have already given birth to one child or who, while old enough to be legally married (age 20 for women), are still below the age recommended for late marriage (24 for women).

One Guangzhou residents committee that I visited in late 1992 had just completed its birth and birth control tally for the first ten months of the year. With a population of 2,303 it reported fifteen births, three pregnancies expected to result in births by the end of the year or very early in 1993, the insertion of more than twenty intrauterine devices (IUDs), nine abortions, and no sterilizations. The degree of compulsion reflected in the abortion figure is difficult to interpret; it includes two cases of presumed accidental pregnancies (those of women who became pregnant with IUDs in place) as well as an unspecified number (possibly zero) of miscarriages, or "spontaneous abortions." All births were first births. In another street committee, I visited a residents committee in which one of the twenty births was a second birth, but this was acceptable because it was a second marriage and one of the partners had been childless.

In 1991 Guangzhou instituted a new rule intended to protect the state from legal challenges to its demand that a couple agree to an abortion. Those wanting to obtain a "birth permit" must now first visit the neighborhood legal services office (a subdivision of the street committee office) and sign a document agreeing to have only one child. Prior to 1991, being married, of an appropriate age, and childless were usually sufficient conditions for the issuance of a birth permit. Those refusing to sign the agreement receive no permit. Those who sign and then go on to have a second child have violated their word and must pay a fine. One or the other partner might also be required to be sterilized.[38] Residents committee personnel conduct household checks at least once annually to determine not only whether local women might have violated the birth control rules but also whether pregnant women from elsewhere might be hiding out in their jurisdiction.

Another demanding activity is mediating disputes among family members or neighbors. Some disputes, such as those involving couples wanting a divorce, can drag on for years (delays were especially frequent during the Maoist and early post-Mao eras, when divorces were seldom authorized); others flare up periodically; and still others are onetime episodes. Neighbors commonly quarrel when fights between children escalate to involve their parents or when disagreements develop over the use of shared living space, such as a cooking area or a common hallway. Lately, inheritance disputes among family members have become increasingly common. The dynamic of these neighborhood disputes is different from that of street disputes between strangers, first, because the parties are known to each other and to the mediator; second, because the mediator has the right and the responsibility to resolve the dispute, and the quarreling parties are obliged to cooperate with the mediator; and third, because the parties may appeal to a hierarchical sequence of mediators if they are unable to resolve their differences. In the event of a deadlock, authority to handle the dispute moves from the head of the small group to the residents committee to the street committee and, finally, to a court of law. One residents committee mediator said with a laugh: "I feel like everybody's mother. Sometimes there is nothing for months, but other times there will be several quarrels on the same day."

Economic and Welfare Functions

Welfare functions in China's cities are a joint responsibility of work units and the local Civil Affairs Bureau, the latter delegating this work to its various subordinate street committees.[39] The handicapped and the childless elderly are the two major categories of people entitled to special governmental assistance, much of which is delivered at the neighborhood level.[40]

The Handicapped

In 1987 Guangzhou participated in China's first national survey of the handicapped. The total number of handicapped in the eight urban districts and the four counties was extrapolated from a random sample of 3,000 households in three street committees located in Yuexiu district.[41] The study revealed the following frequency of disabilities:

Deaf/mute	81,000
Mentally retarded	37,000
Blind (even with vision aids)	33,000
Physically disabled (impaired mobility)	28,000
Multiply handicapped	22,000
Mentally ill	9,000+
TOTAL	210,000

The many different causes of handicaps include congenital defects, diseases, traffic accidents, and work-related accidents. Those whose disabilities stem from accidents on the job or whose conditions, for example, mental illness, develop or manifest themselves only after employment has begun are likely to remain the financial responsibility of their work unit. As the figures indicate, however, the majority of handicapping conditions are obvious even before entry into the labor market, and the affected individuals are unlikely to find employment. In the days when the labor bureau assigned jobs, some of these individuals might have been placed in supportive units. One Haizhu district street committee I visited in 1980, for example, had established a welfare workshop for the handicapped in association with a large rubber factory, whose workers (along with those from neighboring rubber factories) accounted for most of the population in its jurisdiction. In one room of a row of workshops I observed about twenty people, most of whom appeared to be retarded, busily packing condoms. The handicapped who are unemployed remain dependent on their families, for no other financial supports are provided for them.

On May 15, 1991, the national Law on Safeguarding the Legal Rights of the Disabled went into effect. At the same time, the government established the third Sunday in May as annual National Day for Aiding the Disabled. To relieve the financial burden on families, the government has embarked on a campaign to encourage employers to hire the handicapped who are actually capable of work. In Guangzhou it was estimated that 31,000 of the handicapped (not quite 15 percent of the total) fell into this category. Nationwide it was estimated that about 50 percent of the urban disabled who were capable and willing to work were, nevertheless, unable to find employment. In 1991 the municipal government employed 2,300 handicapped workers in its own welfare factories. In addition, another 70-odd factories were sponsored at the county, district, and especially street committee levels.

Besides encouraging street committees to develop work opportunities for the handicapped, the government has also decided to stimulate other employers to hire the handicapped by offering tax incentives. There is a national law that exempts enterprises from taxes if 50 percent or more of their workers are handicapped or reduces their tax payments by 50 percent if 35 percent or more of their employees are handicapped. This incentive has led to some unanticipated creative hiring. For example, when new management took over the operation of a bar and restaurant in Beijing, it immediately fired all the service personnel and replaced them with dwarfs, whom they dressed in tuxedos and trained to provide entertainment as well as service. Not surprisingly, by 1992 a tuxedoed dwarf was in evidence at a similar establishment in Guangzhou.[42] Locally a 1990 law (not implemented until 1991) requires units with fewer than seven handicapped workers per 1,000 employees to contribute a certain amount to a fund used to provide training to the handicapped still seeking employment.

One street committee I visited in 1991 identified a total of 126 of its residents as handicapped (an average rate much lower than that of the city as a whole). Of the handicapped, 54 were considered totally incapable of work (46 of these were under age 60). The remaining 72 included those currently employed as well as those previously employed (even while disabled) but now retired. Forty people (both the still working and the retired) were the responsibility of employers other than a street committee–operated work unit. Nineteen were the responsibility of street committee units, ten were self-employed, and three were without work. As early as 1986 Guangzhou began to establish work information stations for the handicapped who could not obtain regular employment. These stations provide a kind of day care for the handicapped in need of close supervision, thus allowing family members to go to work with their minds at ease. In theory the stations provide work opportunities (usually piecework), supervision, education, and treatment (presumably monitoring medications). A family might or might not have to pay for the program. By 1991 there were 24 such stations, serving 300 or so handicapped persons and their families.

In the normal course of events residents committee workers have little responsibility for the disabled, because they are looked after by their families. Under certain circumstances, however — when the handicapped are left alone, when they become involved in disputes with neighbors, or when the mentally ill experience psychotic symptoms — residents committee personnel are on the front line, as the following episode demonstrates. One day, while walking with Ms. Ma, a residents committee head, I nearly tripped over a man who was squatting in the lane, using his bare hands to scoop cooked rice from the ground and put it directly into his mouth. Ms. Ma made some remark as she passed by that caused the man (Mr. Xiao) to stop eating and stand up. She then turned to me, shook her head, and commented (in Cantonese): "*Soh*" (*sha*, "stupid" or "crazy," a disparaging term used to describe both the mentally retarded and the mentally ill). Later Ms. Ma described Mr. Xiao's situation and how she had come to be involved in it.

The Xiao family has a long history of mental illness. Old Mr. Xiao, who had died in his 60s a month earlier under mysterious circumstances, was himself mentally ill, though he had shown no evidence of this until several years after his marriage, and no one knew for sure whether he had ever been hospitalized for his problems. Though the two Xiao daughters have no mental limitations, the two Xiao sons are both said to be *sha*, and both have spent time in the Guangzhou Psychiatric Hospital in Fangcun. The older son has had multiple admissions and was there at the time I encountered his younger brother squatting in the lane. No one doubts that the two men inherited their condition from their father. There was no hint that the older son was mentally ill until after he had finished school (he graduated from a specialized secondary school and was considered a good student) and gone to work. The state unit for which he is theoretically still working, though he has not reported in for many years, continues to provide him with an income and finances his medical (including psychiatric) care. The younger son had his first mental breakdown before entering the labor force; consequently, he has been unable to obtain employment and is supported by his mother's retirement income. He must take medicine every day to remain mentally stable.[43]

The older son and the father were in the habit of going to have morning tea together. One morning the older son went off to tea by himself, though the rest of the family did not know this because the father had his own room on a different floor. When the younger son happened to go to his father's room, he found him unconscious, with his clothes mostly burned off and apparently still smoking. The younger son had the presence of mind to fill a bucket of water and douse his father. He and his mother called an ambulance to take the father to the hospital, where he died of smoke inhalation. How the father's clothes caught fire remains an open question. Did the father fall asleep smoking, or did the older son set him on fire? Like the father, the older son smokes, and he had once beaten up his father to the point of drawing blood. Not long after the father's death the older son was readmitted to the psychiatric hospital.

All of this had been very hard on Mrs. Xiao. Both Ms. Ma and a neighbor agreed that she had aged greatly in the space of a few weeks. She used to stand straight, but immediately after her husband's death she began to walk bent over. She also developed an enormous bulge in the front of her throat, and her eyes seemed too large for their sockets (presumably because of a thyroid problem). Because of these symptoms she had recently entered the hospital. Her hospitalization meant that there was no longer anyone available to prepare meals for the younger son or to supervise his taking of medication. Ms. Ma had the responsibility of figuring out a solution. She contacted the tenants living on the ground floor of the Xiaos' privately owned building and asked them to prepare meals for the younger Xiao and supervise his medication. When she saw him on the street scooping up the rice, however, she wondered whether the tenants were taking the responsibility seriously.

Although admittedly an extreme case, the Xiao family is not unique. In the same neighborhood was another family with several mentally ill members whose unsanitary habits and carryings-on were frightening their immediate neighbors, and Ms. Ma had had to intervene several times in their affairs. Not far away in another residents committee an elderly woman, who, like the Xiao sons, had spent time in the psychiatric hospital, had driven away two granddaughters who had moved in from the countryside to look after her; she was so threatening to her co-tenants, with whom she shared cooking facilities, that they were afraid to come home to eat. They returned to their dwelling only late at night, when they hoped the old woman would be asleep. Because housing was scarce in Guangzhou, none of these terrified neighbors could pack up and simply move away.

The Childless Elderly

Protecting the childless elderly was a priority of the Chinese government even before it implemented the one-child family policy, but its importance has increased since the early 1980s because of the growing numbers of elderly and the need to assure younger couples that compliance with the policy would not put them at risk of a pitiful old age.[44] The childless elderly in the city proper fall into two categories: those belonging to a work unit and those without one. Only the latter qualify for relief through the Civil

Affairs Bureau; the former are considered the financial responsibility of the work units from which they retired. This distinction is very important because it can result in major differences in entitlements, depending on the work unit from which the elder has retired. To be eligible for relief, a person must have no labor power, no source of income, and no one legally responsible for his or her support.* Although these criteria are not based on age (a young orphan also qualifies), the elderly constitute 93 percent of the urban people receiving relief in Guangzhou.[45]

In the Yuexiu district street committee with which I am most familiar only thirteen people out of a total population of 24,900 were certified as relief households in 1991 and thus receiving support from the Civil Affairs Bureau. Eleven of these households consisted of a single elderly individual; one consisted of a pair of orphans, a seventeen-year-old girl and her twelve- or thirteen-year-old brother. As of August 1, 1994, individuals receiving relief in Guangzhou city proper were eligible for a monthly payment of 170 yuan—up from 130 yuan the previous month. In addition to the monthly stipend there is also a special supplement at Lunar New Year (Spring Festival) that varies over time and from neighborhood to neighborhood but totaled around 200 yuan in 1991. Persons on relief are also entitled to free rent, medical coverage and personal care, funeral and cremation services, and, in the case of children, education through middle school.

In neighborhoods where others are just barely scraping by there is considerable jealousy and resentment of some of these households, for people often suspect that they are not as poor as they make themselves out to be. One elder who was observed smoking became the object of criticism because smoking is an expensive habit, and it struck some observers as a luxury. The woman in charge of welfare at the street committee had to tell the complainant that the smoker had recently been visited by a relative from Hong Kong who had left behind two packs of cigarettes. Of course, having relatives in Hong Kong or overseas generates even more suspicion of hidden income. Until 1990, relief households had had their electricity and water fees covered by the Civil Affairs Bureau, but after many complaints by resentful observers that this encouraged such waste as leaving fans on even when no one was in the dwelling, Civil Affairs decided to make these fees the responsibility of the individual. Because in China's cities electricity fees are normally several times higher than rent (though the ratio is changing as housing reform is implemented), residents are especially envious of subsidies for electricity.

Relief elderly are entitled to live in their own homes (usually single rooms in shared dwellings), or they may apply to live in a home for the

---

* These people are known as the "three have nots." "No labor power" is a direct translation of the Chinese.

aged. Although all street committees in Guangzhou are expected to provide such a congregate facility, in 1991 only 42 of the 90 street committees in the city proper had actually opened one. The homes are normally quite small, seldom accommodating more than ten residents. If a neighborhood has no facility of its own, it may send its relief elderly to a district social welfare home (an option only in Dongshan district in 1991, though Liwan and Haizhu were said to be planning such homes) or to the city-operated home located in a rural area of Baiyun district some 40 or more kilometers from the city core. This large facility has 500 beds; 70 percent of them are occupied by relief elderly, and the remainder, by elderly whose expenses are met out of private or work unit funds. The city home began accepting self-paying residents in 1986, when there was a reduction in the number of relief elderly. By 1991, however, a backlog of 400 relief elderly and 200 self-paying elderly had developed. The fees charged the self-paying residents vary from 180 to 200 yuan a month, depending on the level of care required. Those who are essentially bedridden pay an additional 40 yuan a month. It is also possible, though the city home does not encourage this option, to pay a lump sum of 15,000 to 16,000 yuan upon admission that covers all current and future expenses. Because the home's administrators do not have much experience calculating the average lifetime costs of residential care, they have restricted the use of this option to prevent financial disaster.

It is useful to contrast the rights of the relief elderly with those of unit-sponsored childless elderly, particularly those who have retired from collectives run by the street committee. Whereas the relief elderly are entitled to housing, a minimum monthly income, and all medical care (all their medical needs do seem to be met), the unit-sponsored elderly are totally dependent on the financial circumstances of their work units. Those retiring from well-to-do enterprises, state administrative organs, or nonprofit units such as schools, hospitals, or mass organizations are likely to receive generous pensions, opportunities for postretirement employment as temporary workers, and full or nearly full coverage of their ordinary medical expenses. Those retiring from impoverished units, however, receive minuscule pensions and minimal medical coverage and have little prospect of being rehired by their units.

There are two main reasons that collectives do so poorly that they can barely meet the wages and medical expenses of their current employees, let alone those of their retirees. The first is simply the inability to compete, for example, the failure to recognize that in a market economy products must be tailored to meet consumer preferences. The second is having an unfavorable ratio between current workers and retirees. The 100 or so enterprises run by the Yuexiu street committee, for example, had 472 workers and 573 retirees, for a ratio of 0.8 to 1 — an inordinate financial burden. Under these circumstances the street committee was in no position to send any of its childless elderly to the city home for the aged because it could not pay for them. Until a broader-based system of financial responsibility for retirees that includes all work units is in place, these inequities will continue.*

Conclusions

In this chapter I have described the distinguishing characteristics of the city of Guangzhou; have attempted to demonstrate that despite these distinguishing characteristics Guangzhou is as much a Chinese city as Beijing, Shanghai, Wuhan, or any other; and have given the reader some sense of the texture of contemporary urban life. Guangzhou gains its special feel from its remoteness from Beijing, its centuries-long history of contacts with the outside, the spectacular growth of its economy (particularly in the joint venture and private sectors) since the beginning of the open-door policy, and its position as a leader in setting consumer aspirations.

These factors are, of course, closely interrelated. Both historically and in the present Guangzhou's location far from Beijing has, somewhat paradoxically, made it the national government's preferred site for trade with merchants from other countries. When interested in international trade but concerned about pollution from foreigners, Beijing has authorized Guangzhou (as well as other parts of Guangdong) to take the lead in negotiating deals with outsiders. Because Guangzhou has a long history of such trade, is near Hong Kong and Macao, and has many former residents now living overseas, people there have been exceptionally well informed about goings-on outside China. Their access to foreign broadcasts has even provided them with information about China not readily available to other Chinese living out of range of Hong Kong television.

Despite these special features Guangzhou has remained as subject to the policies of the national government as any other city in China. After 1949 it had no choice but to make itself over in the socialist image required by the Communist Party. It instituted the household registration system, made the work unit a key element of social organization, participated in the Cultural Revolution, enforced the one-child family policy, implemented various post-Mao economic reforms only when authorized to do so by the central government, and followed national guidelines in assisting the handicapped and the childless elderly. Its independence from Beijing is a relative matter,

* In fact, even in 1991 such a broad-based system was in operation in Guangzhou, but participation was not yet mandatory. Participating units must contribute a certain percentage of their income to a common pension fund. The poorest units feel they cannot afford the contribution.

and when push comes to shove, officials in Guangzhou will not publicly disagree with decisions made by the central government, even when they think a particular decision is foolish or outright wrong.

Finally, the chapter has considered the experiences of the ordinary Guangzhou resident attempting to make it through the day. Those who venture beyond their own doorstep inevitably encounter dust, dirt, and crowds. The density of the population and the large number of strangers on the street mean that people traveling outside their own turf must be vigilant. Most encounters with strangers are peaceful. But if a bump or an accident is interpreted as an affront and somehow gets blown out of proportion, the participants can usually count on other members of the public to intervene before serious damage is done. People also are assured that once the perpetrators of crimes are caught, they will be punished by the authorities: sent to a labor camp or prison, put under local supervision, or, if incorrigible, executed.

A deeper understanding of contemporary daily life in Guangzhou requires that we look more closely and analyze how particular reforms have shaped today's circumstances. The next chapter looks in more detail at the most spectacular result of the reforms—the improvement in the material conditions of urban life.

2 | *Living Standards*

*T*he economic reforms have had their most visible impact, not surprisingly, on the material circumstances of daily life. Although the shift to a commodity economy has had its ups and downs, the overall direction has been steadily up. There is simply more of everything around — more food, more clothes, more shelter, more transport, more and better service personnel — and also greater diversity. In addition to buses there are now taxis, motorcycles, and private cars. In addition to electric fans and sewing machines there are air conditioners and videocassette recorders. After decades of forced belt-tightening, China's urban residents can barely contain their enthusiasm for consumer goods. Even though prices have risen drastically, so far wages have largely kept up, leading to an enormous increase in discretionary spending.

State economists view the growth in personal wealth as a reason for the state to reduce the heavy burden of the welfare subsidies it has been providing for years to urban dwellers. In particular, the state has decided to convert housing into a commodity, thus relieving itself of the responsibility of providing housing as a benefit of employment. This new policy has met with little enthusiasm, and its implementation, with many obstacles. This chapter examines the reforms that have improved the standard of living, assesses the changes in the availability and quality of goods and services, and considers what new problems have emerged with the reforms.

In 1980 the economic reforms had barely begun to affect the daily life of Guangzhou's residents, but by the end of the decade the changes brought about by their gradual implementation could not be ignored. In improving living standards, the reforms have been an unqualified success. Although some segments of the population have gained more — and gained it faster —

than others, in Guangzhou, Deng Xiaoping's dictum that "all boats rise with a rising tide" is difficult to refute, as the following brief observations suggest:

In 1980 scarcely anyone appeared overweight. By the end of the decade obesity was officially recognized as a health problem, and consumers were shifting from fatty to lean pork.

In 1980 the shelves on the upper floors of the Nanfang Department Store, the premier department store in south China, were stocked with canned food, thermos flasks (to keep water hot), and plastic inflatable toys for children. Would-be buyers of table lamps had a selection of exactly one lamp at the lighting fixtures counter.* By the end of the decade the Nanfang Department Store had an entire section given over to video games and videocassettes.

In 1980 the quality of goods left a great deal to be desired. Washing dishes was hazardous because drinking glasses disintegrated in one's hand and handles lifted right off the cups to which they were attached. Bicycle tires nearly always needed air. By the end of the decade these particular problems had become less common.

In 1980 plastic and net bags were highly valued items.[1] Purchased goods were usually wrapped in discarded newspapers or tied up with dried grasses or reeds for transport home. Now plastic bags (and styrofoam boxes for take-out food) are ubiquitous and constitute a waste disposal problem.

In 1980 service (or rather the lack of it) was a serious problem. Sales staff seemed not to notice customers hovering around their counter. Restaurant staff avoided looking over at their tables. By the end of the decade selective progress had been made, and more improvements were on the horizon.

In 1980 the urban residents of Guangzhou averaged 4.0 square meters of living space (up from 1960's all-time low of 2.8 but less than the 4.5 available in 1949). By the end of 1993 average living space had more than doubled, to 8.5 square meters.

The difficulties facing urban residents in China prior to the reforms stemmed directly from government policies.[2] When the Communists came to power, they brought with them a profound distaste for cities and city life, which they viewed as unproductive and morally tainted. The wealth

---

* These goods represented a major improvement over what was available in the recent past. A visitor who had last been to the store in 1973 when the shelves were nearly bare was impressed by the variety and quantity of goods on display in 1980.

of large cities, especially of the major coastal cities such as Shanghai and Guangzhou, was disproportionately based on commerce and foreign trade rather than on industry. Commerce and trade were viewed as parasitic and potentially exploitative, rather than productive, activities. This view had a long history in traditional Chinese thought; Communism added to it the highly charged words "bourgeoisie," "capitalism," and "imperialism." Moreover, foreign influence had been greatest in the cities, where affluent and Western-educated residents had adopted foreign ("bourgeois") life styles — for example, a taste for European classical music and Western authors — and had been exposed to Western ideals such as individualism, democracy, and freedom. Furthermore, the enormous variation in living standards among the Chinese population had been most visible in the cities. The wealthy attended fashionable social events and invested in the stock market whereas rural migrants fleeing turmoil or economic hardship pulled rickshaws, begged, or even starved in the streets. These negative images played a major role in formulating policy toward cities until the late 1970s and affected decisions regarding state investment and population migration.

Beginning in the 1950s the state emphasized investment in production, particularly agriculture and heavy industry, rather than in light industry and commerce. Consumer goods and the urban infrastructure, including everything from energy, transport, and communications to housing, were given low priority. Factories received their quotas of raw materials and produced a specified number of goods according to targets set for them by the state plan. Private shops and individual merchants were replaced by state stores that sold only those goods allocated to them under the state plan. Neither factories nor stores were concerned about the quality of their goods or services, because they were not held financially accountable for their behavior and operated in a noncompetitive environment.[3] The state made up their losses from the profits of enterprises or stores that had a surplus.

Workers were assigned to jobs with de facto life tenure, low wages, and few prospects for advancement. Their on-the-job performance would neither raise nor lower their income and would certainly not cost them their job.[4] Such workers were said to have an "iron rice bowl," that is, an unbreakable source of food, and to be "eating from one big pot," that is, from the national or local treasury rather than from the income of their immediate work unit. By the late 1970s there were far more workers in urban work units than there was work for them to do, further exacerbating the problem of worker motivation.

The state was also determined to eliminate hoarding, which created artificial shortages of food and goods. A complex rationing scheme was developed to guarantee every official urban resident access to a certain amount of grain, cooking oil, meat, fuel, cloth, and a wide variety of other goods.[5] These goods could not be purchased without the appropriate ration coupons: as late as 1980 a resident of Guangzhou could not sit down and order a bowl of noodles without first producing a ration coupon in addition to payment. But ration coupons did not end supply problems. Consumers complained that the rationed amount for some items was too small and that sometimes the rationed goods were simply unavailable. The state also set the prices or the range of prices for most foods and deliberately kept them low even when it paid agricultural workers higher procurement prices than it charged urban consumers. Keeping prices low meant that wages could be kept low. The prices of domestic luxury goods, such as home appliances, however, were set artificially high to discourage demand but nevertheless provide an outlet for funds families received from overseas.

While so-called high cadres and individuals receiving remittances from abroad could purchase better goods in special stores, conspicuous consumption was frowned on. Visitors to Guangzhou in the late 1970s were apt to note the limited variety of clothing people wore. In the summer adults of both sexes dressed in white short-sleeved shirts and loose blue or gray trousers. A wristwatch was the only ornament likely to be visible. Women's hair was straight and short and held back from the face by a metal or plastic headband. Young male workers expressed their sense of fashion by wearing semifluorescent undershirts tucked into baggy trousers held up by belts that wrapped one and a half times around the waist. When young women dressed up, they exchanged their trousers for skirts that did not quite reach the tops of their nylon calf-high stockings, and they tied ribbons around the ends of their braids.

The state attempted to guarantee urban residents not only food, clothing, and employment but also a place to live. When the new government came to power, it simply took over the vacated offices and residences of the former government. While private housing was not exactly confiscated, the rights of the owners were severely restricted. They had to give up basic management rights to the municipal Housing Management Bureau (HMB), which assigned tenants to whatever it considered excess dwelling space and set the rent the owner could charge. Prior to the Cultural Revolution the owners continued to collect the minimal rent themselves, but during the Cultural Revolution the HMB took on this task. When housing was owned by absentee overseas Chinese without local agents (i.e., without close relatives), the state acted as agent and managed the property on their behalf. Virtually all housing constructed after 1949 was paid for by the state and assigned work units that made the space available to their workers at very low rents. Much of this housing was built contiguous to the factories where the workers were employed.

Rents were kept low for the same reason that prices were kept low — to allow the state to keep wages down so that it could funnel money into productive investment. Rents were so minuscule, however, that they were insufficient to cover routine maintenance of the buildings, and basic repair work was often long delayed. The World Bank describes the effects of this deferred maintenance as "alarming" even in buildings barely fifteen years old.[6] New buildings have the mysterious capacity to age instantly: housing erected only three or four years ago is easily mistaken for housing built more than fifteen years earlier.[7] Ordinary housing in China was (and still is) presented as ready for occupancy in a much more unfinished state than in North America: floors are normally bare concrete; in Guangzhou there is no means of heating the dwelling; and there are no kitchen appliances. The skills required in Guangzhou for the profession known as decoration differ markedly from those needed in the United States. Chinese "decorators" do carpentry, wiring, plumbing installation, painting, and tiling. They do not concern themselves with window treatments or with matching the upholstery to the wallpaper. Because decorators, until about 1979, could not legally ply their trade and ordinary residents could not get access to the materials necessary to make improvements themselves, most housing interiors remained basically unfinished.

Whereas on the one hand the state, by neglecting infrastructure and maintenance, seemed to condemn urban residents to a life of multiple frustrations, on the other hand, by carefully controlling access to goods and housing, it successfully guaranteed them minimum standards of food, clothing, and shelter. However minimal these standards might appear in retrospect, at the time they were sufficient to make urban life infinitely preferable to the hardships of rural life. Only stringent curbs on migration kept Guangzhou's hills free of the squatter structures common in most cities in developing countries (or even in neighboring Hong Kong). By late 1978, however, the Chinese government was already beginning to authorize a wide range of reforms intended to revitalize first rural and then urban life.[8] These reforms were to have ramifications in nearly every aspect of daily life.

The Decollectivization of Agriculture

The reforms began with the gradual decollectivization of agriculture. Individual households became responsible for producing a certain quota of grain under the "household responsibility system." Once a household had met this quota, it was free to sell excess grain on the newly legitimized open ("free," or private) market or to raise other crops, such as high-yield vegetables, and sell them. Almost instantly private markets materialized on the streets of Guangzhou. These markets charge higher prices than the state markets, but because they also offer fresher food and much greater variety, consumers are willing to pay. Foods on the free market have not been subject to rationing, and consumers may buy as much as they can pay for and consume as much as they can eat — thus the increase in calories consumed and the emergence of obesity as a health problem.

The reestablishment of private markets not only increased the supply of food but also introduced consumers to the laws of supply and demand and paved the way for a (grudging) consumer tolerance of an end to most fixed prices and rationing. When prices were rising rapidly in 1988, Guangzhou's residents were held up as models of restraint for the rest of the country's urban population.[9] At that time, 22 large and medium-sized cities reintroduced rationing of some major nonstaple foods, but Guangzhou did not. While people in Beijing, Shanghai, and Xian were said to complain often about the rising prices, people in Guangzhou, familiar with the phenomenon of price increases, were apparently unconcerned. They had learned from their experience in 1979 (when controls on the price of fish were relaxed), 1985 (when the prices of vegetables, poultry, meat, and eggs were relaxed), and 1987 (when the prices of vegetables, fruit, and fish increased greatly over a period of several months): in each case producers had responded by increasing the supply, so that prices eventually dropped to an acceptable level. The equanimity of the populace was probably also related to wage increases. In the mid-1980s workers' wages in Guangzhou had increased at an average annual rate of 11.3 percent, prices at only 5.3 percent.[10]

Nationally, urban residents did not adjust so easily. In 1985 rising prices had so upset consumers that the state felt compelled to introduce an across-the-board monthly subsidy of 8 yuan to urban workers (including those in Guangzhou) to cover the rise in food prices.[11] In 1988 the state again responded by authorizing an additional monthly subsidy of up to 10 yuan to urban workers, students, and retirees, expressly linking the subsidy to its intention to discontinue setting sales prices (in state stores) for vegetables, eggs, pork, and sugar. According to a Chinese broadcast, the substitution of these direct subsidies for indirect subsidies was expected to

enable people to better understand state policies and . . . help reduce the government's financial burden. Incomplete statistics show that in the past, the state had to set aside dozens of billions of yuan for non-staple food subsidies each year. Take pork for example, the average cost of producing a jin (250 grams) of pork currently stands at 3.6 yuan, but it has been selling at the state-set price of 2.8 yuan, requiring government subsidies of almost 1 yuan per jin.[12]

As agriculture was decollectivized, it became possible for rural households to withdraw from grain production altogether if they wished and apply for the status of "specialized household." This status allowed them to become essentially private entrepreneurs, free to cultivate orchards or ornamental plants; raise pigs, ducks, chickens, or fish (in 1987 prawns were particularly favored); lease or purchase the former collective's tractors or other vehicles and set up their own transport companies; and so forth. In other words, as the communes were disbanded and the role of the collectives redefined, the private sector reemerged. Urban dwellers watched with disbelief as the official media praised the financial acumen of the so-called 10,000-Yuan Households, which used their wealth to finance spectacular wedding banquets and build fancy two-story dwellings for their newly married sons.

The rural construction boom was made possible not only by new wealth but also by labor newly freed from fieldwork. Once a household calculated the labor needed to meet its grain quota, it was free to allocate its excess labor as it saw fit. When villages offer such employment opportunities as factory work, young people are likely to seek work locally. Young people in villages close to urban districts are likely to seek employment in niches avoided by urban young people, such as the service sector — for example, sweeping streets, collecting trash, providing domestic services, or working in the smaller hotels and restaurants. Some rural households have turned their carpentry skills to furniture making. They load the six-foot-long finished cabinets or sofas onto their bicycles, pedal into town, and squat along the main commuting roads displaying their wares.

Villages lacking factories that are also too far from urban districts to make commuting feasible frequently organize their young people into labor crews, especially construction crews, and send them all over the country and even abroad. In addition, hundreds of thousands of individual unskilled or semiskilled rural migrants seeking work arrive annually at the Guangzhou main railway station. Most head south into the counties along the eastern edge of the Pearl River Delta, but many remain in Guangzhou to seek work. They squat along the roadside, hoping someone in need of temporary workers will single them out. Such squatting is technically illegal. The unwary display signs describing the work they are willing to do, but the police sometimes kick them over or rip them up. The more wary simply stand a brick on end as a sign of availability and squat off to the side or even in the bushes. They can thus disclaim any association with the brick should the police take an interest or step forward should a bona fide employer come by.

Both the police and ordinary residents of Guangzhou view these migrants with distaste. Residents of neighborhoods north of the railway tracks, such as Sanyuanli and Xiatang, where there is considerable construction under way, complain that the most devious migrants, especially those from Xinjiang, attempt to squat on the roofs and in the corridors of the as-yet-unoccupied new buildings, scouting out places already inhabited to burglarize. Migrants who use up their limited travel funds have nowhere to sleep except in front of the railway station or in the streets. Even before dark, groups of largely, but not exclusively, young men begin to congregate under highway overpasses, where they carve out sleeping spaces for the night. They wash up as best they can at nearby public toilets or even at the ponds in public parks, but as the days pass, they become increasingly untidy and harder to distinguish from the occasional beggar or mentally disturbed person who is sometimes also found under an overpass. When the authorities perceive their numbers as problematic, they are summarily removed — provided with one-way train tickets back to their place of origin, courtesy of the Public Security Bureau. Around Lunar New Year, which coincides with the slack season for farm work in the north, the number of migrants to Guangzhou is phenomenal. Every year the television news broadcasts show packed trains pulling into the station to be met by police with bullhorns advising those passengers without guaranteed jobs to take the next train back.

That such migrants can literally be here today and gone tomorrow was made clear to me one spring day in 1991 when I suddenly realized that no one had spent the previous evening under our usually jammed neighborhood overpass about a mile from the train station. The reason? "The Trade Fair," explained my restaurant tablemates. Indeed the semiannual Guangzhou Trade Fair was about to start, and the authorities did not want these vagrants to send the wrong message to out-of-town visitors. I had noted a similar phenomenon in the fall of 1987 just before the start of the Sixth National Games, held in Guangzhou, when with equal suddenness the streets were cleared of illegal money changers (black-market currency dealers, at least on the streets, are primarily non-Cantonese). Both these examples make clear that rural migration is tolerated only so long as urban dwellers view it as beneficial.

Enterprise and Employment Reforms

The primary goals of enterprise reform are to make state enterprises more efficient and competitive and to reduce the burden the less efficient ones impose on the state treasury. These reforms, among the first to be aimed specifically at urban residents, are intended to eliminate the practice of eating from one big pot out of an iron rice bowl. To encourage enterprises to take an interest in the quality of their work, be it production or service, the state announced that following the payment of a set amount, they would be allowed to retain most of their profits instead of having to turn them over to the state treasury. This also meant that enterprises that regularly ran a deficit would no longer have their losses covered by the state. They would have to go into debt or even face bankruptcy if they could not balance their books.[13] Although factories would continue to receive target production quotas and be guaranteed supplies of raw materials at set prices, once they fulfilled those quotas they were free to produce whatever goods they thought the market needed, though they would have to obtain the necessary raw materials at negotiated prices from suppliers they located on their own.

Stores, for their part, were expected to sell at set prices certain goods obtained from suppliers, but they could also sell at negotiated prices additional goods obtained on their own. Many of these reforms were tried out in Guangzhou earlier than in the rest of the country, and it was in this environment that the Nanfang Department Store expanded its range of goods and suppliers. In 1983 and 1984 it ranked first in the nation in sales, though as the decade rolled on and the reforms took hold elsewhere, department stores in the larger cities eventually surpassed it. By 1987 its buyers were purchasing 40,000 products from over 2,000 different factories.[14] Thus factories and stores as well as restaurants and hotels were expected to become market researchers, attuned to the needs of consumers and keenly competitive. These reforms played a major role in increasing the variety and quality of goods available to Guangzhou's consumers. Another set of reforms was aimed directly at the workers. By linking performance to wages via piece rates or bonuses, the state hoped to provide workers with personal incentives to work harder (see Chapter 5 for further discussion). Similarly, the management of small state shops was contracted out to individuals or workers whose income was entirely dependent on what the shop took in.

Another wake-up factor for state enterprises was the emergence of a competing private sector when urban excess labor was freed from the burden of "waiting for employment" (just as rural excess labor had been freed from fieldwork). Urban young people, as well as other segments of the population, such as housewives and the retired, who were not then in the labor force, were encouraged to go into business for themselves. In nearly every district of the city, sidewalks and vacant lots have been set aside for the erection of permanent and semipermanent stalls. The distinctive green shedlike wooden structures with their contents, which can be locked up for the night, are assembled into display areas during the day. The operators of these street-side stalls provide a wide array of services, from shoe repair to bicycle repair, and sell a wide range of goods, from take-out foods (cooked pork, chickens, and ducks brought in from elsewhere) to popular magazines and gift cards to fruits, soft drinks, and cigarettes. Vacant lots and back lanes not suited to motor vehicle travel are often set aside specifically for less sturdy, tentlike stalls selling clothing. Hundreds of them are lined up side-to-side and back-to-back, selling nearly identical arrays of high-fashion jeans and elaborately sewn dresses (complete with ruffles, tucks, and flounces) that seem designed to mock the plain styles of fifteen years earlier. Private wholesalers in these goods, who occupy several floors of a large building near the railway station, sell to buyers who bring Guangzhou's fashions to the still stodgy north.

All these sellers are supposed to be licensed and legal, though the person operating the stall at any given moment is not necessarily the person with the license. In addition to those legally authorized to engage in commerce, a host of others not so authorized display their goods from a movable cart or the back of a bicycle, prepared to move off quickly should the authorities crack down and begin confiscating goods. Some unauthorized sellers are simply local villagers without assigned places in the open market who appear at marketing time with a few chickens in a basket or stalks of sugarcane tied to their bicycles. Others sell products they or their associates have made themselves or have taken either on consignment or possibly as unemployment compensation from a small factory. Still others deal in goods that "fell off a truck" (i.e., were procured illegally) or are morally questionable (e.g., foreign videotapes). These irregular sellers are visible primarily on main commuter streets during commuting hours. When the crowds have passed by, they usually pack up their wares and disappear.

That both Guangdong and Fujian are rife with smuggling is no secret. One Guangzhou resident reported seeing an article in the newspaper estimating that 80 percent of the videocassette players for sale in the country are smuggled. In two well-known shopping areas near Guangzhou, including one in Panyu county, nearly all the goods for sale are smuggled. The shops carrying these goods are all run by individuals. Technically, of course, smuggling is illegal, and some people are uncomfortable about its prominence. One man's moral compromise has been to buy nothing himself from these shops but to take visiting friends from the north to them. In fact, he remarked, most people in Guangzhou do not have to resort to this kind of purchase because so many of them have overseas relatives, who are entitled to bring things in as gifts without paying duty on them. The national government charges staggering duties, doubling or even tripling the purchasing price, to enhance its revenues and protect domestic manufacturers. Local governments, however, gain from all these smuggled goods, for as business booms, tax money (to say nothing of possible voluntary and involuntary payoffs) comes in. They turn a blind eye to smuggling, saying, in effect, how can we know that the goods are smuggled — that is the affair of the customs officials.

The customs officials, however, are generally conceded to be a part of the problem. In April 1991 I heard a story in Guangzhou of someone who had been caught attempting to smuggle a car across the border from Hong Kong. The customs officials appropriated the car for their own use by slapping a customs license plate on it. The smuggler could do nothing and was lucky to escape arrest. The customs officials could always justify their actions by saying to themselves they had acted as they did, not for personal gain, but to do their own work better. This thinking resembles that of the local officials who tolerate the blatant sale of smuggled goods in their communities, who tell themselves they are doing it not for themselves but for the greater good of their community or colleagues. Lesser interests are allowed to dominate over national interests. The story of the car smuggler confirmed what I had heard two weeks earlier from senior government officials in Hong Kong. They were lamenting that even though they knew the Chinese authorities had recovered or identified around 150 vehicles stolen from Hong Kong, not one had yet been returned. Worse yet, a group of Hong Kong officials who had gone to Shenzhen to consult on some matter was picked up by an official Chinese government vehicle that gave every sign of being one of these stolen cars. (Cars intended for use in Hong Kong have the steering column on the right, as in the United Kingdom; those for use in China have it on the left, as in North America.)

To encourage Guangzhou's residents to part with their cash, prime-time evening television regularly treats them to a barrage of fast-moving commercials. On Guangdong television these advertisements for local, joint venture, and even foreign-made goods are presented all together in an overwhelming deluge. (I counted 42 in a row beginning around 8:50 one night, followed about an hour and a half later by another 29, including some repeats.) Most of these ads are in Cantonese, though a few, intended for national circulation, are in *putonghua*. The commercials follow formats familiar to North Americans: cartoons, dramatic short skits, testimonials by well-known figures playing themselves or by (apparent) traditional doctors, and so forth. Here is a sample of the deluge:

1. Oil of Ulan (known in North America as Oil of Olay) — a moisturizing lotion by Proctor and Gamble: if you use it, your skin will not wrinkle like the dried-up old apple shown in the ad.

2. Chinese pills to ease aching legs.

3. Sharp (a Japanese company) electronic products.

4. Various packaged food products (of Chinese manufacture) now available at a large department store.

5. Dandruff-remover shampoo manufactured by Johnson and Johnson.

6. Sharp color televisions.

7. A traditional fatty Chinese sausage.

8. Ceramic tiles for beautifying interiors.

9. A spray that removes dust and spots from furniture.

10. Another Chinese pharmaceutical.

11. Candies and sweets from a confectionary factory.

12. An ad for Apollo—the tonic of the sun. A few drops of this and you will acquire new energy and become a big strong boy or man (in Chinese traditional thought the sun is a male symbol).

13. A moisturizer for women's skin.

14. Sharp video camcorder.

15. Manufactured food products.

16. Marlboro cigarette ad—this is a spectacular ad (it went on to win an international award) that I had seen only in a shortened version in Hong Kong. It is done in rich oranges and blues and features a large group of costumed men dramatically performing a martial dance to a booming kettledrum in one of the courtyards of the Imperial Palace in Beijing. Neither the name of the product nor the product itself appears in the ad. The only time the viewer realizes it has to do with Marlboro is at the end, when the final chords of music are played and the Marlboro theme is beat out on the kettledrum. Such a commercial can work only when the audience is already familiar with the musical theme and its link to the product.

17. An ad in *putonghua* for soft contact lenses: a lovely middle school student appears in the doorway. At first people don't recognize her. Then they realize that she is the girl who used to wear glasses but looks so much nicer now.

18. A written ad shown on the screen too fast to read; no dramatic content.

19. Another (different) Apollo ad.

20. A medicine ad.

21. A brand (555) of batteries for toys and other things.

22. Hair spray.

23. A versatile electric rice cooker that not only can be used to boil soups for hours but also can be placed directly over a gas flame if the inner metal part is removed.

24. More face creams.

25. A feminine hygiene product to pour into bathwater (an ad for Whisper brand sanitary napkins is also shown regularly, but it did not appear in this sequence).

26. Packaged foods.

27. Wanbao refrigerators (made by the major home appliance manufacturer in Guangzhou).

28. An ad in *putonghua* for White Cat detergent—a ring-around-the-collar ad, just like those in the United States.

29. Fluorescent bulbs and lamps help the old and the young with hand-work and reading.

30. Toothpaste ad—unfortunately the model is brushing her teeth in-effectually, moving the brush straight up and down.

31. Oyster sauce—a favorite Chinese flavoring.

32. All kinds of batteries.

33. Canned fish (probably dace).

34. Rejoice—a dandruff-control shampoo.

35. Cooking oil that can withstand high heat without smoking.

36. Not clear.

37. Some kind of medicinal tonic.

38. Choose—a brand of men's dress shirts.

39. Ginseng products made in Guangzhou of imported American ginseng.

40. Lux soap ad featuring a Western model (Avon ads also feature Western models).

41. Doublemint gum (Western models)—cures bad breath.

42. Nescafé instant coffee and a nondairy milk substitute (in *putonghua*).

It is noteworthy that not a single advertisement uses patriotism, revolutionary spirit, or socialism to sell its products. All are marketed as making life more comfortable or surroundings more attractive. Materialism is rampant.

Ads like these, along with commercial activity, create an impression of genuine hustle and bustle. The visitor to Guangzhou, whether from abroad or simply from another part of China, is usually genuinely impressed by the range and quality of goods available. Guangzhou is widely regarded as the place to come to buy—though the less accessible Special Economic Zone of Shenzhen is even more favored. The hustle and bustle, however, characterize the private and, to some extent, the collective sectors more than the state sector the reforms were intended to enliven. Those still patronizing state stores in 1987 because of their comparatively lower prices acknowledged as much, with considerable irritation. When I asked a local resident how to tell which shops were state stores and which were contracted out or private, she snorted: "That's easy! Just look in the door and see what the clerks are doing."

Restaurants tell the same story. In 1991 I spoke with a nineteen-year-old worker in a state restaurant that provides meals for guests attending conferences run by its parent unit. It was also open to local residents for an hour and a half each morning for tea, but generally only a few tables were filled because of its poor food and casual service. As a probationary worker, the young woman was earning 180 yuan a month, of which the unit retained 50 to partially defray the cost of her uniform. The monthly bonus in this noncompetitive restaurant was an insignificant 15 yuan. She said these wages were nothing compared to those paid by a restaurant with foreign funds behind it, where one might earn 500 yuan a month. I asked why she preferred to work in this restaurant. The number one reason was the "better work atmosphere," which from this employee's point of view meant that supervision was not strict (*yange*). She said that here she and her co-workers could stand around and joke together, whereas in other places you had to be serious every minute. Furthermore, elsewhere you were constantly on duty because most other places stay open for business all day, whereas her restaurant opens only for specified periods around the mealtimes. Between meals the workers can sit outside, wander around, go back to their rooms, or whatever—thus she was not at all concerned about sitting with me (out of sight of her supervisor) for over an hour between the breakfast and lunch shifts. In addition, other restaurants offer less job security because they do not subscribe to the iron rice bowl concept, but here there is always the chance of securing a permanent job.

But progress is possible. I returned to the same restaurant early one morning in late 1992 half expecting it to be empty. To my surprise the tables were rapidly filling up as local people streamed in. What had changed? "Ha," said my elderly tablemates. "Before, they were the only restaurant around here. They knew we couldn't go anywhere else. But since those other [nearby] restaurants have opened, they have had to find ways to attract us." Indeed, the restaurant now had a *juk* (C. rice porridge) and fried dumpling stand just inside its door so that it could serve both customers seated at tables and those interested in takeout. Restaurant workers, including the young women I had interviewed, were taking orders and pushing dim sum carts up and down the aisles. I was impressed. New management? New bonus system?

Infrastructure: Transport, Communications, and Energy

In 1980 a traveler wishing to cross the Pearl River to or from Haizhu district on the south side could take either of two bridges, one west of the city center, the other leading directly into and out of the center. The first, Renmin Bridge, crossing from Liwan district just east of Shamian, the island to which foreigners had been confined prior to the Opium War, was a narrow and congested bridge predating the Communist takeover. It remains a major bottleneck to this day. The second, Haizhu Bridge, connecting Yuexiu and Haizhu districts, is wider, with three lanes for motor vehicles as well as separate lanes for bicycles and sidewalks for pedestrians.

For the next three decades further bridge construction languished because bridges in the urban districts were officially viewed as serving consumption and not production. With the shift in policy in late 1978, Guangzhou turned its attention to its infrastructure and eventually invested in two new enormous bridges, both east of the city center and, in the spirit of the time, both toll bridges.[15] The first, Guangzhou Bridge, went up in the mid-1980s, crossing the Pearl River east of Zhongshan University and leading traffic toward and away from the Tianhe Sports Center. Although Tianhe was basically an agricultural area when the bridge was built, city planners intended that most of Guangzhou's new residential construction occur in this district. At the end of the decade, Haiyin Bridge, crossing the Pearl River from Dongshan district to the west of Zhongshan University, was opened to traffic. Although these new bridges are assets to motor vehicles, they are of less use to bicycles, and most pedestrians find them too long to walk. A fifth bridge, crossing the Pearl between the Guangzhou and the Haiyin Bridges, is also planned.

Even though motor vehicles can cross the river with greater ease now than a few years ago, travel within Guangzhou itself remains problematic. In 1980 a major impediment was the range of vehicles using the roads simultaneously. Particularly frustrating for the drivers of passenger vehicles and trucks were the small tractors used for hauling goods, especially in Haizhu district, which still had many agricultural villages. (At that time some villagers were still grazing their water buffalo on uncut grass on Zhongshan's campus.) Not only were these quasi-motor vehicles loud and slow, but they also carried awkwardly shaped loads that effectively blocked vehicles trying to pass them. Cyclists and pedestrians still felt they owned the roads and thought nothing of weaving in and out of traffic or darting across the street at will. The response to the chaos was a cacophony of horn blowing and rude aggressive acts by the drivers of trucks and passenger vehicles—mostly, it turned out, demobilized soldiers who had learned to drive in the army. Since so few other people were licensed to drive, they viewed themselves as several cuts above the masses and frequently behaved arrogantly toward them.

By the early 1990s traffic overall had greatly improved. The number of municipal trams and buses had increased substantially (from 899 in 1980 to 1,926 by 1993). More important, over the same period the number of "hire cars" (*chuze che*, taxis and small and medium-sized vans) went from 584 to 12,825 (of which 11,757 were taxis).[16] Tractors had been banned from the city, and horn blowing, though not eliminated, was greatly restricted. Furthermore, although the first-time visitor might perceive only chaos, motorists and pedestrians had become less unruly. Improvement has stemmed from training, education, and law enforcement. The army is no longer the school for most drivers. By the beginning of this decade new drivers, to obtain a license, usually had to pay on the order of 2,100 yuan for a formal driver training course. This course can take up to several months to complete, because there is only one legitimate driver training school, because each trainee needs a minimum number of hours behind the wheel, and because each instructor has many trainees. So great is the demand for a driver's license that by 1993 the cost of the training course exceeded 8,000 yuan.

The mass media regularly expose the public, including motorists, cyclists, and pedestrians, to the consequences of bad driving or walking habits. Particularly bad accidents make the evening news and the daily papers. The bulletin board outside the provincial Public Security Bureau tallies Guangzhou's semimonthly count of accidents, fatalities, injuries, and estimates of property damage. Gruesome color photographs showing crushed bicycles, bloodied pavement, and strewn personal effects add meaning to these statistics. A semimonthly accident report for October 16–26, 1987 (statistics only), listed the following results:

	Bicycles	Motor vehicles	Pedestrians
Injuries	26	17	7
Fatalities	4	4	2
Total Traffic Accidents	88	19	9

  Property Loss: 111,020 yuan

This distribution of accidents is fairly typical in the ranking order of the types, though the number of motor vehicle accidents compared to bicycle accidents is somewhat higher than usual. Paradoxically, however, the estimated property loss is much less than usual.

In November 1987 the bulletin board also displayed a photograph of several handcuffed men in court with their heads bowed. All had been arrested on traffic offenses — either reckless driving or driving without proper papers. Each month (in 1987) Guangdong Television's "Morning Show" featured an interview with a representative from Public Security reporting on the previous month's accident totals and offering safety tips. These efforts produced a noticeable effect in a short time. Between 1987 and 1991 motorists virtually ceased pulling out of line to make a right turn from the left lane; bicycles stayed in the bicycle lanes; and pedestrians thought twice about slipping through metal barriers intended to prevent their crossing heavily traveled roads.[17] The government also moved quickly to prevent the rapid increase in the number of motorcycles from becoming a public menace. For example, fines are immediately imposed on cyclists without helmets or mufflers. During five months in Guangzhou in 1991 I heard only one mufflerless motorcycle, and a friend working in the countryside confirmed that cyclists outside the urban districts do not like to bring their motorcycles into the city because of all the strict enforcement.

Although individual driving, cycling, and walking habits have improved, the sheer volume of traffic has grown enormously, so that getting around Guangzhou can be difficult. Like many old Chinese cities, Guangzhou was laid out long before motor vehicle transport became a consideration. Consequently, the oldest districts (Liwan, Yuexiu, and, to a lesser extent, Dongshan) have few roads with more than one motor vehicle lane each way. Traffic lights give precedence to the few east–west roads through the city, though for several hours each day even these can be subject to long delays. To cross the city along its north–south axis can generally take much longer than a street map would suggest. The main east–west thoroughfare, Huanshi Road, running along the northern edge of the old city, channels traffic from the main railway station past the Baiyun (White Cloud) Hotel, Friendship Store, and Garden Hotel—all located within a few hundred yards of each other about two miles to the east. In 1987, to provide an unimpeded approach to the railway station from the south, an elevated limited-access road was constructed over Renmin Road, terminating near the White Swan Hotel. Foreign observers were critical of this investment since the elevated road, the first in the city core, has only one lane each way and could be completely blocked by a single accident. To have made the road any wider, however, would have meant acquiring the land and housing on one or both sides of Renmin Road and relocating the inhabitants— an expense beyond calculation. Since 1991 the city has built a number of overpasses for traffic crossing Dongfeng Road, thus greatly relieving another major bottleneck. Perhaps most important, to provide an alternative to surface travel, the city broke ground in the winter of 1993–94 for its first subway line, which will run from Tianhe to Liwan district.

Although the number of trams and buses has risen, residents forced to rely on them must still endure extreme crowding and the attendant risk of petty crime. Still, if one can hold on to one's bag, public transport is relatively inexpensive. In 1991 the cheapest (and most crowded) regular bus was a long articulated vehicle with wooden seats. (The length of two buses, it has a flexible joint in the middle that bends as the bus turns a corner.) Slightly less crowded and more costly are the conventional buses with padded seats that charge by the length of the ride. Big spenders can get guaranteed seats on vans or minibuses (sometimes referred to as "bread vehicles" [*mianbao che*] because of their bread-loaf shape) that cruise the main bus routes until all their seats are full, at which point they often take an irregular (faster) route to their proclaimed destination. Their fares seem more arbitrary—whatever the ticket seller says.

At the very top of the scale are taxis. In 1980 Guangzhou had few of them, and they could reliably be found only at the major hotels and transport nodes. By the mid-1980s there had been a veritable explosion in the number of taxis operating within the city, and passengers could easily flag one down on almost any main street. By the early 1990s, although the number had continued to increase, there seemed to be somewhat more competition for them — presumably a sign of greater affluence. In 1994 the meter began at 5.4, 6.0, or 7.2 yuan (depending, apparently, on the quality of the vehicle). But a driver in Guangzhou, just as in North America, could also strike it rich by declining to turn the meter on and taking advantage of someone unfamiliar with charges and routes. The ride from the Baiyun Airport to the American consulate, for example, normally cost on the order of 10–12 yuan in 1991. One consular official, estimating that the typical (naive) visitor to the consulate usually paid about 50 yuan, revealed that the record was held by a visitor who had paid 400 yuan (about U.S. $80 at the then exchange rate). As in the United States, taxi drivers soon became favored targets of armed (usually knife-wielding) robbers. Almost overnight in the summer of 1990 most drivers erected transparent or metal-grill dividers between themselves and the backseat. Signs on the dashboard on the passenger side now state that only women and children are allowed to sit up front with the driver.

Telephones have long been a scarce commodity in China, and understandably administrative offices and work units have had priority in acquiring them. Zhongshan University, for example, had only five outside lines in 1980. At that time there were only 42,640 phones in the city proper, and the city phone directory qualified as a secret document; that is, it was for "internal" circulation only. Ordinary residents had little choice but to use the public telephones operated by the residents committees of some neighborhoods. (Such a phone is public in every sense of the word, for it frequently sits on a table right out on the sidewalk, where both the person responsible for the phone and everyone waiting in line to make a call can overhear.) Receiving a call meant scheduling it in advance or else hoping that the person on duty would run up the lane with a loud summons. Consequently, in 1980 visiting patterns among friends were casual. They made appointments during a previous visit or simply dropped in without notice. Someone unable to keep an engagement simply did not show up.

Beginning in the mid-1980s telephone installations increased rapidly — from 76,554 in 1984 to 105,482 in 1985 to 268,814 by the end of 1989.[18] Most of these phones were installed at work units, and initially even residential phones were ostensibly installed for work-related reasons — and at unit expense. In the early 1990s the installation fee ran around 2,300 yuan because in almost every case the wiring itself had to be put in; the phone company could not simply be asked to turn on the service. In 1987 the wait for a private telephone was two years, but by 1991 most senior cadres and affluent households had acquired one. Indeed, by 1993 there were more than 500,000 regular telephones in Guangzhou, said to be a rate of 20.3

phones per 100 persons, the highest in the nation. Equally significant, some 450,000 beepers (*BB ji*) and 52,000 cellular phones allowed users to bypass the installation fee.[19] People are now calling their friends rather than simply dropping in on them.

In 1980 Guangzhou was plagued by an inadequate power supply, and factories around the city operated on a rotating schedule, closing down on days when their area was scheduled for a blackout. Although increasing the power supply was a major objective of both the city and the provincial government, demand kept up with and at times even surpassed supply. Around 1986 China instituted daylight saving time as an energy conservation measure. By moving wasted (because people are still sleeping) early morning light to the end of the day (when people are still active), the central government hoped to reduce the demand for electricity. People in Guangzhou found it difficult to accept this concept, however, and the local response was a perfect example of how Guangzhou (as well as Guangdong in general) deals with unpopular commands from Beijing. They allowed Beijing to think they were complying but in fact did things their own way, as the next paragraph demonstrates.

On April 15 Guangzhou (like the rest of China) was supposed to move the clock ahead one hour: 8 A.M. suddenly became 9 A.M., and so forth. Because Guangzhou is much closer to the equator than Beijing, it does not experience the seasonal shift in amount of daylight as much as Beijing and did not as readily perceive the advantages of moving the clock. When daylight saving time was first instituted, workers all over Guangzhou groaned so loudly and complained so much that their work units finally gave in. At restaurants, schools, or government offices the scheduled workday was moved ahead one hour, so that workers, who got up at exactly the same real time as before, could nonetheless claim to be following the time change. Because of this change that was not a change some people did not bother to move their watches ahead, and meeting times always had to be clarified.[20] Ultimately, the central government capitulated and in the early 1990s discontinued daylight saving time.

Electricity remains in short supply. Not only factories but also offices, hotels, and ordinary residences have stepped up their consumption. Air conditioners and multitudes of household appliances now compete for power with industry. Hotels and shops have installed their own backup generators or have purchased noisy portable generators, which appear on the sidewalks whenever an area undergoes its scheduled day off the electricity grid. But there are also unscheduled outages. In 1991, for example, a rash of unscheduled power outages around the city occurred in early May. During my last three weeks interviewing in Dongshan district there was no electricity for two consecutive days each week, though it would come on briefly in the evening. Although people remarked on the unusual frequency of the outages so early in the year, the heat at the time (at least five straight days in the low 90s) must have meant that every fan and air conditioner in the city was in use. Fortunately, although the sun was intense enough to "pierce the flesh" (C. *gat yuhk*), the humidity was lower than in March, when walls had dripped and nothing would dry.

On May 27 the government felt compelled to respond (in a newspaper article) to citizen complaints about the lack of electricity. It acknowledged that demand was high because the heat continued (weather forecasts predicted highs in the mid-90s) and that it was also quite dry. Guangdong was in the midst of a major drought: rainfall by early May was only one-third of normal. Some of Guangdong's electricity is generated by hydroelectric plants that were short of water because of the drought; and much of the available water had to be diverted to agriculture. Furthermore, a major coal-burning plant that produces electricity was out of commission. Later in the week the provincial government temporarily banned the use of air conditioners in state residences — a ban easy to enforce because of the sound air conditioners make.

The one area of energy use in which Guangzhou shows real improvement is cooking fuel. Visitors to China frequently remark that in the early morning hours (well before 6:30 A.M. in the summer) the parks and the hills are alive with elderly people doing *taijiquan* or other morning exercises. In the early hours, elders say, they can absorb the fresh morning air. This explanation, which might have its roots in ancient Taoist logic, also makes sense on environmental grounds. In 1980 if one had waited until 7 A.M. to do exercises, there would no longer have been any fresh morning air. By 7 A.M. people would already have prepared breakfast, using for fuel compressed (honey-combed) coal cakes, which would have generated a gray pall over the city for several hours. Even at its worst Guangzhou's air pollution was nothing compared with that of cities further north, where coal is used not only for cooking but also for heating. Nevertheless, since Guangdong has to import coal from other provinces, it was deemed less expensive (and cleaner) for the city to shift to piped gas in newly constructed areas and to liquid petroleum gas (LPG) in the older urban districts. In 1988, when only 15 percent of urban households used gas for cooking, Guangzhou announced that to shift most of the city over to gas within about three years, it was planning to invest 900 million yuan in five gas-producing centers.[21] In fact, within five years 60.5 percent of people living in the city proper were cooking with gas.[22] This changeover measurably improved the air quality, though whether that improvement was negated by a simultaneous increase in pollution from motor vehicles remains an open question.

Household Expenditure Patterns

Another way to consider the impact of the reforms on living standards is to examine how household expenditure patterns have changed. As can be seen in Table 2.1, monthly per capita expenditures in urban households in Guangzhou more than sextupled between 1980 and 1992, increasing from 43.4 yuan to 282.2 yuan.

This increase was accompanied by a parallel increase in monthly per capita expendable income. The pessimistic assessment of this tandem increase would be that nothing has changed, or rather that income has just barely managed to stay ahead of expenditures and that price increases have consumed all wage increases. By 1988 (using 1978 as a baseline) the overall cost-of-living index for Guangzhou had, indeed, gone up 2.7 times. For certain products it had gone up even more: fresh vegetables were up by a factor of 6.7 and aquatic products by 4.8.[23] But over the same period per capita income had gone up by a factor of 3.9.[24] Wages (supplemented by at least two outright increases in food subsidies) clearly kept ahead of inflation.

If price rises took a serious bite out of the monthly budget, one would expect consumers to reduce their spending in the categories with the greatest price increases. In fact, the opposite happened. From 1980 to 1988 annual consumption of grain (a heavily subsidized product) dropped from 161 kilograms per capita to 96.5 while consumption of aquatic products rose from 14.5 kilograms per capita to 24.2. Consumption of fresh vegetables remained more or less steady from 1981 to 1988; in 1980 vegetable consumption in Guangzhou seems to have been unusually high.[25] Furthermore, the proportion of the household budget given over to food dropped from 71 percent in 1980 to 56 percent in 1992 while the proportion given over to electricity rose from an insignificant amount (not even measured) to 2.1 percent. The amount spent on electricity was nearly three times that spent on rent!

Table 2.2 compares per capita monthly expenditures in Guangzhou in 1987 with those in the rest of urban China. Clearly Guangzhou was already substantially ahead of the rest of the country in both overall expenditures and the percentage dedicated to the most expensive category of goods (nonstaple foods). Urban residents in other parts of China spend 2.6 times more on cloth goods (padded jackets, pants, and blankets) because the climate elsewhere is substantially colder than that of Guangzhou. The figures from 1990 reveal variations in spending by income groups. The small size of the sample, however, means that random fluctuations can have a disproportionate impact. Although the pattern of per capita expenditures in Guangzhou in 1990 does not differ significantly from the pattern in

TABLE 2.1
*Urban Monthly Per Capita Living Expenditures for Guangzhou, 1980–92,
and for China, 1987 (in yuan)*

	Guangzhou					China
	1980	1984	1988	1990	1992	1987
Commodity Expenditures						
Food	30.81	43.36	91.39	122.83	158.99	42.51
Grain	4.53	5.58	7.01	8.86	22.57	5.70
Nonstaple foods	21.26	30.53	69.99	92.24	108.60	24.83
Tobacco, liquor, tea	1.43	2.44	4.65	6.75	8.62	4.39
Other foods	3.59	4.81	9.74	14.98	19.20	7.56
Clothing	4.48	4.91	8.97	13.94	21.83	11.18
Articles of daily use	2.05	6.98	16.89	17.16	28.60	9.57
Articles of culture, recreation	1.04	3.06	9.59	8.79	11.02	4.61
Books, newspapers, magazines	0.30	0.62	1.00	1.83	2.49	0.67
Medicine, medical supplies	0.31	0.56	1.59	2.54	5.20	0.63
Housing, construction materials	–	0.41	0.67	4.13	5.20	0.81
Fuel	0.63	0.79	1.65	3.21	5.95	0.91
Other commodities	0.57	0.53	1.01	1.84	2.05	0.98
SUBTOTAL	40.19	61.22	132.76	176.27	241.33	71.88
Noncommodity Expenditures						
Rent	0.70	0.99	1.19	1.37	2.32	0.76
Water fee[a]	0.56	0.35	0.57	0.82	1.03	0.19
Electricity fee	–	1.31	3.05	5.09	6.03	0.74
Gas fee	–	–	–	0.21	0.41	0.16
Urban transport[b]	0.43	0.76	1.02	1.64	4.10	0.32
Other transport	–	0.55	1.00	1.74	1.78	0.57
Mail, telecommunications	0.03	0.04	0.21	0.68	1.86	0.08
Medical insurance	0.22	0.19	0.41	0.80	1.05	0.23
School fees	0.15	0.50	1.48	2.61	5.48	0.89
Child care	0.32	0.21	1.23	1.19	1.76	0.36
Recreation	0.21	0.34	0.89	2.03	2.32	0.29
Repairs and services	0.36	0.79	2.14	5.18	11.79	1.26
Other noncommodity	0.25	0.59	0.67	1.17	0.92	0.80
SUBTOTAL	3.23	6.62	13.86	24.53	40.85	6.66
TOTAL EXPENDITURES	43.42	67.84	146.62	200.80	282.18	78.54
Available expendable income[c]	46.21	69.81	145.30	216.09	310.19	81.95

SOURCE: Guangzhou data for 1980–88 from Guangzhou Shi Tongji Ju, *Guangzhou sishinian 1949–1988* (Guangzhou 40 years 1949–1988) (China: Zhongguo Tongji Chubanshe, 1989), pp. 506–7; Guangzhou data for 1990 from Guangzhou Shi Tongji Ju, *Guangzhou tongji nianjian 1991* (Statistical yearbook of Guangzhou 1991) (China: Zhongguo Tongji Chubanshe, 1991), pp. 324–25; Guangzhou data for 1992 from Guangzhou Shi Tongji Ju, *Guangzhou tongji nianjian 1992* (Statistical yearbook of Guangzhou 1992) (China: Zhongguo Tongji Chubanshe, 1992), pp. 414–15. China urban data from State Statistical Bureau, *The 1987 Survey of Income and Expenditure of Urban Households in China* (Honolulu: China Statistical Information and Consultancy Service Centre and East-West Center, 1990), p. 18.

[a] 1980 water fees include electricity fees.

[b] 1980 urban transport fees include other transport fees.

[c] Available expendable income includes all (reported) sources of income: e.g., wages, subsidies, pensions, self-employment, sales of property, withdrawals from savings accounts.

1987, the pattern of the lowest income group in Guangzhou differs substantially from that of the average and the highest income groups. The lowest income group spends proportionately twice as much money on grain as the highest (indicating a less varied diet) and is severely squeezed by the rising cost of nonstaple foods, which account for 60.5 percent of its expenses, compared with only 43.9 percent for those of the highest income group. Food overall accounts for 75.2 percent of the per capita expenditures of the poorest segment of the population.

Further evidence of a real improvement in living standards is offered by Table 2.3, which shows the steady growth in household ownership of various durable goods from 1980 to 1993. As early as 1980 the vast majority of households in Guangzhou already had at least one bicycle as well as an

TABLE 2.2

Urban Monthly Per Capita Living Expenditures, by Percentages, in China (1987) and Guangzhou (1987 and 1990)

			Guangzhou		
				1990[a]	
	China 1987	1987	Lowest decile	Average	Highest decile
Commodity Expenditures					
Food[b]	53.9%	61.3%	75.2%	61.2%	58.3%
Grain	7.3	4.4	6.8	4.4	3.1
Nonstaple foods	31.6	46.6	60.5	45.9	43.9
Tobacco, liquor, tea	5.0	3.0	1.7	3.4	3.2
Other foods	9.6	7.4	6.8	7.5	8.0
Clothing	15.0	6.5	4.6	6.9	8.2
Articles of daily use	11.6	10.7	4.9	8.5	11.3
Articles of culture, recreation	7.2	5.9	2.5	4.4	5.3
Books, newspapers, magazines	0.9	0.9	0.4	1.0	1.1
Medicine, medical supplies	0.7	1.1	1.0	1.3	1.0
Housing, construction materials	0.7	0.9	0.2	2.1	0.9
Fuel	1.2	1.1	1.8	1.6	1.3
Other commodities	1.3	0.7	0.3	1.0	0.9
SUBTOTAL	92.5	89.1	90.9	88.0	88.3
Noncommodity expenditures	8.0	10.9	9.1	12.0	11.7
TOTAL EXPENDITURE, in yuan	78.5	114.6	116.0	200.8	342.7

SOURCE: 1987 China figures from State Statistical Bureau, *The 1987 Survey of Income and Expenditure of Urban Households in China* (Honolulu: China Statistical Information and Consultancy Service Centre and East-West Center, 1990), table 15, p. 18. Guangzhou 1987 figures from Guangzhou Shi Tongji Ju, *Guangzhou sishinian 1949–1988* (Guangzhou 40 years 1949–1988) (China: Zhongguo Tongji Chubanshe, 1989), p. 509. Guangzhou figures for 1990 calculated from Guangzhou Shi Tongji Ju, *Guangzhou tongji nianjian 1991* (Statistical yearbook of Guangzhou 1991) (China: Zhongguo Tongji Chubanshe, 1991), pp. 322–23.

[a] Because the Guangzhou sample numbered only 300 households, the lowest and highest deciles consist of only 30 households each.

[b] Subcategories under food were calculated from *The 1987 Survey*, table 19, p. 18. The figures do not match the total given in table 15 for the main category Food. Similarly, because of rounding the China figures for 1987 do not add up to 100 percent.

TABLE 2.3

Number of Durable Goods per 100 Urban Households in Guangzhou, 1980–93, and in China, 1987

	Guangzhou						China
	1980	1984	1988	1990	1992	1993	1987
Bicycles	140.0	182.5	177.0	191.7	204.7	208.7	186.1
Electric fans	98.5	204.5	307.3	335.7	359.7	348.7	108.9
Sewing machines	85.0	97.5	91.7	94.3	89.0	89.0	76.6
Black-and-white televisions	49.5	83.5	44.0	36.7	23.7	22.3	69.0
Color televisions	1.5	19.5	72.7	88.7	95.3	99.3	36.9
Mono tape recorders	31.0	45.5	48.3	47.7	53.0	54.0	31.3
Stereo tape recorders	–	40.0	42.3	44.7	42.6	42.0	33.1
Cameras	2.0	10.5	25.0	33.7	45.3	50.7	19.0
Washing machines	1.5	59.0	83.3	87.3	93.3	97.3	71.4
Refrigerators	–	28.0	69.7	87.3	93.0	92.7	26.8
Motorcycles	–	1.0	0.7	4.0	7.0	8.7	1.6
Air conditioners	–	–	0.3	1.3	9.7	19.0	0.2
"High class" sound systems	–	–	–	17.3	27.3	27.0	–
Videocassette recorders	–	–	–	31.0	60.3	55.3	–

SOURCE: Guangzhou data for 1980–88 from Guangzhou Shi Tongji Ju, *Guangzhou sishinian 1949–1988* (Guangzhou 40 years 1949–1988) (China: Zhongguo Tongji Chubanshe, 1989), p. 510; for 1990 from Guangzhou Shi Tongji Ju, *Guangzhou tongji nianjian 1991* (Statistical yearbook of Guangzhou 1991) (China: Zhongguo Tongji Chubanshe, 1991), p. 322; for 1992 from Guangzhou Shi Tongji Ju, *Guangzhou tongji nianjian 1993* (Statistical yearbook of Guangzhou 1993) (China: Zhongguo Tongji Chubanshe, 1993), p. 416; for 1993 from Guangzhou Shi Tongji Ju, *Guangzhou tongji zhaiyao 1994* (Guangzhou statistical summary 1994) (Guangzhou, 1994), p. 65. China urban data from State Statistical Bureau, *The 1987 Survey of Income and Expenditure of Urban Households in China* (Honolulu: China Statistical Information and Consultancy Service Centre and East-West Center, 1990), p. 19.

electric fan and a sewing machine. These items can be considered legitimate necessities in that in 1980 public transport was so overburdened that a bicycle was a rational purchase for anyone who needed to go to work. Similarly, the hot humid climate in Guangzhou makes an electric fan indispensable. Ownership of black-and-white televisions peaked in 1984; subsequently, purchasers bought color televisions (or asked their overseas relatives to bring them in). At about the same time, stereo tape recorders began to be almost as popular as mono tape recorders, and even ordinary folk were purchasing washing machines and refrigerators. By the early 1990s more than half of Guangzhou households owned videocassette recorders, and the affluent were moving on to air conditioners and even motorcycles.

The state, heavily subsidizing the grain purchases and housing of urban residents, took note of this phenomenal growth in apparently discretionary income. In February 1988 an article entitled "A Brief Analysis of China's Consumption Pattern at the Present Stage" appeared in *Guangming Ribao*.[26] The author, Tu Jiancheng, points out that

the key to evaluating whether the consumption pattern and its changes are rational lies in whether they conform to the economic developmental stage's requirements;

that is, in seeing whether they fit the productive force's level, the social political system, and the situation of resources and its changes in the country. They are rational if they fit each other, otherwise they are not.

Using his three criteria, Tu concludes that the current consumption pattern is irrational. First, because production in China is low, the consumption of high-grade durable goods should not be too high. To produce such goods distorts the country's allocation of productive forces, and to import them creates a shortage of foreign exchange. Second, it is unacceptable ideologically at this stage of development to have too great a gap in income between the rich and the poor. Those with excessively high incomes, particularly from nonlabor sources, should be subject to redistribution mechanisms, primarily taxation, whereas those with low incomes should be given some relief. Third, China has relatively low energy resources and cannot afford a pattern of high energy consumption.

To align the consumption pattern with China's developmental stage, that is, the initial stage of socialism, Tu proposes restricting the production and consumption of high-grade durable goods and of luxury goods through taxes and price increases, "constraining" the use of private cars while developing public transportation, and encouraging the production of low- and middle-grade consumer goods that will allow China's traditional industries to flourish. Significantly, he concludes his list with suggestions for housing reform: "The commercialization of housing should be promoted, and the proportion of expenditure on accommodation in the consumption pattern should be gradually increased." When Tu wrote these remarks on China, less than 1 percent of household income in Guangzhou was going to housing, and the state was determined to shift some of the financial burden from its budget to the consumer's. This task has not proved easy.

Housing

At the end of 1978 in Guangzhou, as in other old Chinese cities, living space was cramped (a mere 3.8 square meters per person), housing stock had deteriorated, and ownership rights were unclear. Chinese housing statistics are calculated three ways: the "built-up" or "constructed" area, measured by the exterior dimensions of a building; the "usable area," including all space in a particular apartment plus a fraction of the common areas, for example, hallway and stairs; and "living space," including bedrooms and living rooms in a particular apartment. The figure 3.8 square meters per capita refers to living space. The practice of not including kitchen and bathroom space in calculations of living space might have its origins in the style of the traditional urban dwelling, which was built around a courtyard, frequently without any space permanently dedicated to either a kitchen or a bathroom. Instead, occupants of the dwelling used part of the courtyard for cooking and excreted into chamber pots, which were emptied into larger containers that were then emptied by night-soil collectors. Or it might derive from the conversion into apartments, in the early years of the PRC, of factory dormitories without kitchens and bathrooms. Occupants of these apartments had hearth space set aside in a common cooking area on their floor and shared a common bathroom or used municipal public toilets.

This traditional disregard for kitchen and bathroom space finds expression even in much of the housing built in the 1980s. A kitchen typically consists of a narrow room with a long tiled counter occupying almost half its width. The top of the counter has a set-in sink, and the counter space on either side is used for food preparation and cooking. A double gas burner attached to an LPG canister on the floor is also set on the counter; the refrigerator is consigned to the living room. Beneath the counter is an open storage area. No one can sit and eat in the kitchen. Nor is the typical Chinese bathroom an inviting place for relaxation. For efficiency in plumbing installation bathrooms are usually located right next to kitchens rather than hidden away among the bedrooms. One does not take a bath; one takes a shower in a room that is unheated. Furthermore, the traditional Chinese toilet — still the norm — is not something one can sit on. The user must squat down carefully over a trenchlike fixture, maintain balance for the duration, and then stand erect without a handhold. For these reasons people do not spend much time in Chinese kitchens and bathrooms, nor is their appearance of great concern to the household.

Housing stock was in such poor condition primarily because of low rates of investment in building and maintenance (housing investment was deemed "unproductive") and ideological antagonism to property owners' living off the collection of rents. By 1993 a boom in housing construction brought per capita living space in Guangzhou to 8.5 square meters, and planners were optimistically aiming for a target of 14 square meters by the year 2000.[27] Nationally, by the end of 1988, according to a World Bank estimate, 46 percent of all urban housing stock had been built since the start of the decade whereas only 8 percent predated the establishment of the PRC.[28]

Current Housing Stock

Figures 1–3 show the configuration of some accommodations currently available in Guangzhou: municipal housing, overseas Chinese housing, and new work-unit-assigned housing. The unit in Figure 1 is fairly typical of the

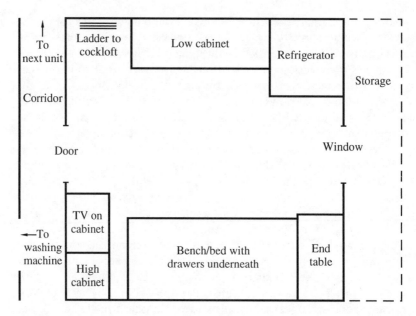

Figure 1. A Housing Management Bureau unit of 7.5 square meters. The tenants added a makeshift balcony, reached by crawling out the window. They also cut through the wall in the public corridor to erect a platform for their washing machine; water for it comes from the building located right below it.

low end of what is available through the Guangzhou Housing Management Bureau (HMB). The 7.5-square-meter room is one of many located in a prewar building in western Yuexiu district. This L-shaped two-story building itself appears to have been a dormitory at one time; each household occupies a single room and shares cooking space in the crook of the L. All residents of the building (and of many adjoining buildings) use a public toilet located just across the lane. The now elderly head of the household was relocated to this second-floor unit in 1952, when the site she, her husband, and son occupied was cleared of squatters for construction. The family now consists of the widow and her son, who will be marrying shortly. Two granddaughters from the countryside, both of whom operate private stalls, occasionally stay here overnight, but usually they stay in rooms closer to their workplace that they share with several other young women. The widow sleeps on the bench/bed against the wall while her son sleeps in the cockloft that has been erected above it. Their monthly rent is roughly 2 yuan.

Many families housed by the HMB actually live in prewar buildings that once belonged to overseas Chinese. The units in these quite narrow buildings are divided into two or three rooms with a corridor leading to the shared kitchen and sometimes to a shared bathroom as well. The overseas Chinese housing in Figure 2, however, is occupied by a single household — a woman and her teenage son — although her parents, who spend half their time in Hong Kong, live with her when they are in Guangzhou. The family pays no rent because the owner, a relative living abroad, has no interest in collecting rent from them. In 1987 the family hired a team of decorators to enclose the rear rooftop and add three small rooms, including a modern bathroom with a Western-style toilet and bathtub.

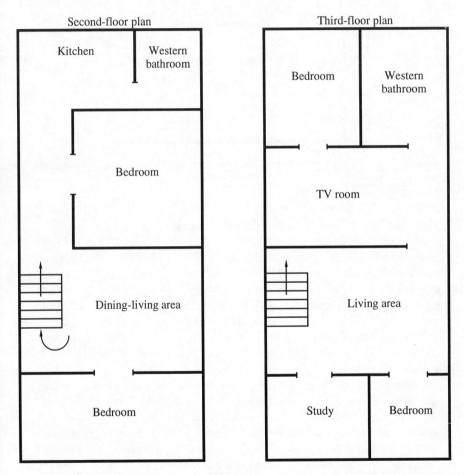

Second-floor plan

Kitchen Western bathroom

Bedroom

Dining-living area

Bedroom

Third-floor plan

Bedroom Western bathroom

TV room

Living area

Study Bedroom

Figure 2. Two floors of an overseas Chinese house. The area including the bedroom, Western bathroom, and TV room on the third floor was added in 1987 by enclosing what had been the rear half of the roof. Total floor space is 100 square meters.

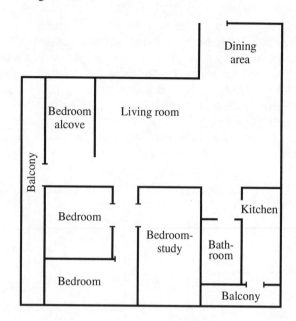

Figure 3. An apartment in new housing constructed by a real estate development corporation.

The upscale housing shown in Figure 3 was purchased by a city work unit from a development corporation. The nine-story building itself, located just north of the railway between Guangzhou and Hong Kong in Dongshan district, was completed in late 1989 or early 1990. The family of six (a middle-aged couple, their two children, the husband's mother, and the wife's niece from the countryside) has been assigned 106 square meters (usable space) and pays 10 yuan a month. The government is especially interested in selling off this kind of heavily subsidized unit to the occupants. The family has creatively redesigned the interior of the sixth-floor apartment to meet its particular needs, dividing space as it saw fit, installing cabinets high up on the walls, and so forth.

Dining takes place in the area at the entry from the corridor. The refrigerator stands against the opposite wall, near the kitchen. The living room used to include what is now a bedroom alcove, but a half-wall with sliding windows to the ceiling was erected to provide a separate bedroom for the nineteen-year-old son of the household. The phone is located in this room, as is the door to the balcony. Because this alcove cannot be shut off from the living room, most of the son's activities are visible, unless he pulls shut a curtain. Most of the time the son is away at school.

The bedroom below the alcove bedroom on the plan is that of the 22-year-old daughter of the household; and below her room is that of the 80-

year-old mother and 12-year-old niece, which has two bunk beds. The older woman sleeps on the bottom of the bunk nearest the door while the girl sleeps on the bottom of the bunk against the opposite wall. The two upper bunks are reserved for guests. Finally, the largest bedroom (identified on the plan as bedroom and study) is the couple's.

The bathroom is small and narrow, with a Chinese-style toilet set into a slightly elevated platform. A water pipe with an attached faucet runs along the wall. A plastic hose attached to the faucet is used to flush the toilet, wash the floor, and (presumably) to shower. The floor slopes slightly toward a drain set near the sink (the sink itself has no drainpipe). Water drawn into the sink flows onto the floor and down the drain.

The kitchen includes a sink, two gas burners, and a long counter for chopping vegetables. Much of the food preparation is actually done out on the small balcony off the kitchen. On the large balcony that runs almost the length of the apartment, clothes are hung out to dry. (The balcony above it provides a roof, making the space below usable except in heavy rain.) In one corner of this balcony fruit peels are set out to dry on bamboo trays.

Real Estate Development and Commodity Housing Construction

Since 1983 few work units in Guangzhou have developed their own housing. Instead they have purchased housing developed by one of the 106 separate real estate development corporations active in the city. As a result of this pattern of purchase, work unit housing is no longer likely to be located on unit grounds, and workers from several different units may live in the same housing block. Over half the real estate development corporations belong to the city; the rest belong to the province, the central government, and the counties, and the government itself provides the initial capitalization. The World Bank has gathered data on the largest real estate development corporations operating in Guangzhou; much of the description that follows is taken from its 1992 report.[29]

The largest of the real estate corporations, the Guangzhou City Construction Development General Corporation (GCCDGC), since its founding in 1983, has been responsible for 30 percent of the housing construction in the city—29,194 units. It has sold 85 percent of its units to enterprises and 15 percent to individuals. Some real estate corporations, such as the Overseas Chinese Property Development Company (OCPDC), aim primarily at attracting overseas Chinese as buyers. In 1987 OCPDC, which had been developing housing in Guangzhou since 1984, began direct marketing to overseas Chinese, who now account for 70–80 percent of its total sales. The proportion of newly constructed housing in Guangzhou sold to individuals (as opposed to work units) by all the development corporations taken together grew from 9 percent in 1985 to 39 percent in 1988.[30] The GCCDGC had a virtual monopoly on construction in Tianhe district, though it sold off some of its land to other firms. From 1983 to 1989 the average sales price per square meter of a GCCDGC apartment increased from 500–580 yuan to 1,300–1,600 yuan. The increase reflected not only inflation but also speculation and a reorientation to producing upscale units with more rooms.

Since 1989 this situation — rapidly rising prices and the limited availability of more modest housing — has gone from bad to worse. By the end of 1993 prices per square meter had risen to 6,000 yuan in the city center, 4,000–5,000 yuan elsewhere in the city, 3,000 yuan on the edges of the city, and 2,000 yuan in the suburbs. With the typical units of commodity housing offering 75 square meters, ordinary families were excluded from the open housing market. Indeed, according to one calculation a household with three workers making average wages and paying 200 yuan a month would require more than 62 years to purchase a 50-square-meter apartment![31]

Apartment prices in a single building vary not only by configuration but also by floor. Residents of Guangzhou strongly prefer to live on the fourth and adjacent floors. The lower floors are considered too dusty, noisy, damp, public, and accessible to thieves and mosquitoes whereas the higher floors, though cleaner and better ventilated, are inconvenient: they can usually be reached only by stairs. Because of electricity and maintenance costs few residences of under ten stories have elevators.

Building in formerly suburban Tianhe seldom involves tearing down existing housing, so that sales prices there are actually below those in the inner city, where property owners and sitting tenants must be dealt with. In 1987, for example, the GCCDGC was selling its Tianhe units for between 780 and 950 yuan, whereas in Dongshan district new units were selling for 1,200 yuan and in even more congested Yuexiu district, for 1,500 yuan.[32] When a unit or real estate company wants to build on an already occupied site, it must negotiate with those who got there first. Owners must be compensated for their property and be provided with equivalent or larger living space in the new building erected on the site. The household, depending on its composition during negotiations, might be entitled to several new units, for example, one for each married child's family. One household in the Family Study managed in 1984 to gain four apartments outright and the long-term rental of another as part of its settlement. If the original occupants are owners, they pay no rent in the new building. If they are tenants, they pay the same rent as those assigned to live there by their units. In addition, each family is given a modest lump sum to cover the moving costs and a monthly per capita sum to cover (or partially cover) the costs of living elsewhere while the construction is under way. In some cases several floors of a new building have to be given away to previous inhabitants of the site, and the buyers of the remaining floors have to absorb the cost of their subsidies.[33]

The skewing of the property market and the tendency of developers to cater to the upper end of the income spectrum have increasingly come to be viewed as inequitable. Few people in Guangzhou can improve their housing in the current market, so alternative routes must be provided for those of modest means. By late 1993 a number of complementary proposals were being considered: accelerating the sale of public housing units (see below under Public Housing Reform), redefining the households designated as facing "exceptional hardship" (*tebie kunnan*), making more funding for housing available to work units, and requiring that a broader range of apartment types be constructed.

For housing purposes only, "hardship" means having less than 6 square meters per person and "exceptional hardship" means having less than 2 square meters per person. Households in the latter category are given a priority assignment (via a lottery) to new housing developed by the government specifically for them. (They may rent or buy this property, depending on their means and their inclination.) In February 1991 Guangzhou held the first of several such housing lotteries. Households certified as eligible by their local government office brought their papers to the Zhongshan Memorial Hall for deposit and were said to have about a one-in-three chance of being assigned new housing. By 1993 most of these families had been relocated, and households with less than 5 square meters per person were being considered for eligibility.

To bring more moderately priced housing onto the market, several proposals were floated. The first was to reduce land costs to developers. The second was to require developers to provide a range of small and medium-sized apartments in addition to the large ones that dominated the market. The third was to require that a precise percentage (on the order of 22–25 percent) of annual residential construction consist of low-cost housing, and the fourth called for the creation of a unified supervisory mechanism that could verify that whatever guidelines were eventually established were being met.[34]

The Restoration of Property Rights

Before the government could allow the sale of housing, it had to define and guarantee the legal rights of property owners. Although rural housing remained in private hands in the Mao era and after, very little urban housing did. The first major change in housing policy to affect ownership rights was the 1956 socialization of property, which restricted the amount of property an owner could control and the amount of rent he could charge. Commercial properties were taken over, though owners were apparently compensated. Owners of residential property were allowed to retain a certain amount of space for themselves, but the excess was to be rented out, and the HMB controlled the assignment of tenants to such places and the amount of rent they would be charged. Rents, set very low, were no longer paid to the owners of private housing, though they were paid to owners of overseas Chinese housing or their local representatives (see below). In September 1966 rents were no longer to be paid even to owners of overseas Chinese housing but only to the HMB. The economic reforms of the late 1970s were supposed to restore to private (local and overseas) owners control over rents and occupancy, but these rights were not easily asserted.

Private (as opposed to overseas Chinese) housing is that housing purchased with money made inside China; the owner is likely to occupy the dwelling himself. Overseas Chinese housing is categorized as old or new. Old overseas Chinese housing generally includes dwellings purchased prior to 1949 by Chinese living abroad. Subsequently, despite efforts to entice foreign capital into Overseas Chinese New Village (an upscale residential neighborhood in Dongshan district set aside for the relatives of overseas Chinese), overseas Chinese purchased relatively little housing until after the Cultural Revolution. Thus, new overseas Chinese housing generally includes dwellings purchased recently with money made abroad (i.e., foreign currency); the owner might or might not be abroad. If abroad, the owner normally designates someone to collect rents and maintain the property. If the owner dies or the representative disappears, ownership becomes clouded. Would-be heirs must certify their claims. If they are scattered, this can take a long time.

One of the households in the Family Study found itself in 1991 caught up in a tug-of-war between two claimants to the property of a deceased overseas Chinese owner. The original owner had gone to Canada long ago and designated one of his daughters living in Taishan county to collect the rent; about twice a year she made the trip to Guangzhou to do so. At one point, however, an adopted son (*yang zi*) showed up, claiming that the old man had turned over ownership rights to him. He moved his older sister into the first floor of the house and demanded that thenceforth all rents be paid to her. People were skeptical of his claim to the house and demanded proof. He produced a letter from the old man saying he was turning over ownership, but the letter was dated *after* the man's death, so everyone knew the document was false. Nevertheless, the family was uncertain what to do about the rent. The Taishan daughter was afraid to come and collect it (the amount involved is minimal), fearing a terrible row with the first-floor usurpers. When the case went to court, it was decided in favor of the adopted son. The family that had lived for over 40 years on the third floor of the old but comparatively spacious house (where they have 40 square meters of living space) has been ordered to move as soon as the appropriate work unit offers them housing. Because the head of the household is a retiree, he has low priority with the unit. So far the family has been offered (but rejected) an apartment smaller than its current one, on the ninth floor of an old building.

Extending rights to owners, however, meant restricting the rights (or the assumed rights) of their tenants. Initially (ca. 1980) the owners were told that besides receiving the rents to which they were entitled, they would receive the rights to any dwelling vacated (and thus permanently forfeited) by the tenants. Tenants who left could not simply pass on their occupancy rights to friends or relatives, as had been common practice in the past, and people occupying a dwelling illegally could be evicted. The owner was then free to decide what to do with the unit: rent it to someone else at whatever price could be gotten, sell it, tear it down and build a new one, or move into it.

The implementation of this policy, however, had unforeseen consequences. Owners demanding back their housing began evicting or trying to evict all kinds of occupants, including long-term occupants who had been paying rent. Even legal occupants were harassed, threatened with lawsuits, and otherwise encouraged to move so that the owner could regain control of the dwelling.[35] These evicted and harassed families in fact had nowhere to go because there was and is no inexpensive housing on the open market. As the situation got out of hand, the government had to revise the policy. Beginning in 1987 (though the new policy did not affect cases already on the books, which were still to be judged according to criteria set earlier) the only basis for evicting legal occupants was the owner's plan personally to occupy the space.

Corporate owners found themselves in a similar dilemma. Among the properties effectively expropriated during the Cultural Revolution were those of religious organizations. Since these holdings were frequently substantial, they had been taken over by comparatively powerful entities, resistant to persuasion. The Buddhist Association, for example, had had to go to court in 1987 to compel the Provincial Antiquities Museum to vacate one of its temples. And as late as 1991 a Christian church in Dongshan struggled to regain property from another unit, which, in an effort to keep the desirable church property it had settled into, offered to swap for it a parcel that was miles away, across the Pearl River.

In 1986 the government did attempt to soften the coming blow to recovery rights by requiring even long-term legal tenants to sign rental contracts with their (private) landlords. Initially the contract period could be whatever the landlord and tenant agreed upon (landlords tended to push for two-year leases), but the rent could be increased by no more than 33 percent each time a contract was renewed. (People signing leases as first-time tenants could, however, be charged whatever the market would bear.) By 1991 leases were to run for a four-year term, with rental increases not to exceed 40 percent upon renewal if the landlord could not get the tenant to leave. These provisions have produced anxiety among tenants whose contracts are due to expire or who have experienced upheavals because co-tenants in multifamily apartments have relocated. One elderly woman in the Family Study discovered that her apartment, once shared by three small households, had been converted into a clothing factory when a new tenant took over the shared living room and one bedroom. Long worktables and suspended metal poles stretched the length of what had been the two rooms. Fourteen workers had been moved into the apartment to live in a cockloft built above the factory floor. The noise and increased burden on the one toilet on the floor was more than the elderly woman could take, but she had nowhere to go. Her lease was due to expire shortly.

Guangzhou has far more private housing than other cities in China, primarily because of the area's wealth, brought about by the flow of remittances from overseas prior to 1949 and again since about 1980. According to officials of the Guangzhou HMB, in 1991 about 33 percent of housing was held by work units, 25 percent was privately held, and 43 percent was held by the HMB. The first national survey on urban housing, conducted in 1985, found a quite different pattern of ownership: 75 percent of housing was held by work units, 16 percent was private, and 9 percent belonged to local housing bureaus.[36] Nationally, given such a pattern of ownership, housing reform focused less on restoring property rights than on relieving the heavy burden on the budgets of the state and of profit-making enterprises. When the state first relinquished much of its control over the budgets of such enterprises, it had hoped that the profits retained would be used to upgrade production capabilities. Instead, the enterprises (and the state itself) went on the construction binge described above and increased their financial obligations by continuing to provide housing at heavily subsidized rents. This outcome was recognized as unsound and uneconomical.

Public Housing Reform

Early in the reforms the state proposed to convert housing from a welfare benefit to a commodity and authorized a number of localities to experiment with ways to effect this conversion. In 1980 both Wenzhou, in Zhe-jiang province, and Nanyang city, in Henan province, began organizing residents to purchase or build their own housing.[37] By mid-decade, however, such purchase schemes were threatened by rapidly rising prices. Other localities, such as Yantai in Shandong, experimented with a voucher system, whereby work units increased both the rentals charged to workers and workers' incomes — but the increased income was in housing vouchers, not in cash. The vouchers could be used only to pay rent. The rent increases were intended not simply to make housing less of a budget-buster for the units but also to induce tenants, now paying higher rents, to consider purchasing a home as sounder financially than paying rent. In February 1988 the State Council, announcing plans to phase in housing reform nationwide over the next three to five years, set the following goals:

To readjust the rent for public housing by factoring in depreciation, maintenance, and management expenses, interest for the funds invested, and real estate tax; to restrain irrational demand for housing; to help workers and staff members buy houses; and to take policy, legislative, and public opinion measures to guide and regulate residents' consumption, rationalize consumption patterns, and lay a foundation for commercializing housing.[38]

In accordance with the State Council guidelines Guangzhou, on October 1, 1989, the 40th anniversary of the founding of the PRC, officially began its housing reform.[39] It set out to unify the rent structure in public housing, provide incentives to purchase instead of rent, and (as already discussed) alleviate the worst overcrowding in households regardless of their unit affiliation. Prior to October 1, 1989, the HMB followed one rent schedule for the housing it supervised, and the various work units followed their own. In 1990, however, the rents for the two types of public housing were standardized at 0.27 yuan per square meter, a rate substantially below what both Chinese experts and the World Bank considered cost-effective. In late 1993 it was raised to 0.50 yuan per square meter, a rate lower than that applied to new housing, for which rents are expected to be high enough to make housing construction a worthwhile investment. (The rate for new housing was raised from 0.50 yuan per square meter to 0.80 at the beginning of 1994.)

A carrot-and-stick approach has been used to encourage both people assigned to new housing and people occupying older housing to buy rather than rent. Negative incentives include the higher rents of new housing; the requirement that arriving tenants put down in advance a rent deposit of 20 yuan per square meter, which they can recover if they move, but not with interest; and the payment of a premium for more space than tenants are officially entitled to occupy for their rank. For example, a cadre already occupying an apartment of 60 square meters who is entitled to only 40 square meters might pay 0.5 yuan for each of the first 40 meters but ten times that amount for each extra square meter.

Positive incentives include a range of discounts on the price initially set for an apartment. For example, individuals who pay for their unit in a lump sum (rather than in installments) are entitled to 20 percent off the selling price. In addition, each year of service with the unit entitles the purchaser to a 0.03 percent discount; that is, for someone with 30 years of service, the price is reduced by 9 percent. Finally, special (unspecified) consideration is given to *lixiu* cadres (individuals who joined the Communists in the fight against the Japanese or Guomindang — thereby earning high credentials — and who have since left the work force because of their age) and other old revolutionaries. These new owners are also exempted from paying any land taxes. By the end of 1993 the incentives had led more than 167,000 households in Guangzhou to purchase their (formerly public) housing.[40]

The large number of purchases in a short time reflects the setting of sales prices for public housing, nationally and in Guangzhou, at only a fraction of true value, with enormous losses to the state as a result. An article in *Yangcheng Wanbao* describes two representative cases of this virtual giveaway.[41] Both involve state employees in their fifties who in 1993 purchased an apartment: Mr. Yang, living in a remote county in Sichuan, and Mrs. Chen, living in a district of Beijing. Mr. Yang's new three-bedroom apartment, which has a constructed area of more than 110 square meters, including a living room of more than 20 square meters, cost 5,000 yuan. The price of such an apartment in this region should have been 15,000 yuan. The discount to Mr. Yang pales, however, when compared with that offered to Mrs. Chen. Although Mrs. Chen's ninth-floor double apartment is actually slightly smaller than Mr. Yang's, it has elevator access, central heating, and piped-in gas. If sold on the open market in Beijing, it probably would have cost some 200,000 yuan, but Mrs. Chen paid only 10,000!

Realizing that work units were essentially giving away their housing, the State Council abruptly intervened, announcing on January 1, 1994, that effective immediately, the sale of public housing in China was to cease until national guidelines could be developed. Would-be and recent purchasers were stunned by the news and by subsequent rumors that those who had already benefited from the low purchase prices might be required to compensate the state in some way.

Why and How People Move

At the time of the 1991 visits to the households in the Family Study, the housing reforms described above had barely gotten under way. Although

TABLE 2.4
Circumstances of Household Moves in Guangzhou,
January 1988 to January 1991 (N = 30)

Reason for move	Outcome					
	To unit housing	Join relative	Temporary relocation	Private purchase	Other	Total
Housing reclaimed by owner	3	6	0	0	0	9
Construction on site	0	1	5	1	1	8
Assignment to unit housing	8	0	0	0	0	8
Personal/unclear	1	2	0	1	1	5
TOTAL	12	9	5	2	2	30

SOURCE: The Guangzhou Family Study
  NOTE: The unit of analysis in this table is the household, not the individual. The number of individuals in the Family Study who moved was higher than that shown (two moved to the United States), but other family members remained in the same housing.

families living in privately owned housing had already signed rental contracts and seen their rents increase, no one had yet purchased a work unit or HMB-assigned apartment, but several were planning to do so. Some families, however, had been affected by real estate developers' or private owners' asserting their right to occupy their property. These families either were assigned to unit housing or moved in with relatives or entered the housing market as renters or prospective buyers. Their experiences entering the brave new world of commodity housing can shed light on the accessibility and cost of free market housing at the turn of the decade.

From January 1988 to January 1991, of the 200 households in the Family Study, 30 changed residence. As Table 2.4 illustrates, the reason for most moves was an owner's assertion of ownership rights (this happened more frequently in Dongshan than in Yuexiu), and the outcome for most evicted households was that they joined relatives elsewhere. Most of these households consisted of elderly couples or individuals not in a position to negotiate a housing assignment from their work units. All the households that moved because their homes were demolished and new housing was built were from Yuexiu district; all were theoretically eligible to live in the new housing on the site when it was completed. Because these households had to find alternative housing within a few months, their circumstances reveal what the open rental market is like for ordinary people.

Three observations come to mind immediately. Most rental housing is in private hands, on the city's outskirts, and is more expensive than what has been left behind. One family of five exchanged its two rooms, for which it had been paying 3 yuan a month, for three rooms (of better quality), for which it had to pay 150 yuan. The family could afford this increase only because the property development company was allocating 35 yuan per person per month toward whatever rent the family had to pay while out of its rightful home. When they move into a new apartment on the old site, they will be allocated 32 square meters and a low rent. The company also gave them a onetime payment for moving expenses of 150 yuan. The family is not happy with its "temporary" quarters, in which it will probably spend more than three years: the apartment has almost no windows, and the expense of electricity is a constant worry. The neighborhood is near railway tracks, next to a coal plant that makes everything around it filthy. The coal plant, however, separates the apartment from the thunder of the freight trains that use this track on the western edge of the city.

Because this building qualifies as a village house (the once rural site was engulfed by urban sprawl), it is exempt from normal building codes and thus occupies every conceivable square centimeter of the owner's property. Although not actually joined to structures adjacent or opposite, it might as well be. Residents of similar urban villages in other parts of Guangzhou joke about being able to shake hands with their neighbors across the street without even having to leave the house. Such houses are built right up to the edge of the lane separating them, and the balconies added to the second and third floors reach halfway across the lane. Thus residents on the upper floors of both houses can reach across from their balconies whereas residents of the ground floor endure the darkness and damp caused by poor air circulation. Pedestrians on the lane below must, in effect, tunnel their way through the village.[42]

Indeed, one of the other families forced to relocate temporarily had moved into such a village in Sanyuanli. The family found the building satisfactory, but not the neighborhood. First, the noise was deafening because the village sits in the landing approach to the airport, near the end of the runway on which planes normally touch down. Second, the villagers put up so much housing so fast that many strangers have moved in. Everyone is leery of everyone else. Instead of sitting outside in the evening and chatting as in the old neighborhood, people come home and lock the door. One family found a quiet place for 140 yuan a month in a village in a still agricultural area. They have peace and quiet, and they know that their neighbors all know each other even if no one knows them, but they also have a latrine that overhangs a fish pond and they are far from the city center, though close to the adults' workplace. (They work in a factory recently relocated from the city core as part of the government's effort to reduce air pollution.)

A family looking in 1991 for housing right in the city—in Xiatang, for example—had to pay anywhere from several hundred to 1,500 yuan a month. Xiatang is a community in Baiyun district just north of the Guangzhou-Kowloon railroad tracks, a ten-minute walk from Yuexiu Park and therefore highly desirable. The original inhabitants are still officially considered rural residents, and they have made the most of their private property rights. In 1985 one family, using funds supplied by relatives living abroad, had its cottage torn down and replaced by a four-story building with a rooftop apartment. The new building occupies an almost triangular corner plot, so that some of the rooms are oddly shaped. The late-middle-aged owners, who live on the fourth floor, have three bedrooms and a living room, kitchen, bathroom, and balcony. They rent out the remaining floors. The first floor is used as a workshop by a Hong Kong company that makes jade ornaments; the second, third, and fifth (rooftop) floors are rented to individual families. Each of the flats is about 80 square meters and in 1991 was being rented out at 1,100 to 1,200 yuan a month. At that time purchase prices in Xiatang were estimated at 2,100 yuan per square meter.

The people who benefit most by exchanging their old housing for something new are those who have long been privileged in socialist China, high cadres and those employed by powerful state units with ready access to construction funds. Among the most privileged are *lixiu* cadres. One of the households in the Family Study moved to a housing estate for *lixiu* cadres that opened in 1989 on the western fringes of Tianhe district in a protected area surrounded by a wall. Although the family includes only three members, because of the father's status it was allocated 108 square meters of living space: three bedrooms and two living rooms (plus kitchen and two baths). The rent was 23 yuan, of which the family pays only about 15 — the difference between its old rent and its new. The father's unit, which pays the old rent, also installed a telephone for them. At the time of the Family Study interview in 1991 the selling of unit housing to the occupants was under discussion, and the family was preparing to buy its apartment in the near future. Although no price had yet been set, the family thought it would be somewhere around 200 yuan a square meter, though the price would be lower to them because of the father's status. This estimate is in line with the prices paid by Mr. Yang and Mrs. Chen for their housing.

How does this price compare with those individuals were paying at the same time on the open market? We can answer this question by considering two families, the Yips and the Chois, who actually did buy housing in Guangzhou during this period. In 1987 Mrs. Yip, aged 82, lived in a 7-square-meter cubicle in housing assigned by the HMB. She paid 1.8 yuan a month and met her expenses through remittances sent by her son living in the United States. At the time, her son had already sent her U.S. $10,000 toward the purchase of an apartment in Baiyun district in a new building that was not completed and ready for occupancy until September 1989.

Mrs. Yip had asked a high-ranking cadre for whom she had once worked as a *baomu* (domestic servant) to write a letter of introduction to the development company so that she would be considered an appropriate buyer.* A total of 60,000 yuan was spent on the new residence: 52,000 to purchase it and another 8,000 to finish it. Mrs. Yip now lives in a dwelling ten times larger than her previous one; she has 70 square meters of living space, including three bedrooms and a living room as well as a kitchen with an attached shower and a toilet near the main bedroom. A young girl who works making clothes rents one of the bedrooms for 250 yuan a month and also pays the electric, water, and trash fees. Seventy square meters seems like a lot of space for one elderly woman, but her daughter-in-law and grandson, who have returned to China, expect to join her. They are currently living in the countryside in the daughter-in-law's natal village, where she is looking after her mother. In two years when the grandson is ready to attend junior middle school,[43] he and his mother will join Mrs. Yip in Guangzhou and look after her.

In 1987 Mr. Choi, aged 82, his two unmarried sons, and a *baomu* lived in a temporary structure beside the site of their previous home, torn down for the construction of new housing into which they expected to move. In the meantime his two unmarried daughters, who live and work in the real estate business in Macao, had decided to purchase an apartment in Baiyun district in a newly completed housing estate a short distance from that of Mrs. Yip. They spent a total of 120,000 yuan for their third-floor residence of more than 70 square meters, which has three bedrooms and a living room, kitchen, and bath — 100,000 yuan for the apartment itself and 20,000 to fix it up. Mr. Choi, his sons, and the *baomu* moved in in October 1989, but they have not transferred their household registration, to avoid forfeiting their eligibility for housing on the old site. To maintain the family presence, one of the sons continues to use the temporary structure as a shop and even sleeps there. The case of Mr. Choi, like that of Mrs. Yip, suggests that purchasing housing on the open market is currently feasible only if a family has access to money from abroad.

Conclusions

This chapter began by contrasting Guangzhou living standards in 1980 with those in the early 1990s, noting the progress made in the abundance and quality of goods. With the partial exception of housing, access to goods

---

* *Baomu* are hired by families as helpers. The *baomu* is often a child's nurse (maid) or a housekeeper, but in actual usage in Guangzhou the term can also mean "personal attendant" (of the sick or elderly). I translate the term here as "domestic servant" because I do not know which role Mrs. Yip played.

is no longer determined by ration coupons and rank but by money. Whereas those with high incomes embrace this distribution mechanism, others are ambivalent. Their appetite has been whetted by the material wealth displayed in stores, on the streets, on television, and in the homes of acquaintances, but they themselves are less able to share in it. Furthermore, even those whose income has risen more than the average are disturbed to see some people in extreme poverty while others have more money than they can easily spend. A consensus has developed — whether the concern is equity or fear of crime — that such a gap must be reduced and that those left behind by the reforms must be helped. The resettling of hardship households constitutes one response; others are discussed in Chapter 5.

How do the people of Guangzhou, in balance, assess the reforms? Where would they like to see more improvements? How are they dissatisfied? To answer these questions we turn to an April 1994 survey, the tenth carried out by a local research institution.[44] These surveys of residents' satisfaction with general economic and "social" conditions as well as their own financial situation have been carried out regularly, twice a year, since 1990; they help the city government measure its progress in addressing the concerns of the citizenry.

The eight questions on the general economic situation focus on residents' satisfaction with the supply of goods available, overall economic developments, the electric power supply, obtaining employment, attitudes of service personnel, the quality of consumer goods, price levels, and the wage gap. People are most pleased by the availability of goods on the market and economic developments overall — 78.2 percent and 62.6 percent, respectively, of the 461 participants expressed their satisfaction on these points. Less than half, however, were satisfied with any of the other economic variables. Indeed, more than 90 percent of respondents expressed dissatisfaction with current price levels and the wage gap. Given the inflation at the time of the survey in Guangzhou and China in general, these findings are not surprising. When asked about their own personal financial circumstances (their ability to purchase things, obtain medical care, and change jobs; their satisfaction with housing conditions, labor welfare benefits, personal income, and opportunities to make money), respondents expressed most concern about housing conditions (the sale of public housing had just been suspended), personal income, and opportunities to make money.

Residents were asked their level of satisfaction with eleven social and cultural issues (though only ten are specifically mentioned in the news reports on the survey): Guangzhou's national status, news reporting, city government, cultural life, educational conditions, public security (crime), supervision of the mobile population, traffic, the social atmosphere, and protection of the environment. Most residents are pleased with Guangzhou's role on the national scene — 58.8 percent expressed satisfaction, though this rate is down from the 65.8 percent reported in the previous survey, in September 1993. Although respondents registered dissatisfaction with public security, supervision of the mobile population, the social atmosphere, protection of the environment, and traffic, all the percentages except the last are actually up over those of September.

The most accurate response to the question raised earlier in this section — In balance how do the people of Guangzhou feel about the reforms? — is that they are ambivalent. Although they are pleased with the abundance of goods now available and rush to buy the newest consumer durable to hit the market, they worry about the government's wish to share its citizens' apparent affluence, specifically, its interest in divesting itself and its enterprises of responsibility for subsidizing workers' life styles. As we have seen, it has already done away with rationing and has begun to sever the relationship between employment and housing. Thus increased affluence has been accompanied by a growing sense of insecurity.

Huanshi Road looking east from the television tower in Yuexiu Park. Nearly all the high-rise buildings in the center have been constructed since the mid-1980s. (June 1991)

The north bank of the Pearl River, looking east from the Renmin Bridge. (February 1991)

The alternate name for Guangzhou in Chinese is Yangcheng, City of Rams, after the legendary visit in 887 B.C. of five rams carrying five immortals. This ram was the symbol of the Sixth National Games, held in Guangzhou in November 1987. It has gone on to symbolize civic virtue and can be seen on posters dropping litter into appropriate receptacles. (November 1987)

The moat separating Yuexiu district (the formerly walled old city) from Dongshan district. In the early 1990s an elevated road was erected above part of the moat. (November 1987)

The Xiatang neighborhood of Baiyun district, just north of the tracks connecting Guangzhou with the terminus in Hong Kong. This area has undergone enormous development since the mid-1980s. (November 1992)

Entering central Guangzhou from the Haizhu Bridge. (February 1991)

An older neighborhood in central Yuexiu district; such areas are rapidly giving way to urban renewal. (November 1992)

New housing in Dongshan district. The building in the foreground was constructed in the late 1970s or early 1980s; that in the background, in the early 1990s. (November 1992)

The Guangta Pagoda of Huaisheng Mosque in Yuexiu district. (November 1987)

Ancient banyan trees shading the courtyard of Chaotian Elementary School. (April 1991)

3 | Family and Household

In Chapters 3–5 we leave behind the larger context of the urban environment to focus on the family, school, and workplace, where individuals acquire the values, attitudes, and practices necessary for successful negotiation of adult life. Two central issues are the effects of the transition to a market economy on these institutions and the lessons they teach — to their offspring, students, and employees.

During and after the Second World War, scholars in the West were much taken by the concept of national character. During this period researchers frequently described populations in terms of their alleged contrasting value orientations.[1] Thus, for example, Chinese were said to be group oriented and to value dependence and obedience to authority in contrast to Americans, who were said to be individualistic, independent, and resistant to authority. Over time these characterizations have been toned down as scholars have acknowledged that reality is better captured by depicting populations along a continuum of values rather than at opposite poles. Thus, although Chinese can be as individualistic, independent, and rebellious as Americans are said to be, the traditional cultural preference has been to restrain these tendencies and to cultivate instead loyalty to the group, responsibility for others, and respect for superiors: parents, teachers, and employers. Far from destroying these traditional values, the Communist government harnessed them for its own ends, replacing loyalty to kin, for example, with loyalty to the party or Chairman Mao and expanding the concept of responsibility for others from intimates to the whole society (or at least to "the people"). The third value, respect for superiors, was made conditional on the superior's correct political thinking.

The reforms and the transition to a market economy, however, have raised the question whether these traditional values are still operative or even appropriate for China. Some argue that they are fetters, holding back adventurous souls on the economic frontier; others claim that the emergence of a private sector, new foreign investment, and an influx of foreign cultural artifacts (films, videotapes, and popular music) have already destroyed traditional values, with crime and corruption the predictable results. Such excessive rhetoric tells us little about the reality of contemporary urban life. Only if we go beyond it and examine concrete institutions and everyday life can we understand how the reforms have affected individuals and their values. This chapter, accordingly, looks at the urban Chinese family, first considering the historical legacy that confronted the Communist government when it came to power, then evaluating the success of the government's effort to bring about changes in the family, and finally examining family dynamics since the implementation of the economic reforms.

The contemporary urban Chinese family cannot be understood apart from its historical predecessors. Although social scientists acknowledge that no single family type can rightfully be characterized as *"the* traditional Chinese family,"* it has nevertheless become customary in writing to accept as the basic model the family type that most closely approximated Confucian norms.[2] This is the same model Chinese Marxists refer to as the feudal family.

From a Confucian perspective the ideal family was a "well-regulated" one in which the whole was more important than any of the parts and in which each person's status was defined according to generation, relative age, and sex. Most important, the living members of a family were regarded as crucial links between its past and its future; and the failure to perpetuate these links (by failing to produce sons) was regarded as the "most unfilial act." Descent was traced only through the male line. Men descended from a common male ancestor (even ten or more generations back) shared the same surname, were likely to live in the same village or cluster of villages, and participated in the annual rituals honoring the ancestors as members of the same lineage. Individuals certainly knew and had contact with their maternal kin but played no role in their ancestral rituals and were not considered members of their mother's lineage. In fact, women were marginal to the lineage system — necessary for its perpetuation but denied full membership. Whereas sons belonged to their father's lineage by birth, daughters were at best temporary members. A son's children were known simply as grandchildren, but a daughter's children were "outside" grandchildren, that is, outside the lineage (this distinction is still current). Unmarried women could not normally have their memorial tablet placed on their natal family's ancestral altar, nor could they be objects of "worship" by their nephews unless special arrangements had been made in advance. A woman's status in her husband's lineage was entirely dependent on the durability of the marital bond.

The political and economic significance of lineages varied greatly across China. They were particularly strong and well organized in the southeast, including Guangdong, where the entire male membership of a given village might belong to a single large lineage. In everyday life they could be more politically significant than the imperial government, whose nearest official representative, the county magistrate, conducted affairs in the county capital. A lineage with a depth of more than a few generations was likely to be divided into segments, each marked off by its own ancestral hall and ancestral estate. Segmentation occurred when the descendants of a particular man decided to honor him (and bring reflected glory on themselves) by setting aside a portion of land and using the proceeds from it to fund ancestor rites exclusively for him. His descendants thus participated not only in lineage-wide rites for their common ancestor but also in rites for their segment founder. The land in an ancestral estate was either rented out to tenants or farmed in turn by the members of the segment. Such lineage land could not be sold unless members of the segment agreed. Most village land, however, was owned, not by lineages or lineage segments, but by individual households that could sell it or add to it.

Authority in the lineage and the family was determined by generational status. A man five generations removed from the founder was ritually superior to a man six generations removed. Although members of a lineage shared a surname, members of the same generation in a lineage customarily shared a common character as part of their personal names. When members of the same lineage from different localities met for the first time, they could easily establish relative seniority by comparing their generation names. This practice survives in an attenuated form when urban Chinese parents give their children (or at least their sons) a common character in their personal names because they think it "sounds nice."

Within the family the generational principle meant that parents, as senior to children, had complete authority over them. Nowhere was this authority more explicit than in the case of a child's marriage. Parents had complete control over the choice of their child's spouse, and, indeed, thought less of choosing a spouse than of choosing a daughter-in-law, who would provide the means to extend the family another generation, bring in additional adult labor power, and serve the parents. With such aims in mind they wanted a girl who was likely to be fertile, in good health, and docile.

The initiative in marital arrangements was usually taken by the would-be groom's parents, who would contact a matchmaker, usually a middle-aged woman knowledgeable about the local availability of brides; she would contact the parents of the most suitable candidate. If interested, the girl's parents would indicate what they required of the groom's side before they would agree to an engagement—engagement being more or less irrevocable. Requirements normally included a "bride price" as well as foodstuffs and cloth to be transferred to the bride's family. In addition, the groom's family provided and furnished the room the new couple would occupy after their wedding. On the wedding day the bride was preceded to her new home by her dowry, which included her own personal effects as well as some furnishings, such as bedding for the bridal chamber.

In the typical "blind" marriage, the young couple met for the first time on their wedding day, and many elderly people I spoke with (in both Hong Kong and Guangzhou) had met their spouses in just this way. Others indicated that though their marriages had been arranged, they either had known the person because he or she was a relative (usually on the maternal side) or from a relative's village or had been given a chance to veto a proposal in its early stages. For example, one elderly woman described how in a department store she and her mother happened to bump into a group of people her mother knew. When after the meeting her mother asked her what she thought of the young man in the group, she realized that the encounter had been designed to give her an opportunity to meet her suitor (and him, to meet her).[3] Even prior to 1949 some couples had met and married without the benefit of parental introductions. A few modern university students had selected their own spouses, and many who had lost their first spouse in the tumult of the Japanese War or the civil wars married someone else whose circumstances were similar.

Although generational status was the prime determiner of authority in the family, relative age (or birth order) was the prime determiner of authority in a single generation. Thus the elder brother took precedence over the younger and stood in relation to him as a father. In the father's absence the elder brother was expected to protect, discipline, and support the younger brother, who in turn owed respect and obedience to the elder. The hierarchy of the sibling relationship was hard to ignore because it was incorporated into the very terms siblings used to address and refer to each other. In Chinese it is impossible simply to say "my brother" or "my sister." The terms that must be used force the speaker to specify older or younger brother or sister. Moreover, older siblings address younger ones by their personal names, whereas younger siblings address older ones by their birth order. Thus the youngest child would call the oldest brother *da ge* (big older brother) and the oldest sister *da jie* (big older sister), the next *er ge* (second older brother), the next *san ge* (third older brother), and so on, similarly for sisters.

An incident that brought home the salience of sibling hierarchy to me occurred in 1973 when I was visiting a village in the interior of Taiwan.

Because I was traveling alone and spoke very little *putonghua* (and no Hokkien, the local dialect of *putonghua*), possibilities for interaction were pretty limited. Consequently, I busied myself with such activities as admiring the kittens a little boy was playing with in front of his home. Noting my interest, the boy quickly pointed out which kitten was the *gege* (older brother) and which was the *didi* (younger brother). I wonder how many American children would know the birth order of a litter of kittens, let alone think to mention it to a stranger.

This attention to relative age also occurs in the workplace and on the street. In the workplace individuals with a higher work status (i.e., supervisors) are addressed by surname and title (at least in an outsider's presence or on a formal occasion) — thus, Principal Dao or Responsible Person Yang. Among people of similar work status, however, relative age becomes a source of distinction. Where workmates' ages differ by roughly ten years or more, it is customary for the older to be addressed (and referred to) as Old X and the younger as Little Y, even when the younger person is approaching middle age. Workmates of similar status and approximately the same age are more likely to address and refer to each other by personal name (or nickname). When strangers meet on the street, they have the option of addressing each other by courtesy titles, such as Miss or Mister, or by kinship terms that take account of relative age. The appropriate term of address is one that shows respect by exaggerating the actual age difference. Someone who is judged a peer or slightly older is called Older Brother or Older Sister, whereas someone substantially older is called Uncle or Aunt.[4]

The final criterion for determining authority in the family was sex. In theory, females were subordinate to males, a concept summed up in the "three obediences," according to which a woman was obedient first to her father, then to her husband, and finally, in widowed old age, to her son. The astute reader, however, will realize that in many circumstances the sex principle conflicted with the generation and age principles. There is no question that mothers had the right to tell their minor sons what to do, including, as we have seen, whom to marry. Furthermore, the realities of family dynamics suggest that a fourteen-year-old girl looking after her six-year-old brother was likely to have been the person in authority. When compared with their male peers, however, females were clearly inferior in both law and custom.

As daughters, females were disproportionately victims of infanticide and underinvestment; that is, they received no education or only a little. In hard times poor parents were far more likely to sell their daughters (to brothels as prostitutes, to rich men as concubines, or to rich families as bond servants) than their sons (to childless couples as heirs) because daughters were viewed as only temporary members of their natal families and because parents expected only sons (and daughters-in-law) to be around to support them in old age,[5] a consequence of marriage patterns whereby girls married into families living in villages other than their own. In the case of single-lineage villages, this pattern resulted inevitably from the requirement of surname exogamy, but even in multi-lineage villages, out-marriage was the norm, probably for two reasons. First, families considered it useful to develop affinal ties with people elsewhere as a personal safety net. If their village was flooded or overrun by bandits, they had a better chance to survive with a refuge 5 or 10 miles away. Links with other people meant potential allies to draw on for support in a dispute, investment in a rotating credit association, and so forth. Second, from the point of view of the groom's family, having affinal kin in the same village could seriously compromise their efforts to control their daughter-in-law. They feared that she might attempt to sneak resources from her husband's household to her parents', and in cases of family conflict she would try to recruit her natal family on her behalf.

As wives, females were disadvantaged in a number of ways. Unlike their husbands, they were entitled to only one spouse. If the bride selected by a man's parents did not please him, he could (if he could afford it) eventually acquire additional wives who did. Even when widowed, a wife was expected to remain faithful to her deceased husband and to continue to fulfill the role of daughter-in-law to his parents. But if her parents-in-law chose to marry her off, she had to leave her children behind, because they belonged to their father's lineage. A husband, moreover, could divorce his wife on various grounds, whereas she had no grounds to divorce him. Finally, a wife had no right to own property, other than what she had brought as a dowry, or to inherit, though she could be a custodian or trustee for her minor sons.

The ideal form of the Chinese family was "five generations under one roof," a goal seldom obtained because of high mortality rates and economic realities. More typically, at least in the rural areas, nuclear and stem forms of the family alternated, with perhaps a brief phase as a joint family. For example, a couple with four unmarried children (two sons and two daughters) would constitute a nuclear family. When the first son married and brought in a wife, the family became a stem family. When the second son married and brought in a wife, the family became a joint family.[6] In the meantime the daughters married out, and grandchildren began to arrive. Ideally the two sons continued to farm the land or operate the family business with their father, who pooled the income so produced and redistributed it according to need. At a certain point, in theory not until the father's death but in practice often shortly after the marriage of the second son, the large household would "divide"; that is, the sons would take their share of the property and form independent economic units, establishing two new nuclear families or a nuclear and a stem family. (Other outcomes were also possible.) The division process determined filial responsibilities for the surviving parent(s) because inheritance and the care of parents were inextricably linked. Normally sons were expected to share equally in the care of parents and would, therefore, inherit equal (or more or less equal) shares of the family's wealth. Daughters had no obligations to provide parental support and no rights to inherit.

Law and the Family in the PRC

Currently the two laws dealing most directly with the family in the PRC are the 1980 Marriage Law, which went into effect January 1, 1981, and the 1985 Inheritance Law, which went into effect October 1, 1985. The 1980 Marriage Law replaced the 1950 Marriage Law, which was the new government's first attempt to abolish the "feudal" family.[7] The very first article of the 1950 law asserted:

> The feudal marriage system which is based on arbitrary and compulsory arrangements and the superiority of man over woman and ignores the children's interests shall be abolished.
> The New-Democratic marriage system, which is based on the free choice of partners, on monogamy, on equal rights for both sexes, and on the protection of the lawful interests of women and children, shall be put into effect.[8]

The new law declared that parents had the duty to rear and educate their children and that children had the duty to support and assist their parents. Furthermore, parents and children were to have the right to inherit one another's property. The 1950 law set the minimum age for marriage at 18 for women and 20 for men, required the registration of the marriage in person by both contracting parties, gave husband and wife the right to inherit each other's property, and allowed either party to apply for a divorce. Grounds for divorce were not specified, but in the event that both partners wanted one, the district government, after making certain that "appropriate measures have been taken for the care of children and property," was to "issue the divorce certificates without delay." In the event that only one party wanted a divorce, mediation aimed at reconciliation was required.

Passing, implementing, and enforcing of the marriage law were three separate issues. Nearly three years after the law's passage, Teng Ying-chao (Deng Yingchao), vice-chair of the Women's Federation (and wife of soon-to-be-premier Zhou Enlai), admitted that despite considerable progress, the law was not being fully enforced and consequently a major campaign was to be launched nationwide to "remould backward outlooks."[9] After an initial period of leniency toward divorce, presumably to allow for the dissolution of forced marriages, the state took a hard line, essentially requiring mediation to continue until the parties wanting a divorce simply abandoned their quest. In rural areas forced marriages and plural marriages remained problems for decades, and education on these matters was still under way in the mid-1980s.

Between February 1986 and March 1988 *Nanfang Ribao*, one of the three major daily newspapers in Guangzhou, ran a feature almost every week entitled "One Hundred Cases to Be Resolved." These cases, culled or synthesized from letters sent to the paper's advice columnist, Li Dongdong, served to educate the public on both ethics and the law. Though problems on a wide range of issues were discussed, all concerned courtship, marriage, or family relations. Two of the cases involving a violation of the right to marry freely are described in the paragraphs that follow.

In the first case a twenty-year-old village girl is on the brink of suicide. She has been brought to this situation because her father wants her to marry a man in his 30s; in exchange, her older brother will acquire a bride from the man's family. The girl is adamantly against her proposed marriage. As the day for the exchange draws near and she shows no willingness to comply despite beatings and scoldings, her father threatens to confine her in a pig cage (these are used to transport live pigs to market) and drown her. What should she do? Li Dongdong, noting that "exchange marriage" is a subtype of arranged marriage, says she has heard recently of such cases occurring in the mountain districts. The girl has a choice: to commit suicide or to struggle for her right to marry freely. The first alternative is unacceptable, so she must take the second. It would be best if she could persuade her father to change his mind, but if he will not, she should appeal to the law. Li Dongdong then describes a similar case from a newspaper account three years earlier. In that case a girl surnamed Zhou had an older brother aged 30 who still did not have a wife. Her father arranged an exchange marriage with another family whereby a son from each family would marry a daughter from the other. Miss Zhou objected, but her father forced her to comply by beating her. On the wedding day the girl, still resisting, was forcibly dressed in her wedding garments and transported by tractor to the groom's house. She spent her wedding night crying on the bed and then tried to hang herself from the window. She was stopped in the act and then appealed to the law. Eventually her father was sentenced to one year in jail, and Miss Zhou regained her freedom. The case demonstrates how the law protects freedom of marriage. Li Dongdong told the letter writer her father would be punished if he persisted in carrying out the exchange marriage, so the girl should abandon the idea of suicide and struggle for her own freedom.[10]

In the second case, recounted shortly after the one just described, the consequences of accepting an unwanted match are spelled out. A youth referred to as Xiao Wang (Little Wang) and a neighbor girl had been in love for more than a year and were preparing to formally register their intended marriage when the girl's parents suddenly changed their minds about Xiao Wang and instead decided, for 1,500 yuan, to marry off their daughter to a middle-aged man living on a state farm. The girl complied with her parents' wishes and married him. But Xiao Wang and the girl still love each other. Although he wants to continue their relationship, he worries about the consequences of doing so. What should he do? Li Dongdong does not mince words. The girl's parents treated their daughter like property and broke up her intended marriage—that is illegal and immoral. Had the girl struggled for her own rights, she and Xiao Wang would face a different situation now. But she is a married woman; she and Xiao Wang no longer have the right to love each other. What they may have is friendship, and friendship does not mean love. Both of them should understand that. Though it is bitter and difficult to convert one's love into friendship, Xiao Wang must do so. It is dangerous for him to think, "She is mine, and we will love each other forever." To persist in such thinking would make him "a third party" (the official term in divorce cases for someone who alienates a spouse's affection) and cause trouble. People these days seem to believe that if the head of a family forces a couple not yet wed to break up, they may continue to love each other even after marrying someone else—and that in doing this they are breaking the bonds of feudal morality and practicing their right to freedom of marriage. They are wrong. If their current marriage is loveless, they may obtain a divorce. To continue to love another while married is to practice bourgeois freedom, which is not allowed in our country. Xiao Wang should restrain himself with Communist morality within the law and not cross the boundary between friendship and love.[11]

Since the implementation of agricultural reforms and the freeing of much rural labor from farm work, many men have moved into towns to seek jobs, away from the supervision of their wives and kin; under these circumstances some have involved themselves in extramarital affairs. Although such affairs usually end in either divorce or the abandonment of the third party, sometimes the husband tries to have his cake and eat it too. A rural woman, married many years, who had already given birth to a daughter, wrote to Li Dongdong that she and her husband had had a good relationship. But after the husband found temporary work in the city, he became involved with an unmarried co-worker, who knew he had a wife. When the writer learned of the situation, she attempted to persuade her husband to give up his affair. Not only did he refuse, but he also told her he loved them both and wanted her assent to his taking the younger woman as a "little wife." He told her that he would wait for her response to this proposal and then would send whatever money she and their daughter needed. What should she do? Not surprisingly, Li Dongdong reminded the writer that China has a "one-husband, one-wife system" and that she should not yield to his threat.[12]

According to Wu Xinyu, vice-chair of the Commission for Legal Affairs of the Standing Committee of the National People's Congress, changing circumstances in China, primarily the need to control population growth and to deal with the multitude of disputes arising from the reestablishment of the private sector, made a new marriage law essential.[13] The changes included increasing the minimum age at marriage from 18 to 20 for women and from 20 to 22 for men. These ages are substantially lower than those the government was actually advocating at the time as appropriate for "late marriage" — one of the cornerstones of the family planning regulations.* For example, the 1980 Family Planning Regulations of Guangdong province state that the late marriage age for women should be 23 and that for men should be 25 in rural areas and 26 in urban areas. Article 4 of the regulations further stipulates that "those who do not meet the late marriage age criteria, but want to register, should be discouraged through education in order that they can voluntarily practice late marriage."[14] The 1980 Marriage Law's minimum ages probably reflect the government's understanding of what was likely to be enforceable nationally.

In addition to setting higher minimum ages, the Marriage Law includes three articles intended, directly or indirectly, to limit population growth. Article 12, for example, specifically requires family planning while articles 8 and 16 are clearly intended to reassure parents who have daughters but no sons that they have not thereby terminated the family line or forfeited their prospects for security in old age. (What the articles mean in practice will be explored later in this chapter.) According to article 8, following the registration of the marriage, "the woman may become a member of the man's family, or the man may become a member of the woman's family, according

---

* Begun in the 1950s, "late marriage" is an official policy of encouraging the delaying of marriage. Initially it was intended as an alternative to parentally arranged marriages of youngsters in their mid- to late teens. By delaying marriage till their later teens or — even better — their twenties, young people would benefit from investing more time in education and work and would approach marriage with greater emotional and physical maturity. By the 1970s, late marriage was also seen as a benefit for society as a whole because it resulted in delayed births and thus helped reduce overall population growth. By this time, "late marriage" generally meant marriage in the mid- to late twenties. But the state recognized that a national marriage law had to acknowledge actual social practice in setting minimum ages for marriage; otherwise large numbers of people would simply fail to register their de facto unions. Provinces and cities that believed they could enforce higher minimum ages for marriage were allowed to designate these ages as "late marriage" minimums and to offer various rewards and punishments to encourage compliance. Couples could still marry if they had reached the national minimum age, but they were required to practice contraception (Tien 1991).

to the agreed wishes of the two parties." Under article 16 "children may adopt either their father's or their mother's family name."

The parts of the Marriage Law that respond to changing economic circumstances deal primarily with property rights and support issues. With the shift from collective to household agriculture, the emergence of private business, and high rates of capital accumulation, the state felt the need to spell out the nature of the property in which husbands and wives hold equal rights. According to article 13, "the property acquired during the period in which husband and wife are under contract of marriage is in the joint possession of the two parties unless they have agreed otherwise." Although Wu Xinyu made no mention of the special needs of the elderly in his remarks, the 1980 Marriage Law, unlike the 1950 law, includes two references to older people, suggesting that they are a population newly at risk. For example, whereas the first law emphasized the special protection of "women and children," the later law protects the "rights and interests of women, children, and the aged." Furthermore, in the absence of the middle generation, grandparents (including maternal grandparents) and grandchildren (including "maternal grandchildren," i.e., the children of daughters) have the duty to support each other.

The 1985 Inheritance Law further clarifies the nature of community property (the joint property of a husband and wife) and details the allocation of property when there is no will (as in the vast majority of cases, at least in the urban areas) as well as the rights of a testator. When a husband or wife dies, only the half of the community property belonging to the deceased is subject to inheritance. The survivor retains all rights to his or her own half and, in addition, inherits, along with the deceased's children and parents, a portion of the deceased's half. Should the widowed survivor subsequently remarry, he or she may "dispose of the property that was inherited without interference from anyone." Although males and females have equal inheritance rights, the law officially acknowledges the legitimacy of the tradition that makes inheritance conditional on support. For example, a widowed child-in-law who has "fulfilled the principal obligation to support" a parent-in-law is to be regarded as a first-sequence heir, that is, on a par with a spouse, child, or parent. Article 13 states in part:

When the estate is allocated, a larger share may be allocated to heirs who either have fulfilled the principal obligation to support the decedent or have lived with the decedent.

When the estate is allocated, either no share or a smaller share should be allocated to heirs who had the ability and means to provide support [but] did not fulfill the obligation to provide support.

The above conditions for the disposition of property apply in the absence of a will. If the deceased left a will, however, the property must be disposed of in accordance with the testator's wishes. The only condition imposed on the testator is that he or she "should reserve a requisite share of the estate for an heir who both lacks the ability to work and is without a source of income." Presumably such individuals would be primarily the elderly, disabled spouses, and dependent children. The need for an Inheritance Law was especially great in rural areas where, in addition to having acquired use rights in land, more and more families have been going into private business or purchasing shares in formerly collective enterprises. In the cities the major inheritable goods are likely to be housing and savings accounts.[15]

In several families of the Family Study inheritance disputes (including those arising from the division of families and property described earlier) had caused serious problems.[16] For example, in 1987, when we visited the Zhangs for the first time, Mr. and Mrs. Zhang, aged 72 and 62, were living in a spacious apartment provided by their unit, where Mr. Zhang had been a high-level cadre. Although their oldest son's son (aged ten) was living with them, their five adult children all lived elsewhere in Guangzhou. When asked to talk about his children, Mr. Zhang forgot to mention his youngest son (aged 28) until later in the interview. This son was the only one of the five children not yet married and, most unusual for an unmarried child, was not living with his parents. In fact, the Zhangs seldom saw him because he worked aboard a ship and during his brief periods of shore leave stayed with friends rather than his parents. These circumstances, together with his having received the lowest level of education among the children, made me wonder whether he was the family's "problem child." Shortly after Mr. Zhang's death from a stroke at the end of 1989, the youngest son pressured his widowed mother to request that his unit (the same unit for which both of his parents had worked) transfer him from ship duty to shore duty on the grounds that she needed a son around now that her husband was dead. Mrs. Zhang, who did not want to apply for his transfer, could not resist the pressure. Once he obtained the reassignment, he moved back into the parental apartment and began to badger her constantly about money or other valuables Mr. Zhang had left behind, because he wanted access to them. None of his four siblings ever raised this issue. Mrs. Zhang became so distressed that she eventually appealed to the residents committee, which instructed the son to drop the matter. A reasonable interpretation of his behavior is that he was angling to set himself up as the primary heir to whatever money and valuables his father had left behind as well as to tenancy rights in the apartment. He might have felt the need for quick action, for at the end of 1990 Mrs. Zhang underwent surgery for lung cancer and in 1991, except for weekends, was spending most of her time in a hospital run by their unit.

In early 1991 the Guangdong provincial government announced a new set of regulations to protect the lawful rights of the elderly. All work units were instructed to enforce these rights, which included, as we have already seen in the Marriage Law, the right to a broad range of support from adult children. In the provincial regulations, immediately following an article emphasizing the freedom of the elderly to remarry and warning against any interference in their family life after remarriage,[17] is a set of articles emphasizing the rights of the elderly (remarried or otherwise) to control their incomes, administer their property, and occupy their dwellings. Adult sons and daughters are warned against forcible attempts to occupy their parents' residence.[18] Though Guangdong was neither the first nor the last of China's provinces to enact such a declaration of rights for the elderly, these regulations seem nearly tailor-made for Mrs. Zhang.

It is difficult to measure the impact of the 1980 Marriage Law and the 1985 Inheritance Law on family formation and family organization. Certainly official norms roundly condemn such traditional practices as discrimination against females, arranged marriage, polygyny, authoritarianism, and loveless marriage and promote equality, affection, and mutual support as the legitimate bases of contemporary family life. Yet judging from the letters sent to Li Dongdong, many people either are unsure of their rights or face opposition in exercising them. Even though the 1980 Marriage Law attempts to ground the right to divorce in the "complete alienation of mutual affection," petitioners for divorce are still subject to mediation by people prepared to argue that a husband and wife who raise a child together and cooperate in managing a household thereby demonstrate the presence of mutual affection.[19]

Although nationally the divorce rate doubled between 1980 and 1990, the actual increase, from 0.7 percent to 1.4 percent, meant that even in 1990, in a population of 1.1 billion, there were only 800,000 divorces.[20] Judging from the figures for Guangzhou, however, the national figure masks great differences between urban and rural areas. In 1992 in Guangzhou municipality, for example, there were 4,990 divorces and 61,201 marriages for an overall ratio of one divorce per 12.8 newly contracted marriages. In the eight urban districts the ratio was one to 9.3, whereas in the four rural counties it was one to 23.6, with extremes ranging from one to 6.2 in Dongshan district to one in 33.9 in Zengcheng county.[21]

Contemporary Urban Family Life

Any discussion of contemporary family life in China must begin with three caveats. First, urban family life is generally recognized as different from rural family life. In the countryside many of the distinctive characteristics of the traditional Chinese family still persist or have reemerged. For example, females still usually marry out of their home communities, villages still consist predominantly of closely related males and their married-in wives, the family is (again) a unit of production. Because urban residence, in contrast, is determined primarily by workplace, there is no concept of "neighborhood exogamy." Although there is a tendency for multiple members of a family to be employed by the same unit, it cannot be said that this phenomenon makes the family a unit of production.[22]

Second, urban and rural family life, even before the establishment of the PRC, were diverging as in other countries, and for the same reasons: migration, leading to smaller kin networks in cities; labor mobility; and greater access to education and new ideas.[23] Finally, the changes that have occurred in urban family life since the establishment of the PRC have not necessarily resulted from the efforts of the Chinese government. Even such a controversial change as the drop in fertility could, as comparisons with other urban Chinese populations suggest, result from a complex of factors.[24]

The sections that follow investigate courtship, marriage, and relations between adult children and elderly parents. The main data sources include the published results of the Five City Family Study carried out (in eight neighborhoods) by the Chinese Academy of Social Sciences (CASS) in 1982; accounts in the local media, including letters to the columnist Li Dongdong as well as local television programs; the Guangzhou Family Study; interviews with other residents or former residents of Guangzhou; and the published works of other writers. The sample of 4,385 households in the CASS study was drawn from Beijing, Tianjin, Shanghai, Nanjing, and Chengdu and consisted entirely of married women (a total sample of 5,057 since some households included more than one married woman). Although the study is dated and does not include Guangzhou, it is nevertheless the only large national data base on the urban family currently available and provides an overall introduction to the topic.

Courtship

Perhaps no aspect of family (or "prefamily") life is believed to have changed so radically as courtship. Visitors to Guangzhou, including former residents returning after an absence of as little as four years, express shock and dismay at the apparent loss of traditional virtue. One 1984 graduate of Zhongshan University reported that today's middle school students are very different from the middle school students of her day. When she was in middle school, even dating was unthinkable, but now, according to her friends and classmates who are teaching in middle schools, "60 percent of the girls are no longer virgins!" In her day there was so much pressure during the school year that it was impossible even to think of anything other than schoolwork (she had attended an elite prep school), but during the summer there were opportunities for recreation. A group of boys and girls who could talk easily together would arrange to meet at a park; they would chat together and get something to eat. There was no pairing off. Even when she attended the university, she knew her husband as a friend for the first three years, paired off with him only in the fourth year, and did not marry until three years after graduation. Now pairing off is common, and even though ten students might share a dormitory room, roommates arrange to be out so that a couple can get together privately.[25]

Miss Mao, a 1991 graduate of Zhongshan, reported that although intense relationships between male and female students are officially frowned upon, dating and even having a special friend of the opposite sex are allowed. If students are suspected of engaging in sexual intimacies, however, they are likely to be dismissed from the school. Surely a good deal of discretion is involved here on the part of both the students and the authorities. According to a friend of Miss Mao's who was attending a university in Shanghai, the authorities had no choice but to take action against seven female students who occupied a room on the floor above her. These young women disappeared one by one in the course of the year—all allegedly expelled for prostitution.

Miss Mao proposed several explanations for the apparent increase in sexual activity among students. First, students identify sexual activity with modernity. They assume that the physical intimacy they see in Hong Kong–and Western-made movies is usual among "modern" people. Second, to behave otherwise may be to stigmatize themselves as tradition bound. Third, some students, mostly males, with little to do at the university expend their excess energy playing games with the opposite sex. Fourth, because playing around is less likely to affect one's marriage prospects if no one knows about it, some students develop casual sexual relationships with people from other parts of the country. After graduation, students from outside Guangdong are expected to return to their home areas. An affair in Guangdong between a student from Hunan and a student from Guangxi is unlikely to become public knowledge in either home community.

A young male faculty member at another university in Guangzhou stated that most students no longer take education seriously but instead spend their time fooling around. He opined that virginity is rare these days and estimated that 30 percent of the female students at his institution will have an abortion sometime or other during their university careers. The consensus is that unmarried women readily obtain abortions in ordinary health care facilities without the news getting back to their work units. As one woman explained, someone who is worried about her abortion becoming public knowledge simply goes to a facility where she is not known and pays for the procedure herself. Even someone who chooses to have an abortion covered by her work unit's insurance plan can save her reputation if the doctor is willing to write that the charge is for unspecified "treatment."[26]

Other sources of data, however, suggest that perceptions of rampant premarital sexual activity among young people in Guangzhou might not be entirely accurate. For example, one day I asked an eighteen- or nineteen-year-old service worker I knew, who called herself Laura, whether I could talk with her sometime about the life of young people in Guangzhou. She agreed, but before we turned to this topic, she asked whether I knew much about psychology. She then explained that she thought that she was abnormal (*biantai*) because when she did not know someone, she would like him, but after she knew him for a while, she would want nothing more to do with him. She meant that as soon as a boy suggested getting physical (for Laura this meant no more than kissing), she would be repulsed and refuse to go out with him again. Her friends often commented on seeing her with different boys but never with the same one more than a few times. Laura said that normally she is very outgoing—when the workers have a complaint, she is the one bold enough to bring it up—but on this matter of boys, she could not figure out what was the matter with her.

Judging from letters to Li Dongdong, others are similarly confused about relations with the opposite sex. These letters, mostly from people in their twenties, reveal a shyness, uncertainty, and immaturity characteristic of a much younger age group in the United States. For example, in one of them a young factory worker, Xiao Li, fell in love with a female co-worker and, for lack of a go-between, expressed his admiration in a letter. To his horror she read the letter aloud in public and ridiculed him as "a frog wanting to eat swan meat." Now he wants revenge. What should he do? Li Dongdong advises him not to retaliate. Everyone knows what the girl did was wrong and sympathizes with Xiao Li. He should learn from this so that next time he will be less rash and will wait until he knows more about the other person before expressing his feelings.[27]

Another letter, from Xiao Zhou, told how his girlfriend of six months has invited him several times to her home to meet her parents. He has always declined. He is shy and fears he will make a bad impression on her parents, but he realizes he cannot put off the meeting forever. What can he do? Li Dongdong advises him that as a future son-in-law Xiao Zhou certainly cannot avoid this meeting. Parents are influential in their children's marriages, so he must treat this occasion as very important. She offers some guidelines: Be polite and bring gifts on the first visit; be clean and neat in dress; if other relatives are there besides the parents and they ask you about your income or your family, answer honestly and avoid getting angry; make sure the host sits before you do; eat in a civilized manner and do not get drunk; when you leave, express your thanks.[28]

Finally, there is the letter of 26-year-old Miss Ping, who through an introduction met a man who had courtship in mind. After their initial meeting, they decided they liked each other and wanted to become friends. But every time they scheduled a meeting, Miss Ping deliberately came late to test her suitor, little realizing that he disliked being tested. Soon he stopped asking to see her. Now Miss Ping is beside herself. What should she do? Li Dongdong tells her that being on time shows respect. Her lateness will make him think she is too proud or uninterested. It is not a useful tactic to test another's interest by deliberately arguing or getting angry. Miss Ping should write the young man or get a go-between to explain the situation.[29]

How does one account for these disparate images of young people: on the one hand sexually experienced, and on the other timid and foolish? Both pictures are correct, though they represent extremes; the behavior of many young couples falls on a continuum between them. The more modern image, however, is more readily noticeable and remarked upon. One couple rolling on the grass in Yuexiu Park makes a much bigger impression than 100 couples chastely sitting on benches eating popsicles. The findings of a national survey of a random sample of 1,642 married males and 1,467 married females carried out from late 1988 to early 1990 offer a less impressionistic picture of urban sexuality.[30]

According to this study both attitudes and behavior are (and have been) more accepting of premarital sex than either Confucian or Communist values would lead one to expect. Although they preferred that their spouse be a virgin, 41 percent of the males and 30 percent of the females "thought that pre-marital intercourse was not wrong and was entirely a private affair. When pre-marital intercourse occurs between fiancés, few think it immoral or unchaste."[31] A more informal survey in Huhhot revealed that 64 percent (23 of 36) of "younger" male informants believed that if a couple is planning to marry, premarital sex is perfectly proper.[32] As for behavior, the national study found that 19 percent of the males and 15 percent of the females who responded to the question (2.5 percent failed to respond) reported engaging in premarital intercourse. Among those aged 20–35 the incidence of premarital intercourse had risen to 25 percent for males and 18 percent for females.[33]

Another factor contributing to the belief that improper sexual activity in China's cities is on the increase is the reappearance of prostitution. In Guangzhou (unless a crackdown is in progress) both foreign and domestic occupants of almost any hotel receive many anonymous phone calls asking if they want company for the evening. Even an unlikely prospect, such as the author herself, can be the subject of these phone calls. On my first day in a domestic hotel in 1991, I received ten calls in a matter of hours. Most of the callers were women, who hung up immediately, but the occasional man who called attempted to start a conversation. A colleague at my unit (the provincial academy of social sciences), a woman in her 50s, reported that when she had received similar calls from males while she was organizing surveys in county towns, she had told them she was "too old" for such activity. These calls are made from rooms in the hotel or from the in-house phones in the lobby. Because hotels are officially supposed to protect their guests from such harassment, legitimate callers from outside the hotel can have a hard time getting through unless they know the room number of the person they are trying to reach. Most of the time in Guangzhou I stayed in a guesthouse belonging to another unit. When I announced that my husband would be coming for a visit, the management immediately contacted my unit, demanding to know how they could be sure he was really my husband.

Some aggressive prostitutes bypass the phone. One long-term foreign resident of a first-class hotel reported that once, responding to a knock at his door, he was nearly knocked over by two young women who charged inside and began to disrobe before he could say a word. Public security officials reportedly flushed 120 prostitutes out of another first-class hotel on a night raid. The short skirts and high heels that some of these young women wear constitute (as elsewhere) an advertisement of their availability. But young women who aim at nothing more than making a fashion statement also wear short skirts and thereby attract the wrong kind of attention.

The inclination to believe the worst about a "modern" young woman was the subject of a March 1991 episode of "One Hundred Life Events," a popular locally produced evening television program. This episode focused on the consequences of rumormongering—how rumors come back to harm those who spread them (a Buddhist notion of retribution). The opening scene shows a woman in her twenties dressed in a miniskirt. She is walking with her mother, who is trying to persuade her to go abroad for more study. The daughter, annoyed at the constant pressure to go abroad, assures her mother that she can get an adequate education in Guangzhou. As mother and daughter go their separate ways, the mother collides with a foreign male. The daughter apologizes to him in English on her mother's behalf, but he responds in unaccented Cantonese that he is a student of Chinese history and culture, that one of his ancestors was Chinese, and so he speaks Cantonese. The young woman then offers to show him the local historical sites. They conclude the day with a snack and beer at a small outdoor restaurant.

At the restaurant another customer—a neighbor of the young woman who with his wife operates a refreshment stall in the neighborhood—takes notice of them. When his tablemate sees him staring intently at the young woman, he at first assumes that he has an eye for the ladies, but the stall operator explains that this is not the case; rather, he is surprised to see this particular person with a Westerner. The tablemate responds knowledgeably that the girl is obviously a "chicken" (prostitute). The stall operator goes home drunk and reports this interpretation to his wife as a fact. She is scandalized that someone in their own building would do such a thing. The next morning while she and a shop assistant are opening up the stall, the young woman, dressed in a jogging suit, runs by and says good morning to them in English. After the young woman has passed by, the wife mimics her "good morning" and comments that she has a lot of nerve acting as she does. The shop assistant is puzzled. In confidence, the wife tells him that the girl is a prostitute and that last night she had gone to a big hotel with a foreigner. The shop assistant is scandalized.

Later, while he is alone at the stall, the woman returns from her jog and wants to buy an ice-cream cone. She presents a large-denomination bill in payment. The shop assistant is nearly overcome. Such a large bill, he thinks, could only have come from her work; thus it is tainted money. He declines to accept it, saying he has no change, but she insists, telling him she trusts him to give her change later in the day. He counters with the assurance that he trusts her to pay him later in the day. They are thus engaged when a woman in her 60s from the residents committee happens by. She proposes that the young woman accept the offer of credit. Immediately after she leaves, the shop assistant grabs a cloth and vigorously wipes off the counter where the suspect bill had lain. The older woman is puzzled, so he explains in confidence how the stall operator had discovered that the jogger is a prostitute who had been with three foreigners the previous night in a big hotel. The older woman goes home to repeat this to her husband and is overheard by a neighbor in the bathroom next door.

The scene then shifts to a lane adjacent to the refreshment stall. The wife is enraged to discover that the residents committee has posted the latest notice on rat extermination on the bulletin board near her stall. Afraid it will affect business, she attempts to remove it. The older woman from the residents committee advises her not to, and as the neighbors gather, the wife flounces off to a beauty shop, letting it be known that her husband was away last night, but that when he returns, he will have something to say about the notice. At this point the neighbor who overheard the conversation between the older woman and her husband announces that the stall operator did not come home the previous night because he was arrested by public security for trafficking in prostitutes and spent the night in jail. The shop assistant runs off to the beauty parlor to inform the wife.

In the next scene the unsuspecting stall operator returns home. His wife immediately assaults him, giving him no time to explain the reason for his absence. The ruckus draws the attention of the neighbors; a young man forces open the door, the neighbors rush in to separate the couple, and mediation begins. We learn that the stall operator had only gone to Shunde county on business — he had not been arrested for trafficking in prostitutes. (Because of the continued shortage of private phones, it is not always easy for people to notify family members of changes in plans or schedules.) He demands to know how she ever got such an absurd idea. She had heard it from the shop assistant, who had heard it from the neighbor, who had overheard it from the woman from the residents committee, who had heard it from the shop assistant, who had heard it from the wife, who had heard it from her husband — the accused himself! Such are the consequences of recklessly embellishing a rumor. We see that merely wearing a short skirt and being seen with a foreign male should not be enough to ruin a young woman's reputation.

The Five City Family Study found that only 33 percent of the most recent cohort of young couples (those married from 1977 to 1982) had initiated their courtship — not surprising, given the shyness of many young people. The others had relied on friends to introduce them (50 percent) or on parents and relatives (16 percent). One percent claimed to have had arranged marriages. Still, these figures represent a major change from the experience of the cohort married prior to 1938, when 55 percent had arranged marriages and only 5 percent found spouses on their own.[34]

According to the authors of the Five City report, young people fail to play the major role in their own courtship because they lack opportunities to meet; feudal thinking (the belief that males and females should have no contact) makes them shy; they have no confidence in their own decision making; and the person who introduces them, who serves as somewhat of a guarantor, makes the marriage more than simply a private matter and enhances its stability.[35] To provide more opportunities for young people to meet and especially to help "over-aged youths" (women 27 or older and men 29 or older) find spouses, the authors recommend that adults provide introductions as part of their personal and social responsibility. They also suggest that introduction bureaus be opened and given serious support. Individuals should be encouraged to place personal advertisements in newspapers and magazines and even on the airwaves.[36] Finally, work units should help their own unmarried young people find a mate by organizing social activities. Those with a heavily female labor force, for example, should organize activities with those whose labor force is heavily male.[37]

Young people in Guangzhou and much of Guangdong have an option not widely available elsewhere in China: they can marry someone living abroad. Commonly an older overseas Chinese male returns to his native area briefly to find a bride to take back with him. A young woman who marries abroad is believed to be marrying a rich man and providing an emigration route for other members of her family. In February 1991 another episode of "One Hundred Life Events" presented a filial young woman's efforts to please her mother yet avoid such a marriage.

In this episode a rich Chinese from America comes to Guangzhou looking for a wife to take back with him. He is in his 50s but wants a younger woman. A daughter of one of the families regularly featured in this program is tapped by her mother to meet him. Initially the daughter refuses, but the mother becomes so upset (she is only thinking of what is good for her daughter, of what this man can provide for her) that the daughter finally consents to the meeting. She is determined, however, to make sure the man does not find her a desirable candidate. She dresses saucily and shortly after meeting him in a restaurant asks him to light her cigarette. She says she hopes he is not upset that she smokes. On the contrary, he is impressed and assures her that in America many women smoke. Indeed, he even pulls out an enormous cigar for her to smoke. She says she smokes *many* cigarettes a day, drinks, plays mah-jongg, and so forth. She then suggests they order drinks. Again he is impressed and suggests they down their full glasses. In the next scene we find her with a terrible hangover, being ministered to by her younger sister. Furthermore, the man wants to meet her again!

In a second effort to deter this man from finding her a desirable mate, the young woman enlists the help of her brother. She arranges that the next meeting take place in a public park but steers him to a bench in a rather isolated section. As they sit there, he moving a little closer to her, a young man (her brother) suddenly bursts out of the bushes and accosts her, demanding that she make good on the debt she owes (presumably as a result of losses at mah-jongg). When the young woman tells the suitor not to become involved, the suitor says he has dealt with many such men in America and knows how to handle them. The suitor comes forward, asks the amount of the debt, and offers to write a check then and there to cover it. The brother and sister had not anticipated this response, but the young man quickly recovers and demands payment in cash. The suitor gives him his hotel address and says to come for the money the next day. The young man, in an effort to frighten him, seizes the suitor's lapel and insists he make good on the payment. The older man, however, is not the least bit frightened. Instead, he asks the young man to remove his hand. The young man refuses, saying, "If you don't like it there, why don't you remove it yourself?" The older man says, "That would not be polite," waits a few seconds, and then belts the young man so hard he is knocked to the ground.

The young woman does not know what to do next, but suddenly hits on an idea that is certain to work. Another family member's sterilization certificate is stored at their house. All she has to do is change the character of the personal name on the certificate, and the suitor will think she herself has been sterilized. Since it is assumed that having children is one of his goals, the sterilization certificate should remove her from consideration. The next scene finds the suitor coming for dinner, at which the mother expects the terms of the marriage to be discussed. The young woman puts the altered certificate in a magazine and contrives so that the suitor reads it while she is ostensibly in the kitchen helping her mother. Sure enough, while leafing through the pages he stumbles upon the certificate. A look of consternation crosses his face. When the young woman comes back into the room, he apologizes, saying something urgent has just come up and he cannot stay for dinner. He rushes out, and the young woman is saved. She has shown her filiality by agreeing to meet this man but has been saved by her wits from marrying him. This story also suggests how difficult it can be to determine whether a particular marriage is truly the result of free choice.

Marriage

The natural outcome of a successful courtship is marriage, and with marriage, in China at least, comes the rearing of children, or rather, in Guangzhou, the single child. Before the child arrives, however, the couple must have a stable living arrangement in which to raise it. According to the Five City Family Study, 47 percent of couples in the most recent cohort to marry (between 1977 and 1982) lived with the husband's family after the wedding, 18 percent with the wife's. Only 32 percent established an independent residence, and just under 3 percent had to make other arrangements — for example, opting to live separately because of work assignments or overcrowding in their natal households that made the addition of even one more adult impossible. The figures for postwedding living arrangements of the oldest cohort (those marrying before 1938) show a higher proportion (60 percent) living with the husband's family and a lower proportion (9 percent) with the wife's but the same proportion (31 percent) living independently.[38] What these figures conceal, however, is that from 1950 to 1965 more than half of all newly married couples lived independently. Even among those couples marrying between 1966 and 1976, 48 percent established their own household, whereas only 35 percent lived with the husband's family and 14 percent with the wife's.[39]

The decline in independent living among newlyweds can be traced to two primary factors: changes in the rates of rural-to-urban migration and changes in the availability of housing. During most of the 1950s enormous numbers of rural laborers came into the cities to participate in China's reconstruction. They came as unmarried young people whose parents by and large remained in the countryside, and they met and married young people in similar circumstances. Thousands of dormitories were erected to house these workers. The cohort marrying 25 or more years later was much more likely to have urban parents with whom they were living prior to marriage. Furthermore, as we have already seen, there was a terrible shortage of housing space that was only beginning to be corrected at the time of the CASS study. Couples were unlikely to be assigned to housing unless they were already married.

During the three-and-a-half-year interval between the first and second interviews in the Guangzhou Family Study (late 1987 through spring 1991) 39 household members, 24 males and 15 females, married for the first time (and one 37-year-old widower remarried).[40] The average age of the men at first marriage was 30 (with a range of 26–36), that of the women, 27.3 (with a range of 21–33). Only two women were under 25 at the time of their marriage; one was originally from a rural area, and the other married a Hong Kong Chinese. These averages are well above the legal minimum age of marriage and also substantially above the provincial minimums recommended for late marriage (see p. 106), but they are not unheard of. Shanghai, for example, has even more stringent criteria for late marriage than Guangdong — 27 for men and 25 for women. A study of the 189,000 marriages registered in central Shanghai between 1977 and mid-July 1980 found that more than 90 percent of marriages met these age criteria.[41]

Apparently pressure from urban work units and a continued housing shortage have resulted in high rates of deferred marriage. Moreover, the factors that have raised the age of first marriage in other urban Chinese communities may be at work in Guangzhou: the increases in education and employment opportunities that lead young people spontaneously to delay marriage. These factors are believed to be primarily responsible for the late mean ages at which Chinese women marry in Hong Kong (25.9 in 1986), Singapore (25.8 in 1987), Malaysia (25.8 in 1984–85), and Taiwan (25.1 in 1987).[42]

Following marriage 63 percent of the newly married men in the Guangzhou Family Study lived patrilocally; that is, they brought in daughters-in-law (64 percent if the remarried widower is included); 33 percent left or separated ("divided") from the parental household; and 4 percent (one individual) remained in the natal household apart from his spouse. By contrast only one woman (6 percent of cases) brought a son-in-law into her natal household,* whereas 67 percent followed their husbands elsewhere.

---

* The woman in this case is an only child. From the time she began going out with her future husband, she made it clear that their marriage was contingent on his moving into her parents' household. Since her father is a high cadre with the provincial government, he was

(Presumably, if symmetry can be relied upon here, most moved in with in-laws.) Another four women (27 percent) stayed with their natal families while their husbands lived elsewhere because of their work. Although the Guangzhou data are not longitudinal, these recent figures do support the CASS study's findings of low rates of independent residence and of residence with the wife's family and high rates of coresidence with the husband's family. A similar shift (declines in coresidence with the wife's family) is documented by Davis for families in Wuhan and Shanghai during the 1980s. Davis attributes these changes to increased control at the family level. In the 1960s and 1970s family strategies were hampered by government policies of job assignment and rustication. Families could not easily determine which children would remain nearby and which disperse. Since the reforms in job allocation and the return of children from the countryside, parents are better able to decide which sex to invest in, and the choice is increasingly to invest in sons, whose economic potential is perceived as greater than that of daughters.[43]

It is critical to note, however, that the immediate postwedding residence is unlikely to be the new couple's long-term residence. Most couples are simply waiting for their housing assignment to be made. For example, a 1985 study of residence patterns in Tianjin revealed that 65 percent of young couples in stem families left the parental household in the first five years of their marriage; another 17 percent left within the next five years.[44] Furthermore, according to a number of studies, most parents and adult children prefer living separately but, if at all possible, in the same vicinity so that they can continue to interact frequently.[45] In fact the nuclear family is the most common family type in China's cities. According to the Five City Family Study 66.4 percent of urban families are nuclear, 24.3 percent stem, and 2.3 percent joint. An additional 2.4 percent are single-person households; 4.6 percent fall into the category of other.[46]

These data reveal that although stem family living is a common experience in contemporary urban China, it is most characteristic of certain age groups: obviously those in their 20s and 30s (the newly married) but also those over 60 (the elderly). In the Guangzhou Family Study, in which all the elderly are at least 70 years old, 60 percent live in stem and joint families and 15.5 percent in nuclear families; only 8 percent live alone. Another 16.5 percent live in other arrangements, such as with an unmarried grandchild or with their long-term employer.[47] A national study of the elderly carried out in 1987 presents the living arrangements of the elderly in a slightly different way, but the message (high rates of coresidence of the

---

slated for reassignment to a new three-bedroom apartment, into which the whole family expected to move in July 1991. Even in their current residence the young couple have a fancily furnished bedroom of their own. The son-in-law's natal family lives in Shanghai.

elderly and their children) is the same. Of the nearly 14,000 elderly living in cities (not including those living in rural townships) 61.8 percent lived in households made up of three or more generations, 26.9 percent in two-generation households, 7.5 percent as couples, 1.9 percent alone, and 2 percent in other arrangements.[48]

Although the contemporary patrilocal stem family shares a common form with the ideal traditional family, its dynamics differ. The senior female of the household (the mother-in-law) generally controls the household budget, but this post is less powerful than is sometimes assumed. Both the Five City Family Study and the Guangzhou Family Study make the same observations on the significance of the household budget. Although others usually contribute a share of their income to a particular person in the household, this share represents the smaller part of their income. Furthermore, the household manager is not free to redistribute this money as she sees fit — for example, to those members in greatest need — but is expected to spend it on food. The junior couple retain the bulk of their income to pay children's educational and clothing expenses as well as their own transport, clothing, meals outside the home, and entertainment. Costly items such as electrical appliances or a new set of furniture are usually purchased by the younger generation, who take them along when they move to new housing.

The strict correlation between seniority and authority characteristic of the ideal traditional family is conspicuous by its absence. In the Guangzhou Family Study elders made it clear that by and large their adult children (even when still unmarried) make their own decisions about where to work, whom to marry, and whether their children (the elder's grandchildren) continue in school. Most of these elders have far less education than their children, are unfamiliar with the job market and the new strategy of locating work on one's own, and are intimidated by their own dependence (financial or physical) on the younger generation. Most freely admit they do not know how to advise on these issues and do not attempt to do so. Though they are happy to be asked their opinions, they usually concur with what the younger generation has already indicated it wishes to do. For its part the younger generation has already factored the elder's likely response into its own game plan. Families that are unable to develop a smooth working relationship usually divide the household if at all possible.

What do families quarrel about? According to a 1987 survey carried out in metropolitan Shanghai that included both urban and rural dwellers, the number one problem is the relation between mother-in-law and daughter-in-law (54.4 percent of respondents selected this from among nine possible subjects of dispute).[49] Other problems include housing (53.4 percent), children's education (49.1 percent), incompatibility (40.8 percent), daily expenses (34.9 percent), caring for aged parents (33.0 percent), life-style issues (23.5 percent), property disputes (20.0 percent) and entertainment (10.7 percent). Rural dwellers are substantially more likely to report family disputes, reflecting their higher rate of intergenerational living and greater stake in controlling family property.

In the Guangzhou Family Study housing disputes loom large. The reallocation of already crowded space or a realignment of social relationships required when a household member, especially a male, marries can make living in a stem family trying for all concerned. For example, when I asked 82-year-old Mr. Lai when he had last seen his son who lives next door, Mr. Lai declined to answer, saying, "I don't consider him my son." Although several years have elapsed since this son's marriage, just the mention of him is enough to raise Mr. Lai's blood pressure. According to his daughters, Mr. Lai has never recovered from having to vacate his own room for the new couple, who quickly divided from the family.

Similarly, when I made my second visit to 80-year-old Mrs. Liao, I found the entire family quarreling about the use of living space. In the three months prior to my visit, both of Mrs. Liao's coresident married sons had moved into housing allocated by their units. By 1987 her older son and his family, though sharing the family dwelling, had already divided out,* and Mrs. Liao was eating with the younger son's family and looking after his two children. By 1991 this arrangement had been terminated, and Mrs. Liao was distressed about the prospects for her future. The building in which she lived was slated to be torn down, and it was clear that members of the younger generation were angling to maintain or establish a claim to live in the residence to be built on the site. Thus, even though the younger son's family had moved, it was attempting to maintain residence at its previous address.

When the younger son left, Mrs. Liao had erroneously assumed that she would be able to move out of the cubicle she occupied in the living room and into the bedroom previously occupied by the couple, which she had vacated for them when they married. Her daughter-in-law, who continues to work in the neighborhood, quickly set her straight, ordering her not to reoccupy the room and not to touch anything in it. To make sure her orders are not violated, she comes back daily to take her lunchtime nap in the room. Furthermore, the daughter-in-law claims she has alerted the police that she has things in the room; if they are disturbed, she will take her mother-in-law to court! Mrs. Liao's two daughters argued their mother's case, demanding to know whether any of this was "right" or "reasonable." Meanwhile her younger daughter, whose husband and older child have

---

* "Dividing out" is an economic issue. To divide means to eat and budget separately. Divided households might continue to occupy the same space, or one household might move to a new location. Both arrangements occurred in the Guangzhou Family Study.

remained at their own residence, has moved in with her younger child to look after Mrs. Liao.

Some arguments seem to be entirely idiosyncratic. A block away from Mr. Lai, 79-year-old Mr. Du was forced to end his relationship with his next-door neighbors, the parents of his deceased daughter-in-law, when his widowed younger son remarried. Mr. Du's younger daughter-in-law died in 1988 of a form of blood cancer. Her parents were Mr. Du's long-term mah-jongg partners and the godparents of Mr. Du's older son's child. In short, the two families were inextricably intertwined. The problems began when Mr. Du's younger son, the neighbors' son-in-law, decided to marry a workmate of his deceased wife. Mr. Du felt that the couple were planning to marry too quickly after the death of his daughter-in-law. He urged them to show some respect by waiting. The parents of the deceased daughter-in-law then indicated that as part of the wedding procedures, they wanted the new bride to knock on their door and offer them tea (a way of formally acknowledging them as relatives of the groom). The bride, however, did not want to do so, and Mr. Du's son supported her in her refusal. Mr. Du's son no longer wants to have anything to do with his deceased wife's parents and has also discouraged Mr. Du from having anything to do with them. Mr. Du sighed, saying that though the couple continue to live next door and remain godparents of his grandchild, the three elders are essentially invisible to each other. When they happen on the street at the same time, they must avert eyes and avoid greetings — a frequent occurrence since they live in adjacent ground-floor apartments.

I provide these examples, not to argue that disharmony is more the rule than the exception in stem families, but to illustrate the tensions that sharing limited space can generate. I also want to point out that in none of these cases does the senior generation feel powerful enough to dictate a resolution. All three of these distressed parents feel they have no choice but to accommodate themselves to decisions made by the younger generation. In stem families where the parents are younger, for example, in their 50s or 60s, or are politically well connected, the junior generation might feel itself disadvantaged in decision-making power. In either case it should not be surprising to learn that nuclear family living has its attractions for both generations.[50]

The primary reason behind the space reallocation following the marriage of a household member is the belief that newly married couples are entitled to a bedroom of their own. Without this minimal requirement for privacy the arrival of the next generation would be delayed indefinitely. China, of course, is world famous (or infamous, depending on one's point of view) for the strictness of its population policy.[51] During most of the 1950s the government's position on population growth was essentially "the more the better"; each additional person was seen, not as a mouth to feed, but as a pair of hands to build the new China. Though there was dissent from this position all along, until the early 1970s dissenters had too little power in the central government to reverse the pronatalist policies. Prior to this time the desirability of reduced fertility had been discussed primarily as a health benefit to mothers and infants, but thereafter the focus shifted to the need to keep down population growth to achieve economic growth. The state began in 1973 to promote the *"wan, xi, shao"* policy: delayed childbirth (*wan*), longer birth intervals (*xi*), and fewer births (*shao*). In the cities this policy was interpreted to mean intervals of at least four years between births and no more than two children per couple. Implementation relied primarily on persuasion, though more forceful measures were available to deal with the recalcitrant.[52] Under this policy the Chinese birthrate dropped from 33.6 per thousand in 1970 to 18.3 in 1978.[53]

This rapid drop, achieved even before any material incentives were explicitly made available, suggests that there was already substantial interest on the part of at least the urban population in reducing family size, probably for many of the same reasons as elsewhere: higher survival rates of children, higher costs in rearing them, more education and increased employment opportunities for women, and so forth.[54] Again, comparisons with Chinese populations elsewhere in Asia are instructive. By 1987 the total fertility rates (average number of children born to women who had completed their childbearing) were 1.3 for Hong Kong, 1.5 for Singapore, 1.7 for Taiwan, and 2.3 for Malaysia.[55] In none of these sites was the pressure to reduce fertility anything near what it was in China.

The pressure increased greatly with the introduction of the one-child family policy in 1979. When it was first announced, there was no consensus whether the policy positively limited couples to one child or set the one-child family as a goal. No national law was passed. Instead, individual provinces were left to formulate their own family planning regulations, and implementation methods (subject to provincial guidelines) were developed at the local level. Each administrative jurisdiction, such as a commune or a work unit, was assigned a quota of births by higher administrative authorities. Jurisdictions or units (or the cadres in charge) that kept births at or below the quota were to be rewarded; those exceeding it were subject to penalties. Given the government's traditional mobilization style, the "bold assault," it should not be surprising that coercion and other abuses accompanied the implementation of the one-child policy, particularly in rural areas, where resistance was greatest.[56]

By 1990 the one-child family policy was understood to mean one child for urban families and up to two for rural families, particularly if a rural couple's first child was a girl. A rural couple may have a second child if one of them (1) is the single transmitter of the line for at least two generations (i.e., the only child of an only child), (2) is the only one in a set of brothers with the ability to procreate, (3) is a male who moves into the household of a woman who is an only child, (4) is an only child married to an only child, (5) is a disabled veteran, (6) is a woman married to a returned overseas Chinese, or (7) belongs to an exceptional hardship household in a remote mountain or fishing district. These exemptions directly address the concerns of rural families who view sons as critical for the continuation of the line and for their own physical survival.[57] Even in the cities a couple may petition to have a second child under certain circumstances, such as having a child who will be unable to earn a living. In such a case a doctor has to certify that the child is disabled and that the disability was not caused by the parents. Some units require that the certifying doctor be from a level higher than a public health station.

Although there was some slippage in enforcement during the 1980s, by 1992, in the wake of tightening restrictions, the birth rate in Guangzhou had dropped to 13.1 per thousand overall and to only 10.9 in the city proper, indicating that compliance with the (modified) one-child policy is high but uneven.[58] For example, although almost 96 percent of births were first births in two of the four core urban districts, in Haizhu district, the most rural of the four, the figure was only 87.8 percent. By contrast, in Guangzhou's four counties, 53–57 percent of births were first births.[59] Such a narrow spread in the rural areas suggests both acceptance and vigorous enforcement of a two-child standard.

Authorities, attributing the excess births to the mobile population, by 1990 had targeted them for special attention. In 1991 the provincial government was requiring all people seeking employment to have a document specifying either that they were single or that, if married, they were in compliance with the one-child policy. Being in compliance means having no child or having one and practicing contraception. In China the officially preferred mode of contraception is the sterilization of one partner or the outfitting of the woman with an IUD before she returns to work. In the event that she is one of those few people who cannot tolerate an IUD and takes the pill instead, this must be stated on the document. Every year work units require a physical exam, to make sure that the IUD is still in place, as well as a urine test, to make sure that the woman is not pregnant. Should she be found pregnant, an abortion is about the only alternative. A woman accidentally pregnant (i.e., with an IUD in place) is not considered blameworthy; her abortion is covered by insurance, and she receives full time off (normally fifteen rest days). An employer hiring people without the certificates takes a big risk because the state conducts periodic inspections. Anyone found to have violated the regulations by hiring someone without evidence of marital and parental status faces punishment. Furthermore, the self-employed must themselves be certified as in compliance before they can obtain a license to set up a business.

Giving birth to a child in Guangzhou requires official authorization. After registering one's marriage, one goes to the local street committee office, which provides newly married couples with a document known as a planned birth certificate, stating that the female applicant is permitted to bear a child in the current year. By tradition, immediate childbearing is the rule, and surveys indicate that 65 percent of Chinese women still conceive within three months of marriage and that more than 85 percent conceive by the time of their first wedding anniversary.[60] Should a woman experience a delay in getting pregnant, there is usually no problem extending the permit to the following year. When a woman goes to a hospital for a prenatal exam (or for any exam at which it is likely to be noticed that she is pregnant), she must present her pregnancy permit. If she does not have the permit, she is immediately called to account and pressured to have an abortion. For this reason women with unauthorized pregnancies frequently do not seek treatment for any health problems until after their baby arrives. If they are employed, however, their co-workers will notice their condition and press for an abortion. If they are not employed, they must stay in seclusion, for should they go out, the neighbors would notice the pregnancy and report it to the residents committee or the street committee. A couple's only hope is for the woman to flee the locality before her pregnancy is obvious. Even so, if her unit or the local government office suspects that she has fled because of a pregnancy, it will be certain to visit both her parents and her parents-in-law to see whether she is hiding out with them. Officials might even chase her to the countryside if they know where she is likely to be. When she finally agrees to an abortion, the unit or government sends someone to escort her to the hospital — to make certain she actually has the abortion.

Every April each residents committee carries out an annual inspection of women of childbearing age in the neighborhood. A representative visits every household in which there is a married woman of childbearing age who has not been sterilized. According to one such representative, who "caught" a rural woman hiding out in her jurisdiction in the 1991 sweep, the inspection is nothing more than eyeballing the woman's abdomen to see if she looks pregnant. If she does, the residents committee pressures her and her family members to agree to an abortion. The residents committee also distributes contraceptives to the few couples with a child who have not been sterilized if the wife cannot tolerate an IUD.

When it comes time to deliver her baby, no hospital receives a woman, even if she is in labor, without the pregnancy permit. A woman under these circumstances either calls in a midwife for a home delivery or attempts to deliver at a public health station. Some such stations will accept her, but others will not, and in any event this delivery is not covered by her medical insurance. Furthermore, the hospital is the only legitimate source of a birth certificate for the baby, and without that the child cannot be officially registered as a resident of Guangzhou (or anywhere else, for that matter). Without registration as a city resident, the child (and thus the whole family) faces educational and employment disadvantages, though these are becoming increasingly less significant. Because these deterrents are well known, it takes a motivated person to buck public opinion and endure the penalties, which include fines and possibly dismissal from one's work unit.

Maternity leave policies vary by unit. State regulations require that a mother be given three months' leave at full pay, but if the mother meets the requirements for a "late birth," that is, is at least 24, she automatically receives an additional month. In the early years of the one-child policy, families that promised to have just one child were given all kinds of incentives, including lengthy maternity leaves. Some units gave one or even two years with full pay, but now that everyone is required to have only one child, this generosity is no longer necessary. Nevertheless, depending on its own financial circumstances, a unit might extend maternity leave to six months or more at 70 percent of pay.

With both spouses in the labor force, young urban couples living in independent households are hard-pressed to care for their child once maternity leave is up, sometimes having to board it during the week with one of its grandparents. Having more than one child, of course, presents even greater difficulties. One day, when I encountered an acquaintance who, I discovered, was the father of young twins (a boy and a girl), I congratulated him on his presumed good fortune (getting around the one-child policy). He shook his head and exclaimed, "It's awful!" Even though his mother-in-law helps them out, "They're always sick. If it isn't this one, it's the other one."

Most parents (whether they live in stem or nuclear families) send their child to day care, because a grandparent might not be available or because the parents worry that the grandparent will spoil the child. The CASS study found that 44 percent of the children under the age of one were already in day care.[61] Though parents are disturbed that children in these group settings get sick frequently, day care is viewed with much less ambivalence in China than in the United States. Freeing women from child rearing to allow them to participate in the labor force is viewed as a necessary step in achieving equality of the sexes. But day care is also viewed as good for children because it exposes them very early to "scientific" methods of rearing. Furthermore, now that nearly all urban children are from single-child families, increased contact with peers and slightly older children is deemed essential for normal social development.

The success of the one-child policy in the urban areas is probably due to a coincidence of personal and official interests. Because pensions are available for most urban workers and those with no pensions and no descendants have a welfare safety net, people no longer perceive children as critical for survival in old age. This attitudinal change is reflected in a survey carried out in Shanghai that asked women why they wanted to have children. Urban women answered that they want children to achieve joy in life, avoid loneliness, have someone who will carry out their ideals, and enhance ties between them and their husbands. These sentimental reasons contrast with the more practical responses of rural women, who want to continue the line, gain security in old age, and increase labor power.[62]

Chinese psychologists and educators worry endlessly about the upbringing of the only child. There is enormous concern that parents will make the child the center of their lives, with dire consequences for the child's development. Some fear the child will become a "little emperor," indulged, doted on, and lacking in self-discipline; others fear the parents will be overprotective, stifling the child; still others fear that the parents, having unrealistic expectations, will burden the child with unreachable goals. The CASS study found, for example, that 87 percent of parents hoped that their child would eventually attend a university.[63]

Adult Children and Elderly Parents

Parents who raise self-centered children may have no one to look after them in old age. The current cohort of elderly raised children for many reasons but certainly expected that their children would care for them when they could no longer care for themselves. When families talk about care of the aged, three words crop up: *yang* (support, provide for), *fushi* (wait upon, attend), and *zhaogu* (attend to, look after), each reflecting a slightly different aspect of care. *Yang* represents the absolute minimum — meeting the material needs of one's parents by making certain they have food, clothing, and shelter. While *fushi* and *zhaogu* are often used interchangeably, some of those I spoke to felt that the terms applied to different situations. *Fushi* implies looking after ("serving") someone of slightly higher status who is probably capable of serving himself. Actions demonstrating *fushi* are carried out respectfully and courteously. *Zhaogu* eliminates the status distinction and assumes a lack of capability on the part of the person being looked after. People in need of *zhaogu* care are children, the sick, and the disabled.

Meeting the material needs (*yang*) of the elderly is not difficult for most urban families, because 58 percent of urban elders receive pensions, which, they indicate, are by far their most important source of income. More men than women, however, receive pensions — according to the 1987 national survey, 84 percent of urban men but only 35 percent of urban women.[64] Men's pensions, moreover, are generally larger than those of women. Those who lack a pension have never been in the labor force, were employed too briefly to qualify, or were employed in the collective sector when only onetime termination payments were made. Retirees continue to receive the same health insurance benefits as current employees, but elderly who have not been employed have either half coverage (as dependents of eligible adult children) or little or no coverage. As with pensions, there are substantial age and sex differences in health coverage. For example, the 1987 survey found that only 20 percent of those aged 60–64 have no coverage, compared with 44 percent of those aged 80–84. Among elderly urban men 79 percent receive full coverage, 12 percent half coverage, and 9 percent no coverage. The comparable figures for women are 26, 31, and 43 percent.[65]

These statistics seem to suggest that medical expenses are not a serious problem for the urban elderly, but the actual situation is more mixed. Paying for ordinary outpatient care is seldom a burden, even for those without insurance, because fees are very low, but the cost of an inpatient's personal, as opposed to medical, needs can strain the budget of even a family with full insurance coverage. For example, one elderly couple in the Guangzhou Family Study, the Jeungs, had combined pensions of about 230 yuan, and as retirees from a state unit, their medical costs (excluding hospital meals) were completely covered. Despite their apparently secure position the Jeungs' monthly health care expenses were more than double their monthly income. In 1987, three months before the first interview, 81-year-old Mr. Jeung suffered a stroke that left him bedridden and in need of 24-hour care in the local district hospital. Feeding, toileting, repositioning, and so forth (all aspects of *zhaogu*) are considered responsibilities of the family, not the nursing staff. Mrs. Jeung, 79, suffering herself from arthritis in her knees and shoulders, could not easily provide this care, nor could her son and daughter-in-law since both are employed. Consequently, she paid a 67-year-old woman (a *baomu*, or nursemaid) over 17 yuan a day to stay at the hospital 24 hours a day looking after Mr. Jeung. She gave 15 yuan directly to the woman and a little over 2 yuan to the hospital to cover the costs of the caretaker's meals. The Jeungs were able to meet these expenses only through the generosity of "friends," that is, contributions from fellow members of their Christian church.

Special medical needs and at-home care can also generate large uncovered expenses. When Mrs. Gunn, a widow in her early 80s, returned from a visit with her daughters in Beijing, her two Guangzhou daughters felt she had deteriorated physically. They worried that she had circulatory problems, so in the spring of 1991 they sent her to the hospital for a general work-up. While in the hospital, Mrs. Gunn had a serious attack of herpes

TABLE 3.1
Living Arrangement of Elderly by Sex, in Percentage, in Guangzhou, 1987

	Males (N = 77)	Females (N = 123)	Total (N = 200)
Living with spouse	76%	15%	38.5%
With spouse only	14	3	7.5
And unmarried child(ren)	12	1	5.0
And married child(ren) and unmarried child(ren)	17	3	8.5
And married child(ren)	21	7	12.5
And married child(ren) but eat/budget separately	5	0	2.0
And other	7	1	3.0
Living without spouse	24	83	61.5
With unmarried child(ren)	3	3	3.0
With married child(ren) and unmarried child(ren)	5	7	6.5
With married child(ren)	6	42	28.5
With married child(ren) but eat/budget separately	1	2	2.0
With other	0	22	13.5
Alone	9	7	8.0
TOTAL	100	98[a]	100.0

SOURCE: C. Ikels, "Settling Accounts: The Intergenerational Contract in an Age of Reform," in D. Davis and S. Harrell, eds., *Chinese Families in the Post-Mao Era*, pp. 307–33 (Berkeley: University of California Press, 1993).

[a] Total is less than 100 because of rounding.

zoster that initially threatened her eyesight and required a great deal of attention. Although a *baomu* was hired to look after her, at least two or three children or children-in-law were usually present also. As a retired kindergarten teacher, Mrs. Gunn receives a monthly pension of 180 yuan and 100 percent medical coverage. Nevertheless, her hospitalization and subsequent care at home cost the family on the order of 4,000 yuan. Part of this sum went for the *baomu*, part of it for an intravenous medication available only from Hong Kong, and part of it for gifts to doctors who came from specialty clinics to treat Mrs. Gunn at home. Fortunately Mrs. Gunn is able to count on her children. When all the children assembled in Guangzhou during the 1991 Spring Festival (Lunar New Year), they decided to formalize their obligations to their mother. The three children in Guangzhou (the two oldest daughters and younger son) are expected to provide housing and the bulk of care. The older son living in Hong Kong and the youngest daughter living in Australia each agreed to contribute H.K. $500 (a total of approximately U.S. $125 at the time) a month to Mrs. Gunn's expenses. The two daughters in Beijing and one in Hunan are expected to be available for emergency assistance, such as looking after her in the hospital or occasionally providing housing. With eight children Mrs. Gunn is in a more comfortable situation than the Jeungs, who have only two (one son in Guangzhou and another in a distant province).[66]

The provision of care is greatly facilitated by coresidence or, at a minimum, nearby residence of the children. As can be seen from Table 3.1, although only 8 percent of the elderly in the Guangzhou Family Study live alone, there are major differences by sex in the actual composition and organization of these households. The typical male over 70 lives with a spouse and is almost as likely to have unmarried children as married ones in the home. The typical female, however, is likely to be widowed and living with a married child (or children) or someone other than a child. These differences occur because the men in the study are generally younger than the women (age-specific mortality rates are higher for men), have spouses younger than themselves, and, if widowed, more likely to have remarried. Women widowed at an early age were less likely to remarry and instead sought security by entering domestic service. Thus several of the women classified as "living with other" are living with the children they brought up in their employer's household. Because they have been such long-term quasi-family members, it is unthinkable for them to live elsewhere in old age. Almost all the other women living with an "other" are living with grandchildren whom they raised for sons or daughters. Table 3.2 reveals that the obligation to look after parents, at least insofar as sharing accommodations is concerned, is still very much that of sons. Of the 117 parents having both sons and daughters, 56 percent live exclusively with sons and only 7 percent exclusively with daughters (an 8 to 1 ratio in favor of the traditional arrangement).

TABLE 3.2
Living Arrangement of Elderly by Sex of Child, in Percentage, in Guangzhou, 1987

	Has sons only (N = 39)	Has both (N = 117)	Has daughters only (N = 28)	Has none (N = 16)	Total (N = 200)
With son	56.4%	56.4%	0%	0%	44%
With both	0	18.8	0	0	11
With daughter	0	6.8	64.3	0	13
With spouse only	10.3	4.3	10.7	18.75	7.5
With other	25.6	8.5	17.9	50.0	16.5
Alone	7.7	5.1	7.1	31.25	8
TOTAL	100.0	99.9[a]	100.0	100.00	100.0

SOURCE: C. Ikels, "Settling Accounts: The Intergenerational Contract in an Age of Reform," in D. Davis and S. Harrell, eds., *Chinese Families in the Post-Mao Era*, pp. 307–33 (Berkeley: University of California Press, 1993).
  [a] Total is less than 100 because of rounding.

Caring for parents does not terminate with their deaths. Children — again particularly sons — continue to have special obligations to their deceased parents. At a minimum, even in the cities, these include arranging a proper funeral and visiting the grave or ash depository annually on Qingming, the spring grave-sweeping festival. Most families also carry out some form of domestic ancestor worship. The Chinese government's official position on these practices has fluctuated since 1949.[67] Objections to the traditional funeral include its expense to the family; its waste of resources (consuming scarce wood and removing land from cultivation); its concern with ghosts, *fengshui*,* and life after death (viewed as superstitious beliefs incompatible with a scientific viewpoint); and its focus on the lineage as an important social group.

Funeral reform has included both recommendations and laws. Thus families have been advised to keep their funeral expenses down and have been offered alternative, inexpensive funerals. Cremation rather than coffined burial has been urged in the cities. The burning of paper goods and setting off of firecrackers in certain public areas have been forbidden. Clan burial grounds have been moved or ploughed under. Initially the state did little in the way of funeral reform, but starting in 1958 at both the national and local levels it began to promote (though not require) cremation rather than burial. In 1958 Guangzhou built its first crematorium, but people were slow to accept the idea, regarding it as too cruel.[68] In the first few years only 8.5 percent of deaths were followed by cremation. In 1962 the Guangzhou Civil Affairs Bureau made cremation mandatory for people in the urban areas. In 1966, with the start of the Cultural Revolution, everyone was too frightened to do anything that might be considered conservative, and the cremation rate shot up to 90 percent. Furthermore, all four of Guangzhou's traditional funeral facilities were closed in 1966, and all subsequent funeral services had to be carried out at the modern facility, which opened that year. In 1973 another law was passed forbidding feudal practices, such as burning things, at funerals.

In 1975 the ratio of cremations in the city began to drop as a result of renewed contact with the outside. In 1985 the national government, concerned about the resurgence of feudal practices nationwide, passed a detailed law requiring that everyone, including rural dwellers, undergo cremation following death. In practice, however, the law is implemented only if there is a crematorium within a reasonable distance; the many places that have none remain unofficially exempt. The law also spelled out exactly what

* *Fengshui*, literally "wind and water," is usually translated "geomancy," that is, a system of beliefs about the influence of topography on a family's or community's fate. There has long been a belief that the correct siting of an ancestor's grave can bring luck and prosperity to his or her descendants.

was and was not allowed at cadre funerals and developed a system of fines to keep cadre funerals in line with policy. The government accommodated certain exceptions to these laws by allowing some of the distinctive minority practices that had been forbidden during the Cultural Revolution, so long as the minorities accept cremation.

In 1986 Guangzhou passed its own regulation following the guidelines spelled out in the national law but specifying even more details. For example, to show respect, exceptions to the cremation requirements were allowed for the families of overseas Chinese and compatriots from Hong Kong, Macao, and (eventually) Taiwan, and land for their burial or that of their kin was made available in a joint venture between the funeral parlor and Hong Kong investors. Under no circumstances, however, may national cadres or members of the Communist Party evade cremation. These 1986 guidelines were to be applied not only to the urban districts of Guangzhou but also to the counties.

In 1990 Guangzhou investigated the "practical consequences" of implementing the 1986 rules, to see how well the new guidelines were working and to plug loopholes people had found to evade them. On November 18, 1990, as a result of this investigation, a whole new set of stricter rules came into effect: (1) The funeral parlor became the only authorized transporter of corpses from the place of death. No one else under any circumstances is allowed to transport the body. Officials knew that families sometimes moved their dead under cover of darkness to evade cremation. (2) The funeral parlor must be notified of a death within 24 hours. (3) If mountainside graves (and their contents) have to be removed because the state is taking over the land for another use, the remains of the individuals concerned may not be reburied. They too must be cremated. (4) Clan burial grounds along roads and highways must be removed, though those not easily reached need not be disturbed. (5) The definition of "overseas Chinese family member" was restricted to those no more than three generations apart. Thus a grandfather in Canada means that two generations of descendants in China qualify for burial or, in the case of a young overseas Chinese, that two generations above qualify. Siblings also qualify. Some people had been claiming overseas Chinese status on the basis of an ancestor who had gone abroad during the Qing or even the Ming dynasty — as early as the seventeenth century! (6) Burial is allowed in mountain villages that cannot be reached by a funeral vehicle. This is being realistic about local conditions. (7) Rural dwellers allowed to have burials may not bury their dead just anywhere. Each community must set aside an area specifically for burials. (8) No feudal practices (e.g., burning of things) may be carried out at or in the general vicinity of the funeral parlor.[69]

Fifty elderly in the Guangzhou Family Study died from December 1987 through May 1991, 24 men and 26 women. Twenty-six died in the hospital (many in the observation room attached to the outpatient clinic or the emergency room), 23 at home, and 1 on the street en route to see a doctor. One family successfully smuggled the body out of the house for burial, and one elderly man returned to his home village, where he died and was buried. Just about every family held one or another version of the standard approved funeral. In the approved version the family rents a room for about an hour at the funeral parlor, during which time the body of the deceased is displayed in the center of the room, surrounded or flanked by wreaths. If the deceased had belonged to a work unit, an administrator or representative from the labor union of the unit makes a brief speech. If the person formerly occupied a high position, several representatives from the workplace might give speeches about his or her contributions. Usually but not necessarily the eldest son then makes a few comments about his deceased parent. Finally, everyone bows to the deceased, walks around the coffin, pauses to console the family members who led the walk, and exits. For Christians a minister makes appropriate remarks. One family even held a regular Christian funeral service at the deceased's church, though only after the body had been cremated. (The ashes were brought to the church.)[70]

The standard funeral service is followed immediately by cremation. Ashes are kept in small containers the size and shape of jewelry boxes or, much less frequently, in small ceramic urns. The containers are stored for a small fee for varying periods in the ash depository at one of Guangzhou's two main cemeteries. These are located on opposite sides of the street; one serves cadres, the other, the masses. At Qingming families go to the cemetery and, instead of sweeping the tombs and cutting back the year's growth of vegetation, dust the box and replace the miniature plastic flowers that share its tiny cubicle. These actions constitute the acceptable maximum for the government and the acceptable minimum for the public, but most families in the Guangzhou Family Study carry out more than the minimum funeral and display more than the minimum filial piety at Qingming.

Many people offered foods and burned paper clothes and paper money for the deceased at home either immediately before or after the official funeral. In addition, most conducted some ceremony, including the offering of foods and the burning of paper goods on the 7th day following the death. A substantial minority conducted the same ritual on the 14th and the 21st days after the death, and at least one family conducted the "seventh seven" on the 49th day following the death—according to traditional beliefs the day the soul is reborn. Seventy-two percent of the deceased, moreover, are memorialized in some form at home, almost always in a small picture. The picture stands on a god shelf (C. *sahntoih*), traditionally reserved for ancestral tablets or statuettes of gods, high on the wall, though sometimes it stands on a secular shelf, and in one case (that of a Christian) simply on a dresser. Besides the deceased's picture, the god shelf normally holds two red electric candles, incense sticks (usually real but sometimes electric), some artificial flowers, and an offering of fruit. Sometimes the picture is accompanied by a conventional ancestral tablet inscribed with the deceased's name. Most of the families burn incense twice a day, though some do so only on the first and fifteenth of the month, when they also offer food and drink.

In six cases (12 percent) the deceased had no domestic memorial. In two of them the deceased left no descendants. In the remaining four (including one party member and one Christian) family members nevertheless regularly visit the ash depository on Qingming. Data are insufficient to account for the remaining 16 percent of the dead. The remains of some were transported back to the village, so it is possible that a descendant in the village has erected a god shelf. Every family in which there are descendants and on which I have information (40 of 48) celebrates Qingming (see Chapter 6).

I found it particularly interesting that not just ordinary families but even high-cadre families performed the "excess" ritual. For example, one 52-year-old man, the party secretary of a large institution in Guangzhou and the sole descendant of his recently deceased mother, carried out elements of the traditional funeral; has the conventional god shelf, complete with electric candles, incense, and offerings of oranges and cakes; and lights real incense daily. He wanted us to understand that none of his actions should be interpreted as expressions of either superstition or feudal belief. His mother had been a party member, a production team leader, and the head of the brigade's branch of the Women's Federation. During the Cultural Revolution she herself had thrown out the family's ancestral tablets. "But," her son said, "she remembered them in her heart." She did not leave her husband's village in Kaiping until she was already 62 years old, when she joined her son in a county town and helped raise her grandchildren; she followed him to Guangzhou when he was reassigned in 1983.

Even though the rituals this son carried out are remarkably similar to the traditional ones, I was assured that other, practical considerations lay behind them. On the evening of the sixth day after his mother's death, the son invited the relatives over to "raise her picture" on the wall, an activity usually carried out on the seventh day. He insisted, however, that the timing was unrelated to the seventh-day ritual and had been chosen solely because it was convenient for the relatives (but it was a Monday — a workday for most people). He also pointed out that the electric candles and incense provide a nice light for people coming home from work ("a custom from the village") and that burning incense is good from a hygienic point of view. (It keeps down the number of mosquitoes.) Finally he leaned over and said that frankly it was important for him to maintain good relationships with his relatives, who are rural people and have certain expectations of what sons are supposed to do for their deceased parents. By doing these things he shows respect for their concerns. No, he did not expect any criticism from the party for doing any of these things.

As the death-related activities demonstrate, although most families have been forced to acquiesce to some of the demands of the state, by replacing burial with cremation and omitting any traditional burning of paper goods and money in the vicinity of the funeral parlor, they have maintained or revived a number of other traditional practices. Some, such as erecting a god shelf and lighting incense, are carried out privately; others, such as "grave" rituals at Qingming, are carried out in public view. The state clearly has chosen to take the hardest line against activities carried out in public, particularly when allowing them might seem to indicate official approval. Because the state participates directly in funerals — it is represented at the funeral parlor by work unit personnel and offers official financial support in the form of labor insurance death benefits to defray some of the costs — its enforcement has been most rigorous at the funeral parlor. Since the beginning of the reforms, however, the state has been much more permissive when activities take place in the private domain, not only ignoring the erection of god shelves and the burning of paper offerings and incense, but also allowing the necessary paraphernalia to be purchased openly from licensed stalls and shops. The party has recognized that filial sons must be allowed to give parents their due.

Conclusions

This chapter has assessed the impact of the economic transition on the family as an institution and on individual family members. It has examined both the "traditional" Chinese family and the prereform efforts of the Communist government to destroy it. When the Communists came to power in 1949, they were determined to abolish the old family system, with its hierarchy based on generation, relative age, and sex, and to replace it with a new family system based on equality, affection, and mutual support. The 1950 and 1980 marriage laws and the 1985 Inheritance Law were intended as instruments for individuals whose new rights were being ignored or violated by family members who clung to the old ways. In addition, the government has engaged in continuing efforts to inform the populace as a whole of its rights and to "persuade" it to comply voluntarily with the government's vision. How successful has it been in reshaping the urban family?

Two problems stand in the way of a complete answer to this question. First, we are not certain of the extent to which either relatively benign Confucian norms or their feudal travesty truly characterized the pre-Communist urban family. Maybe patriarchs were neither so powerful nor so unfeeling as we have been led to believe. Maybe brothers did not take birth order so seriously as linguistic data suggest. Maybe some intrepid middle-aged women ignored the "three obediences" and dominated both their sons and their husbands. Uncertainty about the characteristics of the earlier urban family makes the discussion of change rather difficult. Second, although measurable changes have occurred (e.g., the increased age at marriage and the drop in fertility), it would be foolhardy to attribute these changes solely to governmental efforts, for these same phenomena have been observed in countries whose governments have done little to bring them about.

Perhaps it is wisest to say that the structure and organization of urban family life in contemporary Guangzhou show continuities with the past: in the predominance of patrilocal residence patterns, high rates of stem family living, reliance on sons for support in old age, and the tradition of regularly honoring one's immediate ancestors both privately at home and publicly on Qingming. In some respects, however, these continuities are superficial. For example, although the rates of patrilocal residence are high, few married brothers are actually members of joint families, and almost none pool their income for redistribution by the budgetary manager of the household. Similarly, ancestor "worship" in the city is not focused on a line of ancestors but only on deceased members of the immediate household, whose remains are stored in individual cubicles in a public, rather than a lineage or clan, depository.

Despite the continuities, the contemporary urban family differs in many ways from that of the past. Perhaps most important — because it is causally linked with other changes — is the higher age at marriage. Young people now can play an active role in selecting a spouse and can choose from among a network of acquaintances — neighbors, schoolmates, and workmates. And, generally more mature at 23 than at 17, they may have greater confidence in their own judgment, though as the letters to Li Dongdong and conversations with Laura suggest, not everyone does. Moreover, having chosen one another, the young couple are in a better position to present a united front and defend their interests in the face of opposition from the parental generation. Finally, a higher age at marriage is associated with reduced fertility.

Reduced fertility — more specifically, the one-child policy — represents the greatest break with the past. Although in rural areas the government has had to yield to the need of farmers for sons, it has successfully held the line in the cities. Urban families will have no choice in the near future but to accept daughters as functionally equivalent to sons: in carrying on the family name, remaining in their natal home, and fulfilling traditional obligations to parents. The law, if not actual practice, treats men and women as equals, and the emphasis on female participation in the labor force, facilitated by the relatively positive view of day care for children, offers women the economic means to challenge male authority in the home. A key question raised by the post-1978 economic reforms is whether renewed discrimination against women in hiring will undermine their position in the family.

To learn what specialists in the field think is happening to the Chinese family as a result of the reforms, I interviewed the editors of *Jiating* (Family) magazine in 1987 and again in 1992. This popular magazine, based in Guangzhou, is loosely affiliated with the Women's Federation, though it is responsible for its own budget. It was founded in 1982 as *Guangdong Funu* (Guangdong women) but changed its name to reflect the broader range of topics it deals with and to attract a wider readership. In 1987 it had a national circulation of 2.6 million. The editors see their mission as helping families understand and deal with the new phenomena that emerge as the economic system changes. The problems they saw as meriting special attention in 1987 were the low rates of marriage (for very different reasons) among "intellectual" women and soldiers, objections to the remarriage of the middle-aged and of the elderly, the new mother-in-law and daughter-in-law relationship (with daughters-in-law now having the upper hand), premarital sexual activity, and marital instability. In 1992 marital instability continued to be a major concern, but so too was the growing resistance among women to the idea of marrying at all.

How have the economic reforms affected the marital considerations of "intellectual" women? Quite simply, their enhanced earning capabilities have made them very choosy while at the same time intimidating men used to dominating their wives. Although discrimination against women in the job market continues, highly educated women, particularly in business, have a greater earning potential than other women. That earning potential matters in mate selection becomes clearer when we realize that soldiers cannot find mates because of their low income and their poor job prospects following demobilization. But money has affected family life in other ways as well. Here is the frank assessment a 60-year-old woman gave when I raised this topic at a dinner:

There have been many changes in the family due to the shift to a market economy. Everything has been commercialized. Before, when wages were low and opportunities few, a person's children were likely to have quite similar economic circumstances, but now there can be enormous variation within the family. The one who makes the most money *and* uses it to advance family (parental) comforts is considered the best child.

How to spend surplus funds has become a major source of dissension between husbands and wives and between the older and the younger generations in a family. Such disputes were impossible in the old days when there were neither surplus funds nor consumer goods to spend them on.

4 | *Education*

*I*n any society the goal of education is to prepare the next generation of young people to assume adult roles. This preparation normally involves the inculcation of appropriate values and attitudes as well as the development of practical skills. Equipping young people for the future is a formidable task under the best of circumstances, but when a society is undergoing rapid change, the challenge can be almost overwhelming. Furthermore, education, because it is so vital to a nation, is usually subject to some governmental control. In China governmental control of the content, means, and objectives of education has a long and controversial history.

This chapter looks at the impact on education of the transition to a socialist market economy. From the earliest years of the reforms the leadership was determined to change secondary education, which was seen as too single-mindedly preparing students to take the examinations that would allow them to go on to higher education. Since the vast majority of students who took these exams could not pursue higher education because of the scarcity of places, and because secondary education was too academic, too many of China's young people arrived on the job market without the skills necessary to contribute to the country's modernization. With new jobs emerging as the economy developed, it was critical that training be made available. This thinking led directly to the decision to emphasize vocational education.

But developments in education have not been driven solely, or perhaps even mostly, by pedagogical concerns. Rather they seem to have sprung primarily from the decisions of budget specialists intent on reducing the state's financial obligations and promoting efficiency. In brief, the educational establishment was told that it would have to rely increasingly on its own efforts to procure the funds necessary to keep up with expansion, innovation, and improvements in the wage levels of its personnel.

Efforts to implement this policy have had major repercussions on teacher salaries and recruitment, on school funding strategies, and on student enrollments and morale. The transition to a market economy has slowly but surely eroded the social position of educators and has devalued education in general even as enrollments at the secondary and tertiary levels are rising. How could such a situation have come about? The answer requires a historical overview of both the social position of educators (and students) in China and the nature of education as well as an analysis of the individual changes that in the aggregate and at each level of education have brought about this remarkable transformation.

Normally young Guangzhou residents first encounter the educational establishment when they enter preschool. Here the child comes under the authority of personnel who have been assigned the weighty responsibility of training the next generation of workers and leaders. Educational and governmental circles have debated the goals and the content of that training for more than a century. Today's schools are the products of these debates and reflect to varying degrees the influence of three philosophical orientations, those of the traditionalists, modernizers, and Maoists. Except perhaps for the Maoist, these orientations have been flexible and pragmatic, responding to changed perceptions of China's needs rather than reflecting a rigid ideology. Furthermore, individuals, again with the exception of Maoists, are unlikely to identify themselves as adherents of a particular orientation. For these reasons the account of the three orientations that follows should be understood as a heuristic device to organize the many influences on contemporary educational policy and practice in China.

Key questions have arisen historically in policy debates about education in China: What is the proper moral content of education? Should the schools emphasize the production of generalists or of specialists? How can China maintain its distinctive national identity when much of the subject matter taught in the schools is of foreign origin? To what extent do educators and the educated ("intellectuals") share the same vision of their roles in society as state policymakers? By what criteria should access to education be regulated? Although these same questions have been asked repeatedly, the sociopolitical contexts in which they have been asked—late Qing China, Republican China (1912–49), and the People's Republic of China—inevitably shaped the character of the debates and the range of alternatives considered possible or legitimate.[1]

The traditionalist orientation derives from the educational milieu of imperial China, where the curriculum consisted of the Confucian classics and volumes of scholarly commentary on them. This education was essentially moral and philosophical. The underlying assumption was that the study of the ancient texts would help develop cultivated gentlemen of upright character, who would serve as moral exemplars for both their families and society at large. Moderation in conduct, righteousness, propriety, humanity, and filial piety were virtues of the ideal Confucian scholar that were also seen as critical qualifiers for government service. Indeed, the goal of traditional schools and teachers was to produce bureaucrats to fill government posts throughout the country. Many more aspirants to public service qualified than could possibly serve, and the majority remained in their home communities, where they, in turn, tutored hopeful young scholars.

Gentlemen trained for government service were generalists, who could easily step into administrative posts. Technical or applied training was normally acquired through an entirely different channel, via apprenticeship to a master or simple observation of one's own family members in family shops or enterprises. Although a rigid status distinction existed between mental and manual workers, it did not constitute a caste distinction, for the son of a tradesman who performed well on the imperial examinations was (at least in theory) as qualified for government service as the son of an official. Scholars, even those who never attained a government post, were supposed to be looked up to for their presumed superior practice of morality. A moral lapse was devastating, grounds for dismissal from office and public contempt. That such lapses were not unknown is made eminently clear by the preventive measures the imperial government had developed over the centuries: post rotations every three years, a ban on serving in one's own district, and an entire administrative apparatus dedicated to overt and covert inspection of a magistrate's performance of duty.

When confronted with the superior military capability of the European powers in the mid-nineteenth century, the Qing government was initially uncertain how to respond. Reformers argued that because of the absence of science, mathematics, and engineering courses from the curriculum, bureaucrats were unable to understand the threat facing them from abroad, and thus China itself was doomed. Furthermore, without training in foreign languages Chinese had no access to the technical advances occurring elsewhere in the world. Schools run by foreign missionaries were, in fact, providing such an alternative education — a historical pattern of linkage with ramifications even today. China's introduction to modern science and technology was provided by Christian missionaries, a population with its own agenda for China: the abolition of age-old customs condemned as evils, the saving of souls, and the remaking of the subjugated Chinese Everyman (when it was thought possible) into a self-respecting individual who bowed to no one. Traditionalists warily accepted the need for science and technology for utilitarian ends but maintained that the Confucian classics should remain at the core of educational efforts to preserve the essence of Chinese civilization.

As moral exemplars scholar-officials had two major responsibilities: to perform their official duties in an upright fashion and to remonstrate with those who failed to do so, including even the emperor himself and his advisors. To do so was risky and required great courage. One of the most popular celebrations in all of south China, for example, is the Dragon Boat Festival, commemorating the death by drowning many centuries ago of just such a virtuous official, dismissed from office after warning the emperor of corruption among his advisors. On this June day residents of Guangzhou eat a special food (glutinous rice stuffed with various tidbits, wrapped in a conical shape in leaves, and steamed) said to have originally been dropped into the river to divert fish from the body of the drowned official. For several days, moreover, teams of rural residents compete against each other in highly stylized Dragon Boat races in nearly every waterway in the province.* Thus people are reminded annually of both the responsibilities and the costs of being an honorable official. If an official's advice was not taken and he was dismissed, he was not expected to make public denunciations or organize demonstrations, no matter how worthy his cause. Instead he was expected to withdraw and wait for change to occur more or less spontaneously from within.

Access to office was determined by performance on state-organized and -supervised examinations. A candidate had to pass examinations at the local level to be eligible for each subsequent level (prefectural, provincial, and metropolitan, the last one given in the national capital). Elaborate precautions were taken (and were apparently necessary) to avoid any improprieties in the taking or grading of examinations.[2] Merit rather than birth was firmly ingrained as the basis for occupying public office.[3] Candidates for examination could be from nearly any occupational category of the population, but they had to be male; females could not hold public office. The limiting factors for most candidates pursuing their studies were the ability and willingness of their families to spare them from productive work. Educational expenses, at least at the lowest levels, were the responsibility of the candidate's family. Lineages or wealthy individuals sometimes sponsored promising candidates whose families could not pay their expenses, and some individuals spent their entire lives as unsuccessful candidates. There

---

* Some folklorists speculate that the incident of the drowned official was grafted onto an existing folk festival centuries ago, much as Christian holidays like Christmas and All Souls' Day were grafted onto the pre-Christian festivals of the winter solstice and the end of the harvest cycle.

was no limit on the number of times a person could take the examinations, nor was there any age limit.

The imperial educational system has been dealt with at such length because it is the unspoken model against which reformers have reacted and against which contemporary educators frequently measure their own social status. Though recognizing the many limitations of the traditional system (e.g., disdain for manual labor, a limited and inflexible curriculum, the de facto exclusion of the vast bulk of the population from any education at all), contemporary teachers wistfully contemplate a past in which teachers were respected by their students as well as by society at large and access to public office was determined by unassailable meritocratic principles.

The modernizers, who first emerged in the late nineteenth century, neither disputed the need for teachers to exemplify virtue nor begrudged them societal respect, but they did take exception to the traditional curriculum. Worried about China's ability to mount an effective response to the military threats posed by the European powers, they argued that Western scientific and technological achievements — at least in weaponry and industrial capabilities — were clearly superior to those of contemporary China and that China needed desperately to catch up. Without leaders knowledgeable about science and technology, they predicted, China would be at best at the mercy of foreign experts and at worst at the mercy of foreign governments. Eventually the Qing government was persuaded and began to invite Western experts to lecture in China, to send advanced students abroad for study, and to establish a number of government-supported primary and secondary schools that introduced students to basic science and encouraged them to apply their knowledge to solving practical problems. The modernizers championed the view that education should produce specialists rather than generalists, but they faced a dilemma. So long as the primary route to influence in government was through the imperial examination system, with its emphasis on the Confucian classics, it was difficult both to attract students to the modern schools and to secure their placement in the bureaucracy.

Furthermore, the modernizers' own attachment to traditional Chinese culture and morality was suspect. Initially reformers argued that Chinese learning should remain the core or essence of education, with Western learning adding a utilitarian dimension. As scholars returned from overseas, however, the debate took a decidedly different turn. These scholars, as well as many educated at missionary schools in China, came to believe that Western scientific progress could not be dissociated from the sociopolitical matrix in which it had developed. If science was to take root in China, such Western notions as individualism and representative government would also have to be transplanted. These concepts struck at the core of both traditional morality and the political status quo. Modernizers espousing them found that they were endangering their credentials as reliable supporters of the state — a danger they have faced more or less continuously throughout the twentieth century.

Even though neither the Nationalist nor the Communist government disputed the need for training in science, engineering, and foreign languages, each remained deeply suspicious of what else young people might learn in the schools. This suspicion of students (and their teachers), particularly at the secondary and university levels, stems largely from the political activism that has come to be associated with them. Whereas the traditional scholar-official was expected to remonstrate with the government or to withdraw from it when it was in the wrong, in the early twentieth century modern students (i.e., scholar-officials-to-be receiving nontraditional educations) adopted the confrontational tactics of mass mobilization and public demonstrations. These tactics, particularly when used to protest an unpopular government decision, were perceived as threatening and destabilizing. Consequently, both the Nationalists and the Communists attempted to dictate the ideological content of education at nearly every level and to compel the commitment of intellectuals to this content.

Modernizers have been enthusiastic supporters of academic excellence. They have favored examinations as the basis of both advancement to higher levels of education and recruitment to government posts. Neither gender nor family background is supposed to take precedence over performance in the allocation of places in middle schools and universities. In the first decade and a half of Communist rule, particularly while under the influence of Soviet advisors, the Chinese government subscribed to meritocratic principles but also paid attention to a student's class background. During the Cultural Revolution (1966–76), however, merit was virtually eclipsed. In the post-Mao era the modernizers have regained control over the direction of education, emphasizing examinations, the need for specialists, and practical courses of study. During the 1980s a wave of credentialism swept across China as a reaction to the poor quality of education received by the generation in school during the Cultural Revolution.

The Maoist orientation contains elements of both the traditionalists' and the modernizers' views of educational goals but radically alters content. The Maoist orientation found its greatest expression during the Cultural Revolution, when politics was "in command." During this period, and for several years before, the works of Mao Zedong became the basis for ideological education in both schools and the workplace. The goal of education was to produce young citizens committed to socialism and to destroy some of the traditional cleavages in Chinese society, between urban and rural dwellers, for example, or between those performing mental, and those performing manual, labor. The study of Mao's Thought was to inculcate in young people selflessness and the noble urge to serve the people rather than selfishly advance themselves. In practice this meant initially that students completing their school work would volunteer to go to the countryside for several years to help improve the living situation of rural dwellers. Later this practice was neither voluntary nor temporary. By the end of 1976 several hundred thousand Guangzhou lower and upper middle school graduates had been sent to the countryside. Students still in school (and their teachers) were regularly required to engage in manual labor as part of their class work, for example, tending school vegetable gardens, doing piecework, or cleaning the building and grounds. Moreover, each term they were expected to assist with the harvest or work in factories for several weeks. Mao's position was that only by experiencing the labor of the peasants and workers could intellectuals identify with them and see their interests as their own.

Mao was not intrinsically opposed to specialization. In theory he supported the notion of "walking on two legs" — of being ideologically sound ("red") as well as technically skilled ("expert"). In practice, however, one had to be red to acquire expertise. During the first two years of the Cultural Revolution urban life was so disorganized that schools were either closed or devoted to nonacademic activities. Middle schools resumed teaching in the late 1960s, but new classes generally were not admitted to higher educational institutions until 1971 or even later, by which time the admissions process had been radically changed. Only after demonstrating the correct political attitude through correct political behavior (selflessly and enthusiastically serving the people) did one become eligible for admission to college or university. One could no longer apply directly from middle school but had to spend two years in the countryside or on the job in an urban work unit. Counties and work units had a quota of candidates they could put forward to admissions committees for consideration, and candidates had to win the approval of their peers and supervisors before their names could be forwarded. The admissions process was widely regarded as corrupt. Favored individuals and the children of people in high places were disproportionately likely to be forwarded as candidates.

For example, one Guangzhou resident, the son of a laborer, recounted how in the early 1970s he had been fortunate enough to obtain entry to a college. His then girlfriend, a workmate, was the daughter of a high cadre. Despite the official rhetoric that the children of workers were of good class origin and thus suitable matches for the children of cadres,* the girlfriend's

* Those considered to have a good class background are peasants, workers, soldiers, and their descendants; those with a bad class background are landlords, rich peasants, and their descendants; and those with a middle-class background are entrepreneurs, intellectuals, and their descendants.

father disapproved of their relationship, feeling that the son of a mere laborer was not good enough for her. Nevertheless the cadre's daughter secretly took it upon herself to lobby her father's friends on behalf of her boyfriend. She contacted several well-placed people and made it clear that her boyfriend was her father's preferred candidate when, of course, he most certainly was not. In deference to her father's wishes, his friends then facilitated the young man's candidacy.[4]

The Maoists also regarded teachers and professors with suspicion, doubting their commitment to the Maoist vision, particularly because many of them had been trained abroad, where they presumably had acquired a bourgeois outlook on life. Even those educators trained in China were considered unreliable because so many were of middle (or bad) class rather than revolutionary (or good) class origins. Intellectuals, instead of being respected, became known as "stinking nines," that is, members of the ninth category of political pariahs (behind landlords, rich peasants, counter-revolutionaries, bad elements, rightists, traitors, spies, and capitalist roaders). In the first years of the Cultural Revolution they were challenged, denounced, and "struggled against" by their own students and sent for reeducation to the countryside for months or years at a stretch. When they returned to their classrooms, in middle schools or in universities, they found them occupied by academically uninspired and poorly motivated students.[5]

Teachers were intimidated and students out of control as both realized that the students' futures were by and large unrelated to their academic performance. The vast majority of middle school students were destined for the countryside, whereas most of those who eventually entered the universities were poorly prepared. The correct political attitude rather than academic performance was critical to advancement, and all pretense to the contrary was dropped with the abolition of entrance examinations. Academic performance also declined because the Maoists, believing that much of education was unnecessary obfuscation, reduced the number of years of elementary and secondary schooling required for entrance to institutions of higher learning and also reduced the time devoted daily and over the school year to academic coursework. Moreover, because during the Cultural Revolution more and more students were required to complete lower middle school (instead of ending their education with graduation from elementary school), the schools, increasingly overcrowded, were also increasingly staffed by undertrained teachers.

Following Mao's death and the arrest of his supporters, the "Gang of Four," in 1976, the modernizers gained the upper hand and immediately set about undoing everything the Maoists had put in place. Provincial entrance examinations were reinstituted in 1977, national examinations in 1978. By the summer of 1980 students at Zhongshan University were jubilant.

The last class admitted under the Cultural Revolution political criteria was about to leave the campus; a bright future based on merit beckoned to those left behind. That less than a decade later this jubilation would be replaced by a deep-seated malaise could not have been predicted at the time. The rest of this chapter describes the educational situation in Guangzhou in the early 1990s.

Contemporary Popular Education in Guangzhou

According to the 1990 census only 5.6 percent of the population fifteen years or older in Guangzhou's eight urban districts was illiterate or semi-literate — down from 7.6 percent in 1982 (the date of the previous census). Although the rates vary enormously by age, in the population as a whole at least one-quarter had received an elementary school education, 27 percent a junior middle school education, 25 percent a senior middle school education, and 8 percent a university education.[6] These figures reflect the concentration of highly trained personnel in the provincial capital, with its large number of provincial government organs and 30-odd institutions of higher learning.

Children in Guangzhou are required to attend six years of elementary and three years of junior middle school.[7] The vast majority (around 80 percent) of junior middle school graduates in the city proper also go on to senior middle school. In 1993 the municipal education authorities announced plans to increase the overall (urban and rural combined) proportion of students entering senior middle school to 71 percent by 1997, 85 percent by the year 2000, and 90 percent by 2003.[8] In the city proper in 1992, 99 percent of the students graduating from elementary school entered junior middle school (presumably most of those who did not graduate stayed on to repeat their sixth year); 78 percent of junior middle school graduates went on to senior middle school, and 36 percent of senior middle school graduates went on to higher education.[9]

The field of popular education bears the full imprint of the reformers' goals for modernizing China. Around 1978, in line with national policies, Guangzhou began to reestablish a network of "keypoint" (*zhongdian*) schools for the city's best students at both the primary and middle school levels. These schools receive a disproportionate share of financing, scarce resources, and the highest qualified teachers. To attend a keypoint school is to be assured access to a better education and to have a greater likelihood of going on to higher education. Provincial keypoint middle schools (including boarding schools), located in Guangzhou but with a wider catchment area, also enrolled many students from the city. In addition, keypoint schools (both elementary and middle) were established by city districts.

Many of these schools had been keypoint schools in the early 1960s but lost this designation when it was abolished during the Cultural Revolution.

Opponents argue that such keypoint schools early on stratify the school-age population into those headed for mental work and those headed for manual work. Proponents argue that given China's need for technical expertise and its limited resources, it is necessary and rational to allocate resources where they will do the most good, that is, to the most qualified students as measured by examination performance. By the late 1980s elementary and junior middle schools in Guangzhou were no longer supposed to be designated keypoint schools because with nine years of education mandatory and everyone expected to achieve a certain standard, it was not really fair to distribute resources unevenly. Only upper middle schools were to retain the designation keypoint because it is at entry to this level that students are assigned to one of three channels: the work force, vocational schools, or "ordinary" (i.e., college-preparatory) middle schools.* Students gain entry to lower middle school by passing the elementary school graduation examination and by a complex allocation process that was redesigned in 1992 to further reduce disparities in quality between (former) keypoint and regular schools. Entry to upper middle school is determined by performance on an entrance examination; it is not enough simply to pass the graduation examination certifying successful completion of lower middle school.

Nevertheless it is clear that many people have not noticed the removal of the designation keypoint school. At one Guangzhou elementary school in 1991, for example, the staff readily identified the five keypoint elementary schools in their city district without giving any hint that the designation is obsolete. Similarly, a junior middle school principal commented that since some middle schools contain both junior and senior levels, it is not really meaningful to say that only the upper level is a keypoint school. Finally, the resources poured into the various keypoint schools were not withdrawn when the designation was. Thus the schools with computers, university-educated teachers, and high pass rates into senior middle school (and eventually university) are the same now as before, and ambitious parents seek them out.

Preschool

Most Guangzhou children enter a preschool or kindergarten (*you'eryuan*) before elementary school. In 1989, for example, the enrollment rate for the

---

* The literature on Chinese education refers to these schools as "ordinary" because college preparation was the whole point of middle school until the 1980s. "Ordinary" does not mean undistinguished; on the contrary, the most distinguished schools belong to this category.

municipality as a whole (eight districts and four counties) was 54.4 percent, but in the four central districts it was 98 percent.[10] Preschools in China are primarily a phenomenon of the post-1949 period and provide day care to children of working parents as well as basic socialization. Nurseries (*tuo'ersuo*) provide care to infants and toddlers (those under three), whereas kindergartens normally serve children from three to six.[11] City kindergartens are administered by either the Education Bureau, other government bureaus and enterprises, or collectives. In addition, there are a few kindergartens in Guangzhou that are administered by the provincial government through its Education Department. Their students are not counted in Guangzhou's statistics, such as those that follow. In 1992 Guangzhou city proper had a kindergarten population of 157,116 in a total of 830 kindergartens, of which 67 were administered by the Education Bureau, 426 by other bureaus and enterprises, and 337 by collectives (primarily neighborhood street committees).[12]

Although all kindergartens are expected to meet certain standards set by city and district preschool education authorities (*tuoyou bangongshi*), there is considerable variation in the quality of the physical plant, the availability of equipment, the richness of the curriculum, and the qualifications of the teachers according to administrative body. A major cause of this variation among (and to some extent within) preschools is their source of financing. Most of the kindergartens are heavily subsidized by their governmental sponsors. The neighborhood preschools, however, rely almost entirely on the fees they take in, and consequently they can barely afford the basics and cannot afford frills.

The most highly regarded kindergartens tend to be those directly under the jurisdiction of the provincial Education Department, which accept primarily the children of workers from various (and multiple) government units, for example, provincial schools, hospitals, and administrative offices. In some cases these preschool campuses can be quite elaborate, with multiple buildings, playing fields, and garden plots. City bureaus and enterprises, such as factories, sponsor preschools on their own premises that are primarily for their workers' children. Finally, street committees operate kindergartens for the benefit of the families living (or working) in their neighborhoods. They often have to squeeze the preschool into an old building in an already congested area. There are also some private preschools that must pass muster with the local authorities, but they are said to be a recent phenomenon, uncommon, and usually very small because they are operated out of people's homes.

Certain kindergartens are perceived as exceptionally desirable, and obtaining entrance to them can involve various strategies. The first, straightforward strategy is to meet the basic criterion for eligibility, that is, to be a parent employed at a qualified unit or living in the neighborhood. Even meeting the minimum employment qualification, however, does not necessarily qualify one's child for entry. There might be more children for a provincial or city-sponsored multiunit preschool than can be accommodated. One way of dealing with this is to give each qualified unit a certain number of spaces and leave further allocation up to the unit. The unit might then allocate the spaces on the basis of one per section or office. If this year in your office you are the only one with a child entering kindergarten, your child goes. Or allocation might be on the basis of rank or extenuating circumstances, for example, both parents are out of town a great deal on work-related matters.

A second strategy is to pay a onetime (legal) admissions fee to the preschool, generally 300 to 1,000 yuan (in 1991) but rumored to be as high as several thousand yuan for particularly desirable preschools. One mother cited a construction company working in her neighborhood that runs a kindergarten for its workers' children but will admit others (on a space-available basis) from the neighborhood for 600 yuan. This money, known as a "construction" fee (*jianshe fei*), is supposed to be used primarily to upgrade the physical plant and equipment of the school. In addition, parents must pay the regular kindergarten fees. One reason the government allows the special admissions fee is to provide a means of educating children without local household registration, such as children of migrants. They may not attend unit or government-run schools, but they may attend schools operated by collectives, such as a street committee, if they pay the extra fee. Similarly, units with excess space may make it available to parents from other units. In some cases the parent's unit, lacking its own kindergarten, will "buy" space in someone else's. Alternatively a unit might provide a direct subsidy so that one of its workers can send a child to a kindergarten.

If neither the neighborhood nor either parent's work unit sponsors a kindergarten, parents can pursue a third strategy: to manipulate the household registration of their child from birth. Many women do not transfer their household registration on marriage and therefore register their child at their own parents' address. They do this primarily for their own convenience — they know that the maternal grandparents are available in emergencies and will pick the child up after school lets out. More important, since admission to elementary school is by neighborhood, an artful choice of household registration can make a child automatically eligible for entrance into a desirable elementary school. Many of my informants have used this strategy on behalf of their children.

And, as a final strategy, a parent can go through the back door, relying on personal connections to admit a child lacking proper qualifications. For example, if a relative or friend teaches at the desired school, the lack of proper qualifications could be overlooked.

Jiedao Kindergarten, a typical Guangzhou preschool, is located in Yuexiu district in an old congested neighborhood of shops, factories, and residences.* A school has been on the site for many years, since before 1949. In 1958 the local street committee took it over, and the old building was used as a preschool until 1984, when it was torn down. A new five-story building, hemmed in on all sides by residences, was completed in 1986. There is a little concrete play space in front of the building and a small wading or swimming pool behind it. The pool is in use from May through September or October. An extension of the second floor provides a music/meeting room inside and a shaded outdoor area for play below. Above the second floor music/meeting room is another unroofed play space for the children as well as a pigeon coop with two or three pigeons. There are two classrooms per floor. Several children share a small table, and each classroom comes equipped with an attached bathroom (containing an L-shaped trench along two walls) as well as a sink for washing up. Individual towels are hung from hooks outside the classroom; each child is assigned a distinctive animal that is represented on a sticker next to his or her hook, so that these prereaders can readily identify their own towels. The children sleep either directly on the tables or on sleeping mats on the floor. Their quilts are kept in a closet off to one side of the room.[13] At the entrance to the school there is an archway with benches on either side that provides shelter for children waiting to be picked up by their parents or grandparents. Off the archway on one side is the principal's office, with banners proclaiming various awards, and on the other side another office to take care of general inquiries. The week's menu is displayed on the wall for the benefit of parents.

Jiedao Kindergarten draws its students, or rather "little friends" (*xiao pengyou*), primarily from residents of the neighborhood and secondarily from workers in the neighborhood. Kindergartens normally have three grades: *xiaoban* for three- to four-year-olds, *zhongban* for four- to five-year-olds, and *daban* for five- to six-year-olds. (Some of the more prestigious preschools have added a post-*daban* grade known as *xueqian ban* [literally "prestudy class"] for children who will not reach the age of six and a half by September 1, the start of the school year. These children are too young to start school but have already graduated from *daban*. Some elementary schools have also added this class, which is specifically oriented to the development of study skills.) With 440 students in nine classes Jiedao Kindergarten has an average class size of 49 with two teachers per class.

* *Jiedao* means simply "street committee" indicating that this kindergarten is run by such a group. I have omitted the full name of the kindergarten.

Preschool officials interviewed in 1991 thought that 90 percent of parents would like their children to attend a kindergarten; the remaining 10 percent are those who preferred that the child stay with a grandparent and those who could not handle the expense.

Fees (in 1991) were 22 yuan a month plus 1.5 yuan a day for the two meals and snack. (The provision of meals is one of the big differences between kindergartens and elementary schools. Kindergartens have children the whole day, whereas the elementary schools send most students home for lunch, wreaking havoc with the work schedules of adults unless their own offices have long lunch breaks.) The 22-yuan fee is set by regulations—Jiedao's staff would like to charge a higher fee and thus have a bigger budget to work with. In addition, each semester parents are charged a 5-yuan activity fee (for movies or trips) and a 6-yuan miscellaneous fee (*za fei*—to cover electricity, etc.). (Although Jiedao's miscellaneous fee is relatively modest, the general concept of the miscellaneous fee has proved a real boon, not only to preschools, at which attendance is voluntary, but also to elementary and secondary schools, at which attendance is mandatory and theoretically free—at least in the urban areas. The development of special fees is discussed further below.) Students at Jiedao do not wear uniforms. After a portion of Jiedao's budget is used to cover basic operating expenses, the rest is supposed to be distributed as follows: 30 percent for welfare (of the staff), 40 percent for supplies, and 30 percent for bonus money (discussed later in the chapter). All these budget items must come out of fees. Jiedao has no income-generating potential, so it must rely on its own resources or on donations. (The mirror and piano in the music room were both donated.) The teachers also do as much as they can themselves, for example, painting the chairs as well as colorful and imaginative designs on the building walls and doing maintenance.

The teachers are all women (as is the principal, who came here from the street committee office over ten years ago with no prior experience in education—she had worked as an accountant). They were quite certain that none of the schools training kindergarten teachers would even accept male students. Upon completion of lower middle school, would-be kindergarten teachers attend three years of a specialized upper middle school (*zhuanzhong*). Students trained at public expense in schools run by the government are subject to work assignment by the Education Department; students trained at their own expense find work themselves. Jiedao Kindergarten obtains its teachers from among those who have paid their own way. Whereas in the United States early childhood education is associated with young teachers, in China the preschool teachers are of all ages because until recently people seldom changed jobs. After serving a single trial or probationary year, the teacher is given permanent employment until retirement at

55. Wages in 1991 averaged 250 yuan a month, with a range from 210–220 for beginners to about 300. The lowest retirement wage they could receive was supposed to be 80 yuan.

The two goals of preschool education are modest: morality and culture. Under the rubric of morality children learn correct behavior (conduct and virtue), including courtesy, respect for the elderly, and self-control; under the rubric of culture they learn vocabulary and develop skills in singing and dancing. A typical day proceeds as follows:

6:45   Doors open — children begin to arrive and play freely
7:45   Doors close (no more arrivals allowed) and formal activities start
8:00   Breakfast served in classroom
8:40   First "class" of day (classes are of different lengths to accommodate the different attention spans of the age groups and are followed by activities and play)
10:00   Free play
11:00   Prepare for lunch and eat
12:00   Nap
2:45   Up from nap
3:00   Snack and play until picked up
4:15   Beginning of pickup time

The doors theoretically close at 5:30, but if there are still "little friends" who have not yet been picked up, some of the teachers stay behind with them. On Saturday the school closes at 12:00, immediately following lunch.

Elementary School

In the city proper attendance at elementary school is and has been nearly universal since even before the start of the reforms, and because of the one-child family policy, the size of the elementary school population remained, until very recently, quite stable. In 1980, 534 elementary schools enrolled 291,000 students; by 1985, 543 schools enrolled 272,000 students; and by 1990, 552 schools enrolled 287,000 students.[14] The increase in the number of schools is due primarily to increased dispersal of the urban population from the four old city districts into the four formerly "suburban" districts in which most of Guangzhou's new housing is being constructed. In the early 1990s, however, the incoming classes of elementary school students began to swell because the large cohorts born in the 1960s had reached marital age in the late 1980s. In the fall of 1994, for example, the schools in the city proper braced for the arrival of 58,513 first graders — 13,561 more than the elementary school graduating class—who required the addition of 282 classrooms.[15]

Unlike kindergartens, elementary schools are truly neighborhood schools, and all children from the designated catchment area must be accommodated before a school may consider how to fill any vacancies it might have. Vacancies would normally be made available to children in neighboring catchment areas or to the children of parents working in the general catchment area but living elsewhere. Prior to 1987 keypoint schools recruited their students from within a city district or even from the city as a whole.[16] In Guangzhou elementary schools are normally assigned the responsibility of educating the children from the three or four residents committees (the administrative subdivisions of street committees) in their immediate vicinity. A distinction must be drawn, however, between those children living in the area who are legally registered residents and those who, although living in the area, are not. These children, who usually have rural registration, may not be admitted until all those with legal registration have been placed. In 1990 less than 1 percent of elementary school students (but 2.8 percent of junior middle school students and 1.9 percent of senior middle school students) in the city proper fell into this anomalous category.[17]

For years these irregular students were known as *jidu* ("mail study") students, that is, correspondence school students, although in fact they were physically present in the classrooms right along with the other students. They used to pay an extra 10 yuan a semester for the privilege of attendance, but around 1987 the city converted the charge to a onetime payment at entry of 300 yuan. As in the case of preschools, this payment, known as a "construction" fee, is supposed to be used for such things as extra equipment. Other than this there is no distinction between legally registered and improperly registered students. The authorities decided to allow these children to attend school because, practically speaking, if the parents are in Guangzhou, the children are not going to stay in the village. It was deemed better to accept them, regardless of registration, than to have uneducated youngsters in the city.

One of the more questionable practices currently affecting student admissions is the right of school principals to reserve up to four places per classroom (of 45–50 students) for "selected" (*ze*) students. These are students who, though otherwise qualified, lack the proper residency requirement to attend the particular school but are nevertheless admitted for a fee at the discretion of the principal. Generally such students either have urban registration but live in the wrong neighborhood or have rural registration but come into the city for the superior education available there. The extent to which this student population might overlap with the urban-raised but rural-registered student population is not clear. This formerly backdoor practice, believed in the past to have relied more on connections (*guanxi*) than on money, has been legalized as a way of helping schools meet their expenses. The entrance fee charged these students is referred to as a "selected" student fee and not as a "construction" fee. In any case the fees are substantial — so substantial that in mid-1994 the municipal authorities laid down guidelines for the charges schools could assess entering "selected" students. The higher the level of education, the higher the maximum fee allowed. Thus, for example, students entering typical elementary schools in the fall of 1994 were to be charged a maximum of 2,500 yuan, whereas those attending more desirable elementary schools could be charged up to 3,000. These fees are dwarfed, however, by the 8,000-yuan maximum that provincial and city keypoint upper middle schools (academic and vocational) could charge their entering "selected" students.[18]

Although students attending their rightful school are not subject to this onetime fee, even they have seen the cost of their supposedly free education soar because they are subject annually to a host of miscellaneous charges. At the beginning of each school year, parents are presented with a long list of all the fees they must pay. At one primary school in the urban area the fee list contained 35 distinct charges: 10 fixed by the city, 1 by the district, 14 by the school itself, 8 on behalf of outside units (presumably supplying the school with services of some sort), and 2 by education authorities. To meet these as well as four additional special fees, parents had to expend between 500 and 600 yuan.[19] What do all these fees ostensibly cover? According to one reporter, who obtained a township junior middle school's fee list with 24 separate charges, they cover essentially anything that the school administrators think they can get away with: health insurance, bicycle supervision, sanitation, registration, educational development, library, educational administration, and so forth.[20] In short, these fees are simply a fundraising device.

There is a national curriculum for elementary (and middle schools), but in addition, standards of student achievement are set locally (by city and district). Although technically rural and urban schools are supposed to meet the same minimum levels, they may be hampered by a lack of teachers and by financial constraints. Ambitious individual schools may set higher standards for their students, but even (former) urban keypoint schools do not necessarily exceed their locality's minimum requirements. In one Yuexiu district former keypoint school, for example, English is not started early but rather in fifth grade, as the city requires, because the school has only two English teachers. (Sometime in the mid-1970s Guangzhou was selected by the national government to specialize in the teaching of English, and no other foreign languages are normally taught at the elementary school level. Other cities also specialize — some in Russian, some in Japanese, and so forth.) In 1980 I had visited a nonkeypoint elementary school in Haizhu district that required its third graders to take four English classes a week. The third grade class I visited at the very end of the school year was learning the difference between "some" and "any" while the fifth grade class was studying the verb form "to be going" as in "Is he going to plant trees?" Students were to match a particular pronoun subject with the correct form of the verb "to be."

Elementary school students in the same school work at basically the same pace; there is neither ability grouping within a class nor tracking or streaming of students of different abilities into different classes. Consideration is given, however, to these differences. For example, children with exceptional talent in music or art might be sent to the Children's Palace (a municipal-operated facility) to take special classes a few times a week, and there is an entire separate school specializing in physical education for children being groomed for national athletic competition. Similarly, each school offers a range of extracurricular activities, some of which amount to special classes for the academically talented. Students who take these classes are eligible for entry to the provincial Olympics School, a middle school attached to South China Teacher Training University. This school prepares students to participate in the biannual international academic Olympics. In the fall of 1994 to meet growing demand for this special training, the city opened additional Olympic classes at five junior middle schools. Their opening represented a concession to parents disappointed by the 1992 modifications to the system of assignment to junior middle school.

In elementary (and middle) school students are assigned to a particular classroom under the supervision of a single teacher (*banzhuren*), who also teaches one of their courses. Elementary school teachers in China's cities, unlike those in the United States, are subject specialists and teach only their specialties. Students remain in their own classroom while the teachers circulate. This pattern continues through middle school, though for such subjects as science, which requires special equipment, students venture to the teacher's laboratory. On the order of 10–20 percent of the elementary school teachers in a given school are likely to be male.

In contrast to practice in the United States, the 50 or so children in a particular first grade classroom will remain together throughout their six-year tenure at the school (or three-year tenure at junior middle school). This policy, intended to foster group ties and identification, is abetted by neighborhood stability: given the long-term housing shortage and low rates of parental job change, families seldom move out of their neighborhood. In addition, each classroom has its own quasi-administrative student organization of class head and class committee, responsible for serving as role models and helping to keep the class orderly and well motivated. In the middle school such class officers also take on tutoring responsibilities and organize extracurricular activities, such as athletic competitions.[21]

The elementary school students of today are said to have somewhat different characteristics and needs from those of only ten or twelve years ago—changes viewed as resulting from their upbringing in one-child families and their access to television. At one school these differences were recounted to me so readily and precisely that it was clear the national debate in pedagogical circles on the "spoiled child" was one with which the school's administrators were thoroughly familiar. Today's students were described as "little emperors," used to being doted on and having their every whim met by adoring parents and grandparents who concentrate on this single child. They know only how to enjoy themselves (*xiangshou*) and lack the discipline necessary to attend to things they do not want to do. Moreover, they lack independence in daily activities such as tying their shoes and putting away their blankets after naps because even though they have usually learned these skills in kindergarten, they are not required to use them at home. But they have a general level of knowledge higher than elementary school students of an earlier era because they have been exposed to much more through television and are smarter (C. *lek*).

To overcome some of these problems, educators have sought parental cooperation. In addition to requiring an annual (or semiannual) home visit by teachers, schools also run classes for heads of households on how to help their child make the most of his or her education. Each grade holds these evening classes, meeting for an hour or so, four times each semester. Experts in child development are brought in to explain the child's needs and how the parents can best help the child. If for some reason the class has to be held in the daytime, work units are supposed to grant the parent leave to attend without financial penalty. Attendance by parents is mandatory. One mother, whose son was to begin first grade in the fall of 1991, had already been required to attend such meetings, even though the school year had not yet begun. She indicated that parents have to have a paper stamped certifying that they have attended such sessions; otherwise their child will not be allowed to enter the school. Parents are also responsible for certifying that their child has completed the day's homework assignments and must sign their name to each homework paper. Finally, twice a year, a parent or other senior household member must come to the school on Sunday to obtain the child's grades (on both scholastic achievements and correctness of attitudes) from the class supervisor.

If Jiedao Kindergarten is typical, Chaotian Road Elementary School, not far from the preschool, exemplifies the academic privileges of the former keypoint schools. This elementary school was founded in the Qing Dynasty during the reign of Daoguang (1821–50). The school is built in a U-shape around a large courtyard, which serves as a play area and outdoor gymnasium, and is shaded by two graceful banyan trees. The open end of the U faces the street but is separated from it by a high solid wall. Entrance to the school is possible only through a metal gate. During a tour of the school, I visited a computer class and found every one of nearly 50 students at a computer (an Apple clone). There were also clones of IBM models XT and AT (only one or two of each) in another room for use by teachers or advanced students. Teaching students to use computers is certainly not the norm for elementary schools in Guangzhou. Out of 50-odd elementary schools in Yuexiu district, only 5 have computer classes. Moreover, though all elementary schools in Guangzhou are supposed to teach English beginning in the fifth grade, Chaotian teaches spoken (not written) English in the second grade and has four teachers specializing in teaching English.

In 1991 the school had 1,177 students, somewhat above average for an elementary school. There are six grades (*ji*), with four classes (*ban*) to a grade. The average number of students per class is 49; the range is 46–51. There is one teacher per class. There are 65 teachers at the school, including a few who have retired but continue to work — for example, one of the arts instructors who teaches (unfired) clay figurine making. In the past students entered elementary school at age seven, but legally one may now enter at six. In Guangzhou it is more typical for a student to enter at age six and a half because of a shortage of places. Chaotian Road Elementary School draws about 70 percent of its students from the three residents committees immediately surrounding it and 30 percent from elsewhere. Like other elementary schools, it may accept students from outside the immediate neighborhood only if it has spaces left over.

The traditional route to elementary school teaching has been to take the examination to enter a teacher training school following the completion of lower middle school. More recently prospective teachers have been urged (though not apparently required) to continue at a postsecondary specialized school (*dazhuan*) for two years of college-level training. Elementary schools (including Chaotian) still have many teachers educated under the old standards. The Labor Department assigns teachers, forwarding the names of graduating students to the district Education Department. The Education Department notes which schools need replacements and discusses assignments with the school. Perhaps three candidates are presented as possible teachers; the school principal chooses the most suitable from among them. Apparently to encourage students who plan to teach, the Labor Department allows students graduating from teacher training schools to be placed two months ahead of those graduating from other types of schools. All but one of Chaotian's teachers are from Guangzhou. (In 1990 one teacher came from Wuhan with a spouse — not a teacher — who was transferred to Guangzhou.)

Teachers, considered state workers, are guaranteed a certain minimum basic wage and level of subsidies. Another portion of their income comes from bonus money (some generated by the school itself, some by the government). In 1991 the average monthly income of teachers at Chaotian was between 320 and 330 yuan. The range was from 270 yuan (for someone just out of teacher training school) to 450 yuan (for someone with many years of experience). Of the average monthly income about 200–230 is guaranteed by the state, and the rest is derived from bonuses.[22] Chaotian Road Elementary School obtains its bonus money from several sources: a printing factory it owns and operates itself; arrangements with other, commercial units that use its space, such as a light bulb factory that established a sales outlet at the school; and rental of the school building for adult education classes or evening school.

Chaotian's doors open at 7 A.M., when students on athletic teams are likely to begin practice, finishing at 7:40. The school has swimming, soccer, and track-and-field teams (and possibly others) that participate in district-level competitions and, if they do well, higher level competitions. Classes begin at 7:50 and go to 11:30, with four class periods separated by ten-minute recess breaks, during which the students are free to run about and play. During the three-hour lunch break, from 11:30 to 2:30, most students return to their nearby homes. About 400 students buy lunches at the school and either work on extracurricular projects or just hang around until classes resume at 2:30. The afternoon session extends to 4:00 and includes two 40-minute classes. Students are free to leave after 4 P.M., but many stay on for an hour of extracurricular (e.g., artistic, musical, or computer) activities. Thursday afternoon is entirely given over to extracurricular activities. In addition to regular classes in Chinese, English, math, and science, students also take physical education four times a week. (Two periods are devoted to actual physical activity and two to studying about physical education.) There are also music and arts classes.

One of Chaotian's vice-principals, during a trip in 1988, visited several schools in the United States, among them one in Hingham, Massachusetts. (Guangdong has a sister province relation with Massachusetts.) When I asked him about his impressions, he remarked that in the United States classes are small, with some fifteen to twenty students; that American teachers are casual (*suibian*), interacting with the students in a familiar conversational way; that students have great freedom to select what they study; that teachers are concerned about the students and do not, for example, yell at them or embarrass them; that a relatively high proportion of the government budget goes to education; and that teachers' salaries are good. These comments reflect the comparatively large size of Chinese elementary school classes, the more directive classroom style of Chinese teachers, the fixed curriculum, and the opinion of everyone in the field that education is seriously underfunded.

Middle School

The admissions process to junior middle school has undergone a number of changes since the mid-1980s. Around 1986 responsibility for the sixth grade graduation examination required for entry into lower middle school passed from the city to the district, and students were allowed to apply for admission to only a limited range of schools. Yuexiu district, for example, is divided into northern and southern sections, with Zhongshan Road as the dividing line. Students south of Zhongshan Road, including those at Chaotian, had to select a junior middle school in the southern section, and those north of the road, one in the northern section. Parents indicated their interests in a particular junior middle school, and their child's data were sent there. Highly desirable schools, because they received more applications than they could possibly handle, could be selective; thus, they paid particular attention to such criteria as grades. A school that wanted to be selective was hampered because it could choose students only from among the candidates whose parents had submitted their names.

In 1992 the application rules were revised. First, the special examination for admission was dropped, officially because there are no longer any keypoint elementary schools and it is thus reasonable to assume that all students are receiving the same quality of education. Students able to pass the graduation examinations are felt to be ready for junior middle school. Second, school assignments were mostly taken out of the hands of the school principals and turned over to a computer. This was done to break the stranglehold of the elite schools on the best students. Because all students must now attend school a full nine years, all should have an equal chance (more or less) of attending any junior middle school (in their geographical area). Students may still express their top three preferences, but the best are no longer assured of entry to the elite schools. The authorities hope that sending the best and the worst of students randomly to the various junior middle schools in a particular jurisdiction will eventually even out the differences in educational quality among the various schools.[23]

There is little diversification of curriculum at the junior middle school level. Students continue the Chinese, mathematics, and English they studied in elementary school, and general science is replaced by courses in physics, chemistry, and biology; a new course in politics (essentially the theory and application of socialist ideology) is introduced. This course is by no means the students' first exposure to socialist ideology; their elementary school textbooks (and even preschool games) routinely introduce a socialist worldview, though not as insistently as during the Maoist heyday. It is not clear to what extent the books currently in use have been updated to reflect the orientation to a socialist market economy.[24]

Junior middle school students actually have to meet three different sets of standards (or "examinations") in order to graduate. The first "examination" is intended to determine whether or not a student manifests the right kind of thinking (*sixiang*). When I asked two junior middle school administrators how this could be measured, they admitted it was problematic. Ideally a teacher wants to be able to quantify student achievements in this area, even if only relatively. The practice at their school (where student aspirations and achievements are modest) is for the teachers to divide their students into three categories, such as superior, average, and inferior. Not surprisingly, behavior serves as a proxy for "thinking." Thus in determining a grade, the teacher evaluates the student's attitude toward society, for example, the student's willingness to accept guidelines about dress and wearing ornaments. The second examination measures health and physical ability: all students must pass a physical examination and demonstrate a certain level of physical performance — so many push-ups or whatever. Because senior middle school places are limited, the physical examination is probably used to determine whether the student is physically capable of further education and eventually of work that contributes to society. Suzanne Pepper describes the conditions that disqualify a candidate from admission to university or limit the candidate's choice of specialization. These include, but are not limited to, abnormal blood pressure, epilepsy, diabetes, active tuberculosis, chronic hepatitis, serious kidney disease, and serious physical handicaps or deformities, "such as, for example, the muscular atrophy resulting from infantile paralysis or a difference of more than three centimeters in the length of the legs."[25] Presumably these restrictions would not be applied to students who finance their own education.

The most critical examination, however, is the written one toward which most classroom preparation is directed. All junior middle school students take a three-day series of exams in July to qualify for graduation and admission to upper middle school. These are provincewide unified examinations. Whether a child goes on to upper middle school depends on both examination results and the family's inclinations; compulsory education ends with graduation from lower middle school. Students are tested in mathematics (the maximum score is 120 points), Chinese (120 points), English (110 points), physics (100 points), chemistry (100 points), and politics (100 points). For some reason there is no exam in biology, even though this class is part of the curriculum. The highest possible score is 650 (rarely if ever attained); 300 is passing. The distribution of the points also counts. For example, a student has to pass five out of six subjects, that is, score at least 60 points in each. The student who fails in two or more subjects is not eligible to graduate. Students know their grades within ten days or so of taking the examinations. Those who have too many failures take make-up classes at their own school for about a month during the summer break, after which they may retake the exam; they do not pay to attend these classes.

The evaluation of the exams is structured so as to guarantee fairness. A junior middle school principal with several years experience as a grader explained that each year every junior middle school sends two or three teachers to take part in exam scoring. These graders are sequestered for the week of grading, during which they evaluate on the order of 12,000 exams. Graders for each subject are divided into small groups; the head of each small group looks for obvious errors in a sampling of the exams graded by the group. The different essays of a particular exam are graded by different people to lessen the impact on a student's final grade of any particular grader's harshness or leniency. The student's name is concealed so that grading is anonymous. (Because others are present, no one can easily slip off the stapled cover.) Moreover, the exams of one city district are graded by faculty from another; for example, Liwan district's exams are graded by Yuexiu district faculty. Similar grading strategies are used for the university entrance exams, though in 1990 the total point value of the university exams was raised to 900.

The examination results together with the student's own aspirations are critical in determining the student's subsequent destination: the work force, an ordinary senior middle school, or a vocational school. Students may list as preferences several schools in each of these categories. As I have indicated, in the city proper about 20 percent of junior middle school students seek employment upon graduation. The remaining 80 percent are channeled into either ordinary middle schools or one of a variety of schools loosely referred to as vocational technical (*zhiye jishu*) schools, offering two- or three-year courses of study. There is considerable conceptual and terminological confusion in the field of vocational technical education, reflecting both its diversity and its officially sanctioned rapid growth since the implementation of reforms in the late 1970s and early 1980s.

The early (and subsequent) arguments in favor of vocationalizing the senior middle school are spelled out by Stig Thogersen.[26] He notes that following a speech by Deng Xiaoping at a National Conference on Education in 1978, the media emphasized China's need for skilled workers and mid-level technicians, arguing that because ordinary senior middle schools did not address this need, there was a serious unemployment problem among youth leaving school. By 1983 the national government was calling for a reform that would require giving preference in hiring to those with prior vocational training; its goal was to enroll half of all senior middle school students in vocational schools by 1990. This goal was achieved on schedule in Guangzhou city proper.

According to educators in Guangzhou, vocational technical schools fall into three main categories: specialized or professional (*zhuanye*) middle schools, technical or skilled workers (*jishu gongren*) schools, and vocational (*zhiye*) schools.[27] The last category includes agricultural vocational schools that are not relevant to a discussion of urban vocational education. Specialized or professional schools prepare "specialists" (*zhuanjia*) — for example, nurses, teachers, accountants, and mid-level technicians. These schools are the most prestigious of the vocational schools, and graduates are eligible for higher education, most frequently at a *dazhuan*, or advanced professional school, for a two-year course of study. Most graduates, however, go directly to assigned employment.

Technical or skilled workers schools, which teach basic trade skills, are supported jointly by the city's labor bureau and the various factories that expect to hire the graduates. A student who refuses to accept employment or resigns after only a brief time with the sponsoring work unit must reimburse that unit for the cost of the training. Students in the third category of vocational (*zhiye*) schools also learn technical skills, but these are more broadly defined than in skilled workers schools. The students in these vocational schools prepare for careers in fields as diverse as electronics, plumbing and electricity (*shuidian*), and fashion but apparently choose the service sector most frequently. *Zhiye* schools are usually operated by local departments of education, and ideally their development is closely tied to the specific and emerging needs of local employers. They are the newest type of vocational school in China — both the *zhuanye* and *jishu gongren* schools were established much earlier under the influence of Soviet advisors. The graduates of *zhiye* schools are pressured to seek employment that requires their particular qualifications rather than work whose only prerequisites are attending a school or having a parent employed at (or retired from) a particular work unit.

In ordinary senior middle schools all students follow the same curriculum for the first two years: Chinese, mathematics, English, science, history (world and Chinese), geography (world and Chinese), politics, and physical education. There is no doubt that young Chinese scholars pay a price for all their work. At a national conference on vision problems in 1991 it was reported that whereas the rate for nearsightedness among elementary school students was 11 percent, it rose to 38 percent among middle school students and as high as 75 percent in some keypoint middle schools.[28] Although students are in school for many hours each week and have home-work assignments, it would be a mistake to imagine them exhausted and slumped over their desks as one teacher after another comes into the class-room. In fact, a first-year senior middle school student's Monday schedule reveals ample "down time":

7:35–7:50	Preparation time for first class
7:50–8:35	English
8:35–8:50	Recess
8:50–9:35	Chinese
9:35–9:50	Recess
9:50–10:35	Physics
10:35–10:45	Recess
10:45–11:30	Math
11:30–2:35	Lunch Break
2:35–3:20	Swimming
3:20–3:30	Recess
3:30–4:15	Swimming
4:15–4:25	Recess
4:25–5:10	Do homework

The student's double period of physical education on Mondays accounts for the apparent openness, but even if that is discounted, the student (who attends a keypoint school) has more than three hours for lunch, 5 recess periods, 15 minutes of preparation at the beginning of the day, and a 45-minute study period at the end of the day. Students are free to leave after 5:10, though teachers stay on until 5:30.

On Saturdays there is a regular morning session, but school is over at 11:30. The afternoon session is the official weekly cleaning period. Several students from each classroom take turns cleaning the classroom windows, floors, and blackboards as well as the playground. They also clean the teachers' and administrators' offices. The school has a regular cleaning staff who are responsible for bathrooms and other common areas. Students not on cleaning duty sometimes stay around to play or chat with friends.

Chinese student life is much more organized than American high school student life. There are no electives to speak of. Everyone in the same grade takes the same courses, and members of the same class (*ban*) take these courses together. At this keypoint middle school each class has about 45 students; at other schools classes are more likely to have 50. Each class has one teacher (*banzhuren*) responsible for its students' records, a student monitor (*banzhang*), a number of students each responsible for a particular course (*kedai*, "course representative"), and a class committee (*banhui*), which includes the class monitor as well as a recorder and representatives for labor, music, and athletics.

The student monitor, elected by the students, is primarily responsible for their behavior. The course representatives, usually students who do well in the particular course, are also elected. Their responsibilities include standing at the front of the room and calling the class to order when the teacher enters and helping to hand out homework papers. The class committee members have different duties. The monitor and the recorder have the most responsibility, for together they are supposed to keep an eye on behavior. They usually talk with students doing something wrong to persuade them to behave. Only in exceptional circumstances do they report the misbehavior to the teacher. Students (and adults) are expected to be sensitive to peer pressure, which in China is usually harnessed by the authorities to shape personal goals into conformity with official goals. Students who report on others are disliked by their fellows and are said to be "patting the horse's butt" (*pai mapi*), that is, trying to ingratiate themselves with the teacher. The labor representative organizes students for the Saturday cleanups, whereas the music and athletics representatives apparently organize students when classes are asked to participate in presentations or competitions.

The goals of vocational school students are self-evident and likely to be realized upon graduation. Those of ordinary (i.e., college-preparatory) school students, however, have been more elusive, for until 1994 the number of openings in institutions of higher learning was less than half the number of students taking the entrance examinations. At the end of their second year of senior middle school students must decide whether they wish to be tested in the sciences or the liberal arts. The third year classes are divided up according to which set of exams the students plan to take. Science students take entrance examinations in English, Chinese, mathematics, physics, chemistry, and politics; liberal arts students take exams in English, literature, mathematics, history, geography, and politics.[29] In 1994 a total of 114,193 Guangdong students (not all of them current year graduates) registered to take the entrance exams (this figure exceeded the previous year's by 23,000). Of these, 68,888 took the science exams; 34,887, the liberal art exams; and 4,833, 2,535, and 3,050, the foreign languages, athletics, and fine arts exams, respectively. The number of students taking the exams exceeded the number of openings by a factor of 1.8, a substantial improvement over the previous year's ratio of 2.25.[30]

Passing the exams establishes eligibility for admission to an institution of higher learning; it does not assure admission to the institution of choice or to any institution, because the number of places a given university has in its freshman class is set annually by outside authorities. Students learn their scores quickly and must then calculate their chances of obtaining entry to particular schools. Schools are ranked, according to their source of funding and administrative supervision, into national, provincial, and city institutions. Students may apply to one or more institutions at each level and even to more than one department or program at a particular institution. In fact, they apply, not to a school as such, but to a department or specialization, so that in effect they choose a major before attending the institution; the choice of majors is limited by the entrance exams they take — in science or the liberal arts.

Individual schools and even individual departments in the same school may have different cutoff scores, and passing the entrance exam does not mean that one has scored above such cutoffs. The different cutoffs are largely a function of the desirability of particular fields of study. Undesirable, or "cold," fields, such as geology and teaching where graduation is often followed by assignment to a rural or remote region, necessarily set lower cutoffs to entice candidates. Students rank their choices, and their records are sent to the representatives of their first-choice institution. The representatives are assembled in one spot until all assignments have been made.

This procedure requires that students consider carefully the likelihood of their admission to the first-choice institution and the back-up schools they might find acceptable. Thus one 1990 science candidate from a leading provincial keypoint school obtained an 861 (out of a possible 900) and confidently applied to a single department at a single school, Zhongshan University. He was admitted with no problem. A 1986 liberal arts graduate from another school, however, sized up her chances differently. Her first choice was Shenzhen University (at that time recently opened in the Special Economic Zone of Shenzhen on the border with Hong Kong), followed by South China Teacher Training University and Guangzhou University (a vocational university established in 1983 with two- and three-year courses of study). She was admitted to her last choice.

In 1994 the principles of market economics were employed to tackle the problem that neither lower cutoffs for admission nor persuasion had been able to resolve. To encourage students to enter "cold" specializations, three Guangdong institutions of higher learning (Zhongshan University, South China Engineering University, and Shenzhen University) introduced reformed tuition schedules that base fees on the popularity of the specialization.[31] Students selecting "hot" majors, such as international finance, international trade, computers, accounting, or construction, are now charged according to the principle of supply and demand and pay more than those selecting "cold" majors, such as geology or sociology. At Zhongshan the three-tiered all-inclusive fee schedule (and at South China the five-tiered all-inclusive fee schedule) ranges from 3,500 yuan a year to 1,500, whereas at Shenzhen the fee is either 3,500 or 3,000 (plus a 500-yuan "construction" fee). Four other institutions (Guangzhou Foreign Languages College, Guangdong Commercial College, South China Construction College, and Guangzhou University—all tertiary vocational schools and therefore "hot") have raised their all-inclusive fee schedules to between 3,500 and 3,000.

Such charges are well beyond the means of many prospective students. To make certain that highly qualified students are able to attend university and enter their field of choice even if they lack sufficient funds, each school provides substantial scholarships to the top scorers on the provincial exams. Shenzhen University, for example, offers 5,000 yuan to the top six scorers in Guangdong province, in Guangzhou, and in Shenzhen. Most of the schools automatically offer scholarships to any student exceeding a score of 800; the typical scholarship falls between 2,000 and 3,000 yuan. Less talented students with financial difficulties have the option of entering high priority but undersubscribed fields. They receive financial support in return for a promise (given in a written contract) that after graduation they will accept assignment to hardship posts.

Not everyone has been happy with the return of the entrance examination system. Some have been disturbed by its single-minded focus on intellectual achievement; others have wondered about the political orientation of the students, whose onetime family class background is no longer evaluated. According to Thogersen,[32] the student unrest in the winter of 1986–87 proved to many in government circles that the students were not politically reliable. Consequently, the admissions process began to include consideration of students with lower scores who demonstrated other desirable qualities. These privileged candidates include "three good" students (good in politics/morals, academic study, and physical achievements) and those otherwise exceptional in political-moral attitudes or athletic prowess. Guangzhou has also used these criteria, but no figures are available to indicate their importance or their likely significance under the reformed tuition system.

Higher Education

As of 1992 there were 26 institutions of higher learning in Guangzhou: 9 under the national government, 12 under the provincial government, and 5 under the city government.[33] Some of these institutions existed before 1949 but have undergone such major reorganization, some merging and some splitting, that they are unrecognizable today. Under Soviet influence beginning in 1952 the system of higher education, which had been largely in private hands, was taken over by the government and reorganized. Zhongshan University, for example, was stripped of its professional colleges (engineering, agriculture, medicine, and teaching), which were combined with similar such colleges or departments stripped from other schools to form new specialized institutions.

Early specialization was also required within the standard science and liberal arts curriculum. As I have indicated, students essentially declare their major when they apply to enter a particular department at a university. Once enrolled, they have almost no electives, even within their chosen department, nor are they required to take courses outside their field to fulfill a distribution requirement. Even dormitory living reflects this specialization; so far as possible students in the same major are roomed together.

Until 1989 higher education for ordinary students was virtually free, and becoming a university student meant entering into a contract with the government whereby, in exchange for the privilege of receiving training at government expense, the student agreed to accept whatever work assignment the government provided at graduation. This system of assigning students wherever in the country they are needed is known as "unified assignment." Indeed, although the government still sets annual departmental student admissions quotas with its future work force needs in mind, it experimented for two years (1989–90) with allowing these students some flexibility in work assignment. The class graduating in 1991, however, was told that it was premature for China to have such an open policy, because strategically important projects and institutions in remote areas were unable to compete effectively for graduates, and that "unified assignment" of graduates would be restored.[34]

The fees charged government-subsidized students have been comparatively modest. At Zhongshan University in 1991, for example, students paid 300 yuan a year for tuition and 60 yuan for their (share of a) room. In addition, they were responsible for the cost of their meals, which in any case could be obtained cheaply (for around 2 yuan per meal) at the student canteen. But government-subsidized students are not the only students on China's campuses. In accordance with the policy of shifting the financial burdens of higher education from the state to "society," self-paying (*zifei*) and "commissioned" (*daipei*) students attend classes alongside the traditional government-subsidized ones; the fees they pay have been set substantially higher.

The number of self-paying students, who may be accepted with scores 30 points below those of ordinary (i.e., subsidized) students, is said to have grown nationwide from several hundred in 1985 to more than 30,000 (perhaps to 100,000) by 1988.[35] In Guangzhou in 1989 they already constituted 6 percent (4,227) of the students enrolled in institutions of higher learning. These self-paying students were overwhelmingly (81 percent) enrolled in specialized two- and three-year programs rather than in standard four-year undergraduate programs. Only Jinan University, which has a special relationship with students of Chinese ancestry living outside China, had any substantial presence of self-paying students in its regular undergraduate program.[36] These students are expected to find their own jobs and are not subject to any restrictions in their search for work following graduation.

"Commissioned" students are selected by work units, which pay their educational expenses and expect them to join, or return to, the work unit upon graduation. Their entrance examination scores are expected to be equivalent to those of government-subsidized students. Nationally in 1987 there were 41,000 students in this category.[37] In Guangzhou in 1989 there were 14,464, constituting 22 percent of the students enrolled in higher education. Like the self-paying students, they are disproportionately (74 percent) found in the two- and three-year programs, but they attend a larger number of four-year institutions than the self-paying. For example, they are enrolled in the regular undergraduate programs at Zhongshan University, South China Engineering University, South China Teacher Training University, and smaller schools that do not enroll self-paying students in the regular program.[38]

Beginning in the fall of 1994, however, as part of an experiment in educational reform, seven Guangdong schools (the same seven that introduced a multitiered tuition scheme or raised their tuitions to "reflect the actual costs of education") abolished distinctions among the three categories of students and subjected them to identical fee schedules. (Whether distinctions in entrance examination performance were also changed is not clear.) Except for students who, in exchange for financial support, had signed contracts promising to go to hardship posts (or back to their work units), all students at these schools will be free to find their own employment.[39]

Students enrolled in higher education encounter a classroom organization similar, though not identical, to the one they left behind in senior middle school. Each entering class in a given department is assigned a professor, who is held responsible for it. This professor, who also teaches regular departmental courses, is relatively close to the students. In addition, another person (known as the *fudaoyuan*, "political and ideological assistant") with faculty status, but on the political track rather than the academic track, actually supervises the students' political thinking and behavior; he or she is responsible for two successive classes. This is the person students are most concerned about, for when work assignments are being discussed, the *fudaoyuan* and the departmental party secretary are asked whether they have anything to say about the student's political (including moral) behavior or attitude. Being on the wrong side of this person can be costly. The party secretary, who has overall political responsibility for the department (both faculty and students), resolves problems between the *fudaoyuan* and the students. The students themselves each year elect a class monitor or head (*banzhang*) to serve a one-year term as their representative. The monitor acts as liaison between the students and their supervisors and organizes class activities such as parties, trips, and lectures. Although this student need not have the best grades, to earn students' respect and be able to lead, he or she should not be an obvious academic loser. When issues need to be discussed, the *fudaoyuan* or other concerned leader asks the monitor to present the student side.

The student dormitories are crowded and modestly furnished. Banks of bunkbeds draped in mosquito netting are a common sight in this subtropical region. At Zhongshan University women live six to a room and men, eight or ten to a room. Men may not enter the women's dorms, though women may enter men's dorms. A male student who wants to get the attention of a particular female student in her dorm has to stand outside and call her name. Lights go out at 11:30 each night, and at midnight the front door is locked.[40] After that admission is by ID. Students who have forgotten to bring their IDs do not get into the dorm that night. As Miss Mao indicated in Chapter 3, intense relationships between male and female students are officially frowned upon and draw a comment from one's *fudaoyuan*. Although dating or having a special friend of the opposite sex is allowed, the relationship should not progress to the point where the couple are suspected of having a sexual relationship.

During the 1980s the general mood of university students began to shift from one of relief at the renewed emphasis on academic achievement and optimism about their own future to one of frustration, anger, and alienation, most visibly expressed in the winter of 1986–87 and in the spring of 1989. This shift was the result of major economic and social changes occurring primarily outside the universities but having major repercussions within them. The phenomenal increase in wealth and the concomitant rise in the general standard of living are among the most welcome yet controversial consequences of the various economic reforms enacted in the late 1970s and 1980s. Inevitably this increase in wealth has been uneven; coastal provinces, Guangdong in particular, have surged ahead of inland provinces, periurban villages have surged ahead of more remote villages, and the collective and private sectors have gained on the state sector.

As early as the mid-1980s students began to observe that they were not necessarily going to be among the major beneficiaries of the improved standard of living. Indeed, their early complaints were about the standard of living they endured on their own campuses, and they, like students everywhere who face tuition hikes, were indignant that despite the lack of improvements they would soon have to contribute to the cost of their own education. But even worse in its long-term implications was the system of "unified assignment." Graduates were overwhelmingly likely to be assigned to the state sector, especially to work units with limited opportunities for economic growth, such as schools or administrative offices. Students began to perceive life in a state work unit as possibly less desirable than in a collective, joint venture, or even private work unit. English majors hoped to land a job in a unit involved in foreign trade but feared being sent to the hinterlands to teach English in a rural middle school. Students whose technical specializations more or less assured them an urban assignment fretted that the choicest positions would go to the graduates with connections.[41]

Equally disturbing, not only to students but also to their teachers, was a growing sense of status loss. With the return to meritocratic principles university graduates, as intellectuals, expected to be looked up to and expected their mental work to be compensated at a higher rate than manual work. Instead, they began to suspect that their middle school classmates who had joined the work force instead of going on to university had made the better choice, knew it, and regarded the students themselves as fools. Teachers read about rural households having annual incomes of 10,000 yuan, building fancy houses, and installing all kinds of household appliances when they themselves lived in shoddy apartments of fewer than 40 square meters.

Because one of the key goals of the economic reformers was to put more budgetary responsibility directly on the individual unit in the hopes of lessening the financial burden on the state and stimulating innovation, universities had to scramble to think of ways to generate additional funds to augment the income of their faculty and staff. Admitting self-paying and commissioned students was one solution to this problem; opening night schools and special adult education programs, another; and doing consulting or contract work, a third. But these solutions had negative consequences as well. Generally the faculty who were taking on all these new activities were the same faculty who taught in the regular day program. They spent more time on their new courses or off-campus consulting and less time on their regular courses. The regular students were dismayed; they felt they had been abandoned by the very segment of the population that should have been most understanding of their plight. When they protested in 1986–87, they were denounced for their misguided thinking, and political education was intensified.

This intensification varied according to the administration of the school. For example, the incoming class at one Guangzhou city institution in 1986 underwent a weeklong military training session the first week of the fall semester (before the first wave of student unrest). According to a student who went through it, the training consisted primarily of marching and drilling, though students were also expected to read materials about the army. In the fall of 1987, however, the training was more serious, including athletic maneuvers as well as opportunities to handle weapons. The student concluded that the purpose of this training was "to teach you to follow orders." Students from another institution who were interviewed on "The Morning Show," a locally produced television program, offered a more benign interpretation of the 1987 training: they uniformly described the training program as desirable because it had taught them to take care of their own clothing and hygiene and had instilled in them a concern for public places. (Soldiers, for example, keep their barracks clean and place their mugs and toothbrushes in a neat line on a shelf.) The students claimed that they had also learned self-discipline and perseverance, important lessons, they agreed, for those living away from home for the first time, whose parents no longer direct their daily lives.

A student at a national institution in Guangzhou described the rocky course of military training at her school from the fall of 1987 through the fall of 1990 as follows. The whole class of 1987 had to spend a month at a military base to undergo a version of basic training, which she described as very laborious (*xinku*).* They were not allowed to go to sleep until midnight but had to get up at 6 A.M. each day. Furthermore, they could never get a good night's sleep because they knew that at any moment the training officers might get them up to dress and line up for inspection. They had to do an hour's worth of exercise before they could have breakfast. They had to attend lectures on China's military equipment and learn about self-defense and defense strategy, for example, the best way to defend a site from capture. They never knew from one day to the next what to expect or even in the morning what to expect in the afternoon. If they asked the instructors any questions about scheduling, they were told not to ask questions — all they needed to know was the importance of following instructions. The students hated the military training and complained bitterly about it when they returned to school. Consequently the program was made less rigorous for the class of 1988. Following the June 1989 confrontation between the military and the students, school officials were so afraid of a violent clash between the students and the military that the military training of the classes of 1989 and 1990 was held on campus. Yet none of this training can compare with the year-long military program required of the class entering Beijing University in 1989.

* The Chinese describe a class by its year of entry, not the year of its graduation. The class of 1977, for example, is famous because it was the first class to enter college after the reintroduction of entrance exams in 1977.

Throughout the 1980s the relevance of Marxism to China's modernization was widely debated in the official media, at research institutes and think tanks, and among students. The increasing adoption of practices that smacked of capitalism but were justified in socialist terms seemed illogical and stimulated a search for a new ideology or at least a new set of guiding ideals. Nearly every political or social theory from the West, historical or contemporary, was scrutinized in the hope it would help to resolve this confusion. According to various writers the period 1979–82 was characterized by "Sartre mania," 1982–84 by "Freud mania," and 1984–86 by "Nietzsche mania." By 1985 so many theories had their moment in the sun that strict periodization was no longer so simple.[42] Even Confucius was reconsidered. In this chaotic atmosphere, the authorities say, students lost their bearings, fell prey to "spiritual pollution," and became the victims of a "bourgeois liberal" mentality. The renewal of student unrest in April 1989, continuing into June and culminating in what Chinese officials obliquely refer to as the June 4 Incident (known to outsiders as the Tiananmen Massacre despite disputes as to the exact number and location of the deaths) spurred the government to further intensify political education. The official story (with its distinctive flavor) of what took place in 1989 in Guangzhou is summarized below.[43]

According to the authorities, in the beginning of 1989 some students in higher educational institutions in Guangzhou were influenced by foreign counter-revolutionary forces and by bourgeois liberal counter-revolutionary propaganda materials brought into China. In mid and late April, under the influence of students in Beijing, students demonstrated and marched in the streets of Guangzhou. In mid-May the "Guangzhou Institutions of Higher Education Patriotic Student Alliance" was established and began carrying out activities. It organized a twelve-day sit-in and hunger strike (May 17–28) at the gate of the provincial government; under the banner and slogans of the "Patriotic Movement" of the students in Beijing, who were staging a sit-in and hunger strike, it instigated and organized students and workers in the Guangzhou area to demonstrate in the streets; it printed and distributed inflammatory handbills distorting the facts, and with counter-revolutionary writings and slogans against the party and socialism created disorder among the students and populace; it entered school office buildings and occupied, or cut the electricity from, school broadcasting stations; it obstructed bridges and roads to the point of creating a de facto strike, because workers could not get to the workplace; and it organized students to empty the schools. On June 4 students in Guangzhou obstructed bridges and roads for more than a day and even blocked the Guangzhou–Shenzhen trains for several hours.

This official version leaves out such interesting facts as the level of cooperation that apparently existed prior to June 4 between the students and local government officials. For example, at one point representatives of the provincial government met with student leaders, pointed out that their demonstrations were disrupting the daily flow of workers, and asked the students to reschedule their activities so as to minimize this disruption. The students complied. Local authorities were also instrumental in arranging for buses to transport students from the site of their sit-in back to their campuses at night because the regular bus lines had already closed down.

All the students' actions are then explained away as a consequence of the students' failure to understand the position of the government. To change their position and transform their attitude, they were brought back to school and, as soon as the formal semester was over, required to study documents from the fourth plenum of the Thirteenth Party Congress and the speeches of Deng Xiaoping. No explanation other than problems in their thinking is offered as a rationale for the students' actions. None of the underlying issues is addressed.

Yet it is clear that in the course of the next five years the government did attempt to address at least one of the students' concerns — the unpopular system of unified assignment — though the solution introduced is probably not the one students themselves would have chosen. More and more students have been told they have the freedom to choose their workplace after graduation, but at the expense of losing their subsidized education. At the seven experimental institutions, government-funded students have been transformed into scholarship students, and the scholarship determines the student's degree of freedom. Those whose scholarships are based solely on merit, as opposed to need or choice of specialization, can now join the self-paying students in seeking the most desirable type of employment. No longer will they, at least, have to join a state unit with limited financial prospects.

Conclusions

The beginning of this chapter noted that despite increases in student enrollment at the secondary and tertiary levels, both respect for the traditional curriculum and the relative social and economic positions of educators have declined. These developments can be traced directly to the reformers' goals of promoting applied (vocational) education at the expense of the liberal arts and requiring schools to generate an increasing proportion of their own funds. These policies are directly responsible for declining teacher salaries (relative to those available in the private sector and in successful state enterprises), difficulty in recruiting and retaining qualified teachers, and the treating of education at every level as a commodity to be sold to the highest bidder. Increasingly education is looked on by both its consumers and its producers as a means of making money rather than as a process of moral training or an end in itself. One should not overstate the change, however; it is certainly the case that previous generations also sought education and government service because of financial considerations.

Though there is general agreement that preparing young people to make money is the rightful task of educators, government officials charged with ideological work still express concern about their moral training. Social instability is officially ascribed to failures in the ideological training of young people. The Chinese government is fully aware that the situation is far more complex than this moralistic interpretation indicates, but for various reasons it is unable or unwilling to address the underlying causes. Although many political educators seem prepared to give lip service to the official interpretation, they remain uncertain how to address the problem because there is still no well-thought-out alternative to the now stale Marxist ideology of the past. The moralists' dilemma is further complicated because much of the advanced knowledge China needs to continue its modernization can be obtained only from abroad. It is unclear how much Western knowledge can safely be brought into the Chinese curriculum without threatening its Chinese or socialist foundations. Because of China's historical experience as an object of Western missionaries' "civilizing" goals, Chinese authorities are acutely sensitive to any efforts by Westerners to provide (or attempt to impose) their own moral standards as a model.

In January 1994 Chinese President and General Secretary of the Chinese Communist Party Jiang Zemin addressed a six-day party conference on the topic of ideological work. His speech echoed traditional Communist rhetoric and simultaneously called on party workers to share their experiences and help solve problems that have emerged in the course of the reform. According to an article in *Beijing Review*, Jiang stressed that ideological work should create an environment favorable for further reform, for the building of a socialist market economy, and for the development of productive forces. In this context, his remarks on education — that it should initiate patriotism, collectivism, and socialist values as well as raise ethical and moral standards — seem almost like an obligatory aside.[44] Quite clearly the development of individuals capable of continuing the process of economic reform is the main goal on the educational agenda.

Residents committee members attending to business in their tiny office. (November 1987)

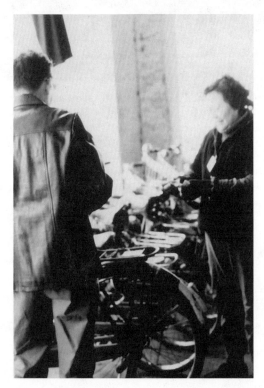

An attendant collects fees at a bicycle parking lot operated by a residents committee. The lot occupies half the width of the sidewalk, obstructing the flow of pedestrians. By the early 1990s this lot also had a section for motorcycles, further disrupting foot traffic. (November 1987)

Even in winter fresh vegetables of all kinds can be found in Guangzhou's street markets. (November 1987)

Freestanding specialty stalls operated by private entrepreneurs in Yuexui district. (November 1987)

A private shop in the front room of an apartment in Yuexiu district; such business locations are generally available only to those living on the ground floor. (November 1987)

Sunday barbers practice their craft along the promenade on the south bank of the Pearl River in Haizhu district. (February 1991)

Paraphernalia for bird fanciers in a shop in People's Park, Yuexiu district.
(November 1992)

A boy helps prepare a meal in a modern kitchen equipped with gas for cooking.
(February 1991)

A flowering peach tree takes pride of place in this household display of fruits and flowers during the Spring Festival. (February 1991)

The Hong Kong and Guangzhou members of this extended family (only some of whom appear in the photograph) invited the anthropologist to share in their first big meal of the Spring Festival. (February 1991)

5 | Employment

Reformers realized that if China was to move from a centralized planned economy to a socialist market economy, modifying the employment system was likely to be one of their most important and difficult tasks. To improve the financial situation of the various enterprises, service institutions (such as schools and hospitals), and government administrative offices, it was essential to reform the employment system, because providing employment entailed much more than simply paying wages. As in the West, but to an even greater extent, Chinese work units (*danwei*) have been required to provide a host of welfare benefits, such as housing, medical insurance, pensions, sick leave, and so on, to their employees.

At the same time, individual worker productivity in the late 1970s was very low (for reasons discussed below), and the system of permanent employment meant that units could not easily dismiss poor performers or release excess labor. To break this cycle of excess and unmotivated labor, high benefit burdens, and rising deficits, the state decided to shift substantial financial responsibility to the individual work unit, especially to those directly engaged in market activities, that is, such business enterprises as factories and department stores. Hand in hand with this increased financial responsibility went increased autonomy in production and marketing. Despite this new autonomy, however, the lack of a job market made it difficult for units to release redundant personnel, and the state still required units to provide their workers with extensive welfare benefits.

For their part, Chinese workers were concerned about the impact of the transition to a market economy on their own security. What would increased efficiency mean for them: Unemployment? Loss of benefits? If so, the state was likely to be faced with major social unrest. To forestall these eventualities, the reformers moved relatively slowly in implementing new policies after their official announcement so that those affected could adjust to the idea. Moreover, they introduced gradually such politically sensitive changes as withdrawing permanent employment and certain benefits, applying them first to new entrants to the labor force and extending them only later to other segments of the labor force. Finally, they remained alert to the social and economic consequences of the reforms and to public opinion. When necessary, they were prepared to halt or modify unpopular policies and mitigate their impact on those most disadvantaged by the new economy or unable to participate fully in it.

It was difficult for the state to take the initiative in reforming the urban workplace, however, when there was a much more visible and compelling problem in the late 1970s: millions of unemployed youth.[1] Until this problem and the unease it created in those already employed could be resolved, it would be pointless to talk about releasing redundant workers in the name of efficiency.

Youth Unemployment

In the late 1970s youth unemployment was high for two main reasons. First, the number of middle school graduates waiting for work was steadily increasing because of an increase in the population. Restrictive family planning policies had not been in effect long enough to reduce the numbers then entering the work force. Second, millions of young people who had been sent to the countryside during the Cultural Revolution were slipping back into the cities and beginning to demand employment, including many former Red Guards, perceived as an undisciplined and potentially dangerous lot.[2] Other unemployed people in addition to these youth sought work: people released from labor reform camps, the disabled, housewives who had never been in the labor force, people who had lost jobs, and retirees who still wanted some form of employment.[3] The total number of urban unemployed was reliably estimated to have exceeded 15 million.[4]

These young people were normally referred to as "waiting for employment" (*daiye*), rather than as unemployed (*shiye*), for two reasons. First, they could not locate jobs on their own because urban labor allocation was almost entirely in the hands of the state; they had to wait until the state found some way to employ them. Second, it was not politically acceptable to admit that China had an unemployment problem until after the Cultural Revolution. In socialist societies employment has strong political overtones because in socialist theory access to and control over the means of production are the basis of political and economic power. A person who is unemployed by definition has neither access to nor control over the means of production. For many years this critical link between employment and power (in the minds of theorists if not in those of workers) made any discussion of unemployment politically unacceptable. The revolution that brought the Communists to power was carried out to make the masses (or proletariat) the masters of society. Unemployment would beg the question of how successful the revolution had really been. Even in 1980 in Guangzhou I was quickly corrected when I slipped up and inquired about unemployment.

The central dilemma for the state was that it did not want to allocate state jobs to these millions of "waiting" people because it recognized that state organs and enterprises already had far more workers than they could actually use. Out of desperation, perhaps, policymakers authorized two options, one short-term and one long-term, to provide jobs to young people without unduly burdening the state: expansion of the "stand-in" or "substitution" policy (*dingti*) and the reestablishment of the urban private sector.

The Substitution Policy

Dingti, normally the substitution of a child for a parent, had existed for many years. In some cases this substitution occurred when a parent died while still employed, but it was more common when the parent retired and the child was given the parent's position. "Position" is being used loosely here: the position given the child was not identical to that of the parent being replaced, although some effort was made to match the work status of child and parent. Thus an office worker's child was more likely than a production worker's child to obtain a white-collar post. Substitution should be understood in relation to the number of permanent positions or slots a work unit is authorized to fill at any given time. These slots are included as fixed items in the work unit's budget; if one is vacated, it remains on the budget. The death or retirement of the parent results in several other workers' being promoted or moved around, thereby freeing up lower-level positions suitable for a young and untrained person.

Beginning in June 1978, the *dingti* policy was officially expanded, and personnel in state work units were actively encouraged to retire, even to take exceptionally early retirement.[5] The policy had almost immediate results. According to one study,[6] in eight large Beijing enterprises in the early 1980s the average age of retirement among male workers dropped 6.5 years and among women workers 5.6 years—over the short space of four years! In 1977, 411 workers retired from these eight enterprises; in 1978, 700; and in 1979, 1,941—an increase of 4.7 times. In Guangzhou at least 40 parents (in 35 households) in the Family Study exercised the *dingti* option, though this figure is surely an understatement because I did not systematically ask about the practice.[7]

The wide application of *dingti* substantially reduced unemployment among young people. In the Beijing study, for example, stand-ins filled an average of 74 percent of the positions opened up by both scheduled and accelerated retirements. But the policy had its critics. Alleged disadvantages of *dingti* included premature exit from the labor force of talented parents and their replacement by those offspring otherwise unlikely to obtain placement because of disabilities, criminal records, ineptitude in studies, and so forth. The policy was also inequitable because it was available only to young people whose parents worked in the state sector. For these and other reasons the Youth Problem Study Group argued in 1982 that the policy should be regarded as only temporary; it made the following suggestions for improving the quality of the labor force.

1. We must fully emphasize the principle of hiring on the basis of superior ability and qualifications.
2. We must control the gender ratio more strictly.
3. We must improve the system of retirement and arrange for the numbers of retiring personnel in a more rational way.
4. We must put in a great effort to develop vocational education in order to enhance the standards of science and culture among young workers. Vocational education must be practical and feasible, and gradually systematized.
5. We must deepen the basis of the construction of a spiritual civilization, in particular paying attention to educating young people to establish for themselves a correct sense of values and a philosophy of life.
6. We should gradually enhance the status and vocational reputation of collectively owned economic units and individual business operations.[8]

Although the *dingti* policy was officially repealed in September 1983, it did not finally lapse until 1986 with the national implementation of the labor contract system.

The Return of the Private Sector

The gradual reestablishment of the urban private sector via self-employment in individual businesses began in the late 1970s. Initially the option of self-employment was discussed primarily in terms of the rural economy with the legitimation, for example, of private plots, rural sideline activities, and market trade. In July 1981, however, the State Council issued a set of regulations for urban nonagricultural individual businesses.[9] At first, presumably because of ideological discomfort with enterprises in which the workers were not clearly the owners, such businesses could hire no more than seven employees. In practice this limit was frequently exceeded, and finally at the Thirteenth Party Congress in the fall of 1987 official recognition as private (as opposed to individual) businesses was given to enterprises hiring eight or more employees.[10] On June 25, 1988, the Provisional Regulations of the People's Republic of China Concerning Private Enterprises were promulgated; they went into effect the following February. These regulations, which do not apply to individual businesses, specified, among other things, that private businesses must obtain insurance for their workers and comply with the requirements of all labor protection legislation; for example, child labor is prohibited and the workday is limited to eight hours. Their workers must have contracts filed with the local labor administration authorities and must be free to organize labor unions.[11]

The development of the urban private sector faced many hurdles, including the absence of an experienced entrepreneurial class, ideological hostility, and public contempt and distrust of entrepreneurs. Under these circumstances only those individuals with no alternative means of making a living were likely to embark on a career in the private sector. And indeed the state itself, at least initially, restricted business licenses to youths awaiting employment, unemployed employables, and retired persons with urban registration who had the approval of their street committee.[12] Most cadres with state jobs were not prepared to consider venturing into the private sphere until after the implementation of the 1988 regulations.[13]

The near-elimination of the private sector in the 1950s and its disappearance in the 1960s understandably contributed to skepticism about how long the new private sector would be allowed to last. Doubts about continuing opportunities to pursue business have sometimes led to a get-rich-quick mentality that neglects the long-term interests of both the business and the community.[14] Public contempt and distrust of entrepreneurs is founded not only on decades of indoctrination against capitalists and the bourgeoisie but also on centuries of Confucian indoctrination against the merchant class, which was depicted as motivated by greed and self-interest rather than concern for the community as a whole.

Because of the extent to which private businesses are regulated, they are exceptionally vulnerable to bureaucratic interference. In the legal domain all manner of approvals are required, and all kinds of special taxes and levies have been introduced by creative local officials. Being outside the state plan, private businesses do not have preferred access to credit or to raw materials. When the state feels it necessary to restrict credit or the circulation of scarce materials, as in the late 1980s, the private sector is hit disproportionately hard. Given the weak bookkeeping skills of both entrepreneurs and tax officials, authorities have difficulty knowing the extent of a firm's profits or the honesty of its tax payments. Both officials and the public assume that tax evasion is rampant. Because of this assumption about entrepreneurs and their high incomes they are pressured to contribute to community projects, thus sharing their wealth. Consequently, many de facto private businesses mask their identity by registering as cooperatives or collectives.[15]

Tax evasion is frequent in private firms but not limited to them. According to Kraus, an investigation by "the finance ministry concluded that 70–80 percent of the private firms evaded taxes, but also that 50 percent of the state and collective companies were not above tax evasion."[16] Along these same lines, in 1991 in Guangzhou the manager of a state company related how he was learning the fine art of tax deductions from a book published outside China. He commented that from what he had heard about tax collection in the United States, the tax agency (the IRS) was even more clever than the public security bureau (the FBI) in ferreting out criminals. He was certain this was not the case in China.

The state regularly employs the mass media to educate both the public and the entrepreneurs themselves in appropriate business behavior. For example, a locally produced television program featuring a *geti hu* (individual household, or entrepreneur) was shown in Guangzhou in late December 1987. The story conveys a mixed message: although it is sympathetic to the young *geti hu*, it also affirms the viewer's suspicion that the business world is full of swindlers.

The episode features a young woman who runs her own fashionable clothing stall (a typical individual enterprise), but whose heart is clearly not in it. She cannot concentrate on her work but instead spends much of her time studying English (presumably so that she can find other work). She complains that she is discouraged because people look down on *geti hu*. Sometimes one or another of her neighbors, who are also entrepreneurs, stands in for her at her stall while she goes to fetch more clothes or attend to other errands. One of these neighbors is a middle-aged, generous, and good-natured man who runs a canned and bottled foods shop; the other is a middle-aged, narrow-minded woman who also runs a shop. One day the narrow-minded woman is tending the stall when a customer comes by and attempts to return a garment. The customer pulls the garment out of a plastic bag and explains that after she got home and examined it closely, she saw many indications that this was an old and not a new garment. She wants her money back!

The neighbor does not know what to make of this, but basically dismisses the woman and says the stall policy is that goods are not returnable. The male neighbor happens by, recognizes the customer because he had sold her the outfit earlier in the day, and is puzzled by the situation. At this moment the young owner herself comes out of her building. She is surprised by the charge that her goods are used but intervenes and asks the customer who sold her the item. The customer points out the male neighbor. The young woman gives her a refund. Later two more customers come by with the same complaint, and though quite disheartened now, the young woman also returns their money. The two customers praise her "service attitude," saying that she is not like some of the entrepreneurs (individual households) written about in the paper who are devising schemes to make money — even doing such things as passing off old clothes for new. They then hastily apologize and explain that they did not mean she was doing this. Apparently the young woman's inattention to her work had caused her to buy a batch of clothing without inspecting it very closely herself; thus she wound up as someone else's victim. The male neighbor consoles her, and she is last seen pedaling off to fetch another batch of goods for her stall.

In October 1992 there were 3,877 private enterprises (not including individual businesses) in all of Guangzhou, constituting 5.3 percent of all enterprises and employing 42,953 workers. Growth was particularly rapid in the early 1990s, increasing more than fourfold between April 1989 and late 1992. Most private businesses are capitalized at between 300,000 and 500,000 yuan.[17] The reestablishment of the private sector, of course, served other ends than simply absorbing the unemployed or underemployed. As I indicated in Chapter 2, private shops made available to urban residents a whole range of goods and services that were otherwise in short supply or unavailable. Furthermore, because of their dependence on their own profits for income, proprietors and workers in private enterprises were likely to provide higher quality goods and better service than those in other sectors of the economy and thus, through competition, to serve as models of efficiency to enterprises in the more sluggish sectors.

In this regard it is appropriate to mention the reestablishment of foreign direct investment in China, officially authorized in 1979. Both joint ventures and wholly owned foreign enterprises were also expected to serve as models for the state sector — less by direct competition (most of their products are for export rather than domestic consumption) than by their innovations in managerial responsibility and decision making and in labor relations. In 1991 the total number of Chinese managers in such firms was estimated at between 45,000 and 55,000.[18] These managers are relatively young (in their 30s and 40s) and are all highly trained, mostly in engineering. The attractions of working in the foreign sector include high wages, greater decision-making power, opportunities to travel abroad, and freedom from the politicized atmosphere characteristic of state enterprises. Managers are also able to change jobs more easily in the foreign sector.[19]

Stimulating Productivity

"Eating from one big pot" is an expression describing the forgiving relationship that long existed (and, despite the reforms, continues to exist) between the higher and lower levels of any governmental hierarchy. The various enterprises under a particular central ministry, provincial department, or municipal bureau were said to be eating from the same pot because they were not independently accountable for their own profits and losses. Rather the gains of profitable enterprises were sent to the top of the hierarchy and redistributed to the unprofitable. In Guangzhou this relationship is sometimes described as "eating Grandfather's rice," an apt allusion to the ideal traditional extended family in which the earnings of the junior generation are pooled by the senior generation and redistributed according to need. Just as no one was supposed to lose his or her job, so no enterprise in the state sector was supposed to be shut down. (In the collective sector, individual factories or shops are responsible for their profits and losses and can, indeed, fail, but they employ only a minority of the urban work force.)

Financial Reforms

One of the reformers' early goals was to make enterprises responsible for their own profits and losses on the theory that they would focus on profitability once they realized they could keep their profits (if they were efficient) or would go out of business (if they were not). First, enterprises were allowed to retain a certain proportion of their profits. Later this policy was replaced by a more straightforward tax on profits. Apparently the reformers expected that the profits would be reinvested to modernize antiquated plants, but in fact most of them were immediately ploughed into workers' benefits, such as bonuses and housing construction.

The reformers recognized that simply giving greater financial responsibility to enterprises without allowing them additional freedom would not increase productivity. Consequently a whole set of reforms affecting production decisions, wages, labor recruitment, labor mobility, and social security issues were also gradually implemented. All these reforms were intended to afford the enterprises the maximum flexibility they needed to increase their profitability without seriously disrupting the employment security to which China's urban workers had become accustomed. These policies resulted, at least initially, in distinctive cohort differences in employment opportunities and benefits, for those already privileged by lifetime employment sacrificed nothing until years later whereas those new to the labor force entered it on less favorable terms.[20]

Although state enterprises remained subject to some state planning and were assigned annual production quotas, they were encouraged to expand their production or to develop in new directions appropriate to their locale. These endeavors outside the state plan fell under different rules; for example, the enterprises were granted more price flexibility, could obtain raw materials where they desired, sell their finished goods where they desired, and hire workers on temporary rather than permanent terms. As the *dingti* option faded, state enterprises welcomed these additional off-plan employment opportunities that could be filled by the children of their own workers.[21]

Labor Reforms

The system of lifetime employment of state workers is usually referred to as the "iron rice bowl" because the workplace essentially constituted an unbreakable vessel from which the worker would always be able to eat, that is, obtain an income. Entering workers were assigned to the lowest wage grade of, for example, production worker, clerical worker, technician, or cadre, and expected over the years to be promoted to higher levels. Promotions were based primarily on seniority (years in grade) rather than on performance. Such promotions, however, were not as frequent as one might expect. Around the time of the Cultural Revolution, for example, promotions were more or less frozen for fifteen years. Since wage increases were associated with seniority and not with performance, failure to perform up to standard was not penalized.[22]

When the reformers noted that worker motivation in the late 1970s was very poor, they proposed to stimulate it by linking performance and wages. The lack of motivation was apparent to anyone visiting a Chinese state factory at the time: machines stood idle and workers played cards and sat around smoking while on duty. The Chinese press regularly talked about poor discipline and high rates of absenteeism, but these problems had less to do with the wage system than with shortages of materials and energy, which regularly disrupted production, or with overstaffing, which meant that many people had nothing to do. As one state employee memorably explained to me: "Two can do the work of one. Even three can." To motivate workers, piece rates and the payment of bonuses were reintroduced.

Wage Reforms

Piece rates had been used in the 1950s, prior to the Great Leap Forward, and again in the early 1960s, but they had been discredited during the Cultural Revolution, when egalitarianism was emphasized. They were gradually reintroduced in the late 1970s, though they were not allowed to account for all of a worker's wages; instead, they were applied only to production above a certain quota, for which the basic wage was essentially guaranteed. Piece rates, however, are suitable only for certain kinds of work, in which increases in production can readily be measured — on the assembly line, at the sewing machine, or in the packing room. To improve service in hotels and restaurants, sales in shops, and efficiency in offices, the bonus system was deemed more suitable. Under it, everyone is assured the basic wage but receives an additional amount (sometimes varying monthly) depending on both the overall fortunes of the enterprise and individual performance. Ideally each department of an enterprise receives each month a share of the take to distribute as bonus money among its workers.

It is difficult to measure precisely the impact of the bonus system on worker motivation and performance. In some units it probably had no major effect.[23] For example, in 1987 one young service worker in a state-run hotel in Guangzhou indicated that at her workplace there were three levels of bonus, with 1 the highest and 3 the lowest, and that every month people were evaluated by their supervisors. The majority of workers were automatically rated a 2. Those who were enthusiastic might rate a 1; those who were indifferent (but made no serious errors) might rate a 3. Those whose attitude or performance was really poor, however, might forfeit the bonus entirely. This pressure to treat workers more or less equally doomed one scheme to promote worker motivation at Guangzhou's Baiyun Airport. In 1991 two foreigners, hired to upgrade the skills of aircraft mechanics, perceived great variation in the motivation and aptitude of their trainees. They wanted to start a "Worker of the Month" program to acknowledge outstanding performers. They were informed, however, that they could not select just one worker each month; they would have to select 25 for the designation. And the next month they would have to select another 25 until all workers in the program had been honored. They decided not to implement the program.

Because workers in different departments in the same enterprise are not necessarily treated equally, those on the losing end have been discomfited. Prior to the economic reforms office workers in factories almost always had higher wages than production workers, but this is no longer the case. One woman working in the office of a state factory producing medical equipment, for example, has watched her income fall below that of the production workers. Although their basic wage is actually lower than hers, part of their income is based on piecework, whereas there is no equivalent of piecework for the office staff. Furthermore, the bulk of the bonus money distributed to both office and production workers goes to the production workers on the grounds that they generated it.

Paradoxically, perhaps, the bonus system has also served to motivate both managers and workers in units where one might least expect it — in such nonprofit institutions as hospitals, schools, and research institutes. Because the fees these institutions are allowed to charge patients, students, and government clients are deliberately set low by the government, their workers, many of them highly educated, have had to endure the indignity of watching the wages of the relatively unskilled and uneducated zoom past their own. This inequity has generated enormous discontent as well as innumerable strategies to increase the institutions' incomes. I have already noted that schools, to make a little money, rent out excess space and even, in the evenings, classroom space to businesses. More important, as I indicated in Chapter 4, college professors and researchers have been required to increase their work loads. In addition to their regular duties, they teach special courses offered by their own institutions, translate works, serve as consultants, carry out contract research, and so forth. Although these activities inevitably impinge on their work with their regular students, the official government position is that it is right and proper for them to increase their incomes in this way so long as they do not exploit their own students.[24]

Many individuals, however, have acute "second-job fever" that leads them to work outside their units (while still officially on the payroll). According to a 1993 article in *China Daily*, 40 percent of the nation's scientists and technicians, underutilized by their units, have an overabundance of free time.[25] At Beijing Union Medical College Hospital, for example, the 200 doctors licensed to perform surgery are each limited to nine operations a month because of a shortage of space in the operating theaters. Consequently, many such doctors choose to work at district hospitals and clinics in their spare time. The same article reported that one in three state employees and two of five scientists and technicians in Guangzhou have second jobs, and in Chongqing, in Sichuan province, more than 40 percent of government functionaries moonlight.

Some units have found even more creative ways to make money through their personnel, although these are seldom officially reported. For example, one Guangzhou employee was in a quandary because he wanted to leave his (nonprofit) unit and take a job with a better-paying foreign work unit. The foreign work unit, however, could not provide him with housing, and his original work unit wanted to be able to continue him on its roster (and thereby continue to receive wage and benefit allocations from its supervisory organ). The compromise: the worker could stay on the roster, keep his housing, and go to work for the foreigners, provided he remitted part of his new salary to his original unit. In the same vein, in Beijing another nonprofit informed its professional staff that they would have to pay what amounted to a substantial annual affiliation fee for the privilege of retaining their work-related benefits. They were expected to pay this fee out of their extra income-generating activities.

An article in *Economic Daily*, arguing that this trend was disturbing, suggested that one way to stop it would be to pay workers in government departments and institutions a meaningful wage.[26] The article pointed out that although the wage reforms of 1985 allowed state enterprises to link economic performance and workers' salaries, workers and staff in other types of state work units still follow the old pattern of wage distribution; that is, the wage scale is the same regardless of the functions of these very diverse work units. The suggested solution was to create a single civil service wage system for people employed in government administrative departments and different wage systems for those employed in medical, research, or cultural fields. For example:

In educational, scientific and health care sectors, the employees' performances should be connected with their academic credentials; in geological, meteorological, and topographic fields, the professionals' income should be related to their working environments and their physical exertion; and in sports, arts and literary circles the income should be more connected with their prime age.

Most important, the article argues that the wage standards in government departments and institutions should be roughly the same as those in enterprises, where wages are currently 20 percent higher. This wage differential is widely regarded as an important stimulus not only to moonlighting but also to corruption.

To boost the income of their workers, state institutions and organizations have developed special programs and have even participated in joint ventures. Hospitals, for example, have attempted to develop special services, such as long-term care and cosmetic surgery, that are not covered by insurance regulations. Clients interested in these services must pay for them directly. In Guangzhou an official of the Communist Youth League estimated that only one-quarter of its budget is actually provided by the provincial government. To obtain the rest it has organized a "company" and started three major enterprises: a joint venture with the Japanese raising cultured pearls out toward Huangpu, a clothing factory employing 100 workers on Guangzhou's south side, and a ceramics factory in Mei county.

Recruitment Reforms

Reforms in labor recruitment and retention are intended to ameliorate two closely related problems: inefficient use of personnel and overstaffing. Prior to the reforms, recruitment had meant either "unified assignment" or district labor bureau assignment. Chapter 4 discussed unified assignment as it applied to government-funded students graduating from specialized secondary schools, colleges, and universities. To fulfill national work force needs, these students could be sent anywhere in the country. Because it was difficult to turn down even the most undesirable or illogical placement, many graduates found themselves assigned to jobs they would never have accepted had they been free to choose, and work units found themselves stuck with individuals they would never have chosen to hire.

Under these circumstances students, and their parents on their behalf, naturally angled to gain favorable placements — at a minimum to remain in Guangzhou rather than be sent to a remote or rural area — but because the location of openings was literally a state secret, it was difficult, though not impossible, to influence placement. Connections (*guanxi*), of course, could be helpful. For example, one family with a son graduating in an athletic specialty desperately wanted to keep him in Guangzhou. On learning through connections the location of the single local opening in this field, the parents went in person to the head of the relevant work unit, explaining how important it was to them to keep their son in Guangzhou. The head responded sympathetically, saying he had no objection to their son's assignment to the work unit. The parents then rushed off to their son's school to speak with the person in charge of matching graduates to openings and explained how the head of the work unit had indicated his willingness to receive their son. The desired match was made.

In another case a young man learned of an opening in a certain large *danwei* with several subunits below it. He pleaded with the school assignment officer not to write so specifically that he was being assigned to one of the less desirable subunits; instead, the officer should write that the graduate was being assigned to the *danwei* as a whole. The student then went to someone he knew high up in the unit, pointing out that he was being assigned to it in general, and asked whether there was a place in the unit (other than the one he did not want) where he might work. The official asked around and found a superior placement. These machinations have proved less necessary in recent years with the introduction of labor fairs (discussed below), which allow college students in their last year of school to meet face-to-face with potential employers.

Students either graduating from junior middle school or failing to qualify for postsecondary education were the responsibility of their local (district) labor bureau. Prior to the reestablishment of the private sector, they had been assigned to work in state or collective units in their general area of the city. Predictably under this system many young people were assigned to the work units of their parents entirely independent of the *dingti* option. During the late 1970s and early 1980s, when there were many more people to place than there were openings, the street committees were charged with developing new collectives and cooperatives, largely in the service sector, to employ neighborhood young people.

Since the beginning of the reforms there have been three major changes in labor recruitment: the reestablishment of the private sector (discussed above), the shift from labor bureau assignment to labor company facilitation, and the introduction of the labor contract system. Labor companies (which are like quasi-governmental job clearing houses) usually operate at the city district level, and contact with them is optional rather than mandatory. When a work unit needs additional employees, it may notify the labor company, which then makes efforts to publicize the opportunity. Or the work unit might choose to notify only its own employees and limit its publicizing to posting a notice on its gate.

In an attempt to get around this continuing tendency of *danwei* to give preference to the children of their own workers regardless of their credentials, Guangzhou in 1989 began to implement the principle "first train, then obtain employment" (*xian peixun hou jiuye*). In other words, prospective workers had to demonstrate that they already possessed the skills appropriate for the positions they were seeking. One suspects, however, that work units will easily find ways to bend this principle to their own inclination to hire the children of their workers. Students enrolled in technical or skilled workers (*jishu gongren*) schools, for example, are disproportionately drawn from the children of workers at the factories that co-sponsor the schools. Young people looking for work may go to the labor companies to learn what is available, but they are not required to, nor, if they do go, are they required to accept any job recommendations the company might make. As might be expected, without compulsory assignment, hiring has become difficult for work units with unpleasant working conditions—for example, those whose work involves public sanitation or exposure to high temperatures or toxic chemicals. These jobs must now be filled by workers from the countryside.

Although there have been a few experiments temporarily suspending or modifying the system of unified assignment, it basically remains in force for students whose education or training has been funded by the government. The state briefly considered letting university graduates, beginning with the entering class of 1989, find jobs on their own. To prepare for this eventuality, cities in the late 1980s began sponsoring labor fairs, especially around the Spring Festival, when students studying elsewhere return to their home communities. At these fairs graduating seniors were able to meet face-to-face with personnel from *danwei* expecting to have positions available the following summer—thus making open what had previously been a state secret. If a student and a work unit were mutually attracted, the representative of the work unit would notify the student's school that it

TABLE 5.1
New Workers in State Work Units in Urban Districts of
Guangzhou, 1990

Source	N	Pct.
Unified assignment	20,393	45%
Graduating students	19,113	
Military	1,280	
Recruited from cities and towns	13,779	30
Promotion of temporary workers	6,066	13
Recruited from rural areas	2,621	6
Other [a]	2,882	6
TOTAL	45,741	100

SOURCE: Guangzhou Shi Tongji Ju, *Guangzhou tongji nianjian 1991* (Statistical yearbook of Guangzhou 1991) (China: Zhongguo Tongji Chubanshe, 1991), p. 359.

[a] Includes 756 persons shifting in from joint ventures, 584 children of retiring staff and workers or of people whose official residence is a state farm, 518 persons who had resumed their state posts following a period of unpaid absence, 312 persons shifting in from collectives (or, possibly, whose collectives had been taken over by the state), and 712 persons with unspecified origins.

wanted him or her for its opening. Two problems quickly became apparent: undesirable work units could not attract candidates, whereas desirable work units that could pick and choose among candidates tended to discriminate against women. Because of these problems the state decided not to allow graduates of the class entering in 1989 and thereafter to find jobs on their own, and in 1991 Guangzhou announced that henceforth it would restrict labor fairs to students with Guangzhou household registration, a rule rendered obsolete in late 1992 by a central government decision to make Guangdong an experimental labor market. By 1998, however, nearly all graduating students (from seven schools experimenting with this reform in Guangdong) will find jobs on their own. Self-paying students, however, have been expected to find their own jobs all along.

Table 5.1 shows how state sector openings in Guangzhou were filled in 1990 — 45 percent of them through unified assignment. The labor contract system was implemented nationally in October 1986, although Guangzhou had been experimenting with it since 1983–84. Under this system, at least in theory, the iron rice bowl was smashed, and incoming state workers were no longer guaranteed lifetime employment. Instead, new entrants to the labor force are now required to sign term contracts for two, three, five, or even more years. When the contract expires, the worker is free to seek other work, and the employer can refuse to negotiate a new contract. Compensation may be required should either party break the contract. Several caveats are necessary here. First, the labor contract system applies only to workers entering the labor force since its implementation; those hired prior to this date still have lifetime employment (unless they had been hired as temporary workers). Second, many of these contract workers are automatically rehired at the expiration of their contract period, and particularly desirable workers are known to have been offered contracts with such long terms — for example, twenty years — that they are de facto permanent workers. Third, substantial numbers of new entrants to the labor force have continued to join their work units as permanent members.[27] A primary reason for introducing the labor contract system was to make it possible for enterprises to gain greater control over the number of their workers. Hiring on time-limited contracts allows enterprises to shed excess labor rather than keep it idle and on the payroll. Nevertheless, at present this reform affects only a minority of the state work force because most workers over 30 were hired under the old terms of lifetime employment.

Labor Mobility

In the early 1980s the issue of labor mobility was given a great deal of public attention. It was widely recognized that many work assignments had been mismatches, and enterprises were urged, in the interests of modernization, to let talent flow where it was most needed and best suited. Although both employers and workers could see advantages to themselves of a free flow of labor, they could also see disadvantages so severe as to constitute major barriers to the development of a viable labor market. Enterprises with redundant permanent workers were, of course, happy to see them go, but not when such departures represented the loss of a major investment.[28] In Guangzhou, for example, in the early and mid-1980s several thousand workers wanted to leave their jobs to become taxi drivers. Their units balked, saying they would be difficult to replace and/or that the unit had paid for their training and was entitled to reimbursement; thus the workers often had to pay what amounted to a severance fee. Similar thinking lies behind the requirement that state-supported university graduates work several years for the state before going abroad for study or else reimburse the state for the cost of their education.

For their part state workers had neither experience in seeking jobs nor access to information about job availability. Those who resigned their positions and either found no satisfactory new job or were discharged from one had no means of financial support. Furthermore, until very recently permanent workers who resigned, rather than arrange a transfer within the state sector, compromised their eligibility for health insurance, pensions, and other benefits if they shifted to the collective or the private sector. For these same reasons *danwei* have been reluctant to shed their excess workers, viewing discharge as the moral equivalent of abandonment. Consequently, most labor mobility occurs among young workers on contracts and not among redundant lifetime employees.

To promote job mobility among permanent workers (as well as to protect contract workers), the state has introduced talent exchange centers, has expanded labor fairs, has developed an unemployment compensation program, and has provided guidelines to work units to allow them to discharge excess workers humanely. Talent exchange centers, which help state workers get around *danwei* resistance to the movement of skilled personnel ("talent"), became important in Guangzhou around 1990. Under most circumstances state units will not hire (or accept on transfer) any permanent employee without first examining the candidate's dossier (*dangan*) for evidence of qualifications, work attitude, and (until very recently) political reliability. If the personnel department holding a worker's dossier refuses to allow another unit access to it, that worker is effectively barred from leaving the workplace (except to go to the collective or the private sector, either of which is less likely to take the absence of a dossier so seriously). One of the most important functions of talent exchange centers is to serve as *dangan* depositories. For a monthly fee those interested in changing jobs can transfer custody of their dossiers from their unit's personnel department to the talent exchange center, which then takes responsibility for maintaining them, that is, keeping them current with entries of achievements, awards, and so forth. Employers may then go to the talent exchange center to look over the dossiers of prospective candidates. The state does not allow individuals to keep their own dossiers for fear that damaging information will be removed or false credentials inserted.

As the capital of Guangdong province, Guangzhou also serves as a magnet, attracting from all over the country personnel interested in employment in the city itself, the general region, and even overseas. During a gigantic three-day labor fair held in late February 1993, some 41,500 people from more than 20 provinces and cities came to Guangzhou seeking one of the nearly 44,000 posts being offered by 714 institutions and enterprises.[29] Up to 65 percent of the job seekers, who included government officials and clerks, workers, farmers, college graduates, and unemployed people, were eventually employed. Most of the skilled labor went to the Special Economic Zones of Shenzhen and Zhuhai as well as to prosperous delta cities, such as Zhongshan, Shunde, and Panyu.

In theory Guangzhou introduced a system of unemployment compensation as early as 1986 in conjunction with the contract labor system, the idea being to give contract workers some security between jobs. By late 1992 more than 4,000 state enterprises in the city with more than 900,000 workers were participating in the unemployment insurance program. Under the program eligible workers are entitled to income support, job introductions, retraining, and assistance in setting up their own businesses. More than 20,000 workers were said to have already enjoyed these benefits while unemployed, including more than 4,400 who became self-employed.[30] A survey of workers, however, suggests that eligibility criteria and benefits are not widely known: 40 percent of those surveyed knew little or nothing about their own unemployment insurance.[31] In January 1993 Guangzhou extended unemployment insurance coverage to contract workers in collectives and in March 1994, to contract workers in private enterprises of all types.

Dealing with redundant permanent workers remains a seemingly intractable problem for the state. In 1992, despite years of calling on enterprises to shed workers, nonproductive state enterprises across the country received 22.4 billion yuan in subsidies,[32] much of it necessitated by wage and benefit obligations. In 1993 the state announced its intention to move about 17 million workers to other jobs over the next few years. Of these only 7.3 million were expected to obtain jobs newly created by state enterprises. The rest were going to have to find work on their own.[33] In April 1993, claiming that enterprises had hesitated to discharge excess labor because they did not know how, the State Council issued guidelines on legitimate termination and the obligations of enterprises to terminated workers.[34] The guidelines encouraged state enterprises to set up subsidiary service units (responsible for their own financing) to absorb some of these workers. Such service units would be given a 100 percent tax exemption for two years and a 50 percent tax exemption for the next three years. Workers could be put on leave and paid a stipend (as opposed to wages); women could be put on maternity or nursing leave for two years and paid a stipend. The stipend would be set by the enterprise itself but could not fall below the minimum established by the local government. Workers within five years of retirement could agree to take early retirement. In the interval they would receive a stipend, to be replaced by their normal retirement pay when they came of age. Workers could even simply resign and receive a onetime severance payment. All these regulations suggest a state hard-pressed to lay off redundant personnel.

Welfare Reforms

A major factor affecting the financial performance of any state enterprise is the heavy welfare burden it has been required to shoulder on behalf of its workers. So substantial is this burden that in any other system it would serve as a major disincentive to hiring.[35] Welfare services include an array of subsidies embedded in the monthly wage package as well as health insurance (which usually includes dependents), sick leave, maternity leave, pensions, and, when feasible, housing. An enterprise has to be mighty profitable to have a surplus for reinvestment after meeting all of these obligations. Large collectives attempt to provide the same benefits as the state sector, though small ones, such as those run by street committees, generally do not. Smaller collectives usually have less generous health insurance and seldom offer coverage for dependents. In some cases their pension payments have been so small as to fall below the official provincial minimum. Workers in joint ventures between Chinese partners and foreigners normally receive the same coverage (plus higher wages) as workers in Chinese enterprises.[36] Owners of private (Chinese) businesses (but not of individual businesses) have been required since 1988 to provide similar benefits to their workers.

Different benefit obligations affect the competitive positions of the different classes of enterprise, to say nothing of the well-being of their workers. The most exploited workers seem to be those in enterprises owned by foreign investors, mostly from Hong Kong, who deliberately moved their operations to Guangdong to escape Hong Kong's stricter protective legislation. In January 1994 the provincial general trade union reported on a survey of twenty different kinds of foreign enterprise carried out in ten cities around the province. They uncovered widespread ignorance among workers of their rights and, predictably, widespread abuses.[37] For example, 32.8 percent of the workers did not have a signed contract, and another 7 percent did not even know what a labor contract was. Workers were regularly required to work many hours of overtime. A large proportion had no social insurance: 44.2 percent lacked any medical coverage, 31.6 percent lacked accident coverage, 27.8 percent had no pension coverage, and 55.3 percent of women had no maternity coverage. Furthermore, their living conditions were often pitiful: 26.7 percent of the workers were housed in dormitories with less than 2 square meters of living space per person. In March 1994, to eliminate these abuses and to even out differences among the various classes of enterprise, the provincial government put into effect comprehensive regulations meant to apply to *all* enterprises. These required them to participate in all the social insurance programs, to provide medical coverage, to meet the local minimum wage, to restrict overtime, to have labor unions, and so forth.[38]

Income Subsidies

Table 5.2 shows the monthly wages of urban workers in Guangdong. Because both for-profit and nonprofit units are included, the average bonus for state sector workers is less than that of workers in collectives, who are more likely to be in for-profit (i.e., production or commercial) enterprises than state workers. Subsidies in the state sector, however, are double those

TABLE 5.2
Average Monthly Wages by Ownership System in Urban Areas of Guangdong, 1990 (in yuan)

	Basic wage	Bonus	Subsidies	Total[a]
State				
Lowest decile	102	38	40	184
Highest decile	127	105	74	320
Average	112	72	54	246
Collective				
Lowest decile	88	42	22	155
Highest decile	125	183	37	350
Average	108	83	26	222
Other[b]				
Lowest decile				154
Highest decile				480
Average				236

SOURCE: Guangdong Sheng Tongji Ju, *Guangdong tongji nianjian 1991* (Guangdong statistical yearbook 1991) (China: Zhongguo Tongji Chubanshe, 1991), p. 360.

[a] The totals exceed the sum of their parts by anywhere from 3 to 14 yuan; this discrepancy is not explained in the original table.

[b] Includes various forms of joint venture, both those between domestic partners, e.g., state and private or collective and private, and those between a Chinese partner and a foreign one.

in the collective sector, reflecting the numerous additional ways the state attempts to increase workers' incomes. These subsidies are of two types: standard of living subsidies (*butie*) and work-related subsidies (*jintie*). The first are mandated by the state to almost all urban workers and are intended to reduce the burden to the worker of price increases in such necessary goods and services as meat, nonstaple foods, electricity, and fuel. The second in some cases are mandated by the state, as in the single-child allowance, and in others are more at the discretion of the work unit. Most of these subsidies are directly tied to the performance of work, for example, a grooming allowance for service workers in the tourist industry, a uniform allowance, a cold drink allowance in the summer, and a hot drink allowance in the winter. Retirees continue to receive *butie* but not *jintie*. The average income of workers in the state system is higher than that of other workers, but income potential, as measured by the income of the highest decile, is clearly greatest in the newer ownership systems.

With their greater financial responsibility, work units, whenever they can, now avoid incurring obligations to pay subsidies. For example, one couple, both employed by provincial government units, found their respective units haggling over the details of their one-child family subsidy and their daughter's overnight preschool (*quantuo*) subsidy. As parents of a single child, they are entitled to a payment of 7.5 yuan a month—a sum their units split, each paying 3.75 yuan. The daughter stays at the *quantuo* four nights a week; on Wednesdays and on weekends she comes to stay with them. The fees for the *quantuo* amount to 100 yuan a month, but 10 yuan can be reclaimed from the parental work unit. The two units split the 10 yuan: one pays for the even- and the other for the odd-numbered days. At one time the wife outranked her husband; she became eligible for a housing assignment in her unit before he did in his. The apartment offered was in an old building and not especially desirable, but they were told they could move into a unit on a higher floor when it became available. In 1991 they prepared to move into the now vacated apartment when the wife's unit suddenly balked. Since the husband had received a promotion in the interim, he now outranked his wife, and her unit attempted (unsuccessfully) to foist responsibility for a housing change onto his unit.

Health Insurance

In 1952 Guangdong (and the nation as a whole) established a system of free medical care (*gungfei yiliao*) for people working in government organs or in the technical, educational, and health fields as well as for certain disabled members of the military. Coverage under this program was later extended to college and university students. Workers in state enterprises have been covered separately under the labor insurance program and have generally received the same entitlements as those under *gungfei yiliao*. Workers in urban collectives have received some medical coverage, but because the necessary funds have derived from the income of the individual *danwei*, the extent of coverage has been variable and, frequently, minimal.

Health coverage of staff and workers under *gungfei yiliao* has been comprehensive. Outpatients normally have paid only the nominal registration fee at the appropriate clinic or hospital. Inpatients have paid a similar nominal registration fee plus meals. If patients required a personal attendant, however, the family had to provide or pay for the service. (Dependents, in contrast, have been accountable for 50 percent of their medical costs.)

By the mid-1980s the costs to the state of providing health care coverage had grown astronomically for several reasons: the epidemiological transition from acute diseases requiring a single intervention to chronic diseases requiring multiple interventions; the aging of the population with a high prevalence of chronic disease; and the efforts of hospitals to increase their own incomes by introducing high-tech diagnostic equipment and expensive medications. Patients were also suspected of abusing the system by seeking medical treatment for trivial complaints or even engaging in fraud, as when they sought medicine actually intended for someone else. Such fraud is so common that the perpetrators barely acknowledge that it is illegal. For example, on one occasion, I was struck down with a fever and respiratory distress. I had already visited, as a private paying patient, the special clinic for overseas Chinese in one of the district hospitals (this choice allowed me to bypass several long lines) and had also been seen as a courtesy by a doctor attached to the unit in whose guest house I was living. I had an adequate supply of medication. Nevertheless, when an acquaintance learned on the phone that I was sick, she immediately came to visit me with four or five freshly prescribed pharmaceuticals in her handbag. When I protested that she should not have spent so much money and that I wanted to repay her, she laughed and said the medicine had cost her nothing.

In 1987, to deal with these rising health costs, the provincial government decided to introduce a system of copayments for medical care. Outpatients were to pay 10 percent of their costs whereas inpatients were to pay 5 percent. Veteran cadres, however, were to be exempted from these new rules. For a few months in 1988 provincial *danwei* attempted to implement the copayment system, but it was considered such a nuisance and there was so much resistance that the government was forced to abandon it before the end of the year. Other cost-reduction strategies, implemented independently at the *danwei* level, included various exclusionary rules; that is, certain medications, tests, and surgical procedures were made the financial responsibility of the patient and not the unit. Some units set a maximum on the amount they would pay. The issue of providing long-term care was ignored; the costs were left to the family.[39]

In 1994 the Guangdong provincial and Guangzhou city governments felt confident enough to attempt another "major surgery" on *gungfei yiliao* and hope this time for success. Health care costs had continued to rise since the first major reform attempt in early 1988. Provincial per capita expenditures on the health insurance program for 1993 were up 50.6 percent over 1992; in Guangzhou city proper they were up 39.9 percent, to 1,129 yuan.[40] In this economic context, the state introduced simultaneously, effective July 1, 1994, a set of reforms that included copayments, an annual maximum limit on copayment expenditures, a medical subsidy, and expanded benefits for dependents; thus from the beneficiary's point of view the reforms include both gains and losses.

Employed beneficiaries of *gungfei yiliao* were made responsible for 20 percent of outpatient costs and 10 percent of inpatient costs, and retirees were required to pay 10 percent and 5 percent, respectively. The annual maximum copayment for an employed person is 500 yuan, for a retiree, 400 yuan. Old members of the Red Army, *lixiu* cadres, and certain disabled military were not affected by these changes. To help beneficiaries deal with their increased financial responsibilities, they were simultaneously given a medical services subsidy consisting of a monthly payment based partly on rank and partly on age.[41] Although beneficiaries now have 10 yuan (as opposed to a formerly nominal payment) deducted from their wages for each dependent who is insured, the dependent's coverage has been upgraded to the same level as that enjoyed by the primary beneficiary.[42]

Retirement and Pensions

As an institution, retirement serves multiple functions. First, it allows workers who reach a certain age to leave the labor force but continue to receive income; second, it provides a convenient mechanism by which work units may legitimately reduce the size of their labor force; and third, it opens up senior positions to the succeeding generation. The statutory age for retirement in China is 50 for women workers, 55 for women cadres and staff, and 60 for men. Until about 1978 each age indicated eligibility for retirement, but the unit, and to a lesser extent the individual, could decide the age of actual retirement. Senior cadres, however, maintained full control over their own retirement; and many had no interest in retiring.

Until the mid-1990s the rules governing pensions for workers were the same as those established shortly after the Communists came to power. To be eligible for retirement, one had to work at least ten years, and one's pension was based on years of service and wages prior to retirement. Those retiring with only ten years of service would receive 60 percent of their previous wages; with fifteen years, 70 percent; and with twenty or more years, 75 percent. Pensions were calculated without regard to the bonuses that might have greatly augmented actual preretirement income. Former model workers (individuals who had been publicly recognized as exceptional performers) were eligible for an increment of 5, 10, or 15 percent, and those who participated in the Communist revolutionary movement left (and continue to leave) work under more favorable terms (see below). With the beginning of the reforms in 1978 the state had several reasons to promote retirement among both workers and cadres: high rates of unemployment among youth, low levels of education and in some cases of performance among the old, and the possibility of political obstructionism by "conservative" cadres opposed to the reforms.

Retiring workers proved to be an easier task for the state than retiring cadres. Indeed, the policy of reversing verdicts and restoring to their positions cadres who had been criticized during the Cultural Revolution ran exactly counter to the policy of encouraging their retirement.[43] Nevertheless, by about 1982 the state began to insist on retiring all but a few of the highest ranked cadres, who were either exempted from retirement altogether or allowed to become members of advisory commissions. Cadres were divided into two broad categories: those who had participated in the revolution (veteran or revolutionary cadres) and those who became active only after the establishment of the People's Republic on October 1, 1949 (ordinary cadres). Veteran cadres were entitled to a whole set of privileges not available to ordinary cadres, including 100 percent or more of their salary, access to restricted documents, special assistance in meeting their needs for housing and medical care, and continued involvement in political affairs, though not daily affairs. In fact, these cadres are said not to retire but to "take leave for convalescence" (*lizhi xiuyang*, usually abbreviated to *lixiu*), indicating that though their formal duties have been reduced in deference to their age, they continue to work for the goals of the revolution.[44]

Since the institution of retirement reforms, the retired population has grown rapidly, though not solely because of mandatory retirement. Millions of people have reached pensionable age and survive into advanced old age thanks to improvements in public health and the availability of medical care. In a 1991 interview with an official from the provincial labor department I was told that 7–8 percent of the population in Guangdong was 60 or older. It is estimated that by 2020 Guangdong will have an "aged population," with 10 percent or more aged 60 or older. Between 10 and 11 percent of the population in Guangzhou city proper is already aged 60 or over. The retired population of the province is currently increasing by about 8 percent annually as each year some 90,000–100,000 people retire. At the end of 1990 the total number of retired people in the province was 1.24 million. By 2000 there will be 2.2 million retirees, with the peak expected to be reached in 2030. In the early 1990s the ratio of workers to retirees was roughly 6 to 1. By 2030 it is expected to fall to 2 to 1. Of this retired population 830,000 are retired from state units, 405,000 from collective units, and 5,600 from other units.

Prior to the reforms this pension burden had been treated as part of the "one big pot," so that each ministry was responsible for the retirement payments of all the workers under it regardless of their actual work unit affiliation. As individual enterprises became responsible for their own retirees' pensions, they thereby assumed unequal burdens because of differences in the age composition of their work forces. For example, in 1980 a factory established in the mid-1950s was likely to have a middle-aged work force, with most people in senior grades or retired, whereas a factory established in the late 1970s was likely to have a young work force in the lowest pay grades and no retirees. The different wage and retirement burdens of the two factories would have a major effect on their competitive position.

To deal with this new inequity Guangdong in 1983 (and the central government in 1984) began a new system that was intended, ultimately, to shift responsibility for financing retirement from the individual enterprise to employers and workers as a whole. Under this system enterprises in Guangzhou contributed 15–18 percent of the wages they paid monthly to a social labor insurance company, which pooled contributions from its jurisdiction and redistributed them to retirees (although, in fact, retirees continued to pick up their monthly checks from their own units). In August 1993 the whole province became a single jurisdiction. Not all of the money is available for disbursement. A certain proportion is to be set aside each year to build up a retirement fund for the time when the ratio of workers to retirees is less favorable than now.

Prior to 1993 all funding for the state pension program was provided by the individual state work units themselves; collective work units, because of their weaker financial position, had already had to consider alternative funding strategies. Liwan district, for example, when setting up a pension scheme for its collectives in 1985, had relied entirely on contributions from the participating *danwei*. By 1990 the economic condition of many of these collectives, combined with rapid increases in the number of their retirees, made it impossible for Liwan to meet its pension obligations. The 467 district collectives had a total labor force of 29,559, of whom 15,064 (51 percent) were retired! As a result of a financial restructuring carried out at the end of 1991, the municipal labor bureau, the district treasury, and the workers themselves joined the individual enterprises in making contributions to the collective pension funds. This new strategy netted the retirees an average monthly pension of 92.9 yuan, an increase of 12.85 yuan.[45]

Before the labor contract system was implemented, individual workers had not paid into their own retirement funds. Once it was introduced in Guangdong, however, contract workers each month contributed 3 percent of their pay. In 1990 new permanent workers fell under the same requirement, though permanent workers hired previously remained unaffected. Then in October 1991 the State Council announced plans for the eventual restructuring of the pension system. Under the new system, parts of which were put into effect in Guangdong in August 1993, all staff and workers (permanent, contract, and temporary) in units, regardless of ownership (state, collective, and foreign funded) and type of work (production, service, administration, culture, etc.), must contribute the equivalent of 2 percent of their monthly wages to the pension fund. Similarly, all units are required to contribute 2 percent of their monthly payroll to the pension fund.

A second reform governs the calculation of benefits. Starting in January 1994 the monthly pension is based, not solely on the worker's own previous wage, but also on current wages; that is, retirees are to receive a minimum pension equal to 30 percent (35 percent for *lixiu* cadres) of the average monthly wage for the current year in their locale. This base pension is to be augmented by a fixed percentage for each year the recipient contributed into the system.[46] These various reforms have greatly reduced the disparities in pension eligibility and benefits that characterized staff and workers of different tenure only ten years ago. The creation of a pension system that makes the worker rather than the enterprise or government department the owner of the account should remove one of the major obstacles to the free movement of labor across ownership systems.

The Danwei

For most urban residents the unit (*danwei*) or workplace is the most significant social organization beyond the family.[47] More than simply offering employment, it gives workers an identity in their own and others' minds. For example, a stranger arriving at the entrance or reception desk of a factory or government office is likely to be asked, "What unit are you from?" rather than "Who are you?" or "What do you want?" Similarly, a caller, especially one from a high-ranking unit, telephoning an office in another unit might simply announce, "This is Unit Such-and-Such" or "*I* am Unit Such-and-Such," even if he or she has a low-ranking position in the *danwei*. Identification of one's *danwei* membership is important because it immediately establishes one's position relative to the other and alerts the other to the possible consequences of acceding to or ignoring one's requests. For example, in 1980 a representative of my unit (Zhongshan University) and I attempted to purchase a ticket for me to go to Hong Kong. When we were curtly told that none was available, we remained at the counter, unsure how to proceed. The clerk, sensing he might be missing an opportunity, suddenly asked us what unit we were with. When we said Zhongshan University, he merely snorted and turned his back to us.

Although differences among units, particularly those involving the rights and opportunities of workers and staff, have been systematically lessened with the reforms, these differences, until very recently, were of overwhelming significance. Depending on their administrative level, their ownership system, and their function, units differ fundamentally in the resources they have and can make available to their workers (and, through their workers, to outsiders). For this reason until recently most young people have thought less about the kind of job they are likely to have and more about the kind of unit they want to join.

The higher its administrative level, the greater the resources to which a *danwei* has access.[48] To belong to a unit that is on the central budget, such as the customs service, national railway, or various ministries, is to enjoy the greatest access not only to income but also to such perquisites as housing. Next, in decreasing order of resource control, are provincial, municipal, (urban) district, and neighborhood (or street committee) units. The second important criterion used to distinguish among units is ownership system. During the Maoist period, urban work units were owned either by the state or by a collective. The major distinction between state and collective units is financial or, more specifically, budgetary. State units historically were funded out of the "one big pot," which, depending on administrative level, meant out of the central, provincial, or municipal budget. This is decidedly not the case for collective units, which are, in theory at least, completely responsible for their own profits and losses. If they lose money in their operations, they must either obtain a loan, merge with a profitable unit, or dissolve. The smallest collectives keep their costs down by not offering the same range of subsidies as units in the state sector or by cutting back on them. Their workers can lose their jobs if the collective does not recover quickly from its losses.

With the introduction of the reforms came new forms of ownership: joint, foreign, cooperative, and private. As their names suggest, the new work units, with the partial exception of joint ventures, derive their funds from nongovernmental sources. They depend on their profits for survival and, unless well connected, are highly vulnerable to tax assessments and other types of financial extractions. In the first few years of their existence, these *danwei* did not have to provide the full range of welfare benefits given workers in state *danwei*, but gradually they have been required to bring their practices in line with those of other enterprises.

The third criterion that distinguishes units is their function — whether their primary role is to generate profits or to provide public services, such as public administration, education, health care, and the maintenance of the urban infrastructure. Generally speaking, the service *danwei* were the more prestigious, because of their higher proportion of educated personnel, greater financial security, and closer association with the Communist Party. At first the economic reforms were intended to help sluggish enterprises become more profitable (or at least break even). But as profitability increased, the hierarchy of the *danwei* began to shift: nonstate enterprises began to outperform state enterprises, and profit-making enterprises began to provide higher wages to their workers than public service *danwei*.

Within each *danwei* there are additional distinctions based on position (job title), rank, and tenure. Formerly seniority and rank basically coincided, but now, with the new emphasis on specific qualifications, it is possible, though not very common, for someone junior in age and seniority to outrank elders. Although people in different ranks receive different salaries, income is not the most significant aspect of rank; rather rank establishes priority of access to scarce goods allocated by the *danwei*. Workers in a unit are distinguished by tenure, or the security of their employment; only permanency makes them eligible for the full range of unit-provided benefits, such as housing, employment for children, tickets to cultural events, and so forth.[49]

The unit looms large in the lives of urban residents for three reasons: it provides employment; it is (or has been) the source of a wide variety of goods and services not easily obtained elsewhere; and it is a mechanism through which political and social control is exercised. Let us consider these characteristics of the unit in more detail.

The *Danwei* as Employer

Because a *danwei* is a work unit, it is the primary source of its employees' income and fringe benefits. Prior to the relegitimation of the private sector a person without a work unit had no means of employment and was completely dependent on others (usually family members) for income and for access to other unit-provided goods and services. Being employed (in China as elsewhere) means more than simply having an income. Employment is also a source of self-esteem, a means by which one establishes oneself as an adult in the eyes of others, and a way of contributing to society.

As I indicated earlier, because unemployment, from the government's point of view, was politically unacceptable, membership in a *danwei* became virtually irrevocable. Redundant staff were kept on and paid even when there was no work for them to do. Individuals under a cloud because of political campaigns were often removed from their offices or from factory floors and sent home or to the countryside to change their thinking. They were seldom, however, discharged, nor were they permanently deprived of their wages. Most received their wages throughout the Cultural Revolution; those who did not usually received their back wages when they returned to work. The other side of irrevocable membership, however, has been that the worker has not been free to leave.

The major reason a *danwei* has been (and in many cases remains) inescapable is that until the 1980s job mobility was frowned upon and likely to be possible only when it served the interests of the *danwei* or the party. No new employer could or would consider hiring someone already working without examining the contents of his or her *dangan*, which until the opening of the talent exchanges was in the custody of the current employer. With the emergence of the private sector and a new commitment to profit making, some unit heads are prepared to overlook the absence of a *dangan* when they believe the individual will be of value to their enterprise. Even employers in the state sector (according to one such employer) are now willing to take this gamble, believing that once the original unit realizes the worker has taken a new job, it will give up, say "Forget it!" (*suan le*), and eventually forward the *dangan*. Nevertheless, many highly skilled workers, especially those who received their jobs through state assignment, believe themselves trapped. Here are a 33-year-old male educator's frank comments in 1991 about opportunities for job mobility in the field of higher education in Guangzhou.

There is not one faculty member who wouldn't choose to leave China if given the chance. The status of intellectuals in China is pathetic. The traditional precedence of brain work over manual labor has been completely reversed. Factory workers make three or four times the monthly income of professors and have better living accommodations as well. My own income is 120 yuan a month, and as a single person I am entitled to only 9 square meters of living space. The most living space a professor can aspire to, regardless of the size of his family, is 40 square meters.[50]

A professor can do little to improve his situation. For example, one cannot transfer to another university; there is no job market. Before Liberation Chinese used to talk about the three mountains that obstructed China's development as feudalism, imperialism, and bureaucracy, but now these three mountains have been renamed the *dangan* [dossier], *hukou* [household registration], and *danwei gongzi biao* [unit payroll]. Because university graduates are subject to unified assignment, normally to state units, they cannot easily leave. Were they to leave, they could not get another teaching job, for no unit could accept them. Universities and other state organs are allotted a specific amount of money to use for wages and are authorized to hire only a specified number of people each year. They cannot afford to hire anyone outside the budget because they have almost no other source of income. Any income that they do manage to scrounge up is used for the benefit of those already in the unit who are so badly underpaid!

The *Danwei* as Provider of Goods and Services

As indicated in Chapter 2, prior to the 1978 and subsequent reforms Chinese cities, where consumer goods were generally in short supply, experienced rationing. The work unit became the primary administrative mechanism for distributing both rationed and other scarce goods. In Guangzhou, although rationing has ended, work units continue their other distributive functions. Although some goods and services are available to all members of a unit, others are distributed according to a complex calculus of rank, seniority, merit (such as being a model worker), and, perhaps, personal relationships. All members of the work unit, for example, are eligible to receive packages of foodstuffs at the Lunar New Year or to attend films or dances sponsored on weekends by the work unit. Similarly, just before the start of the cold season some units allow everyone to bring their bed quilts in to be sent out for washing and fluffing. Other goods and services, however, are not generally available. Tickets to major cultural activities, such as the Sixth National Games held in Guangzhou in November 1987 and attended by then Party General Secretary Zhao Ziyang, are often distributed through work units.* Similarly, only a limited number of slots in a coveted

---

* Tickets were also distributed another way. The games, held in Tianhe Stadium, opened with the release of thousands of homing pigeons and thousands of balloons. Residents who raised homing pigeons were given one ticket for every ten birds they contributed to the cause. One household in the Family Study donated 30 birds and netted three tickets.

day-care center or kindergarten might be allocated to a particular *danwei*, which can then make them available to only a limited number of families.

Housing has been the most important good distributed by the work unit, although in the past few years the Chinese government has embarked on a course to cut the link between housing and employment. Nevertheless, the majority of Guangzhou residents realize that even today their best hope of moving into new, spacious housing is to work for a unit that provides housing (or, failing that, to live on a site destined to be taken over for housing construction). Living in unit-provided housing often means much more than simply having a place to live. When housing is located on the same site as the workplace, there is virtually no distinction between neighbors and workmates. Privacy is difficult to maintain, and family problems quickly come to the attention of superiors at work, just as problems at work quickly become known to neighbors.

This coincidence of workplace and living place occurs most frequently when the *danwei* has occupied a large campus-like site or when the *danwei* offices or factories and housing have been constructed at the same time. In *The Chinese Hospital* (1984) Gail Henderson and Myron Cohen describe Hubei Provincial Medical College and its Second Attached Hospital, a *danwei* of the first type in which they worked and lived for several months in 1979–80. In Guangzhou's Dongshan district, Zhongshan Medical College and its First Attached Hospital form a similar unit, as does Zhongshan University (in Haizhu district), where I lived for three months in 1980. At that time the campus was bounded on the north by the Pearl River, on the south by Xingang Road,[51] on the east by a shipbuilding factory, and on the west by the vegetable fields of a nearby village. In practice in 1980 faculty or staff members of Zhongshan University could meet almost all their needs on its grounds, which contained an elementary school, a clinic, a swimming pool, a restaurant, a service area with small shops specializing in minor repairs, haircuts, and canned or bottled goods as well as grain- and coal-rationing stations, and a pool of cars and drivers, to say nothing of housing, student dormitories, classrooms, and a library. To buy fresh produce required only going out to the main gate, where private vendors sat with their fresh vegetables, or taking a short bicycle ride down Qianjin Road, where a state and a large private market coexisted, to obtain meat and fish and a wider variety of fresh fruits and vegetables. Because the campus was and remains walled, anyone attempting to enter it by vehicle was readily noticed and, if conditions seemed to warrant it, challenged at the main gate.

Although the campus-style environments of schools and hospitals built before 1949 often allow some distance between dwellings, those built later are likely to be more crowded together. These newer units, many of them factories built in western Haizhu district, are located cheek by jowl with the several-story apartment blocks that house their workers. Units located in the center of the city, whether old or new, are less likely to have housing contiguous to the workplace, though there are scattered housing blocks that are under unit control. Because of the disproportionately high percentage of housing that is under the Housing Management Bureau (HMB) or privately owned in Guangzhou, the city's residents are less likely than those elsewhere in China to have neighbors who are also workmates; thus they are probably able to maintain somewhat more separation between work and private life.

The *Danwei* as a Mechanism of Political and Social Control

In addition to its various distributive functions the *danwei* also plays an important role in political mobilization, in enforcing compliance with a wide range of government policies, and in otherwise dominating the lives of its workers. Most *danwei* of any size contain a local branch of the Chinese Communist Party, whose members occupy all or most of the important leadership or managerial positions in the unit. Units whose work is in the political or intellectual sphere have a high proportion of party members, whereas those whose work is in (nonstrategic) production or distribution have a relatively low proportion. When the Central Committee sends documents for study to the local party branches, party members are responsible for communicating the relevant contents to the administrative hierarchy of the *danwei* (with which, as I have indicated, there is substantial overlap in membership) and, if appropriate, for mobilizing ordinary workers. This mobilization may take the form of organized study groups held after regular work hours in which the workers memorize various texts and/or discuss how the texts have helped or will help them to improve their work or their political attitude.[52] Alternatively it may require the workers to put all work aside for weeks or months and participate wholeheartedly in some political campaign, put up posters, criticize selected individuals, and join in massive public demonstrations as during the Cultural Revolution.[53]

In the late spring or early summer of 1980, for example, the provincial government issued a warning advising Chinese citizens to limit their contacts with foreigners. This warning might or might not have stemmed from government concerns about the activities of an American doctoral student who at that time was conducting anthropological research elsewhere in the province. In any case, it was clear that the personnel of our *danwei* had been duly warned to restrict their contacts, as two incidents illustrate. In the winter of 1979–80, several months before my planned stay in Guangzhou, I had briefly met in the United States a professor from Zhongshan University with whom I had seemed to hit it off. Although she could not accept my offer to tour a local shopping mall, her warmth suggested that I would have a friend when I arrived in Guangzhou later in the year. Yet during my stay, although she knew I was on campus, she never contacted me. Even more pointedly, when we once found ourselves accidentally walking toward each other, the sole occupants of a long shaded walkway from which we could not exit, she managed to walk past me with her eyes averted.

The second incident involved a student majoring in English who had been introduced to us by his English teacher, a "foreign expert." He was very knowledgeable and forthright, so that when we learned that he was a native of an area we would be visiting for several days, we requested (eventually insisting, since our request was initially ignored) that he be allowed to accompany us (at our expense) as a valuable resource person. He was allowed to accompany us but, we learned later, was told that he was to have no contact thereafter with us. Shortly before we were to leave the university to return to the United States, we ran into him near the foreign experts guesthouse. My husband tried to engage him in conversation and to encourage him to return with us to our residence. With evident reluctance, he walked a few steps with us, but as it became clear that our path would take us near the university administration building, he bolted without a word. Had these two encounters occurred on the street, away from the watchful eyes of the *danwei*, it is unlikely they would have taken quite the same form.

Although it is generally believed that political supervision became more lax during the 1980s, the unrest of both the winter of 1986–87 and the spring of 1989 served as a clarion call to conservatives, who attributed that unrest to failures in political indoctrination. As I noted in Chapter 4, in 1989, immediately after the end of the academic year and in the aftermath of the Tiananmen demonstrations, students were called back to school to study the collected works of Deng Xiaoping. Furthermore, intellectuals must continuously be prepared to verbalize their support for the party's interpretation of events. For example, one intellectual (a party member), who had visited the United States in the early 1990s, demonstrated on his return his support for the party line that the United States was directly involved in attempts to destabilize the Chinese government. At a party branch meeting at his unit (which was still dominated by leftists), he announced that all kinds of people are kidnapped in the United States: rich people for ransom, spies by the government, high foreign officials whom the U.S. government wants to compromise, and potential converts by religious groups. He claimed that he himself had nearly been kidnapped during his visit. Another intellectual (also a party member) at the same unit, when required to comment on his experiences in the United States not long thereafter, limited himself to describing the good "service attitude" of salesclerks in a department store, thus subtly supporting the goals of the reformers. More open dissent is costly, for each person's political attitude is duly noted by superiors and peers, recorded in his or her dossier (*dangan*), and in all likelihood recalled when the person asks the unit's assistance in obtaining a transfer, a position for a child, or housing.

The *danwei* also supports the implementation of state policies and regulations, such as those concerning migration, rationing, and birth control. For example, a work unit in Guangzhou cannot hire whomever it wants without regard for the household registration system. A unit has to be able to make a strong case that no one with urban registration in Guangzhou is available to fill a particular position before it may hire someone from outside. The *danwei* issues ration coupons (though this function has disappeared in Guangzhou) and, as we saw in Chapter 3, is also the locus of rewards for people following, and punishments for those defying, the one-child family policy. When workplace and residence are the same, supervision can be all the more pervasive. This enforcement role has probably contributed substantially to the authoritarian image of the Chinese workplace, but as Andrew Walder points out,[54] this authority is exercised less through force than through a complex net of mutual obligations that bind the individual worker to his or her immediate superiors and thereby to the unit as a whole.

Worker dependence is the critical issue in the dynamic behind any authority relationship in a unit. The absence (until after 1978) of alternative employment and of housing and a multitude of goods and services meant that the worker was entirely at the mercy of immediate supervisors for access to highly valued scarce goods. Thus workers' own self-interest has motivated them to keep on the good side of their superiors (without alienating their workmates). Superiors, for their part, have been inclined to take seriously the various social welfare functions that have come to be associated with the *danwei*. To some extent this attitude is the logical outcome of their own self-interest: because they cannot easily discharge disgruntled and unmotivated workers, they must try to keep them reasonably happy. But Chinese supervisors genuinely believe that the unit should try to meet a wide variety of needs that employers elsewhere would probably consider none of their business.

For example, most units still feel a responsibility to employ their workers' children if they are unable to obtain work otherwise. Foreign investors are quickly socialized to these expectations. In 1987 the foreign partner in a joint venture in Guangzhou expressed his amazement on learning that his factory, producing or assembling automobiles, was situated on land ample enough to support a vegetable crop. His partner insisted that the joint venture raise its own vegetables and use them in the unit canteen. He then learned that the surplus vegetables would be used in a roadside restaurant or sold at roadside stands in front of the factory by the children of the employees. He believed that several other creative employment schemes were still in the pipeline. Such ventures are off the state plan, either self-supported or funded out of the profits of the parent *danwei*.

Units are also expected to function as social work agencies. They intercede on a worker's behalf with other units, such as the HMB or the courts (and vice versa—they supervise the worker for the courts), and they become involved in the resolution of family disputes.[55] Furthermore, termination of employment does not mean an end to these social welfare functions. Beyond continuing health insurance and providing pensions, the *danwei* remains completely responsible for the well-being of any of its childless retirees and must both assure them of a minimum standard of living and housing and meet all the costs of their medical care, including that of a personal attendant when necessary. Thus from the point of view of workers the *danwei* not only supervises but also looks after them, creating a psychological bond that can be difficult to break. The section that follows looks at how people decide whether a particular *danwei* is good or bad.

Good and Bad Danwei

Everyone in China is aware that just as individuals are constrained by circumstances beyond their control, so too are *danwei*. Thus no one expects a street committee–run collective to provide the same benefits as, say, a provincially administered hospital. Nor do people expect units to ignore the larger political context in which they must survive. If the government calls for political study sessions or stricter enforcement of certain regulations, people may moan and groan, but they do not generally blame the *danwei*. Instead, when people evaluate a *danwei*, they look at how well it attempts to meet the needs of its workers in those areas where it actually has some discretion. In short, a good unit is a humane and compassionate one that will decide a difficult issue in the worker's favor. A bad unit is one that puts its own interests first. These attitudes, obviously held by workers, are not uncommon even among managers, as the case that follows illustrates.

Humane Units

Case 1. Mr. Zhang was the 40ish manager of a *danwei* of ambiguous type; although it was formally considered a collective, it was in a sense both a collective and a state enterprise. Not long ago the unit was hived off a provincial administrative unit and told to go it alone—to become a service company responsible for its own profits and losses. It received its initial capitalization, personnel, and various other assets from its parent unit, but was expected to meet its payroll and benefits out of its own earnings. Unfortunately, the staff did not have the vaguest notion how to function in a competitive environment. Mr. Zhang was advised by his superiors to fire the incompetent.

Had it involved only one or two people, maybe I could have done it, but to really change the situation would have required dropping about half the staff. Almost every one of these people is over 40 and would have nowhere to go. I've known these people for most of my work life. They haven't done anything wrong. I told my leader that if he insisted I fire them, then *I* would leave the unit rather than comply.

Ultimately the parent *danwei* dissolved this unprofitable company and redistributed its workers to other subordinate units.

But before it did so, Mr. Zhang had to wrestle with another headache — how best to allocate his unit's medical insurance funds. For ordinary outpatient care each member of the unit automatically received 35 yuan a month; the unit covered basic inpatient costs. As I noted in Chapter 3, however, many inpatient costs are not normally covered; this was the experience of an older man in Mr. Zhang's company who was in the hospital with cancer. His wife came to Mr. Zhang, begging him to reimburse the family for certain additional costs, including gifts to doctors, payment for an attendant to look after the patient in the hospital, and airfare for that attendant to fly to Guangzhou.

All told, his wife wanted 600 yuan reimbursed. She herself ran a small shop or stall and couldn't look after her husband in the hospital. They *had* to put out this money. I decided to reimburse her, but some people griped. They resented treatment that was not going to save this person's life — so why pay? This kind of petty thinking is very common in financially weak units.

In both situations, Mr. Zhang based his decision on his sense of fairness to the workers and not on the financial consequences to the *danwei*. He put compassion before profits, and the company failed.

Case 2. Mrs. Gui is a 52-year-old widow who spent most of 1992–93 looking after her husband as he slowly succumbed to brain cancer. During the last several months of his illness he was virtually immobile, incontinent, and unable to speak, though he could accept food by mouth. Mrs. Gui had hired an attendant to look after him 24 hours a day in the Guangzhou #1 People's Hospital, but she herself also stayed at his bedside 24 hours a day, spending the night on a cot. In the midst of all this, Mrs. Gui confessed that she had not shown her face at her unit (a provincial nonprofit) for months, and after her husband's death she confessed that during the nearly two-year course of his illness, she had been unable to carry out her work at all. Yet her *danwei* did not complain, nor did it suggest she go on leave or dock her pay. In fact, it even contributed 500 yuan toward her husband's hospital care. Why? On the face of it, the circumstances were exceptional; the unit was highly unlikely to face a similar event again, and Mrs. Gui's devotion and self-sacrifice were inspirational. But the unit did not actually have an assignment for Mrs. Gui (or for many of its other staff). She could, in fact, read and write reports or not as she liked; she would receive her salary in either case. Even a decade after the start of the reforms Mrs. Gui still had an "iron rice bowl," and therefore her *danwei* could be accommodating without obvious cost to itself.

Case 3. Mrs. Bo works as a freelance *baomu* in the orthopedic section of a hospital in Liwan district, providing personal care, performing tasks that nurses regard as family responsibilities. She is responsible for up to eight patients at a time, each of whom pays either 5 or 10 yuan a day, depending on the amount of care required. Altogether Mrs. Bo earns about 50 yuan a day, but she does so by being on duty 21 out of every 24 hours. Except for the three hours a day she takes off to check up on affairs at home, she eats and sleeps in the same room as her patients. Yet the hospital is not Mrs. Bo's legal *danwei*. In fact, Mrs. Bo is on the official roll of another unit for which she used to work. It has retained her name, though it is no longer paying her any wages. By retaining her name, however, the *danwei* allows her to enjoy certain important fringe benefits, in particular the right of her child to attend the unit's *quantuo* (overnight preschool). Without this benefit (for which she must nevertheless pay), Mrs. Bo would be unable to work through the night at the hospital. This arrangement, in which she is employed as a private worker yet retains a position in a *danwei*, is one of the new phenomena that have emerged to permit state workers to experiment with nonstate employment. Ideally, if they are successful in the private sector, their names will eventually be removed from the state's rolls. If they are unsuccessful, however, they might be allowed to reassume their old position.

Selfish Units

Case 1. Although 77-year-old Mr. Shen had had only two years of schooling, he learned enough characters to be able to perform his job of compounding the various medical ingredients that make up traditional Chinese prescriptions. His 60 years of service were acknowledged by a special document displayed on the wall of his one-room dwelling and signed by Peng Zhen (chair of the National People's Congress in Beijing in the 1980s). It had not been Mr. Shen's aim to work so long. In fact, he had tried to retire when he reached the age of 60 and again when he reached the age of 67, but his unit refused to let him go. Finally, in desperation, at the age of 76 he went over the heads of his immediate superiors and presented his retirement request to a higher-up. That leader was outraged by the treatment Mr. Shen was receiving, scolded Mr. Shen's supervisors, and allowed Mr. Shen to retire immediately. What kind of unit would refuse to allow a 76-year-old worker to retire? One that had no prospects of finding a replacement. Mr. Shen's job was so repetitive, boring, and unlikely to lead to advancement that no younger person would consider it. The medicine shop could replace him only if the local labor bureau assigned someone in his place, but the labor bureau no longer had this kind of power.

Case 2. Mrs. Ming, who is about 30 years old, had an experience similar to that of Mr. Shen — a unit that would not let go. She had been assigned to a factory that made monosodium glutamate and worked there for more than ten years before leaving on her own initiative in 1990. The factory was not happy to see her go because it has had trouble finding new workers — the work there is simply too laborious. Even though Mrs. Ming had left the factory more than a year ago, it still had her *dangan*. She said it was more *mafan*, "troublesome," than anyone could imagine trying to get it back. Although they refused to release it, Mrs. Ming was hired by the street committee office without any fuss because she knew someone there who was willing to overlook the missing dossier. Apparently they needed someone (residents committee work is not popular), and she was eminently qualified because she already knew most of the residents.

Mrs. Ming wanted to leave the factory because it was located on the south side of Guangzhou in Haizhu district, a 50-minute bicycle ride each way — too far to allow her to look after her family. She also had to work different shifts, including the night shift. When Mrs. Ming left the factory, her years of work there could no longer count toward her pension. She now has just a year's worth of work counting for her in her new job. She also suffered a drop in wages and a shrinkage in welfare benefits. Her factory did not offer housing, so she lost nothing there. Although her work hours at the residents committee are longer than her work hours at the factory, the job is much more convenient to her home. Mrs. Ming's situation epitomizes the dilemma (and the tactics) of *danwei* that have difficulty attracting workers in a free labor market. One unit, attempting to restrict labor mobility, illegally retained her *dangan*, and another, attempting to promote labor mobility, illegally hired her without it.

Case 3. Finally, there are corrupt *danwei*, or at least corrupt individuals in strategic positions within them. When 35-year-old Mr. Ruan returned from study overseas in 1988, he joined a prestigious unit under the direct control of the central government in Beijing. He was temporarily assigned to sub-standard housing with the expectation that he would shortly be moved to accommodations appropriate to his rank. Yet as the months went by, nothing happened, and all his efforts to have his case heard went unheeded. Gradually friends and colleagues suggested he pay a private visit to the person in charge of housing assignments. Mr. Ruan began to get the picture. During the visit he learned what was expected of him. The housing office was short of foreign exchange; surely Mr. Ruan had acquired foreign currency while abroad and had brought some of it back to China. That being the presumed case, all he had to do to obtain his housing was exchange his money for 1,000 yuan of the housing office's money. The precise exchange rate for this private transaction was unclear, but of course the legal rate would have been well below the black market rate. Either way this was an illegal transaction, but Mr. Ruan did not see that he had any choice. He paid up and got his housing.

As all the cases demonstrate, *danwei* have not necessarily responded to the economic reforms as planners hoped. State units with financial backup (or the expectation of financial backup) are still soft on the workers—Mr. Zhang could not sacrifice his incompetent old associates or deny the honest request for reimbursement of health care expenses from the wife of a colleague. Mrs. Gui's unit was also prepared to overlook her two-year unofficial leave of absence, just as Mrs. Bo's unit pretended she was there, thus protecting her right to the services of its *quantuo*. Disadvantaged units, however, put their own needs ahead of their workers' interests. Unable to attract workers, they refuse to let the old ones retire or the young ones transfer, regardless of the regulations on retirement and labor mobility. Short of foreign exchange, they force their workers (such as Mr. Ruan) to make it available to them by withholding their rightful benefits.

Employment Patterns

In 1992 in Guangzhou city proper 10.9 percent of the population was employed in the primary sector (agriculture, forestry, animal husbandry, fishing, and water conservancy). The vast majority of this population lives in formerly suburban Baiyun district, the largest and most rural of Guangzhou's eight urban districts. The secondary sector employed 42.9 percent of the population (34.8 percent in industry and 8.1 percent in construction), and the tertiary, 46.2 percent. The most important fields in the tertiary sector are commerce, accounting for 15.6 percent of total employment; transport and communication, 8.0 percent; real estate supervision, public utilities, and other resident services, 6.8 percent; education and culture, 5.0 percent; and government, party, and mass organizations, 4.1 percent.[56]

Almost no urban youths, unless they are already holders of rural household registration, seek employment in agriculture. Nearly everyone expects to find work in the secondary or tertiary sectors.

Excluding agricultural workers, in 1989 in Guangzhou city proper 72 percent of urban workers belonged to state units, 19 percent to collectives, and 5 percent to other (private or joint ventures); 4 percent of the employed population consisted of individual entrepreneurs (*geti hu*).[57] The latter two categories have been steadily expanding since 1979 and, compared with the state and collective categories, contain a disproportion of youth hired under the labor contract system. For example, in 1990 in Guangzhou as a whole (data for the city proper are not separately available) only 2 percent of the total employed population but 12 percent of contract workers fell into these two categories. By contrast, in Shenzhen, the Special Economic Zone that came into existence with the reforms, 27 percent of the total employed population and 35 percent of contract workers were employed in joint ventures or private and individual businesses.[58] All these figures suggest that high rates of state and collective employment are the legacy of past policies whereas new employment is increasingly being found outside these two sectors. The retirement of older workers and the transfer or resignation of others will gradually reduce this legacy. A comparison of Tables 5.1 and 5.3 reveals that in 1990 in Guangzhou city proper there were 45,741 entrances into the state sector but 63,747 exits, for a net loss of 18,006 persons.

There is more than a touch of flimflam to these figures, however. First, temporary workers are not included in the tables. Because they are not entitled to the full range of benefits, increasing their numbers at the expense of contract and permanent workers is one way of hiring and not hiring at the same time, for temporaries do not go on the books in quite the same way. Interestingly, it is not unusual for state units to retire and then immediately rehire as temporaries workers who reach the age of (now) mandatory retirement. Since retirees are already entitled to 60 to 75 percent of their basic salary and *butie*, all the unit has to do to regain an experienced worker is add to the basic wage, bonus, and *jintie* out of its own pocket to make up the difference between the preretirement wage and the pension. This type of rehire is likely only when workers have valued skills or when the units have difficulty attracting new workers. Second, as note *c* to Table 5.3 indicates, at least 8 percent of those counted as leaving state work units are in fact on a temporary leave that might or might not become permanent.

To get a sense of employment patterns and employment mobility in contemporary Guangzhou, I analyzed the households in the Family Study whose members entered and left the labor force (Table 5.4) and changed jobs.[59] Although the bias of the sample (the disproportionate representa-

TABLE 5.3

Reasons for Leaving State Work Units in Urban Districts of Guangzhou, 1990

	N	Pct.
Retirement [a]	23,557	37%
Transferred to joint venture	11,514	18
Discharged [b]	11,296	18
Dismissed	2,308	
Name removed from roll	8,145	
Expelled	843	
Contract expiration or termination	6,239	10
On leave [c]	3,306	5
Off payroll but position retained	2,008	3
Died	1,403	2
Transferred to collective	1,267	2
Resigned	855	1
Other (unspecified)	2,302	4
TOTAL	63,747	100

SOURCE: Guangzhou Shi Tongji Ju, *Guangzhou tongji nianjian 1991* (Statistical yearbook of Guangzhou 1991) (China: Zhongguo Tongji Chubanshe, 1991), p. 359.

[a] Includes 1,556 *lixiu* cadres.

[b] These are grouped together because the outcome for the affected individual is the same: loss of job. According to one informant, "dismissed" (*citui*) implies the worker was simply let go without a fuss; "name removed from roll" implies the individual refused to go gracefully; "expelled" (*kaichu*) means the individual lost his job as a punishment for some offense.

[c] "On leave" implies an indefinite absence, whereas "off payroll but position retained" implies a fixed term of absence. Such absences are frequently permitted to allow state sector employees to try their hand at the private sector.

tion of the elderly) means that these statistics cannot be generalized to the Guangzhou population as a whole, the patterns they reveal are suggestive. Those entering the labor force were, with one exception, in their late teens or early twenties. The one exception was a man in his 30s whose *dangan* had been confiscated by the police for four years following his arrest for complicity in a scheme to smuggle antiques out of the country. Those retiring were mostly women in their 50s or men of 60, whereas those newly entering postretirement positions (having been out of the labor force as a result of retirement at the time of the first interview) or leaving them were (in all but one case) in their 70s.

To some extent the private sector serves as a haven for the elderly, who are almost as likely to seek postretirement employment in the private sector as in the public. For example, Mr. Zhou, a man in his 70s who had retired from a small collective haircutting shop, was in 1987 being allowed by his former employer to come in on a semiregular basis to cut hair. By 1991, however, the collective had been contracted out to a manager, who was determined to make the shop truly profitable.[60] He dismissed Mr. Zhou, whose skills were limited to the simple cuts favored by the elderly, because he brought in little income. With a total monthly retirement income of a mere 88 yuan, Mr. Zhou had no choice but to set himself up privately. In an open space behind his residence he opened his "shop," which consists of a windowsill where he keeps his combs, scissors, and mug. Some tiny chairs and benches (each capable of seating only a single person) are off to the side. Mr. Zhou sighed as he described how unscrupulous young hairdressers are able to make a living.

Some people can earn 1,000 yuan setting a bride's hair. I saw a story in the *Yangcheng Wanbao* [the evening paper] of a couple from abroad who were charged this much. When they complained to the police, the hairdresser had to pay a fine. . . . I earn about 7–8 yuan a day. I'm down here almost all the time. Some days are better than others. Right now because of the New Year nobody wants to get a haircut. . . . I charge 1 yuan. . . . No, *very few* people give tips. I deal with retired people, and they don't have much money.

Although the ages of those entering and leaving the labor force are relatively predictable, the ages of those simply changing jobs, that is, *danwei*, are less so. Of the 39 individuals who changed units, 15 were under 30, 16 were between 30 and 49, 7 were in their 50s, and one was in his 70s. The nature of the job changes clearly varies with age. For example, young people change jobs easily because their contracts expire, giving them the opportunity to sample other kinds of work. These young people are likely to be

TABLE 5.4
Work Force Entries and Exits, by Sector, for Households in Guangzhou,
January 1988 to January 1991

	Public	Private	Unspecified	Total
Entered labor force	5	1	5	11
Unemployed	3	1	2	6
Retired	15	0	2	17
Rehired	6	0	0	
Found Other Work	0	0	2	
Exited labor force	9	0	0	
Postretirement work[a]	7	6	1	14
Rejoined labor force	3	1	0	
Reexited labor force	4	5	1	
TOTAL	30	8	10	48

SOURCE: The Guangzhou Family Study. In the 200 households 48 people entered or exited the labor force.

  [a] Applicable only to individuals already retired at the time of the first interview in 1987. "Rejoined" indicates that the person subsequently rejoined the labor force. "Reexited" indicates that the person had been working following retirement but has since left the labor force.

those with only a junior middle school education; many senior middle school graduates and postsecondary graduates obtain their positions under unified assignment. All the people in their 50s who changed jobs were men, and most, but not all, of them were being promoted to senior positions in other state units; for example, one man went from party secretary of one educational institution to party secretary of another. In this regard the different retirement ages for men and women probably result in discrimination against women, for the unit gains little benefit by promoting them into senior positions since they retire five to ten years earlier than men and would not serve long enough to make much of an impact. Even when changing jobs, people tend to remain within the same sector. Of the 29 cases for which sector movement is identifiable (ten of the job changes were unspecified), 18 people (83 percent) took a new job in the same sector as their old one (intrasector movement); of the five people changing sectors, all went from the public to the private. Six people changed jobs within the private sector. The two cases that follow give an account of life under the new employment system.

Miss Lin is eighteen years old and a duly registered urban resident of Guangzhou who left school following graduation from junior middle school, when she was not yet sixteen. She had no interest in continuing school and told her mother so when she was in the second year of junior middle school, asking her not to press (*bi*) her about this. Neither Miss Lin's older brother nor her older sister had gone beyond junior middle school. Miss Lin's father died when she was only twelve, and besides not liking school, she felt that by going out to work she would lighten her mother's burden. Even though married, her older sister had been contributing some money to her mother's household, but when Miss Lin went out to work, the sister cut back her contribution. Miss Lin's brother still lives at home but is not yet married.

Miss Lin has held four jobs since leaving school — all of them temporary positions. The first and the one that she most enjoyed was working as a switchboard operator. She next spent some time at the Nanfang Department Store, took another job that I cannot remember, and now serves as a waitress in a large restaurant in a hotel owned by one of the Special Economic Zones. Miss Lin explained her passage through four jobs in three years as a consequence of her wish to look around and see what society is like. When I asked her what she thought of society, she replied that it is *fuza* (literally "complicated" but carrying the connotation of unwholesome or unsavory complications). Indeed, this was precisely what she meant, I realized, when she explained why she liked being a switchboard operator. Miss Lin pointed out that a service person has contact with all kinds of people; in the morning the young hoodlums and other undesirable types make all kinds of comments that are impossible to avoid. If they make these comments to you on the phone while you are operating a switchboard, they know only your voice and not what you look like. When they start making improper remarks, like "My room number is . . . ," you can just cut the connection, but when you work in a restaurant, you cannot just cut contact. You have to take their order and serve their meal. It was clear that she found this aspect of her work very trying.

I frequently ate in this restaurant in the evening in a quiet alcove at a private booth, where I could write up my interview notes while they were still fresh in my mind. One evening I overheard another patron freely conducting his business on a cellular phone in the next booth. After assuring the caller that he could speak freely — that the phone call could not be traced because it was being made on a cellular phone — he asked which girl the caller wanted and his location. On learning that the caller was in Foshan, a neighboring city, he assured him that he could get a girl over there in about a half hour. It is easy to understand the hassles Miss Lin has to put up with in the course of her work.

Unlike Miss Lin, the Yang family has been trying to make a go of it in the private sector, but the experience has proved difficult. In 1987, 53-year-old Mr. Yang ran his own business repairing motor vehicles. His 28-year-old son, who never completed upper middle school, was studying driving with the aim of becoming a taxi driver. Within less than four years the Yang ventures had all collapsed. In 1991, 56-year-old Mrs. Yang, who in the interim had retired and immediately been rehired by her unit (a kindergarten), offered the following analysis:

The more open the system, the worse things have become. Everyone is motivated to make money any way they can. Drivers are terrible — failing in their responsibility to get their vehicles repaired. Drivers used to just take their vehicles to my husband's station for repairs, but in the past five or six years all kinds of people, including *leng jai* [C. literally "clever boys" but carrying the connotation of slickness], who falsely claim to know how to do repairs, are setting themselves up as masters. Now that there are so many repair stations, the drivers require anyone wanting to do the repairs to pay them 100 yuan for the privilege. To make up this money all you have to do is pad the repair bill, and the unit owning the vehicle will give you back your 100 yuan.

But Mr. Yang was not quite up to this kind of competition. Consequently he had fewer and fewer repair jobs, and his station failed. He then attempted to open another one elsewhere, but that failed too.

In the meantime, when the Yang son completed his driving course, he and a friend jointly leased a taxi — each driving it twelve hours a day. They had to put up a hefty security deposit for the duration of their lease; only if they served out the lease would they get the money back. In addition, they guaranteed the taxi company 150 yuan a day (75 yuan per shift), or 4,500 yuan a month, and were responsible for gas and repairs. Mrs. Yang commented with a sigh:

Think about it—the vehicle never gets to rest. [It was not new to start with.] Nobody stops to do any maintenance until something goes wrong, and, of course, several things go wrong at once. This is loose and that is broken. The place you take it might find even more things wrong with it and not have the necessary parts.

Her son and his partner had to give up driving, but the family did have a backup plan for the son to operate a small shop from the front of their ground-floor dwelling, which faced onto the street. To this end in 1989 the Yangs had had a one-story structure with a shop-front window added to their living space, but they had not reckoned with their status as tenants in a privately owned building. The owner's representative, who lives on the third floor, objected (at the instigation, the Yangs suspect, of their co-tenant on the ground floor) to their opening a shop. Both the Yang men are currently reduced to doing casual labor while Mrs. Yang and her daughter-in-law hold on to their jobs in the state sector.

Conclusions

The changing organization of employment since the start of the reforms has been intended to revitalize the economy without generating social unrest. Specific objectives have been to reduce youthful unemployment and to increase productivity in the state sector through a variety of incentives. The spur of competition has been applied to both workers and managers, who are increasingly expected to generate the profits that mean bonuses and to assume more of their real expenses. With piece rates and bonuses workers can directly affect the amount they earn, and the labor contract system lets enterprises get rid of poor performers or excess labor. At the same time, new workers' wages are now subject to deductions for their future pensions, and work units are backing out of providing housing and struggling to limit their health insurance costs. In periods of serious inflation (in 1987–88 and again in the early 1990s) most workers, no matter how well they have fared, feel uncomfortably exposed financially. This problem is most serious for those hired under the labor contract system and for the self-employed, who must meet their expenses out of whatever income they generate. The elderly whose pensions are small or whose preretirement (but not postretirement) income included a large percentage of bonus money also feel the financial pinch.

From the workers' point of view one of the best things about the reforms is the opportunity to choose a field of work. It is a great relief for those changing jobs within the same sector to find a workplace closer to home or one that makes better use of their talents, and for many who shift to the private sector, escaping the oppressive political supervision of the *danwei* can be a special bonus. Although the cases of Mr. Zhou and the Yangs suggest that workers in the private sector do not do well, they represent only part of the story. Vogel, for example, describes one Guangzhou family that opened a tailor shop and was so successful that in 1986 they paid 50,000 yuan in taxes, and a couple who started out selling Chinese sausages from a stall and wound up with a restaurant employing over 30 workers.[61] Successful entrepreneurs (though on a lesser scale) can be found even among the households in the Family Study, for example, a middle-aged couple who have gone into the wholesale clothing trade and a young man who purchased a new pickup truck (on which he lavished considerable attention) to start a delivery service. But these entrepreneurs remain vulnerable to economic downturns in a way that state workers (such as Mrs. Gui) by and large do not.

6 | *Leisure Activities*

Whether the economic reforms have brought increased leisure to China's urban residents is difficult to say. Certainly the amount of discretionary time available has increased as people have been relieved of tedious tasks that occupied their nonwork time in the past. With the loosening of restrictions on commerce and the development of the private sector, Guangzhou residents no longer have to spend so much time meeting basic needs: they no longer have to stand in long lines for rationed goods, struggle to get things repaired, or scour state stores for clothing or ordinary household items. The elimination of rationing, the return of the small repair business (along with the increasing ownership of laborsaving household appliances), and the expansion of commerce have made it easier to meet basic needs and still have time left over.

Furthermore, the official workweek was cut from 48 to 44 hours in early 1994 and from 44 to 40 hours in May 1995.[1] This reduction, however, has not necessarily led to increased interest in leisure. For many workers it has simply expanded the time available for a "second job." Certainly individual entrepreneurs will not reduce their hours because of this legislation. Given that in the past workers in collectives and foreign enterprises have routinely worked far more than the number of hours allowed, it is likely they will continue to do so. Nevertheless, in principle workers now have more time available to use as they like.

The economic reforms, besides leading to the development of commerce and the spread of laborsaving devices, have also had a profound effect on the operation and content of the mass media, which play an important part in the typical urban resident's daily life.[2] Newspapers and radio and television stations, like factories and schools, have been made financially responsible for generating more and more of their own funds. They have accomplished this goal primarily by selling advertising. Advertisers spend money, however, only when they are reasonably sure that people are reading, listening to, or watching the relevant medium. Their desire to reach the broadest audience possible has attuned them to program ratings.[3] Thus the new financial regimen has led directly to a change in the articles or programs presented to audiences. This chapter examines this fare later in detail. But first it considers what leisure was like before the introduction of the reforms.

Until the 1980s urban residents of Guangzhou confronted few options when deciding how to spend their leisure time. They were constrained by a relative lack of free time, by the narrow range of activities considered permissible, and by practices affecting access to entertainment. Participating in the labor force, in the recent past as now, consumed an enormous amount of time and energy. Not only do most urban workers still work 40 hours a week, but they also face time-consuming commutes by bicycle or public transportation. Although workers housed adjacent to the workplace do not have this additional burden, other household members employed elsewhere can have long commutes to their workplaces. In the Family Study some couples were forced to live separately (in Guangzhou) at least part of the time because of the inconvenience involved in getting to work. Given the historical problem of job mobility, permanent workers cannot easily seek more convenient work, but they frequently use the forced separations to negotiate with their units for transfer.

The decade of the Cultural Revolution was characterized by a repressive atmosphere. Cultural works based on traditional themes were condemned for inculcating feudal values — for example, those that encouraged respect for the old class system by portraying "good" gentry — whereas works from the West were condemned as bourgeois. The only works deemed suitable for public consumption were those glorifying socialist values, patriotism, and loyalty to Mao. A limited repertoire of operas, songs, and skits was endlessly recycled, and the audience soon knew the works by heart. Even with the economic reforms, screenwriters, directors, and performers still fall under the scrutiny of the Ministry of Radio, Film, and Television, and movie theaters, the stage, and the mass media remain under government control.

Foreign investors, however, have challenged this official monopoly by financing creative proposals in filmmaking and popular music that cannot obtain official backing. In some cases these joint venture productions find an audience first (and possibly only) overseas. For example, Hong Kong–funded Zhang Yimou's *Raise the Red Lantern* received an Academy Award nomination for best foreign-language film in 1991 but was not authorized for domestic release until the autumn of 1992. Indeed, Chinese theaters have not been among the beneficiaries of the reforms. Attendance at movie theaters dropped from 21 billion in 1982 to just 4.5 billion in 1991, primarily because of competition from television.[4] Foreign-funded popular music (underground rock), however, is consumed almost entirely in the domestic market.[5]

During the Cultural Revolution the Chinese population gained access to entertainment in several ways. A resident of Guangzhou could simply buy a ticket to a movie, but admission to other entertainment was likely to depend on rank and unit membership. Works considered inappropriate for the masses were not necessarily forbidden to everyone. People working in culture needed to know (within limits) what was going on in the field and to keep abreast of technological innovations abroad. Indeed, one of the leaders of the Cultural Revolution, Jiang Qing, Mao's wife and a onetime film actress, was reported to view many foreign films.[6] But only the most politically trustworthy were likely to have access to such foreign works. Those with a high status in a work unit had a better chance of getting a coveted ticket to public concerts or other stage entertainment, because government organs or other large work units often purchased blocks of tickets for distribution either as rewards to model workers, or on the basis of rank, or by similar criteria.

Even more important than giving their members access to public entertainment, work units frequently provided entertainment themselves. During the summer of 1980, for example, Zhongshan University erected an outdoor screen and set up a movie projector every weekend to show its staff and workers current Chinese films. Hundreds of people sat on straw mats or on folding stools at these showings, complaining about the mosquitoes. Even now when a great deal of public entertainment is available to anyone willing to pay for it, work units continue to sponsor movies, day trips for retirees, and dances or karaoke competitions for their workers as well as special holiday events.

For most working adults, before and since the implementation of the economic reforms, finding things to do in their free time has not been an issue. The activities they most frequently indulge in are logical extensions of everyday life such as chatting with neighbors, going for evening strolls, visiting relatives, reading newspapers, and sitting at home watching television (as early as 1980 half the households in Guangzhou owned a television; see Table 2.3). Those most likely to take a serious approach to leisure or entertainment are the young and unmarried, retirees, and people in business for whom entertaining partners and clients is part of business.

The favorite activities of the young and unmarried vary by sex and educational level. Like their elders young people chat with neighbors, visit relatives, and watch television, but they also listen to popular music or watch videocassettes from Hong Kong, Taiwan, and elsewhere. Because of crowded housing conditions, however, groups of young people spend much of their time together in public spaces. Young women, regardless of educational level, go window-shopping, stroll about, or stop for snacks at fast-food shops. Although some young men indulge in these same activities, those with less education may also spend time gambling or watching others gamble. Although gambling is officially illegal, knots of male cardplayers can be seen during lunch breaks and in the early evening at most parks. So long as money is not visible, the authorities are not likely to intervene.

Retired people also gamble, mostly playing mah-jongg in their own homes with their neighbors while the working adults and school-age children are elsewhere. Retired people are viewed as entitled to relax and enjoy themselves after all their years of hard work. In reality, however, they live lives of leisure only if their family situation permits. Older men are better able to realize the ideal than older women, who might still find themselves responsible for marketing, cooking, picking up grandchildren from day care, and looking after a husband's needs. Hobbies, such as tending plants or raising carp or songbirds, are almost entirely the province of men. Both sexes, however, take seriously the need to preserve their health, and most who are physically able rise early several days a week to exercise in a nearby park. There both men and women — as couples, in mixed-sex groups, or in single-sex groups — can be seen practicing *taiji* (a series of meditative movements derived from the martial arts, sometimes known in the West as shadowboxing), doing stretching exercises, and even participating in aerobic dancing classes. After these activities the men usually go to a nearby teahouse to drink tea and read the newspaper. Increasingly they are joined by their female peers, who until the last few years would have hesitated to be seen so obviously idle. The women stop at the market on their way home to pick up vegetables and meat or fish for the noon meal.

Ordinary urban residents see the expensive restaurants and night clubs, with karaoke equipment and prostitutes, that have sprung up all over urban China as places of employment rather than entertainment. Among the few who can generally afford the prices charged by such fancy establishments are officials whose units actually pick up the check, visitors from abroad (including business representatives and returning relatives), and the newly rich private entrepreneurs. The average person in Guangzhou dines at these restaurants only as a guest — when a relative returns or a wedding banquet takes place.

The remainder of this chapter focuses on the leisure activities of daily life and on those that are seasonal, such as the celebration of traditional and official holidays.

The Mass Media

Prior to the economic reforms the mass media, including films, newspapers, radio, and television, depended almost entirely on their sponsoring national and provincial government departments for funds. Their role was primarily to support the policies of the party and the government and to educate the Chinese population as concerned and responsible citizens. To ensure that the content of articles and programs presented by the mass media conformed to official guidelines, only the most politically reliable individuals were appointed to such positions as editor or head of a broadcasting station. Similarly, reporters and production crews were required to have a correct understanding of their mission. Because the government had a monopoly on publishing and broadcasting, cultural workers and audiences had almost nowhere else to turn.

To win an audience, however, newspapers and radio/television programs could not focus solely on their supporting or uplifting roles. Consequently, the mass media also took on a public service role, publishing or broadcasting such useful information as movie theater schedules, weather forecasts, missing persons reports, and the results of sports competitions. Different newspapers catered to different segments of the population, with those aimed at the least educated publishing more stories and oddities to pique the interest of their readers than those aimed at secondary school graduates. Similarly, broadcasting stations had to include something for everyone or no one would listen.

The post-1978 reforms have brought major changes to the operation of the mass media. While they continue to be charged with supporting official policies and educating the masses, they are expected to carry out these responsibilities in an entirely new fiscal environment. No longer able to rely on the sponsoring government department or organ for funding, they must generate most of it by their own efforts. By the early 1990s advertising had become the most significant source of funding for both newspapers and broadcasting stations.[7] Advertising, scarcely necessary in the days when raw materials and finished products were distributed according to the plan, began to make sense only when enterprises were given the opportunity for off-plan buying and selling and had to locate their own suppliers and markets. As Chapter 2 demonstrated, the prime-time television viewer in Guangzhou today is subjected to a veritable barrage of advertisements for all kinds of products.

Reliance on advertising has stimulated competition for viewers among stations and led to greater diversity in programming. This competition is enlivened by the new "open-door" policy. Chinese television stations rent or purchase from abroad materials to enhance their market position that will not set them at odds with the guardians of public morality. Thus when looking for traditional Chinese opera, martial arts serials, films made in pre–World War II China, or contemporary sentimental dramas set in Chinese communities, broadcasting personnel turn to Hong Kong, Taiwan, and occasionally Singapore. They also look to the United States, Great Britain, and Japan for everything from discontinued serials such as *Dynasty*, slapstick comedies, and children's cartoons to serialized films of literary works such as *Wuthering Heights* and *Tender Is the Night*. Most foreign works are translated into *putonghua* (if translated in Guangzhou, however, they are translated into Cantonese as well). Works intended to help viewers improve their foreign-language skills, like the two films mentioned above, are shown in their original language with Chinese subtitles.

The funding and programming innovations described above apply throughout China. Broadcasters in the Pearl River Delta, however, face exceptional competition because viewers there can opt out of Chinese television entirely and watch live Hong Kong television (in Cantonese and English) instead. Hong Kong broadcasting has long been a thorn in the side of the Chinese government because it provides, intentionally or otherwise, an alternative view of the world and of China itself. The government has alternated between jamming broadcasting signals from Hong Kong and grudgingly tolerating them. Distinctive ("fish-bone") antennae on the roofs of dwellings in the southern Pearl River Delta readily reveal Cantonese viewing preferences. When oriented to the east, they indicate that the household is watching a program from Hong Kong. When oriented otherwise, they are probably picking up domestic stations. In 1987 the provincial government forbade the population to orient the antennae to the east during the National Games, which were being played in and broadcast from Guangzhou.

Guangzhou residents cannot pick up Hong Kong stations without a special antenna. By 1991 it had become possible to subscribe through Guangdong Television to the Eastern Network, which provides cable access (at 5 yuan a month) to all four regular Hong Kong channels. Viewers who understand English now have access (via Hong Kong) to CNN and even the CBS news. But the Eastern Network remains vulnerable to politics: it mysteriously went off the air for most of June 4, 1993, the fourth anniversary of the Tiananmen disturbances, presumably so that Chinese citizens would not be able to watch foreign newscasts about goings-on in China. Similarly, although the range of themes deemed suitable for mass consumption has broadened substantially, the huge debate over the showing of the television documentary *Heshang* (known variously in English as *River Elegy*, *River Dirge*, *The River Dies Young*, and *Deathsong of the River*) in 1988 revealed just how contentious the issue of "suitability" remains.[8] This six-part program took a dim view of China's past, arguing that its earthbound, inward-looking orientation had led to stagnation (symbolized by the silt-bearing Yellow River) and that rejuvenation would be possible only when China began to look outward. Some commentators felt this perspective belittled thousands of years of philosophical and cultural achievements and demonstrated a lack of patriotism and a love of things foreign. The creators of the program are among those who went into hiding or fled the country in the aftermath of the 1989 demonstrations at Tiananmen.

Perhaps the greatest stimulus to innovative programming in China has been Satellite Television Asia Region, better known as Star TV. Since 1991 this Hong Kong–based company has been broadcasting on five channels, and by 1993 was said to be reaching at least 4.8 million homes in China alone.[9] Star's five channels originally included BBC World Service News, MTV (Music Television) Asia, Prime Sports, Star Plus entertainment, and a *putonghua* station (the Hong Kong government would not allow Star TV to broadcast in Cantonese because it did not want to weaken the market position of the preexisting Hong Kong stations). In 1994 Star TV replaced the BBC news station with a subscription movie channel, a change attributed to the company's efforts to placate Beijing, which wanted more control over the news.[10] It seems to me, however, that the more subversive station is MTV Asia, whose programming features, for example, angry rap groups acting out violent scenarios (e.g., setting everything in sight on fire) and displaying a generally anti-establishment stance. As I watched these videos in Guangzhou, I felt I was witness to a second "cultural revolution."

To provide a better sense of the contemporary mass media in Guangzhou, the paragraphs that follow briefly describe the main local newspapers and radio programming before turning to a more extensive examination of the local television scene.

Newspapers

The variety of newspapers available at any street stall in Guangzhou is amazing. Dailies, weeklies, and monthlies abound; they range from the all-purpose daily paper to more specialized papers (to say nothing of magazines) dealing with sports, the entertainment industry (featuring stories about pop music stars, film and television actresses, etc.), hobbies, and crime or targeted at particular readers such as overseas Chinese, children, youths, parents, and old people. In addition, visitors to hotels catering to foreigners have access to the *International Herald Tribune*, the *Asian Wall Street Journal*, and Hong Kong–based English- and Chinese-language dailies.

Guangzhou has three major local dailies: *Southern Daily* (*Nanfang*

Ribao), *Guangzhou Daily* (*Guangzhou Ribao*), and *Ram City Evening News* (*Yangcheng Wanbao*). *Southern Daily* puts more emphasis on national and provincial news than the other two papers. Excerpts from the column "One Hundred Cases to Be Resolved," presented in Chapter 3, were drawn from 1986 editions of *Southern Daily*. *Ram City Evening News*, with a total circulation estimated in 1992 at almost 1.6 million, ranks first among the three locally published dailies.[11] Until quite recently, when it was surpassed by Shanghai's *New People's Evening News*, *Ram City Evening News* was the leading local daily in all of China, trailing only the national newspaper, *People's Daily*. Significantly, many subscribers, including over 100,000 in Shanghai, live outside the province. *Guangzhou Daily* has an estimated 1.3 million subscribers, and *Southern Daily*, an estimated 800,000.

Circulation figures are not necessarily the most reliable guide to popularity or total readership because official newspapers — those committed to reporting on party and government affairs — are likely to rely on mandatory subscriptions from government offices and mass organizations. Another way to estimate the size of a newspaper's readership is to consider what advertisers are willing to pay. In 1992 a full-page black-and-white ad in *Ram City Evening News* cost 100,000 yuan; a 3-by-6-inch ad on the upper right corner of the front page cost 12,000 yuan; the same size ad in two colors (black and red) cost 15,000. These were believed to be the most expensive rates in Guangzhou and add weight to the relative accuracy of the circulation estimates. (Further confirmation comes from the households in the Family Study, which were much more likely to purchase *Ram City Evening News* and *Guangzhou Daily* than *Southern Daily*.) Ads now account for the bulk of a newspaper's income, though interest-free loans from the government are used to buy new equipment or to fund construction.

Prior to 1980 the local dailies usually consisted of no more than four pages, printed on the front and back of a single folded sheet of newsprint. By the early 1990s the papers had grown to eight, twelve, and occasionally sixteen pages an issue; even *Southern Daily* usually put out eight pages at least twice a week. To provide the reader with a sense of the topics and coverage typical of these daily newspapers, we will look closely at an issue of *Southern Daily* and more cursorily at an issue of *Guangzhou Daily* from the same week.

Southern Daily

The lead story of this eight-page edition of Sunday, November 8, 1992, takes up half of page 1 and all of page 2 except for two 3-by-6-inch ads and presents the text of Provincial Party Secretary Xie Fei's November 1 address to the Fourteenth (Provincial) Party Congress. The address emphasizes the need to speed up modernization of the economy. Most of the remainder of page 1 is given over to short political and economic articles. The ads on the bottom of page 2 are really more on the order of announcements: one by Shunde City Overseas Chinese Middle School inviting alumni and former staff to a celebration of its 35th anniversary and another by the Jiangmen City Labor Bureau announcing that it will hold a three-day labor fair at which employers and prospective employees can meet face-to-face. Shunde and Jiangmen are located south of Guangzhou on the west side of the Pearl River Delta.

Page 3 is headed "Timely Affairs," a catch-all phrase to describe general news items from around the country as well as news about Chinese living elsewhere. The articles include human interest stories and not necessarily fresh news. On the fold between pages 2 and 3 are the schedules for movie theaters and other places of entertainment in Guangzhou, a description of a missing person, an announcement to shippers that work is scheduled to be carried out in Shenzhen harbor, and a request for help identifying a man killed in a traffic accident in Panyu. The reverse of the fold, between pages 1 and 4, contains announcements by two training schools of their openings for students, course offerings, and fees. The top half of page 4 is devoted to miscellaneous articles on sports, for example, preparations for upcoming athletic competitions and the experiences in Guangzhou of a Russian trainer who signed a one-year contract to work with a provincial team. The bottom half of the page is given over to a celebratory announcement in red and black by the Shunde City People's Government of a program to be held to honor overseas Chinese and compatriots from Hong Kong, Macao, and Taiwan whose efforts have promoted vigorous growth in the area. At the celebration 35 named individuals will be awarded honorary citizenship in the city, 350 individuals will be commended, and the inauguration or completion of ten construction projects will be noted.

The top half of page 5 (the first page of the second folded sheet of newsprint) is devoted to "Science, Education, and Hygiene News." This section contains articles describing, for example, the graduate student openings at Shantou University in the coming year, the improvement in the inspection of foods for sale on the street, and the various services that street committee–organized "service stations" provide to local residents.* On the bottom half of the page, in red and black, 120 units (presumably exhibitors) from all over China extend their congratulations to an annual sales show being held in Zhongshan (in the southern Pearl River Delta) that features motorcycles and associated products. Page 6 is devoted to "Financial and Real Estate" news. The various articles educate readers about the workings of stock and property markets. Readers are taught, for example,

---

* "Service stations" are hole-in-the-wall collectives that provide such services as sewing repairs, medicine boiling, or the preparation of takeout foods.

the ins and outs of acquiring rights to property (e.g., required forms and eligibility criteria) and learn about the misconceptions or difficulties of people moving into new housing as owners. Occupying the bottom third of page 6 are three advertisements: one announcing a contest to choose an emblem for a city in Shunde, another for heavy-duty trucks, and a third announcing contest winners. Page 7 encourages tourism and travel and features stories dealing with various domestic destinations. Occupying the bottom third of the page is an advertisement for Wu Yang–Honda (Five Rams–Honda) motorcycles. This joint venture is based in Guangzhou.

On the fold between pages 6 and 7 are more missing persons ads as well as requests for information leading to the recovery of stolen motorcycles and so forth. Nothing is printed on the reverse of the fold (between pages 5 and 8). Page 8 itself is divided in half, with six attractive scenic or human interest photographs in black and white on top — the winners of a contest held by a photography periodical. The diverse pictures include a young woman jumping backward off a high diving board, sheep grazing with the Great Wall in the background, the conductor of a Western orchestra seen from the vantage point of the harpist. On the lower half of the page is a red-and-black advertisement announcing the establishment of a pharmaceutical and medical supplies company in Chaozhou (a city on Guangdong's northeast coast).

Southern Daily has a visually appealing layout. Just about every page has reproductions of black-and-white photographs. Individual stories are boxed off from one another by differently patterned lines (solid circles, twisted ropes, strings of beads) and are introduced by vertical or horizontal headlines printed against pale, medium, or dark gray backgrounds. Various sizes of print are used, and fanciful or semiabstract drawings are occasionally interspersed among the stories. More visuals are contributed by advertisements that include drawings of trucks and motorcycles (in this particular issue) as well as faint red background drawings of lanterns, fireworks, and other indicators of celebration in announcements of the opening of a new company. In content and style *Southern Daily* is the most politically oriented of Guangzhou's three daily papers.

Guangzhou Daily

The layout of *Guangzhou Daily* is similar to that of *Southern Daily*, but the two papers differ in the relative allocation of space. Page 1 of the sixteen-page four-section edition of Wednesday, November 11, 1992, contains much more news and information that is specific to Guangzhou (warnings about counterfeit currency, a number to call at the mayor's office to complain about unsanitary or unsafe environmental conditions) along with familiar stories (in the spirit of the Fourteenth Party Congress industrial output in Guangzhou reaches new heights; party members must learn how to manage the "three relationships," i.e., take a more laissez-faire approach to the commercial sector). Page 2 is headed "Guangzhou News," but as in the case of *Southern Daily* not all the content is timely, though the exchange rates in the center of the page are up-to-date. Typical articles (there are about seventeen on the page) report on progress in accounting, a manager who helped two guests at his hotel recover stolen property, and a survey of Guangzhou residents' satisfaction with this year's reforms.

Page 3 is given over to international news, with a photograph of a big fire in France and articles, for example, on trade with the United States and a friendship treaty between England and Russia. Various advertisements and announcements occupy the bottom third of the page: an ad for Orient (a Japanese brand) watches, an announcement of forthcoming openings for students at the Dongshan district branch of Television University, an announcement that the assistant general manager of a local restaurant will be returning to Hong Kong at the end of the month. As in the *Southern Daily*, the movie schedule appears on the fold between pages 2 and 3. The newspaper's address and phone numbers appear on the reverse of the fold. The top of page 4 is headed "Southern [Guangdong] Towns" and features items about towns in the Pearl River Delta, for example, Foshan and Shenzhen. The bottom half of the page contains an advertisement for luxury apartments (three bedrooms, one and a half baths, telephones with international direct dialing) in a new high-rise complex in Panyu county. Prices start at 3,000 yuan per square meter; apartments start at 120 square meters. Page 5 (the first page of the second section) features news from other parts of China and a "Look-out Post on Hong Kong and Macao"; the top halves of pages 6 and 7 focus, respectively, on "Sports" and "Economic Information"; the bottom halves and all of page 8 contain advertisements.

The third section (pages 9–12) of *Guangzhou Daily* is primarily concerned with entertainment and cultural matters. Articles about contemporary performers and stage productions appear on page 9, whereas works of fiction appear on page 11. Page 10 deals with consumer issues, such as the cost of living, that would be of interest to the ordinary person. The bottom portions of these pages plus all of page 12 are full of advertisements. The fourth section is divided into four parts: page 13 focuses on family matters (how a couple planned the birth of their child, what women need to know about men); page 14, on contemporary science and technology (how engineers are being trained abroad, how rice production can be increased scientifically); and page 15, on education (including a picture of students at a middle school receiving military training and a story on the acceptance of an American teacher at Puizheng Middle School). Two-thirds of page 16 consists of black-and-white photographs of events or persons outside China.

This particular issue is dominated by pictures of the aftermath of the recent American presidential election (a sad-faced President Bush in the back of a limousine, a victorious president-elect and Mrs. Clinton) as well as photographs of an estranged Prince Charles and Princess Diana, a blond in a bustier dancing in New York, a French farmer emptying grapes from a basket. The bottom third of every page in this final section consists of advertisements.[12]

Radio

By the early 1990s Guangzhou radio listeners had ready access to six different domestic broadcasts, five operated by the province and one by the city, the city station having gained its independence from the province in 1991. In addition, strategically situated residents of Guangzhou can pick up transmissions from nearby county or city stations such as Nanhai and Foshan as well as FM broadcasts from Hong Kong. According to one radio official, television programming is seen less as a competitor to radio programming than as a complement. Though the two media broadcast at the same time during much of the day and night, only radio broadcasts 24 hours a day. Furthermore, radios dominate daytime listening when people are on their way to and from work, on their lunch break, or relaxing in the park. The number of radio channels, moreover, has expanded right along with television. Like the newspapers radio has become heavily dependent on advertising for its funds. About 75 percent of Guangdong Radio's operating budget comes from advertisements; prior to 1980 the government provided all funds.

Though there is overlap in programming among the various channels, there is also substantial differentiation. One channel, which broadcasts in *putonghua*, aims at providing the public with news, service, and social education programs, which acquaint listeners with the significance of laws, technical innovations, and events that affect their own lives. The so-called economic channel, the most popular channel, broadcasts a diverse range of programs primarily in Cantonese — everything from call-in shows to interviews, music, entertainment, and stories. The music channel, which began broadcasting in 1991, plays all kinds of music (provided it is "healthy"): Western classical music; popular music, both Chinese and foreign; and specialty music. For example, on the day I visited the station, country music (with lyrics in English) was being broadcast during the American Music Hour.

The literature and arts channel specializes in more traditional fare: plays, all kinds of (Chinese) operas, comic dialogues, stories, news, and music derived from movies. It regularly broadcasts (in Cantonese) serials that can run for several months. These serials are immensely popular. In 1987 a Judge Bao serial, about a virtuous magistrate in the distant past, was being broadcast (on another channel) twice a day—during the lunch break and again in the early evening. One could not walk down the street without hearing the narrator's voice issuing from one shop front after another. At the time of my visit to the station in 1992, a serial set in the Song Dynasty, *Yang Family Generals*, was on the air. Using *putonghua*, the educational channel provides formal instruction in various subjects including Chinese, Japanese, English, and even German. Finally, the English channel, which began transmission only in 1992, is aimed at the foreign community and local residents who want to improve their language skills; it focuses on news, foreign events, and introducing foreigners to China and Chinese culture.

In mid-1992 a new experimental service channel, Ram City Traffic, went on the air. This station is intended to help taxi drivers make their way around the city by providing up-to-the-minute reports on traffic accidents and congestion. Between traffic bulletins, it plays music "suitable for taxi drivers." When I asked about this phrase, I learned that the station plays music that helps to keep drivers calm and thus to reduce the likelihood of traffic altercations. Drivers do, in fact, tune in to this channel.

Television

Television broadcasting began in Guangzhou in 1959 with the establishment of Guangdong Television (GDTV). By the early 1990s Guangzhou residents could routinely tune in to six domestic channels. Four of them— Pearl, Lingnan, and two (of which one is educational) China Central Television (CCTV) stations—are broadcast by GDTV, the provincial station. The fifth, Guangzhou Television (GZTV), the municipal station, began broadcasting in January 1988 and added an educational channel in 1993. The programs of these stations (minus the educational stations) are regularly published in *Guangdong TV*, the local weekly equivalent of *TV Guide*.

GDTV has a potential viewing audience approaching 100 million. Its broadcasts are accessible via relay to about 90 percent of the provincial population as well as to another 35–40 million people living in adjacent provinces. Because GDTV attempts to reach a more diverse audience than GZTV, including villagers living in "backward" mountainous areas, the general rural population, and the urban population, it must present a range of programs geared to different levels of sophistication. Furthermore, as a provincial rather than a municipal unit, GDTV is expected to take a broader view of its mission, to demonstrate its shared concern for the national interest by broadcasting programs from Beijing and using *putonghua*. GDTV meets these requirements by employing one channel exclusively to relay programs originating on CCTV in Beijing and another for national educational programs, including formal courses in foreign languages, engineering, and other technical specialties; both these channels use *putonghua*.

On the two channels reserved for its own programming GDTV broadcasts an average of just over 23 hours a day: 18 on Pearl, primarily in Cantonese; and 5½ on Lingnan, primarily in *putonghua*. According to GDTV's own province-wide ratings, which include CCTV, Pearl, Lingnan, the various municipal television stations, and the Eastern Network, at almost any given moment half of the provincial viewing audience is likely to be watching Pearl. In Guangzhou itself, however, a substantial proportion of the viewing audience is likely to watch the municipal station or cable, and in the delta many viewers watch Hong Kong channels without the benefit of cable.

About one-third of the programming on Pearl and Lingnan is produced locally. The remaining two-thirds of GDTV's daily broadcasting consists of domestic and foreign programs obtained directly from other provinces, foreign programs obtained directly from abroad (GDTV has movie catalogues from all the major American studios, such as Disney, Fox, and Columbia), and programs, primarily news, obtained from CCTV. GDTV has two large studios (one of 800 square meters and another of 600 square meters) for shooting movies, operas, and various extravaganzas (arrangements are made with opera troupes, movie companies, etc., to perform on the premises) and eleven smaller studios for its own in-house productions, such as the news, "The Morning Show," or cooking demonstrations. GDTV camera crews also visit different parts of the province to make documentaries of historical sites and local customs. In addition to being aired locally, all these various cultural programs are made available for sale (or exchange) to other provinces or abroad.

Although some productions are short subjects with only 10 or 20 minutes of footage, others are multiple-episode documentaries or dramas that are shown over weeks or months. For example, the documentary "The New Image of Guangdong" consists of nine 20-minute episodes and

provides a close look at the achievements and social changes in Guangdong Province during the past twelve years of reform and since opening its doors to [the] outside world. It also depicts the new upsurge of economic development in Guangdong after Deng Xiaoping's tour to southern China in the spring of 1992. Large scale, newly invested projects, high-tech enterprises and new development goals of the special economic zones, are all introduced. The Program not only shows fully the great aspirations of the Guangdong people to catch up with Asia's "Four Dragons" in economic development, but also reveals the new trends and tendencies of reform in this area.[13]

The monumental drama "Hong Kong in Turmoil," produced in 1991, consists of 55 episodes, each 50 minutes long. Aired three times a week during the spring and early summer of that year on Pearl, it regularly sat at the top of the charts. The story concerns

two half sisters, who had been separated for a long time, and how they become involved in the inheritance of a large fortune left them by their father. It vividly presents the ways of the society of Hong Kong in the 1930's–40's, involving the commercial world, the police, the court, the film-making industry and the underworld.[14]

Prior to 1980 about 90 percent of GDTV's operating budget came from the government and 10 percent from other sources; by the early 1990s, however, the proportions were reversed, and revenues from advertising now account for 90 percent of the operating budget. There are four grades of advertising time, with prime-time (from 7 to 10 P.M.) the most expensive. In 1992 a 30-second prime-time advertisement for a domestic product cost 2,200 yuan but for a foreign product, U.S. $1,400 (four to six times higher, depending on the exchange rate). As an alternative to buying an ad, a company may provide goods and services to the production crew while it is out in the field, for example, making premises available or supplying assistance with logistics. In this way it can have its name mentioned in the credits.

GZTV is on the air a little over twelve hours a day—from noon to nearly 1 A.M.—and has a potential viewing audience of 10 million (i.e., people living in Guangzhou as well as in the densely populated areas of the Pearl River Delta). GZTV sees its mission as different from that of GDTV; specifically, it aims at urban dwellers and tries to help them modernize. It also hopes to market its programs to the interior provinces and introduce them to all the changes that are taking place in China's southern gateway. In the early 1990s GZTV operated only one channel, but it expected to start a second, less powerful, channel sometime in 1993. Both channels will carry programs in Cantonese and *putonghua*. GZTV produces only 1½ to 2 hours of its own daily programming, a rate that is considered quite good for a municipal station. Prime-time advertisements on GZTV cost about one-quarter of those on GDTV.

Pleasing viewers is tricky. One GZTV official emphasized that people flip channels all the time. But an attractive program—one that is lively, stylish, and fashionable—is bound to catch and hold a large audience. The closer a show is to the viewers' own concerns, the more likely they are to watch. This does not mean that in programming "anything goes." On the contrary, broadcasters have their own sense of professional ethics and define their role in educational and psychological terms: to help people feel good and to promote social stability. The television audience in Guangzhou has a wide selection of programs from which to choose: variety shows, short subjects, news, and dramas. The paragraphs that follow examine the range of Chinese programs in some detail.

Variety Shows

Many Chinese variety shows do not originate with the TV stations themselves; rather they are taped versions or excerpts, of theatrical performances, for example, or of entertainment for some special group (the military, retired cadres, government officials). These origins leave their mark. Stylistically the variety shows tend to be the most conservative — the most old-fashioned and least innovative — of all the programs on television. They regularly feature small children with rouged cheeks and frozen-faced smiles, decked out in national minority costumes, performing some song or dance number. When members of the audience are panned by the camera, they look pretty bored. Adult dance routines, again usually featuring a national minority dance or a Han folk dance, are also common. Acrobatic routines or mixed acrobatic-dance routines are often featured. The participants hold sticks to which long ribbons are attached and twirl or unfurl them in colorful patterns.

Variety shows also feature vocalists singing in either the traditional high-pitched Chinese operatic voice or the more conventional popular music voice similar to that used in the West. Although popular music predominates even in these settings, patriotic songs about military sacrifice or heroism are frequently sung, with forced Cultural Revolution–style enthusiasm, by individuals or groups dressed in army uniforms or in tuxedos, usually by singers with powerful voices. (The vocal power of the operatic star Pavarotti probably accounts for his passionate reception on his China tour.)

Adult audiences especially appreciate the traditional stand-up comedy act (*xiangsheng*) that is also a part of these variety shows. In these routines two men carry on a dialogue in which current issues or popular concerns are humorously lampooned. Typical topics include using one's connections or expressing false enthusiasm for the one-child family policy.[15] Variety shows might also feature short dramatic skits from traditional Chinese operas or more contemporary dramas. With the exception of the comic dialogue, most of the acts in a typical variety show have a strong visual component — lots of color and action — a combination likely to appeal to the less sophisticated among the audience.

Short Subjects

Short subjects might best be thought of as fillers between regularly scheduled programs; they are certainly treated this way, cut off whenever it is time for something else. Snippets from variety shows also fall into this category, but so too do snippets of popular music videos that are tame and unimaginative compared with American popular music videos (or those on StarTV) but not too far behind those produced in Hong Kong. (Indeed many of those shown are produced in Hong Kong and Taiwan.) More flamboyant and provocative tapes produced by freelance musicians and vocalists circulate outside official purview. Songs of lost or unrequited love seem the dominant genre, and the (usually) female vocalist does a lot of staring into the distance, posing against a tree or a wall, or walking through fields of flowers. Minority songs with sweeping views of mountainous or wind-swept Chinese landscapes are popular fillers.

Foreign fillers include ballroom dancing competitions in Europe, ballet performances, classical music orchestral performances, animal tricks shows, and foreign tourist spots of scenic or historical significance. In the early 1990s GDTV featured on most mornings a leotard-clad young woman who, to the accompaniment of mournful soul music, did stretching exercises (bordering on the erotic) in front of the Tianhe Stadium. Another young woman (less often featured) did light aerobic exercises to music. Other short subjects might have an educational component: the history of a temple in a popular tourist spot, the distinctive cuisine of a particular locale (lots of food preparation shots), the art of flower arranging, or a special look at airplanes.

News Programs

News programs are on several times a day. Depending on the particular program, national, local, or international news is included. The local stations have their own news reporters who make on-the-scene reports with their own camera crews. There is much more economic news and fewer crime reports than on national and local news programs in the United States. Anyone who believed that television news told the whole story (no one does) would have a very optimistic view of the country. Economic progress seems to be occurring everywhere, and although the death sentences of batches of criminals are reported, crime itself is given only modest attention on the TV news. Traffic accidents, fires, and major natural disasters (in China and abroad) do receive substantial coverage. Sports, both national and international, account for only a small proportion of the news.

The list that follows of the news stories broadcast on February 12, 1991, gives a more concrete sense of GDTV's Nightly News program (which starts at 10:13 P.M.). The reports begin with national and local news (1–9 in the list that follows); present (in Cantonese) international stories, many from CNN or American network news programs, probably purchased from Hong Kong (10–12); and conclude with more local news (13–19):

1. Premier Li Peng talks about the need for enterprise reform. (The next morning this story dominated the newspapers as well as television.) A

full ten minutes of news time was given over to a view of Li Peng, dressed in a Western-style suit, reading a report. The *putonghua*-speaking narrator prefaced nearly every point with "Li Peng said . . ."

2. A Guangdong vice-governor meets with uniformed people — presumably the police or military.

3. Municipal government cadres hold a meeting.

4. The processing of thousands of travelers at the train station and the ports proceeds efficiently as Spring Festival (Lunar New Year) approaches.

5. The Guangzhou flower markets (associated with the festival), selling peach blossom trees, ornamental orange (C. *gat*) trees, and so forth, opened today. (See "The Seasonal Round" below for an extensive discussion of this celebration.)

6. Shots of the Hong Kong flower market.

7. Repeat of the Guangdong vice-governor meeting with the police or military.

8. Exhibition of products made in Shenzhen.

9. Report on the trial of Wang Juntao (one of the "Black Hands" behind the prodemocracy demonstrations of 1989) in Beijing.

10. President Bush on the situation in Iraq.

11. Bridges and civilian areas in Iraq damaged by American bombing.

12. Concerns of the USSR about the situation in Iraq.

13. Feature on the business of raising potted plants.

14. A ballroom dancing contest.

15. Snakes, turtles, and owls are released from captivity in Shaoqing, a tourist destination two or three hours' drive west of Guangzhou; it is not clear what this is about — either opposition to cruelty to animals or protecting endangered species.

16. Men are tried for some kind of stampede or building collapse — it is not clear whether this is taking place in China.

17. Tennis match.

18. Weather report.

19. Financial report: exchange rates for yuan, prices on the Hong Kong stock market and Hong Kong gold market.

Dramas

The three different dramas recounted and analyzed below aired during prime time about three times a week during the first half of 1991.

A Historical Martial Arts Tale

For most of the month of March and into April GZTV ran a twenty-installment martial arts serial entitled "The Valiant Woman" from 8:45 to 9:30 P.M. Like most, if not all, the martial arts programs shown on television, it was set sometime in the dim past (perhaps the Song or Ming dynasty) and was made in Hong Kong in Cantonese. The plot centers on the relationships among five families of the gentry, drawn into conflict by the ambitions of the unscrupulous ones among them.

The A Family consists of Chau Leuhng, the heroine or "valiant woman" after whom the story is named, and her parents. Everyone in, or associated with, the A Family is virtuous. Chau Leuhng herself is highly motivated to do good and secretly apprentices herself to a female *shifu* (martial arts master) who wants her to renounce her affiliation to her natal family because it interferes with her ability to concentrate and be a good student. This request presents Chau Leuhng with a major dilemma, for her mother's health relapses every time Chau Leuhng disappears for her lessons. The *shifu* grants her leave to visit her parents for a month, but after that if she is serious about her commitment to learning, she must come back and completely forget about them.

The B Family consists of a father and daughter. Associated with them is Yeuhng Daaih Go (Big Brother Yeuhng), who heads up the B Family guards and with whom the B daughter is in love. Yeuhng Daaih Go is ever courteous to her, but he is not in love with her. In fact, he has fallen in love with her visiting friend Sigei. In the beginning everyone in this family seems virtuous, though the father is a little on the crafty side. Ultimately he becomes the archvillain.

The C Family includes a father (who frequently dresses in black, has a sinister laugh, and pulls on his moustache) and son. From the beginning of the story the son is unbearable: ambitious, exploitative, sneaky, and arrogant. The C father is just a shade less unpleasant.

The D Family consists of a young man and his parents. Everybody in the D Family is good. The young man, in fact, frequently acts as a kind of Robin Hood, going into the town market in disguise and defending the populace when the guards of the C Family storm in to steal from merchants, push people around, and possibly grab good-looking women for their young master.

The E Family is represented by a single young man, who lives alone in a nice house adjacent to the town market. (The others all live on their estates.) His circumstances are unclear; perhaps he is the sole survivor of a once wealthy family. At the beginning of the story E seems a trifle simple. He sells brass mirrors for a living, but his real passion is reciting poetry.

Early in the story E gets kicked around by the C guardsmen, and the baby rabbit he has been carrying in his hand is crushed in his fall. With tears in his eyes E puts the dead rabbit on a leaf bier, lights candles, places them on leaves, and sends the rabbit and candles all floating out to sea. E is observed doing this by Chau Leuhng (home on her month's leave). She has no idea who he is but, on a whim, announces to him then and there and later to her parents that he is the man she wants to marry. Her parents, disturbed by her frequent absences, have concluded that the best way to curb her restlessness is to find her a husband. Chau Leuhng reluctantly agreed to marry provided she could choose her own husband. By selecting E, she hopes to put off the pressure from her parents, for E is hardly the highborn type they would have chosen for her. E does not know what to make of her attentions and tries unsuccessfully to elude her.

The story then takes several complicated turns. Sigei visits the B Family and is noticed by the scheming father of the C Family, who eventually manages to make her a voluntary prisoner in his home by threatening to kill Yeuhng Daaih Go, whom he has taken captive. Sigei feels she must turn herself over to him because earlier Yeuhng Daaih Go had rescued her from a difficult situation. She manages to keep Father C at bay, however, by pointing out that taking her by force is not the way to build a relationship. Since he claims his goal is matrimony, she asks if it would not be better for that marriage to be founded on respect. And what better way to express this respect than to give her time to develop feelings for him. Father C accepts this line of reasoning, although his wicked son constantly tries to sneak into Sigei's room and have her for himself.

There is also a subplot concerning two martial arts *shifu:* the woman who is training Chau Leuhng and a man who is apparently in the pay of Father C. At some point in the past the two *shifu* had been on intimate terms. At present the male *shifu* goes about in disguise (wearing flowing white robes, a white wig, and a long white beard) and has forced a young woman who works in an inn to become a spy for him. The young woman falls for a mysterious guest, Son D ("Robin Hood"), who is nice to her but does not reciprocate her affection. The young woman is essentially in bondage to the male *shifu*, who proves to be a mean man. Whenever she fails in any task, he punishes her cruelly, stomping on her hands, beating her up, and even raping her. To redeem herself in his eyes and possibly to save her own life, she makes a number of unsuccessful attempts on the lives of various good people. During one of them she is caught and is about to be killed when Son D, one of the defenders, realizes who she is and asks (offering no explanation other than that she is a "friend") that she be spared. In the end the young woman redeems herself by rescuing Son D from the dungeon of the C Family. Unfortunately, she is fatally wounded during their flight by the female *shifu*, who is back on good terms with the young woman's master. With her dying breath the young woman warns the female *shifu* that the male *shifu* is using her for his own purposes, just as she herself has been used. With this warning she reveals her true good character.

Another subplot (I will not mention them all) involves two brothers who are seeking a map that will lead them to the location of a classic work on the martial arts. Whoever obtains this book will be able to fly through the air, loft boulders about as if they were beachballs, and cause people to burst into flames with a mere gesture of his hand. This map was stolen by a man who is something of a Taoist free spirit, good-natured but given to drinking and freeloading. He has successfully bamboozled E into giving him free food and lodging. Eventually, however, he begins to teach E the rudiments of the martial arts, and this softhearted young man quickly becomes skilled.

Much of the plot revolves around the switches of loyalty that occur as various people realize the importance of the map and guess at its location, and thus that of the classic work itself. The C Family tries various cruel maneuvers to obtain the desired information but is outwitted by Father B. Both Father C and his son are eventually killed by Father B or his under-lings. (Actually Son C accidentally falls on a sword he intended to use on Yeuhng Daaih Go and kills himself, thus saving Yeuhng Daaih Go from sullying his reputation by killing a wounded and weakened opponent. Ear-lier, while hanging in chains from a dungeon wall, Son C had tried to taunt Sigei into killing him. She was tempted because he had tried so many times to dishonor her — and, I think, ultimately did — but when faced with the opportunity to take revenge against him when he was defenseless, she re-sisted the urge, thus maintaining her virtue.)

In the end, through various machinations and deceptions, Father B ac-quires the ancient martial arts classic and develops the skills it teaches. Unfortunately, the intensity of physical and mental concentration required to exercise these skills just about exhausts the practitioner's vital forces (qi). Father B goes on to become a kind of cannibal, drawing out other people's qi with the power in his hand in order to replenish his own. The viewer sees healthy, vital people wither into corpses at his touch or even the mere pointing of his hand. His own daughter and Yeuhng Daaih Go have long since abandoned him, and the evil male *shifu* has become his follower.

Finally, realizing the terrible deeds he is perpetrating, five people resolve to kill Father B: Sigei, Chau Leuhng, E, Son D, and Yeuhng Daaih Go all take up arms against him. In a fierce struggle Father B is overpowered and strangled by the long scarves flowing from the sleeves of his opponents. The story ends with all the young couples now free to begin their lives anew: Yeuhng Daaih Go and Sigei, Son D and Daughter B, and Chau Leuhng and E. Indeed, the final scene of the program shows the last two standing in a small boat, which E is poling through the mist. Tucked into the corner of the boat is a small basket containing two little rabbits.

The martial arts genre is extremely popular with Chinese audiences both young and old. It draws on the same traditional plot repertoire as Chinese operas and storytellers — *The Romance of the Three Kingdoms, Water Margin* (also known as *All Men Are Brothers*), and *Journey to the West* (also known as *Monkey*) — as well as on innumerable semihistorical and legendary events.[16] The moral virtues stressed in the program include loyalty (to family, *shifu*, lord, and/or subordinates); a sense of justice (embodied in outrage when others are treated unfairly or in vengeance when others are wronged); sensitivity to others' feelings; respect for the powerless (women and the lower classes); and stoicism in the face of one's own pain and suffering (embodied in sticking to one's ideals despite torture or in refusing to acknowledge the extent of one's suffering to family or friends). Moral dilemmas frequently involve choices among these virtues, for example, what to do if one's father (like Daughter B's) is revealed as irretrievably corrupted or one's *shifu* insists that the price of being her student is to sever ties with one's family.

Moral failings include greed, abuse of power, disregard for the sufferings of others, a readiness to switch sides when it is to one's own advantage, and selfish ambition. Evil people abuse the weak, exploit women, and are cruel to their own subordinates. Basic themes, perhaps drawing on Buddhist conceptions of retribution, include the punishment of true evildoers and the ultimate redemption of relatively innocent evildoers (whose actions result from a lack of knowledge or an untenable situation), by their own good deeds. Unfortunately, these usually entail their sacrificing their own lives when the true situation becomes known. The martial arts themselves are essentially neutral. Virtuous people use them for moral purposes, wicked people, for immoral purposes. All these action-packed lessons are taught by stereotypical characters decked out in beautiful costumes.

A Contemporary Drama

About a month before "The Valiant Woman" was shown, another prime-time program, "Mother," dominated the Guangzhou airwaves. This dramatic serial, shown on GDTV's Pearl channel, was dubbed into Cantonese from *putonghua* and appears to have been made and set in contemporary southern Taiwan or possibly Singapore. "Mother" is an extremely intense program with multiple tragedies in nearly every episode. American audiences who viewed the Chinese-American–made film *The Joy Luck Club* have been exposed to a mild version of this popular genre. A plot summary and an account of a typical episode follow.

The story focuses on an attractive, honest, and trusting young woman, I Ling, with whom A, the given-away son of the Mother of the title role, is in love. I Ling is actually going with B, the son of a wealthy businessman, but A manages to convince her that B is deceiving her. With the help of his no-good real younger sister, C, who is a compulsive gambler, A makes it appear that B has another girlfriend. I Ling is shocked and dazed by the discovery that B is cheating on her. In total confusion she allows herself to be convinced by A that B cannot be trusted whereas A will truly look after her. I Ling agrees to marry him, though she is clearly unhappy about this outcome.

A's birth mother, who had had to give him away to be reared by someone else when she was widowed, knows that I Ling loves B and vice versa and that A contrived this deception. She knows further that if I Ling marries A, everyone will be unhappy in the long run: A, B, and I Ling. She tries to locate C so that she will admit the role she played in the deception and convince I Ling that B is worthy of trust. The Mother manages to do this just in time to stop I Ling from saying "I do." A is furious at his mother for giving preference to an unrelated male over her own son. He determines to get I Ling back.

A tracks I Ling and B to a beach where they go swimming. In the course of the struggle he initiates with B, A bumps I Ling so hard that she is knocked unconscious in the water and is submerged for a long time — so long, the viewer learns, that she has been left a semivegetable. Although she can sit up in a wheelchair and accept spoon-feeding, she has no memory and no capacity for interaction. All this lovely young woman can do now is stare straight ahead. A, unable to understand what he has done wrong, is sent to jail for two years while B attempts to provide all the stimulation possible to I Ling so that she will eventually regain her personality. He encounters many obstacles in doing this because I Ling's scheming older brother, her legal guardian, prefers not only that she not recover but that she die as soon as possible so that he can gain control over her share of the family property.

In a representative episode three plots are interwoven: I Ling as vegetable, A's birth mother's older daughter and her marital problems, and trouble at B's father's business. B's father has long been irritated at B's spending so much time (two years have already passed) on I Ling at the expense of his work for the family business. An employee who has been involved in some illegal activities in the business tries desperately to talk to B, but B is lost in thought about I Ling and tells the man to talk to his father. B then goes on an outing with I Ling (in a wheelchair) and A's newly pregnant older sister, whose marriage is in trouble. As they return and are carrying I Ling's wheelchair up the stairs, they encounter the desperate employee, who seizes B's father (who has just arrived) and begs him not to turn him over to the police. During the struggle the employee knocks over I Ling's wheelchair. Everybody dashes for it. A's pregnant older sister falls to the ground trying to reach it — and loses the baby. B's father tries to push the wheelchair out of the path of an oncoming car only to be struck down himself. He needs a lifesaving operation.

In the final episode (which topped provincial ratings for the week) we learn that the events we have witnessed are the reminiscences of Mother herself as she relives on Mother's Day all the experiences she had raising her children. Everything has turned out well, often because of Mother's persuasion and wise counsel. I Ling and B are married. After four years of tending I Ling without so much as hearing a word from her, B, distraught, finally brought her back to the scene of her near-drowning to commit suicide with her by carrying her into the water. As she started to go under, she awoke from her semicoma entirely well. A got over his infatuation with I Ling and returned to his first love, I Ling's older sister. I Ling's scheming older brother has been forgiven by his two younger sisters. A's older sister's marriage worked out. A's no-good younger sister reformed. The final episode concludes with all the young adults, their spouses, and numerous descendants coming to celebrate with Mother, the true heroine of the series. Mother now has a fashionable haircut and is relaxing in a luxurious setting, totally different from that in which she spent most of her life and most of the series. Presumably this outcome is all made possible by the joint contributions of the younger generation. (Mother never remarried or even had a boyfriend.) Thus the trials and tribulations of motherhood are ultimately rewarded by successful, loving children whose goal in adulthood is to make Mother happy!

The drama and sentimentality of this program are typical of Chinese-made products from outside China. Crying, by both men and women, is common. A similar tendency is creeping back into the domestic product but has not yet been given free rein.[17] The overall message is fatalistic: life is hard, nice people die all the time, jealousy and deception ruin lives, anger is frequent and dangerous, causing people to do foolish things like seeking vengeance. But nonetheless, personal commitment is important, people should requite those who have helped them, and young people should accept good advice and not bullheadedly do as they wish.

An Educational Drama Program

As I have indicated, GDTV produces a substantial portion of its own programming. Several episodes from one of its programs, "One Hundred Life Events," aired weekly in 1991 during the early prime-time hours. (A similar educational program was shown in 1987.) Each episode of "One Hundred Life Events" is self-contained, with a single event or problem introduced and resolved in the space of a half hour, although all episodes feature the same cast of characters in the same setting. In its style, goals, and emphasis on timely topics this Guangzhou product is nearly indistinguishable from a popular program produced and aired in Hong Kong in the early and mid-1980s, known as "Hong Kong 1982," "Hong Kong 1983," and so forth, and is clearly modeled on it. Reruns of "Hong Kong 1984" were being played on Hong Kong television in 1992.

The two programs are similar in focusing on ordinary local people with modest jobs (the central family in the Hong Kong version operated a fast-food shop; two of the central characters in the Guangzhou version operate a sidewalk refreshment stall) and their moral dilemmas and misadventures or those of their relatives, friends, or neighbors. The educational goals of the programs are revealed by the questions they address, questions assumed to be in every viewer's mind: How is an ordinary decent person like myself to handle all the challenges and temptations of life in this changing society? Whom can you trust in this day and age? Are there standards of right and wrong anymore? My employer, parents, spouse want me to do such and such, but I do not really want to. How can I remain a good employee, adult child, or spouse if I do not do what they want? Without being heavyhanded each episode helps the perplexed character (and viewer) find moral bearings in this seemingly rapacious world. As in the martial arts and contemporary serials described above, the characters in these programs are more stereotypical than a viewer accustomed to realism might like, but they are more believable than the archstereotypes of Cultural Revolution–era productions.

Episodes from "One Hundred Life Events" have already been presented earlier in this book (see Chapter 3). The first was the story of the young woman who was mistakenly assumed to be a prostitute by one of her neighbors; the second dealt with the efforts of another young woman to comply with her mother's request that she consider a visiting overseas Chinese as a marital prospect and yet avoid marrying the man. Here we will look briefly at two additional episodes, one about the karaoke craze and the other about the role of the broker in private business.

In the early 1990s Guangzhou was in the grip of a karaoke craze. The first Japanese-style drinking establishment, or karaoke bar, opened as a joint venture in the Dongfang Hotel in January 1988. Some 210 more opened in Guangzhou between late 1989 and the end of 1991, most of them (180) in the city proper. By 1992 the repertoire of officially sanctioned karaoke songs exceeded 2,000.[18] Every new bar/restaurant proclaims its karaoke equipment, and karaoke competitions are a television staple. (Young) people are so caught up in this activity that they practice at home. That their practicing results in unpleasant noise for the neighbors is clear.[19]

In the episode depicted in "One Hundred Life Events" the selfish wife of the sidewalk refreshment stall operator has gone to a karaoke establishment with her workmates and has returned very excited. She wants to participate in a contest and begs her husband to help her buy the necessary equipment. To his regret he does. Not only is this woman a terrible singer, but she practices regularly until all hours of the night, driving the neighbors crazy. When she refuses to listen to either her husband's requests or their complaints, two young neighbors conspire to cut off her electricity while she is practicing. She is outraged when she catches them; her practicing continues as before.

Finally the neighbors, with the husband's collaboration, decide that since she does not listen to reason, she should be given a taste of her own medicine. The neighbors in the apartment immediately above her pretend to take up another fad, tap dancing, and practice it through the night. As soon as the karaoke buff begins her practice, they beat the floor with their tap shoes, distracting her and making it impossible for her to practice. She decides to give up and go to bed but finds the neighbors tapping like mad right over her bed as well. She complains to her husband that she cannot sleep, but he is unsympathetic, explaining that just as she has freedom to practice her singing, they have freedom to practice their dancing. The wife then proposes that they could dance at more reasonable hours, and he counters that they probably feel the same way about her singing. He finally suggests that if she limits the hours of her singing, they will probably agree to limit the hours of their dancing. After some bargaining, she agrees to the limits he suggests, at which point he bangs a broom handle on the ceiling and the tapping comes to a stop.

The husband is shown in a less sympathetic light in the second episode. One day while he is operating his sidewalk refreshment stall (selling ice cream, soft drinks, beer, etc.) an older man, obviously from the countryside, happens by and asks for help locating an address written on a piece of paper. He explains that he has been asked by his fellow villagers to arrange for the shipment of several tons of fresh flowers to the village for a big celebration. The old man is looking for a former resident of the village who has become a high cadre with connections, who can help him locate and purchase the flowers. The stall operator, seeing an opportunity to act as middleman, tells the villager that the cadre is now retired and that his contacts are useless. He whips out a card with the name of his own "company," with himself as "manager." He assures the old man that for a percentage he himself can arrange everything within the necessary three days. The old villager agrees to deal with him.

The stall operator then goes into action. He knows a neighbor who is an official in a factory with connections to places dealing in flowers. He approaches this neighbor (who just might be the former villager the old man was seeking), inviting him to become an "advisor" to his company and offering to pay him 300 yuan a month for his services. It is not stated but clearly understood that advising means arranging contacts. A dinner is held to celebrate this man's agreement to become an advisor. The first 300-yuan payment is made. Almost immediately the stall operator asks the advisor to facilitate contacts with people in the flower trade. This turns out to be more difficult than anyone had anticipated. The relevant people are out of town; they do not return the advisor's phone calls. The three-day time limit is running out. The frustrated advisor admits he cannot deliver and resigns his position. The stall operator realizes that in his greed he has overreached himself.

Both these episodes reflect the changed tenor of the times. Although the first story depicts concretely the boundless enthusiasm of a student of ka-raoke and its consequences for her neighbors, its real concern is a much larger issue — the need for self-restraint in an era when it seems that any-thing goes. Now that the bonds of authority have been loosened, some people, maybe even most people, no longer have any sense of limits. They need to realize that the exercise of "freedom" does not mean freedom to do anything (within the law) one wishes. They must consider the conse-quences of their actions for others and voluntarily set limits on their own behavior. Some people can appreciate the needs of others only when they are dealt a taste of their own medicine.

The second story takes up two aspects of the role of the broker, a role that has evolved along with the private sector. Although middlemen (and women) have long played a role in interpersonal and intergroup relation-ships in China, the opening of the economy has increased the demand for their services. Now, with the supply channels that existed under the state plan disrupted, a wider variety of goods and suppliers on the market, and the demand for many of these goods frequently in excess of supply, buyers depend on third parties to assist them in locating the best deals. Ambitious individuals who have established "companies" and have given themselves a string of impressive job titles come forward to offer their services, even when their only credential is that they themselves know someone else they presume is well connected.

As we see in the story, such people then invite others, who they assume are even better connected, to become their salaried advisors, with the clear understanding that advising means using official connections on behalf of the advisee. In this case the advisor is promised a monthly income and given a welcoming banquet (free meal) in exchange for his services. Viewers know, of course, that many so-called advisors demand and get much more for their services. They also know that such practices are one of the most common forms of corruption. In this case ambition did not pay — at least not for the stall operator. He lost his investment as well as his reputation and had to make restitution to the villager to whom he had promised delivery of the flowers.

The Seasonal Round

In traditional Chinese society the drudgery of daily life was relieved by a great variety of popular festivals.[20] Some, such as the "birthdays" of particular deities, were only local, others, regional or even national. A visitor to contemporary Taiwan or Hong Kong can still see vibrant public celebrations of such traditional holidays as Lunar New Year (in China now referred to as Spring Festival), Ching Ming (in China spelled Qingming), the Dragon Boat Festival, the "Hungry Ghosts" Festival, and Mid-Autumn Festival.

From the time of its founding in 1949, however, the Communist government has been ambivalent about these festivals. It opposes the celebration of various holidays for reasons of ideology, politics, and economics. Ideologically the Communist Party is atheistic, viewing religion, the basis of many of the holidays, as the "opiate of the people." Belief in spirits and such popular religious practices as divination and the appeasements of ghosts are officially dismissed as "superstition," the unfortunate outcome of ignorance. Although formal organized religions came under tight control, the government was less confident of its ability to control popular manifestations of religion, whether domestic or public. Ideally, through education the masses would come to appreciate the triumphs of science and recognize it as superior to religion. In the meantime, however, the government discouraged the practice of popular religion by restricting the availability of the necessary paraphernalia. Incense sticks, god shelves, and paper goods such as money and garments for the dead went out of circulation. During the Cultural Revolution homes as well as shrines, temples, and monasteries were ransacked by Red Guards seeking material evidence of religious worship. Ancestral tablets were smashed, ancient structures and scriptures were destroyed, and believers were thoroughly intimidated.

Political opposition to the festivals derives from the opportunity their public celebration presents for rival forces — temple associations, organized religion, lineages, or, in a worst-case scenario, secret societies — to display their mobilization skills and strengths. The state has no interest in facilitating the survival of extensive social networks beyond the bounds of party control. From an economic perspective the festivals have been viewed as a waste of resources that could better be used for national development. This line of thinking is also responsible for the state's efforts to streamline weddings and funerals.

The state, however, does not exist in a vacuum. It has all along had to consider the effect on citizen morale of the rigid enforcement of its beliefs and policies. When the Communist Party embarked on a new economic course meant to stimulate the development of the private sector and increase consumer demand, it realized that if it loosened ideological controls, citizens would recognize that the reforms represented a genuine reorientation of party priorities. Furthermore, the effort to open China up to the outside made it desirable to present a more hospitable environment to overseas Chinese and other foreign investors. Consequently, the state selectively lifted the controls on the public manifestation of traditional beliefs and practices. Religious paraphernalia have now been widely available on the market for over a decade. Christians may attend Sunday services and hold rituals such as funerals in their own churches. Religious associations have been able to use the courts to oust illegal occupants from their properties.

The state, however, has continued to hold the line on practices that it believes to be either utterly superstitious or politically dangerous. Thus although scores of blind soothsayers are allowed to ply their trade periodically outside of the Guanyin Temple, almost immediately behind the headquarters of the provincial government, the work of spirit mediums is still officially proscribed. And although weddings have turned into lavish events complete with videotaping of the joint banquet held by the families of the bride and groom, funerals, at least in the city, remain modest affairs. And even though foreign religious organizations may now donate funds to local private, nonprofit institutions, such as a school for the mentally retarded, political activity by any religious organization continues to be firmly discouraged.

This official ambivalence toward traditional and religious practices is reflected in celebrations in contemporary Guangzhou. The major festivals most closely associated with the family or domestic religion, such as Spring Festival and Qingming ("clear and bright," the spring grave-sweeping festival), are tolerated and their celebration even assisted, whereas those associated with organized religion, such as the Hungry Ghosts Festival, are not. The two major festivals are discussed below.

Spring Festival

The date of the Spring Festival, determined by the lunar calendar, usually falls in February of the solar calendar. Officially employees of state organs are entitled to three days off, beginning with the first day of the new year; if one of those days falls on a Sunday, they are entitled to a fourth day. Similarly, most shops and restaurants are completely closed down for these three days. Other units, such as factories or construction companies, shut down for as much as one to two weeks to allow their mostly rural workers to return to their home communities at a time when public transportation is strained way beyond its capacity. In fact, the holiday begins earlier, on the last day of the old year, when all pretense of work is abandoned. On that day only a skeleton crew reports to the workplace to tidy it up while the rest of the workers clean their own residences so that when the new year starts, everything will be in good order — actually and symbolically.

Before the workers disperse for the holiday, which traditionally lasted two weeks, they usually receive gifts of foodstuffs from their unit. In addition, depending upon their resources, units provide a variety of preholiday activities. For example, one municipal unit that served as a conference site and operated its own restaurant and hotel began holiday celebrations three days before the official start of the 1991 new year (the year of the ram) by showing a movie in its meeting hall at 2 P.M. and holding an "evening party" in its attached dance hall at 7:30 P.M. The next day I noticed a boisterous crowd made up of staff and workers in the unit's restaurant at lunch. The diners came in carrying cases of beer, liquor, and soft drinks; the din in the eating area was almost overwhelming. The lack of curtains or rugs to dampen the sound did not help. As the platters of food arrived, conversation quieted down a bit, but the volume still exceeded what would be tolerated in a Western restaurant. Periodically everyone at a table would stand and toast someone at the table.

As stomachs began to fill up, the eating pace slowed down, and people started moving about to other tables to make toasts. One man stood at a table with his empty glass, into which others tried to empty a bottle of hard liquor. He steadfastly kept his glass close to his body to shield it from others' efforts to fill it. If he took his eye or hand off the glass for one second, there was always someone nearby who would try to take advantage of his lapse of attention. Finally, he persuaded the boisterous group to pour the liquor into the glass of a man seated at the table. But they poured out only half of it and then insisted the visitor accept the rest of it and *ganbei* (drink it down). He did so, but no sooner had he finished than someone from another table rushed up to refill his glass with a newly opened bottle. He protested strongly and was rescued by an older man from his original table, who came over to retrieve him.

People left the restaurant fairly quickly after the meal, though there were some stragglers. People were clearly feeling the effects of the liquor. One young man snatched the cap off the head of an older man and put it behind his back and then on his head. The old man seemed a bit befuddled, and eventually the younger man clapped the hat back on its owner's head. Moments later the same old man approached a tall young woman walking with someone else and indicated he wanted to whisper something to her. She stepped aside to listen to him and at first seemed to have trouble understanding him; then, abruptly but not harshly, she hit him and pushed him away. Further down the road another young woman was busy hitting a young man every time he came near her. When she refused to proceed further down the road until he stayed away from her, two other young men put their arms around the offender and steered him clear of her. I am certain that both young women were responding properly to inappropriate comments from their inebriated male co-workers. All this behavior called to mind the stereotype of the American office party at Christmas.

On the last day of the old year people rush about to complete preparations for the arrival of the new year. Because the renewal of social ties, expressed in visiting, is an important part of holiday activities, families purchase and prepare snack foods in anticipation of guests, stuff small sums of money into red packets to distribute to the unmarried children of visiting friends and relatives, and decorate their apartments with an assortment of flowering and fruiting plants. Flowers and fruits are a major part of Spring Festival. In particular every household should have a big peach tree in bloom. (These are cut off at the ground with their branches bound up by rope for easy transport, like Christmas trees elsewhere.) One might or might not decorate the tree with red packets or with strings of little lights; the quantity and quality of the flowers are the most important considerations. Historically, the quantity of peach blossoms is associated with fertility whereas the fruit itself is associated with longevity. Every household should also have a living (i.e., potted with roots intact) tree bearing orange fruit. Kumquat, *gat* (C.), *gam* (C.), and similar auspicious plants are especially desirable. The golden fruits symbolize the money that will flow into the household in the coming year, and the names of the plants conjure up good fortune. *Gat*, for example, is a homonym for luck, *gam*, a homonym for gold. People also buy narcissus bulbs or nearly blossoming narcissus in the hope that they will bloom on the first day of the new year. If they bloom earlier, you lose the next year's luck, but if they bloom for the first time on the first day of the new year, you will have a lucky year. Narcissus are also valued because of their strong sweet fragrance. Various cut flowers (chrysanthemums, gladiolas, and dahlias) and even peacock feathers are frequently displayed in vases in the home. All the major hotels and restaurants also put up new year floral displays with a huge peach tree as the centerpiece, surrounded by many plants bearing orange-colored fruit. In addition, hotels, shops, and large units put up strings of lights and banners with new year's greetings and hang lanterns around their entrances.

Although the various plants can be purchased just about anywhere, the most popular places to buy them are the specially established flower markets. Various streets are closed to traffic, and bamboo stands are erected on which sellers can display their wares. These markets open on the 28th day of the lunar month and remain open until midnight on the 30th day. I had been to the flower market in Victoria Park in Hong Kong in 1976 and found it jammed with people. With considerable trepidation I set out on new year's eve to visit Guangzhou's largest flower market, on Jiaoyu Road in the center of Yuexiu district. Despite the number of people and the density of the crowds, Guangzhou's flower market was more orderly than Hong Kong's because in Guangzhou the police were directing pedestrian traffic as well as vehicular traffic. The crowd was allowed to walk only counterclockwise around the bamboo stands stretched down the middle of several streets. Just as the best way to get around on a bicycle is to travel at the same speed as everyone else, getting through the flower market required a similar adjustment of walking pace. It was nearly impossible to fall over because the people were so thick they would have supported a falling body with their own. It also was very difficult to see how many purchases could be made, for the band of people passing the sellers at any given moment was at least ten to fifteen people wide. Someone at the further edge of this band would never have been able to cut across it to reach the sellers. Remaining stationary was not an option either.

Except for a late evening excursion to the flower market, Guangzhou residents generally spend new year's eve at home, sharing the last meal of the year, snacking, chatting with family members, watching holiday fare on television, or (prior to 1993, when they were banned) setting off firecrackers, which periodically drown out conversation. Although some people stay up until dawn to welcome in the new year, most fall asleep shortly after midnight. The first three days of the new year are said to set the tone for the rest of the year. Everyone goes out of the way to be nice to others, avoids saying unlucky things, and otherwise strives to create a vision of family harmony and to maximize good luck.

Not all households in Guangzhou celebrate the new year in the same way. Young couples who live apart from their elders are likely to skimp on holiday decorations because they usually spend new year's eve and most of new year's day with the husband's family and later visit the wife's family. Other young people whose cadre families came from the north are cut off from their own traditions and have adopted only a few of the local practices. Even when a family does celebrate the new year wholeheartedly, it often does so in relative privacy, decorating the interior of its dwelling but avoiding any public display such as posting pictures of door gods or lucky sayings around its entryway. The character of the neighborhood affects public displays. Lucky sayings and burning incense sticks are rare in areas where cadre housing is concentrated but proliferate in formerly rural enclaves swallowed up in the past decade by urban sprawl. Neighborhoods having a high concentration of families with connections overseas fall in between.

I spent much of the first two days of the new year with the Yuan family, half of whose members reside in Guangzhou and half in Hong Kong. The

Yuans had all the appropriate flower and fruit trees. A truly beautiful flowering peach tree with a few chrysanthemums at its base was set in a ceramic container on a cabinet and dominated one corner of the room. Adjacent to it on the cabinet were potted narcissus, potted roses, and a potted *cha* (C.) plant (with carnation-like flowers) as well as an arrangement of cut flowers. In the dining corner of the room was a potted tree with a huge number of big *gam*-like fruits on it.

The first big meal of the new year is supposed to be meatless, but the Yuans did not follow the old rule. Their concession to the custom was to include a Buddhist vegetarian dish more or less identical to one I had been served on new year's eve by another family. The meal started off with a soup, but then our bowls were filled with white rice, and we were free to help ourselves to all the accompanying dishes. Besides the vegetarian dish the selections included a boiled and cut-up chicken with side dishes of ginger and green onions, a dish of (cooked) dried mushrooms and lettuce, a boiled and cut-up goose, a small dish of preserved salted vegetable, boiled or steamed pigs' feet with rehydrated daylily buds, a mixed meat dish (several different meats, including roast goose, arranged separately on a plate), and others I cannot recall. We had nothing to drink with the meal. Afterward we were offered tea, melon seeds (some the size of pumpkin seeds and others the size of watermelon seeds), peanuts, preserved fruits, and so forth. Seeds, of course, symbolize fertility. *Ji* (C. seed) is also a homonym for *ji* (C. son). Similarly *fasang* (C. peanut) is close to *faat saang* (C. producing birth).

I was urged to return for dinner on the second day of the new year. This meal is said to "open the year" and is supposed to be the one at which meat is consumed for the first time. The Yuans, as I have indicated, had eaten meat the day before. They asked what foods Americans eat at Christmas, and I thought to myself that the typical American Christmas menu lacks the symbolic content of the meal that opens the year, at which nearly every dish is aimed at bringing good fortune. We started with chicken soup, and then moved on to the various dishes, including a lettuce dish (lettuce is *saang choi* [C.], a homonym for *saang choih* [C. give birth to wealth]); a dish of pigs' feet and turnips (eating pigs' feet enhances one's ability to grab all the wealth that comes along); steaks, or *faai* (C. slices), of *saang yu* (C.), a kind of fish (*saang yu faai* is a homonym for *saang yuh faai* [C. give birth to much happiness]); a Buddhist vegetarian dish composed primarily of *hoi sin* (C. seafood), a homonym for *hoi sihn* (C. open up [for] happiness). Essential ingredients of this seafood dish are *houh si* (C. dried oysters), a homonym for *hou sih* (C. good things/events) and a very fine black seaweed known as *faat choi* (C. hair-like vegetable), a homonym for *faat choih* (C. produce wealth). We also had mushroom caps stuffed with ground pork and topped with a bit of duck egg yolk; the round dried mushrooms symbolize old coins, and the egg yolk, the hole in the center of the coins through which a string was passed to make a string of cash. We also had roast goose (with red skin) and boiled chicken (with yellow skin); I could not catch their significance except that the color of the skin had some relationship to the eater's good health. There was also a beef dish with *chou gu* (C. grass mushrooms) that happened to be placed near me. Except for me and the person next to me, who picked out some grass mushrooms but left the beef behind, no one so much as touched it. People are reluctant to eat beef during the new year because of compassion for the water buffalo whose life is spent in servitude to humankind. Other dishes included a large, steamed fish, preserved sliced duck eggs (a green gelatinous kind of egg), and vinegared diagonally sliced carrots and daikon. This last dish is intended to assist digestion. The vinegar is said to counteract all the fat and oil consumed.

I had originally assumed that the point of this dish was to have something *syun* (C. sour), a homonym for *seuhn* (C. favorable or smooth, as in favorable circumstances or smooth going). A related good luck symbol is a *syuhn* (C. boat), another homonym for *seuhn;* thus a boat with billowing sails concretely suggests smooth sailing in the new year. This boat motif is often found on new year's cards. On the fourth day of the new year I had lunch at the White Swan Hotel coffee shop. A man dressed as the god of wealth, accompanied by an assistant beating gongs, made the rounds of the tables distributing red packets, each containing a coin-shaped piece of chocolate wrapped in gold paper. Stamped into the paper was this same image of a boat in full sail. Along the rim, half-encircling the boat, were the words in English APLEASANTJOURNEYTOYOU. This was all very appropriate for a hotel located on a river bank and catering to tourists!

Qingming

The official date of Qingming, the most important annual festival of the dead, is April 5 (by the solar calendar). In fact, however, because of the crowding that would occur were everyone to visit ancestral graves on the same day, it is customary in urban Guangzhou to celebrate Qingming as early as two to three Sundays before this date. (Because workers are not given time off for this holiday, most families have no choice but to visit the cemetery on a Sunday.) If a family member has died since the previous Qingming, it is essential to perform the grave-sweeping ceremony on behalf of this person on or just before April 5. If no person has died since the previous Qingming, anytime around April 5 will do. I was warned when I set out with a local resident on the Sunday immediately before Qingming in

1991 that the cemetery would be unbelievably crowded, but because of bad weather (rain, wind, and cold) it was not. Although there was no tie-up, plenty of police were in evidence to control traffic.

We went first to the Silver River (i.e., Milky Way) Revolutionary Public Graveyard, which is directly across the street from the Silver River Public Graveyard. The revolutionary graveyard is for cadres above a certain rank, the other for the masses. These are the only legitimate cemeteries for Guangzhou's urban residents.[21] Adjacent to the graveyard for the masses is the crematorium, which was spewing forth smoke with a distinctive odor at the time of our arrival. The cadre graveyard actually has a few graves in it—those of people who died in the 1950s, before cremation was made the official rule. Just below these graves are rows of what look like very small graves, each with a distinctive headstone. In fact, they are burial plots for boxes containing ashes. Several such plots had sticks of incense burning before them, and a few families were setting up candles and offerings in the narrow space separating the rows of headstones.

As I indicated in Chapter 3, the ashes of most of the deceased are kept at the ash depository (a building at the cemetery), in a container reminiscent of a small jewelry box. The boxes sit in glass-fronted compartments about 10 inches wide, 5 inches high, and 18 inches deep in a tall, cabinet-like structure that extends nearly the width of the building. The box of ashes occupies the rear center of the compartment, with the remaining space decorated as family members consider appropriate. One family, for example, had placed a teapot to the left of the box because the deceased had liked to drink tea. Otherwise they had put in the standard tiny arrangements of artificial flowers: tiny memorial wreaths (inexpensive miniatures of the real ones used at funerals), with streamers listing the names of those who sent them, or vases of flowers. Along the route to the graveyard there were many people selling these floral arrangements as well as incense, candles, hell bank notes (from Hong Kong), and gold-marked papers.*

The ash compartments are arranged in rows eight compartments high and twenty compartments long, so that there are 320 compartments on each aisle of the depository. There were probably six aisles on either side of the center of the building, making for some 2,000 containers. Presumably the other side had the same number. Thus around 4,000 people were accommodated in a small space—one of the professed goals of those who

---

* According to folk beliefs a soul, before it is reborn, spends 49 days traversing hell. Inevitably it has expenses during this journey. Bank notes drawn on the Bank of Hell are the primary acceptable currency. These are manufactured in Hong Kong and are burned at the grave (or elsewhere) for the use of the soul. Even better than currency is gold itself. Thus gold paper or squares of paper with embossed gold centers are also available. Burning transmits the essence of the currency or gold to hell. In Hong Kong mock U.S. dollar bills, Japanese yen, and credit cards are also believed to be negotiable in hell.

advocated replacing burial by cremation. The people eligible to have their ashes kept here for a small rental fee are cadres above a certain rank and those who "sacrificed" themselves for the sake of the country, that is, died in the line of duty. Thus the ashes of doctors and professors as well as of military and administrative cadres are deposited here. In a more exclusive but otherwise quite similar depository elsewhere on the site families had added to the compartment party flags or pictures of the once prominent deceased in his office or at his desk.

People constantly came and went through the depository door, removing boxes of ashes from their compartments (grave sweeping has necessarily been replaced by box dusting) and taking them outside to areas set aside for "worshiping" activities. The boxes were carefully carried from their compartments in both hands with the front of the box facing forward. Both worshiping areas are sheltered by tin roofs; under them tables can be rented for a short period for the family rituals. There were about 30 tables, each occupied, though there was no conspicuous crowd waiting to rent a table. The box of ashes was centered squarely at the rear of the table (the rear being whichever side faced out), with incense sticks, candles, fruit, sugarcane, and meat offerings arranged before it. The meat was either a steamed chicken propped forward to bow, a roast duck or goose, or a roast suckling pig. Many families were burning paper money for the spirit of the deceased. Although the family eats some of the offering at the "grave-site" ceremony to share the meal with the ancestor, the real consumption occurs later when the family returns home.

It is worth noting that these traditional rites were being carried out in the *cadre* graveyard and were facilitated by the state. At the same time they were clearly domestic and not lineage rites; that is, the rites were performed by individual families for their immediate ancestors and not by lineages for their collective ancestors. Nor did all cadre families make offerings to their deceased. Some restricted their activities to dusting the ash box and its compartment and bowing three times before it.

When I crossed the street to visit the cemetery for the masses, I noticed a wider variety of traditional items for sale than on the cadre side. For example, whereas stalls on the cadre side sold incense, candles, hell bank notes, cut flowers, and miniature artificial floral arrangements, those on the other side also offered *fengche* (pinwheels that draw in good luck) as well as miniature paper or plastic replicas of TV sets (showing cartoons), refrigerators, combination washer-dryers, and radio-cassette recorders (at 2 yuan apiece). Here the compartments in the depository were slightly larger than those for the cadre, but they were split into two levels, so the total space per person was actually less. Ashes in this section were deposited not only in the boxes I had seen earlier but also in white pottery urns painted with blue designs. In addition, more conspicuous displays of concern for the well-being of the deceased were observable from the placement of miniature cars, refrigerators, sets of chairs, and even modern bathtubs and shower fixtures along with the usual artificial flowers. The rows of compartments reached nearly to the ceiling, and a high ladder was required to fetch remains from the upper levels. Public ritual activities were similar to those in the cadre area but a little more elaborate: paper garments were being burned for the deceased, and the volume of exploding firecrackers was deafening. A heavy pall of smoke from these rituals hung over the whole area.

People in Guangzhou became bold enough to explode firecrackers and burn paper offerings at Qingming only in the mid-1980s. During the Cultural Revolution people had not dared to do so, though they would come and bow and dust off the boxes. The debate over the extent of this return to traditional practices was still going on in the early 1990s. In 1991 a member of the Provincial People's Congress proposed a ban on firecrackers at Qingming. (This was passed in 1993.) A few weeks later a provincial report was publicized expressing special concern about funeral practices in the rural areas, where the transition from burial to cremation has not been carried out, a deviation from the ideal tolerated because of the shortage of crematoria in the rural areas. The report said people were disturbed by the reversion to tradition and superstitious practices and noted that burials waste resources (wood, land, and funds). Families have also found themselves the objects of extortion. When they assemble at an ancestral grave, two or three scythe-bearing men suddenly appear, begin cutting grass before a word can be said, and then demand payment for their unsolicited services. Furthermore, the resurgence of organized ancestor worship has been leading to disputes between groups and is socially disruptive.

Yet the state can restrict only so much; as we saw in Chapter 3, nearly everyone regards participation in Qingming as essential. This is one of the two occasions of the year (Spring Festival is the other) when all the relatives gather; furthermore, they gather in a spirit of cooperation. Whatever their individual disputes, these will not be allowed to interfere with worshiping their ancestors. If you neglect the ancestors, they might become irritated with you. Certainly the relatives who are still alive will take a dim view of your behavior. For these reasons urban dwellers even send money back to their ancestral villages to contribute toward the worship of grandparents and other, more remote, ascendants.

Other Traditional Festivals

The Dragon Boat Festival falls in early June, but because it remains primarily a rural festival, it has little impact on the lives of urban residents, who receive no time off for it. At most, official travel to the countryside is curtailed for several days, for everyone knows it will be nearly impossible to conduct business while the locals are out viewing the dragon boat races. During the festival both urban and rural families eat the traditional dish of steamed dumplings made from sticky rice and wrapped in leaves.

In Hong Kong the "Feast of the Souls," or Hungry Ghosts Festival, is one of the most publicly celebrated holidays. It falls during the seventh lunar month, at which time the souls of the dead are said to wander the earth. Although educated people ignore the holiday, the more tradition oriented are likely to participate enthusiastically in both the domestic and public arenas. One's own ancestors are welcomed back on their annual home visits, and unrelated ghosts are pacified with offerings made at the entrance to one's dwelling. (In 1983 I had to interrupt an interview with an elderly woman in a public housing estate because she was eager to begin burning her offerings. As I left her apartment and entered the public corridor, I was startled to find that about 20 percent of the households had metal wastebaskets full of burning paper in front of their doors.)

In the public domain various groups of donors sponsor several days of entertainment for the wandering ghosts on stages hastily erected on public playgrounds or in the courtyards of housing estates. Buddhist monks and nuns are hired to chant for hours on end. Goods are donated and auctioned off for charity. Beggars (future hungry ghosts) gather for the distribution of sacks of rice. In short, with neither government sponsorship nor censorship there is more than enough popular enthusiasm in Hong Kong to make the Hungry Ghosts Festival a grand occasion. In Guangzhou, however, evidence of this holiday is conspicuous by its absence. Occasional bursts of firecrackers (in 1987) indicated that at least some households acknowledged the ghosts, but there were no public displays analogous to those in Hong Kong.

The holiday traditionally known as "Double Nine," because of its arrival on the ninth day of the ninth lunar month, is celebrated in Guangzhou as both a "height-ascending" festival and the autumn grave festival (a pale imitation of Qingming). Because this is not a public holiday, celebrants usually climb hills (to improve their luck or just to enjoy the scenery) or visit graves on Sunday or their regular day off. The favored mountain to climb in Guangzhou is Baiyun, or White Cloud.[22] One middle-ranking cadre (a 38-year-old university graduate) I know well laughed, embarrassed that he and his wife had climbed White Cloud Mountain on this date in 1992 on the advice of his wife's younger brother. He himself had no interest, but his wife really wanted to go. Because people climb as couples, he reasoned that he could not really let his wife go alone. He took a nap when they reached the top; when they started their descent, he was amazed to see the whole mountain swarming with people! The couple's luck changed within months of their climb: the wife received a promotion (she had feared she was slated to be let go), and the husband changed companies. Of course these things had nothing to do with the ascent, but his brother-in-law argues that surely he feels better now than before the climb and insists that to maintain the luck they must repeat the climb for the next two years. They will probably do so — just for the good feelings.

Official Holidays

The Chinese government has introduced its own set of national holidays to promote a belief system and set of values different from those represented by the traditional festivals. Nearly all these holidays ostensibly promote socialist values: Women's Day, March 8 (women have the day off); Workers Day, May 1 (one day off); Youth Day, May 4 (no day off but young people have meetings or parties); Children's Day, June 1 (children have the day off, receive presents, are taken on outings); Party Day, July 1 (no day off); Army Day, August 1 (no day off); and National Day, October 1, celebrating the founding of the People's Republic of China. Spring Festival and National Day are the only holidays when everyone has the same days off. The two-day vacation for National Day is usually spent visiting family and friends.

In 1991 I had the opportunity to participate in some of the Women's Day afternoon activities sponsored by the Women's Federation at the Dongfang Hotel. The purpose of the gathering was to allow foreign and local women to get a chance to know each other; at least 200 people were present. Although all the Chinese guests were dressed nicely, many of the foreign women, underestimating the formality of the occasion, had come in casual attire. Unfortunately, it was difficult to get to know others because of the simultaneous activities going on. As people talked around the tables of food, officials from the sponsoring organizations gave speeches from the stage that were translated in segments into English. Thus it was hard to know what the officials actually said. It was my sense that the speeches focused on women's contributions, for every now and then I caught snatches of production figures.

Following the speeches we were invited to eat from the various tables and get acquainted. No sooner had we started to eat, however, than the entertainment began. Most of it was high-volume music and singing by a live band with a female lead vocalist/drummer. She was very good, but while she performed conversation was impossible. After this performance we were asked to volunteer for two teams, one of foreigners and one of Chinese, to compete onstage in learning a little dance to the song "You Are

My Sunshine." The Westerners, embarrassed, proved inept. After the dancing a skit was presented involving a bride sitting in a basket hung from the groom's carrying pole. Next two more teams, again one of foreigners and one of Chinese, were culled from the audience to play a version of musical chairs. The winners of one competition received electric irons. To a Westerner the iron seemed an odd prize to be offered by an organization officially promoting the rights of women. To the Chinese, however, the electric irons probably symbolized progress and modernity.

Conclusions

The post-1978 reforms, in particular the reestablishment of the private sector, the creation of a new fiscal environment, and the cultural openness have had a major impact on how the people of Guangzhou spend their leisure time. Although each reform has been significant in its own right, together they have had a multiplier effect. First, the reestablishment of the private sector has permitted the establishment or expansion of commercial and service industries — for example, fast-food restaurants, home appliance repair shops, and "decoration" companies. These ventures reduce the burden of shopping, food preparation, repair work, and housing maintenance and thereby free up time for other pursuits, including leisure. Second, foreigners have proved willing to invest directly in the entertainment industry, in films, music, and nightclubs, thereby providing new diversions for the masses and making cultural workers less dependent on state work units. Such investments have, on the one hand, broadened the range of acceptable cultural work and, on the other, created the role of the freelance artist.

The creation of a new fiscal environment means much more than simply the possibility of foreign funding. By requiring state units, including those in communications, to become increasingly self-sufficient, the state has forced the mass media to be responsive to market forces. Now that newspapers and broadcasting stations must derive most of their funds from the sale of advertising, they must demonstrate that they reach a wide audience. To attract that audience they must produce newspapers or programming with popular appeal. Articles or programs with heavy-handed ideological content lack such appeal and consequently have been almost entirely displaced.

The new cultural openness is intimately connected with increased diversity in programming. Because China itself still does not produce enough popular works to fill the television airwaves, local broadcasters inevitably look abroad for suitable material. In this way the population of Guangzhou has become accustomed to viewing reruns of martial arts films and of contemporary dramatic serials and soap operas from Hong Kong, Taiwan,

Japan, the United States, and Great Britain. The values implicit in these works are seldom compatible with the socialist values officially espoused by the party. Indeed, instead of being called upon to serve some greater common good, today's television viewers are being encouraged implicitly, through programs such as *Dynasty*, and explicitly, in advertisements, to focus on becoming affluent so that they can lead glamorous or at least comfortable lives like the people they see on television.

The state has not, however, stood idly by. News coverage remains consistently supportive of official national goals, and newspaper editors and broadcasters continue to promote moral development. Thus *Southern Daily* hoped to keep youth on the right path through its column "A Hundred Cases to Be Resolved," and GDTV's program "One Hundred Life Events" guides people facing novel situations as a result of the reforms (or other policy changes). Similarly, although the state may be relatively tolerant of behavior it would have condemned a decade ago as "bourgeois," it remains less tolerant of behavior viewed as "feudal superstition." Thus the public celebration of traditional holidays in many cases remains muted, however elaborately individuals may celebrate in the privacy of their own homes.

| *Conclusion*

*T*he preceding chapters examined the post-Mao reforms and the experiences of the people of Guangzhou as they have adapted to the nation's transition from a planned to a market economy. Broadly speaking, the reforms have aimed at "enlivening" the economy and "opening up to the outside." Enlivening the economy has meant finding alternative employment for millions of surplus agricultural laborers, re-creating a vigorous private sector, increasing the efficiency of state enterprises, enhancing urban job mobility, and reducing the welfare obligations of the state by shifting some of the financial responsibility for funding onto the individual. Opening up to the outside has entailed seeking foreign investment, creating a hospitable environment for compatriots and over-seas Chinese (the primary foreign investors), and tolerating cultural and ideological incursions from abroad. In carrying out these reforms Chinese leaders have been largely pragmatic, first speaking vaguely of developing a "commodity" economy or "socialism with Chinese characteristics"; later justifying their policies in Marxist terms, which theoretically allow a private economy in a country, like China, still in "the initial stages of socialism"; and most recently emphasizing that ownership and not management of the means of production is the essence of socialism and that therefore China is not betraying socialism by developing a market economy.

Have these reforms improved the standard of living for China's urban population? Let us look at two kinds of data: per capita income and overall economic development. In 1978 the national annual per capita income (including basic wage, bonus, and subsidies but not noncash benefits such as housing or health insurance) of urban residents amounted to 316 yuan. In 1992 this figure had risen to 1,826 yuan — a nearly sixfold increase if one ignores the impact of inflation. But even when price rises are taken into account, real incomes grew by a factor of 2.3 over this period.[1] This improvement results directly from four different factors. First, the overall rate of employment has gone up. (Recall all the efforts to employ those millions of youth "awaiting employment" in the late 1970s.) Increased employment brought the dependency ratio (the number of persons supported by each employed person) down from 2.06 persons in 1978 to 1.73 in 1992. Second, the government deliberately kept incomes ahead of price increases by raising the wage scale, introducing the bonus system, and increasing the amount and kinds of subsidies included in the wage packet. Third, the greatest income growth and the widest spread in income have occurred in the newly sanctioned private sector. Finally, as we have seen, many people have increased their incomes by either taking on second jobs or rejoining the labor force immediately following retirement.[2] In 1993 incomes continued to soar, increasing by 28 percent to 2,337 yuan per capita. Although 1993 was a year of high inflation, this figure nevertheless represents real continued growth of 10.2 percent over 1992.[3]

In 1978 Deng Xiaoping proposed the year 2000 as the date by which all of China's major cities would achieve a living standard of "relatively well-off." According to a survey conducted by the Chinese Academy of Social Sciences (CASS), 24 of China's cities, mostly in coastal areas, had already achieved this objective by 1993.[4] Employing data from the State Statistics Bureau, CASS set up six indices (based on a total of 31 items) to determine the relative ranking of the 24 cities. Beijing, Shanghai, and Changsha were highest in the cultural category, Hangzhou, Suzhou, and Anshan, in social stability. Guangzhou was rated high in economic efficiency and quality of life but relatively low in population quality and social stability.* The reformers seem to be achieving their economic targets for China's citizens. This success is important not only in and of itself but also as a prerequisite to the continuation of the reforms. Without confidence that their own living standard would not fall, China's urban dwellers would have been ill prepared to tolerate the other primary objective of the reformers — decreasing the enormous burden of welfare and subsidies the government has had to bear so that its enterprises could become more efficient.

Over the past fifteen years China has chosen to bring about this economic transition in its own way. It has taken a gradualist approach, testing out a myriad of local experiments before deciding which to make national policy and requiring that implementation take account of local financial

---

* The *China Daily* article does not explain the terms "cultural category" or "population quality." The first may relate to the number of educational and cultural institutions in the city and the second to the level of education or literacy of the population or even to life expectancy.

conditions. It has also attempted to minimize disruption to the lives of the adults already in the work force by applying the most worrisome reforms, at least initially, to newcomers but not old-timers. The state has also been attentive to the results of individual reforms and has backed away from or modified them when they did not work. Most important, the state has recognized that it cannot rely entirely on market forces but must continue to play a role in protecting its citizens from a too freewheeling economy.

Let us review some of the state's attempts to reduce its responsibility for employee welfare by shifting it to individual work units and to the workers themselves before we consider how the state has compensated those who have benefited least by the reforms. Prior to the reforms individual workers were not required to contribute toward their pensions or, except for a nominal registration fee, to their medical treatment. As we have seen, the proportion of the population receiving pensions grew rapidly during the 1980s, as did the per capita costs of the health insurance program. If these expenses were not controlled, enterprises would not be able to manage their budgets and would sink further and further into debt. Contract workers were the first to be asked to contribute part of their monthly wage packet toward their future pensions, but eventually all workers were brought in.

Initial attempts to reform the system of free medical care (*gungfei yiliao*) in 1988 in Guangdong were less successful — perhaps because all insured and not just newcomers were expected to assume a share of the costs. When the provincial government tried to introduce a modest copayment scheme, it found that staff and workers were simply not ready for it and quietly backed down from enforcing its own regulations after only a few months. Not until six years later, in mid-1994, was the government confident enough to attempt again to require copayments from the insured, and this time it offered the carrot of a special monthly medical subsidy so that for most of the insured the additional costs would be easily borne.

In the same spirit of reducing state financial responsibility, but this time in the field of higher education, the government authorized the admission to colleges and universities of students paying their own tuition, giving them the carrot of freedom from compulsory job assignments. As household incomes went up, it became easier for the state to require even government-funded students to pay for their meals and, by the late 1980s, a portion of their tuition. Then in 1994 government funding was restricted (experimentally in several schools) to only a small minority of the students with the highest scores on entrance tests. All others were put on their own financially *and* freed to search for employment without interference after graduation. Students who could not otherwise afford to go on for higher education were granted scholarships if they agreed to major in specializations where candidates were in short supply and, upon graduation, accept whatever employment the state assigned.

A similar tentative approach was used to introduce the concept of housing reform. First an enormous amount of new housing was built. Because this was higher quality than the old housing, higher rents could be justified, though in fact higher rents were charged even for older housing. Then the state attempted to rid itself of the expense of maintaining all this housing by making it financially attractive for occupants to purchase their dwellings. So attractive were the terms in Guangzhou that tens of thousands of housing units were sold off within two years. During this same period, however, because of a phenomenal real estate boom, the actual value of the housing skyrocketed, and the state was left feeling that *it* had been expropriated. Consequently, housing reform was suspended at the beginning of 1994 until the state could determine a more equitable way of arranging a transfer of ownership.

At the same time that the government was trying to reduce some of its traditional welfare responsibilities, it realized that some segments of the population had not benefited financially from the reforms to the same extent as others and took steps to reduce the gap between the new haves and have-nots. Two factors probably motivated these compensatory actions: the genuine belief that by definition no socialist society (or even a socialist market economy) can tolerate great differences in income among the wage-earning population and a concern about the possible destabilizing effects of highly visible and major differences in wealth. To cope with these problems the state slowly created a minimal financial safety net, including unemployment insurance, extension of worker protections to those employed in foreign firms, the setting of a minimum wage, and a new means of calculating pensions.

Unemployment insurance was initially presented as a means of promoting labor mobility and protecting workers whose contracts had expired. Only later was the rest of the labor force (those who thought they had iron rice bowls) informed that they too would be eligible for these benefits if their units went bankrupt or merged with others. So worried was the state about the consequences of actually laying off workers that nationwide only 300,000 people were laid off by state enterprises in the five-year period 1986–1991. But as the unemployment insurance system became more familiar to the populace and as the state gained confidence, the number of layoffs began to accelerate; in 1992 alone, 340,000 people laid off from state-owned enterprises received unemployment compensation, and in the first six months of 1993 the number doubled to over 700,000.[5]

When the state reestablished the legitimacy of the private sector, it at first said little about the rights of workers—how, after all, could the self-employed (*geti hu*) be said to need protection from themselves? Similarly, in the early 1980s the state was so eager to encourage foreign investment that although joint ventures were required to participate in the developing social insurance schemes (pensions, medical insurance, disability payments, etc.), for all practical purposes most wholly foreign-owned firms were not. Even in Guangdong (a province nominally requiring foreign firms to participate in the social insurance system) 44 percent of the workers in foreign firms in late 1993 lacked medical coverage. In early 1994, when the national (and provincial) government felt that foreign firms were sufficiently established (and that their owners had more than made their money's worth), it announced the extension of the social insurance schemes to all workers in all enterprises. No longer were the profits of the private sector to be allowed to rest so heavily on the exploitation of its workers.

The state also eventually took steps to protect the incomes of the most disadvantaged workers and retirees. Because the least desirable jobs were likely to be held by migrant workers desperate for employment and with little knowledge of the local wage scales, it was easy for employers to pay them low wages. In early 1994, following a period of price increases, all provinces and municipalities were required to establish a minimum wage based on local economic conditions and to implement it by July 1. The minimum wage was pegged at not less than half the local average wage. Shanghai, for example, set the minimum monthly wage at 210 yuan whereas the Special Economic Zones of Shenzhen and Zhuhai set theirs at 280 and 326 yuan, respectively.[6]

At just about the same time, the state announced a new system of calculating pension payouts. Previously retirees' incomes had been based primarily on a fixed percentage of their last basic wage. Those who had retired prior to or in the early years of the reform period had retired when wages were still very low; consequently, despite periodic subsidies given to all urban workers (and retirees) to compensate for inflation during the 1980s and early 1990s, their monthly income remained extremely low. Recognizing the erosion of the retirees' standard of living, the state announced that beginning in January 1994 the retirees' incomes would be based on current wages; that is, they now receive at a minimum a pension equal to 30 percent of the average monthly wage for the current year in their locale. Both the pension standard and the minimum wage standard are to be redetermined (indexed for inflation) annually.

Housing policy represents another example of state efforts to reduce the developing gap between the new haves and the have-nots. As we saw in Chapter 2, households occupying very small dwelling units were classified as hardship and exceptional hardship households on the basis of their per capita living space. In Guangzhou in 1991 this population was targeted for accelerated housing relief; the state built special housing and made it available by lottery and at low cost to those experiencing "exceptional" hardship. Over the course of the next two years additional lotteries were held until nearly all such households had been relocated, and plans were made to extend the lotteries to the next (nonexceptional but still disadvantaged) hardship category.

As all these examples illustrate, unlike some of the countries of Eastern Europe or the former Soviet Union, China did not believe that the best way to reform the economy was to apply shock therapy. Nor, despite the staunch belief of Western political scientists that economic and political reform must go hand in hand, did it intend that economic reform be accompanied by political reform (democratization). Indeed, the collapse of the Soviet Union has confirmed the Chinese government's view that political stability is the bedrock of economic reform. Interestingly, many dissidents, active in the Tiananmen demonstrations in 1989, have been converted to this view or at least have abandoned their more radical proposals. Although I encountered many ordinary people who were discontented with the Communist Party ("It's rotten") and especially with corruption in high and low places, they did not have a clear vision of an alternative; few had strong convictions. Most merely hoped that the party would simply fade away or evolve into a nonideological body. Chaos, political or economic, is greatly feared by both the government and the people.

Defenders of the current course argue that in fact the process of democratization has already begun. They point to Beijing's increased difficulty in its tax and budgetary negotiations with the provinces as indicating the increasing decentralization of political power. They point too to the occasional assertion of independence by the provincial and city people's congresses, which have refused to ratify party candidates for appointment to high office. Furthermore, the party's own policies of both freeing enterprise managers from party control over economic decision making and expanding the proportion of the economy that is outside the state plan reduce the party's sphere of influence. Whether Western political scientists will interpret decentralization of power and an overall reduced role of the state in the economy as processes equivalent to democratization remains to be seen. There are currently few signs that the Chinese leadership is prepared to go much further than this. Indeed, if the government is able to sustain economic growth, it may not need to go further for quite some time.

Yet despite the economic progress and the overall improvement in their standard of living, urban dwellers remain worried. The increasing disparity in income across different segments of the urban population is the single most remarked upon negative associated with the transition to a market economy and is also, as I have noted, of enormous concern to the government. The nature of this concern, however, reflects different interests. Some discontent is ideologically driven; that is, longtime members of the Communist Party simply cannot accept what they perceive as the restoration of capitalism. When they see the return of flashily dressed prostitutes and foreign businessmen on the one hand and shabbily dressed rural migrants on the other, they wonder why they fought the revolution. Some discontent is politically driven; perceptive observers question just how long workers will tolerate these disparities without resorting to demonstrations and demands for change. They worry about the potential for chaos. And, finally, much discontent is personally driven; segments of the population feel that although they may have benefited somewhat, others (less deserving) have benefited even more. Thus urban workers are dismayed when rural entrepreneurs have incomes approaching theirs. Workers in the state sector are irritated when workers in the collective and private sectors make more money than they do. Office workers and intellectuals are angry when production workers' incomes increase more than their own. And almost everyone is angry that who-knows-how-many cadres have enriched themselves through a combination of bribes and embezzlement.

There is a pervasive sense of disillusionment—a sense that even though the standard of living has gone up, something else has been lost. Human feelings and relationships seem to have been replaced by a drive to make money no matter what it takes and no matter how dishonest the means. One senior cadre who in 1987 had been an all-out advocate of reform had this to say in 1993:

The level of morality has dropped drastically. Girls think nothing of coming from villages for a short stint as a prostitute and then going home proud of the money they take back. *Nothing* is guiding people—not Marxism, not Confucianism, not religion. At least religion put the fear of hell into one [he describes various scenarios from popular renditions of Buddhist hell], but now people don't believe in these things.

Along with this sense that anything goes is an underlying fear that although one may have done well so far, something terrible, such as an announcement from one's factory that 100 people are being put on leave, could be just around the corner.

Yet perhaps this pessimistic assessment is a bit overdrawn. After all, there really is agreement now that (at least in the moral domain) things have gone too far. People are beginning to think seriously about issues of equity, and popular television programs such as "One Hundred Life Events" are offering guidelines for people who did not at first understand that "freedom" does not mean the absence of all limits. It is important to keep in mind that China is in transition, not in a permanent state. Readers whose experience extends back to the 1960s in Hong Kong and Taiwan will not be shocked by the free-for-all in Guangzhou today. In fact, this experience allows us some perspective. If Hong Kong and Taiwan could survive the tumult and moral murkiness of their day, one suspects that Guangzhou will too.

Reference Matter

Notes

1 | The City of Guangzhou

1. Its popularity, however, was not new. For example, in "Wonderful Canton," a poem of 50 stanzas written in 1959 by the then mayor of Guangzhou, we find the following paean to the *hongmian*.

> Wonderful Canton
> The cottonwood tree seems so noble when the leaves fall
> and the flowers open.
> They fly like the flaming phoenix,
> Their flowers are like red dragons rising to the sun.
> And in March the spring breezes begin to blow.

The whole poem is found in Vogel 1969, pp. 358–68.

2. This patriotic, revolutionary history begins with the unsuccessful Chinese effort to confront the imperialists with Commissioner Lin's confiscation of opium from the British in Guangzhou in 1839. The leader of the Taiping Rebellion and two leaders of the 1898 Reform Movement were Cantonese. In the spring of 1911 Sun Yatsen staged an unsuccessful armed uprising against the Qing Dynasty governor of Guangdong and Guangxi. The Huanghuagang Park in Guangzhou contains the remains of 72 of the revolutionaries who lost their lives in the battle. In yet another unsuccessful venture in December 1927 the Communists in Guangzhou attempted a coup against the Guomindang government, which earlier in the year had purged the Communists from its ranks. A memorial to this event occupies 260,000 square meters of prime real estate in western Dongshan district.

3. The following account of the history of Guangzhou is drawn from Chang 1986, *The Archaeology of Ancient China*; Guangzhou Social Sciences Research Institute 1986, *Handbook of Investment and Tourism in Guangzhou*; Fairbank 1992, *China*; and Vogel 1969, *Canton Under Communism*.

4. Vogel 1969, p. 19.

5. The following works (among others) discuss the origins of the Chinese in the United States: Fessler 1983, *Chinese in America*; Miller 1969, *The Unwelcome Immigrant*; and Sung 1967, *The Story of the Chinese in America*.

6. See Vogel 1969, pp. 102–3, for a fuller discussion of this problem.

7. See Vogel 1989.

8. Guangzhou Shi Tongji Ju 1993, p. 433.

9. The text of the regulations can be found in Guangzhou Social Sciences Research Institute 1986, pp. 246–50.

10. Guangzhou Shi Tongji Ju 1992, table on the fifth of a set of unnumbered pages of tables at the front of the yearbook.

11. Ibid., p. 307.

12. See, for example, Whyte and Parish 1984.

13. See, for an example of the conventional view, Ramsey 1987. Speaking for the opposing view, DeFrancis 1984 suggests the neutral and intermediate term "regionalect" to describe the Chinese languages.

14. Reported in the *Cleveland Plain Dealer*, Mar. 1, 1992.

15. The text of the law is available in Guangzhou Social Sciences Research Institute 1986, pp. 175–80; regulations (promulgated in 1983 to take effect in 1985) to implement the law can be found on pp. 181–221.

16. All these changes are detailed in Vogel 1989.

17. Vogel 1969, pp. 22–24. These are the same four subpopulations described in Blake 1981.

18. The reader interested in a fuller discussion of the meaning of urbanization in post-1949 China is referred to the following works: Guldin 1992, *Urbanizing China*; Kojima 1987, *Urbanization and Urban Problems in China*; Kwok et al. 1990, *Chinese Urban Reform*; and Whyte and Parish 1984, *Urban Life in Contemporary China*.

19. Guangzhou Nianjian Bianzuan Weiyuanhui 1992, p. 68.

20. Dutton 1988.

21. Guangzhou Shi Tongji Ju 1992, p. 360.

22. Kohut 1992.

23. Jankowiak 1993, especially pp. 125–64.

24. The mediation of disputes in China also contrasts with urban behavior in the United States, or at least in Boston. At the time I was writing this section, the *Boston Globe* carried reports on three consecutive days of fatalities in traffic disputes involving strangers. The triggering offenses were passing in a no-passing zone (causing no harm to the occupants of the vehicle that was passed), failure to respond quickly enough to a light that had just turned green, and some similar insult. No racial or ethnic motivation was in evidence. All the incidents involved youths and alcohol and occurred in the absence of neutral observers. One youth was twice run over by his antagonist, a second was stabbed to death, and a third was shot. The dangers inherent in attempting to mediate in these circumstances serve as effective deterrents to any would-be judicial samaritan.

25. Butterfield 1982. For reports of extramarital sexual activity in rural China during the Cultural Revolution, see the accounts in Chan, Madsen, and Unger 1984, *Chen Village*, for rural Guangdong; for similar reports during the reform era, see Huang 1989, *The Spiral Road*, for rural Fujian.

26. Jankowiak 1993, p. 188.

27. It is difficult for a Westerner to know whether her own experiences of sexual harassment in China are typical of those of Chinese women. In the fall of 1987 I had a particularly bad run of luck. In the park an exhibitionist exposed his genitals as I jogged by (this has happened more than once in the United States under the same

circumstances). While I was walking in the Nanfang Department Store with my husband, a man openly grabbed my breast, and while I was inquiring about a guest at a hostel on Shamian, someone patted my backside. But when I related any of these incidents to Chinese women, they readily recounted their own similar experiences.

28. Kohut 1992. According to Kohut, the existence of the serial killer has not been mentioned by Guangzhou's media. Police fear that reports of the crimes would stimulate others to copycat behavior or help the killer elude detection.

29. *Boston Globe*, Dec. 13, 1992.

30. Because these crimes occur most frequently in crowded circumstances, Guangzhou residents take various defensive actions: avoiding certain buses if possible, wearing a shoulder bag bandolier style, and holding one's shoulder bag in front of oneself so that it can be kept in sight at all times. Despite following these precautions, I nearly fell victim to one of the standard ruses — the distraction routine. As I mentioned earlier, although public buses are often unbelievably crowded, people usually stand so as to minimize the inconvenience to others (relatively speaking). Thus they shrink from inappropriate contact with other passengers and avoid forcing others into an uncomfortable position. One evening, however, a tall young man pushed his way into the bus. He grasped the overhead poles on either side, and his elbow was so close that I had to cock my head to avoid having his elbow in my eye. Furthermore, I had to move slightly to evade the unacceptable intimacy of frontal contact. The aggressive posture, I realized in retrospect, is calculated to distract a woman whose purse is the true object of interest. As I maneuvered, my purse shifted (quite possibly with an assist) so that it was behind me. I felt fumbling behind my back and turned to stare at a man who I assumed was searching his own back pocket for bus fare; I was wary lest he use this opportunity as a cover for physical contact. In fact, I am pretty sure that what I felt was the man's slashing my purse. The two men had me sandwiched between them, one creating a diversion while the other worked with a knife. I did not discover the two long slashes until the next morning. Fortunately, the knife had failed to penetrate the lining. I lost nothing.

31. Whyte and Parish 1984, p. 270.

32. "Attack Black! Attack Black! Pay Close Attention to Attacking Black," *Nanfang Ribao*, Apr. 24, 1994, p. 5.

33. Deng 1987, pp. 137–38. That Deng's concern with crime was not new can be seen from his Oct. 22, 1984, "Speech at the Third Plenary Session of the Central Advisory Committee of the Communist Party of China," reprinted in the same volume. In this speech Deng mentions that he concentrates his attention on only a few very important issues each year. "Last year [1983] I devoted myself to only one thing: a crackdown on criminals" (p. 74). Indeed, in the spring of 1983 in Kunming I encountered on public bulletin boards not only notices detailing recent crimes and sentences carried out but also photographs of the executions themselves. Some 10,000 criminals were said to have been executed in 1983 as part of this crackdown.

34. For example, according to an Associated Press report appearing June 27, 1992, in the *Boston Globe*, 88 convicted drug smugglers were executed in China on June 26, International Anti–Drug Abuse Day, in 1990 and 1991. A total of 866 people were given death sentences for drug crimes in 1991, though some of these

sentences were suspended. On June 26, 1992, in Kunming, the capital of Yunnan province, 21 drug traffickers were executed and in Gansu province, 6.

35. For one woman's account of the activities of her residents committee during the Cultural Revolution in Shanghai, see Frolic 1980.

36. See, for example, Whyte and Parish 1984, pp. 284–85.

37. For the results of a survey of street committees in Guangzhou, see Chan 1993b.

38. According to consular officials in Guangzhou, Chinese visitors or illegal immigrants wanting asylum in the United States now use a new tactic: they produce a letter from their unit ordering them to report for sterilization.

39. For a fuller description of the delivery of welfare services in three Chinese cities, including Guangzhou, see Chan 1993a and Chan and Chow 1992.

40. Other categories of the population are also entitled to assistance, but because either their numbers are small (e.g., orphans) or they become eligible only under special circumstances (e.g., dependents of revolutionary martyrs or families of personnel in the armed services who have fallen on hard times), they are not discussed here. It is also highly likely that the categories childless elderly and dependent of revolutionary martyr overlap.

41. Officials were vague on the exact population included in the survey. Published sources suggest that the population surveyed was under the age of 60, but some local officials thought that those over 60 who had been handicapped most of their adult lives were also included, but not those whose handicaps were associated with the arrival of old age.

42. *South China Morning Post*, Apr. 8, 1991. It is also widely suspected that factories pad their payrolls with handicapped workers who are not required to show up for work.

43. For a thorough discussion of both inpatient and outpatient care of the mentally ill in China, see Phillips, Pearson, and Wang 1994.

44. The fullest account of the special programs available to the elderly since the establishment of the People's Republic of China is available in Davis-Friedmann 1991.

45. According to an official of the Civil Affairs Bureau in 1991, all but 200 out of about 3,000 people on relief were elderly. The population base for these figures is the urban population of Guangzhou municipality, i.e., people with urban household registration living in Guangzhou city proper as well as in the towns of the four counties. An additional 8,000 people (also overwhelmingly elderly) living in villages receive the benefits of the rural welfare plan — the so-called Five Guarantees. A higher proportion of rural childless elderly receive assistance because they have no formal affiliation with a work unit. Until 1983 or so, the only rural work units likely to be available were village production teams and village-run collective factories. Some of the income from village-run collectives is now channeled into a welfare fund that helps to support the Five Guarantees program.

2 | *Living Standards*

1. I presented a neighbor with a small gift of litchis in a plain plastic bag. He took the bag into his room, emptied out the litchis, and without a word returned the

bag to me. It was apparently self-evident that one would want one's plastic bag back. On another occasion I attempted to appropriate what I thought was an abandoned net carrying bag. When its owner, who had misplaced it, saw me carrying it, she angrily rebuked me.

2. A thorough discussion of the policies and their consequences can be found in Whyte and Parish 1984; see especially chapter 4.

3. These features were more characteristic of the state sector than of the collective sector. The distinctions between the two sectors are developed in detail in Chapter 5.

4. Off and on, particularly in the early 1960s before the Cultural Revolution, there had been attempts to link performance and wages via piece rates, but this system was at best an alternative for a minority of workers and at worst totally condemned and abandoned.

5. See Whyte and Parish 1984, pp. 85–98, for details on the rationing system and its limitations.

6. World Bank 1992, p. xii.

7. Over the space of several months in 1987 I observed the conversion of part of an old residence to a day-care center. As a special decorative touch, the interior walls were painted green. In less than a month, however, it was impossible to tell that this had been done. Either the poor quality of the paint or the texture of the wall surface (or both) caused the paint to fade into insignificance. Even with adequate money and materials such an outcome could only discourage the would-be home decorator.

8. Guangdong rural life in the mid-1970s is thoroughly covered in Parish and Whyte 1978, *Village and Family in Contemporary China*; the transformations of that life in Dongguan county are covered in Potter and Potter 1990, *China's Peasants*; and the post-1978 reforms in Guangdong are covered in Vogel 1989, *One Step Ahead in China*, especially chapter 3, "A Decade of Reforms." For a brief chronology of the national reforms, see Davis and Vogel 1990, *Chinese Society on the Eve of Tiananmen*, pp. 307–14. For a broader discussion of Chinese rural models of development, see Nolan and Dong 1990, *Market Forces in China*. For the impact of the reforms on various segments of the Chinese population, see Watson 1992, *Economic Reform and Social Change in China*; and for the most voluminous (954 pages) account of the reforms, see Joint Economic Committee 1991, *China's Economic Dilemmas in the 1990s*.

9. *Renmin Ribao*, May 9, 1988, p. 2; trans. in *FBIS-CHI*-88-091, May 11, 1988, p. 29. *FBIS-CHI* is *Foreign Broadcast Information Service–China*, published in Washington, D.C. It makes available on a nearly daily basis translations of current Chinese newspaper and journal articles as well as translations of broadcasts (and transcripts of foreign-language broadcasts) from selected countries.

10. *Renmin Ribao*, May 11, 1988, p. 2, in *FBIS*, May 11, 1988, p. 29.

11. Xinhua News Agency English-language broadcast, Apr. 28, 1988, in *FBIS-CHI*-88-082, Apr. 28, 1988, p. 35.

12. Xinhua News Agency English-language broadcast, May 5, 1988, in *FBIS-CHI*-88-087, May 5, 1988, pp. 16–17. The state had to backtrack on this intention to institute direct subsidies. Instead of decontrolling prices, it merely adjusted them. Nevertheless, over the course of the summer the politburo committed itself to

eventual decontrol of most commodity prices. This statement of commitment at a time of high inflation — the highest since 1949 (nationally the retail price index rose 19.2 percent above that of July 1987 while in urban areas of Guangdong it rose about 30 percent) — touched off a wave of panic buying. By the fall the state had announced that price reform would be put on the back burner indefinitely.

13. For a variety of reasons too complex to go into here, the state has found it difficult to enforce these regulations. Enterprises with poor financial records have repeatedly been allowed to borrow funds and have not had to face actual bankruptcy.

14. Vogel 1989, pp. 205–8.

15. In fact there was a burst of bridge building all over the Pearl River Delta. In 1980 traffic between Guangzhou and Macao faced a long wait at each of several ferry crossings. By 1991 all these ferry crossings had been replaced by bridges.

16. These figures are from Guangzhou Shi Tongji Ju 1989, p. 527, and 1994, p. 39. No data are available for the number of trucks or unit-owned vehicles in the city, but certainly these have also increased.

17. Unfortunately, however, motorists out of sight of the law relax this discipline, though not to the same degree as in 1980. At that time motorists on county roads blithely went around curves the shortest way, even when this meant crossing into the lane of oncoming traffic. Sometimes the driver would hit the horn as a preliminary, but only to say, "I'm coming. You'd better get out of the way." An oncoming bicycle was expected to dive into a ditch. Not surprisingly, I saw a number of vehicles that had taken the ditch option. By 1987 drivers kept pretty much to their own side of the road, but nonetheless passing, particularly at night, entailed considerable risk. It was difficult to estimate the speed of oncoming vehicles or even identify them. One time the driver of a vehicle I was in, assuming that the single light in the oncoming lane was that of a motorcycle, attempted to pass. When the "motorcycle" turned out to be a bus with its left light (the one nearer the center of the road) out, he abruptly abandoned the attempt.

When accidents occur on these country roads, there are no breakdown lanes for the damaged vehicles, and there are no flares to warn approaching drivers. In the daytime the evidence of an accident just around the bend is often the unexpected appearance of a leafy tree branch in the road. Drivers break one off the nearest tree and deliberately place it to ward off a rear-end collision, but such a warning is scarcely visible at night, when drivers use only their parking lights to avoid night-blinding approaching drivers or cyclists. A much more sinister finding is the presence, night and day, of large boulders in the middle of a road. They appear to come from nowhere since there is no nearby slope from which they could have rolled down. In 1990 I saw several such boulders along the main road between Guangzhou and Huizhou. Since these areas were inhabited, I wondered why no one bothered to move the boulders to the side of the road. Later I was told that they are deliberately set out by villagers hoping to precipitate accidents, so that they can carry out repairs for the hapless drivers.

18. Guangzhou Nianjian Bianzuan Weiyuanhui 1990, p. 57.

19. "Guangzhou's Telephone Dissemination Rate First in the Entire Country," *Nanfang Ribao*, Dec. 23, 1993, p. 1.

20. All of this could work havoc with people's travel plans. Soon after the sup-

posed time change one of my acquaintances was spending the week taking a Hong Kong relative around to places of interest. He discovered that flights and trains to other provinces followed the new time schedule, but that buses operating within the province followed the old time schedule. Even greater confusion was possible because counties near Hong Kong explicitly followed Hong Kong time, i.e., old time (Hong Kong does not go on daylight saving time).

21. Xinhua News Agency English-language broadcast, May 11, 1988, in *FBIS-CHI*-88-093, May 13, 1988, p. 48.

22. Guangzhou Shi Tongji Ju 1994, p. 38.

23. Guangzhou Shi Tongji Ju 1989, pp. 518–19.

24. Calculated from ibid., pp. 506–7.

25. Ibid., pp. 511–12.

26. *Guangming Ribao*, Feb. 13, 1988, p. 3; trans. in *FBIS-CHI*-88-052, Mar. 17, 1988, pp. 30–31.

27. "Guangzhou: Residents Have Their Housing," *Nanfang Ribao*, Oct. 4, 1993, p. 1.

28. World Bank 1992, p. 6.

29. Ibid., pp. 157–66.

30. Calculated from ibid., p. 158.

31. "Average Citizens Hope for Glad Tidings," part 1, *Guangzhou Ribao*, Dec. 3, 1993, p. 4.

32. The prices were reported by government officials from Dongshan and Yuexiu districts in an interview, December 1987.

33. According to World Bank 1992, p. 163, the Guangzhou Suihua House Property Development Company, an operating unit of the Guangzhou Real Estate Management Bureau, is committed to redeveloping old urban areas, but these are so densely settled that rehousing their residents consumes up to 70 percent of the newly constructed buildings — leaving only 30 percent to be sold commercially. Consequently Suihua has had to limit redevelopment projects to less than 25 percent of its construction.

34. "Average Citizens Hope for Glad Tidings," part 3, *Guangzhou Ribao*, Dec. 17, 1993, p. 9.

35. The following case is reasonably representative. In the 1950s a unit assigned the first floor of a privately owned building to one of its workers and his family, which consisted of more than ten people (eight children, the couple, the wife's mother, and possibly others). One of the building's owners (the other had fled to Hong Kong) retained use of the second floor. The first-floor apartment had a large living/dining room, a bathroom, a cooking area, and at least two, possibly three, bedrooms. This was a great deal of space by local standards, but it had originally been assigned to a very large family. The monthly rent was on the order of 20 yuan. Because no one had invested in upkeep or improvements, however, the general appearance of the unit was quite poor — dark and unadorned. Gradually the members of the family married and dispersed. Three children went to Hong Kong. Their mother, born there, was able to go back long enough to apply for them to leave China legally. Four of the other children still lived in Guangzhou, and another had taken a job in Beijing.

By 1987 the apartment had only six occupants: the grandmother (aged 86), the sixth child (fourth daughter) with her husband and three-year-old daughter, a young household worker, and the visiting son from Beijing. The couple originally assigned the housing had retired from their unit (a newspaper), but as retirees they were entitled to remain. In fact, however, they actually lived around the corner with their third daughter and her husband and nine-year-old son in a dwelling belonging to a relative living overseas.

The co-owner living on the second floor wanted to regain control of the first floor. He had his Hong Kong relative come with documents certifying his claims of overseas Chinese status and ownership of the house. But the occupants did not want to move, and the local owner had to find a judge (one he personally knew) to review the facts of the case and determine whether the household would have to vacate on the grounds of semi-illegal occupancy. The local owner also went to the newspaper and insisted that it chase out the occupants because none of them actually worked for the newspaper or had retired from it. In the end the decision rested with the retired newspaper editor who had originally been allotted the dwelling. When he decided not to continue the fight and agreed to withdraw his claim of occupancy, a new residence had to be located for the young family being evicted. Although housing was available through one of the units to which the couple belonged, it was unsatisfactory from the couple's point of view because it was much smaller than their present quarters and was in the suburbs.

To hurry the young couple on their way, the owner resorted to petty harassment, as I discovered one evening when I arrived on a visit. As I entered the gate, rain seemed to be falling in the front entrance area. I looked up and saw a heavy spray of water issuing from a dark window: someone was watering the plants in the window box, even though the household below had laundry out on the line. When the old grandmother went to bring in the clothes a bit later, she found them soaked. She was not surprised.

36. See the table in Ekblad and Werne 1990, p. 76.

37. Zhu 1987, trans. in *FBIS-CHI*-88-019, Jan. 29, 1988, pp. 10–13.

38. State Council Leading Group for Reforming the Housing System 1988, Xinhua Domestic Service, Mar. 9, 1988. Translated in *FBIS-CHI*-88-057, Mar. 24, 1988, pp. 41–46.

39. Interview with municipal housing officials, June 24, 1991. Interviews with residents, however, suggest that implementation of these reforms was delayed a year or more. For example, a housing lottery to alleviate extreme overcrowding was not under way until February 1991, and the actual prices to be charged for already occupied housing under the home purchase scheme were still under discussion in the early summer of 1991.

40. "Average Citizens Hope for Glad Tidings," part 3, *Guangzhou Ribao*, Dec. 17, 1993, p. 9.

41. "Evening Meeting Special Feature [on Housing Reform]," *Yangcheng Wanbao*, July 9, 1994, p. 7.

42. Readers who have visited the once notorious Kowloon Walled City in Hong Kong will experience a shock of recognition on visiting such sites in Guangzhou. Overbuilding has not yet created the warrens characteristic of the Walled City, but the trend is ominous.

43. Writers differ on the translation of the Chinese term *zhongxue*, the five or six years of formal schooling that fall between elementary school and college or university. A literal translation is "middle school"; a conceptual translation is "high school" because the years of *zhongxue* correspond more or less to the years an American student would spend in high school. The first three years of *zhongxue* are usually translated as "lower middle school," "junior middle school," or "junior high school," whereas the last two or three years are usually translated as "upper middle school," "senior middle school," or "senior high school." In this book *zhongxue* is translated as "middle school."

44. The data from the survey were published piecemeal in the following newspaper articles: "Guangzhou Residents Again Look at Guangzhou," *Nanfang Ribao*, Apr. 24, 1994, p. 2; "How Has the Degree of Satisfaction of Guangzhou's Residents Changed?" *Nanfang Ribao*, May 30, 1994, p. 2; and "How Do Residents Evaluate Guangzhou's Developments in Economic Livelihood?" *Guangzhou Ribao*, July 20, 1994, p. 7.

3 | Family and Household

1. See, for example, Hsu 1952, *Americans and Chinese*; and, for Japan, Benedict 1946, *The Chrysanthemum and the Sword*. For a more contemporary example, see Chu and Ju 1993, *The Great Wall in Ruins*.

2. An enormous literature depicts and analyzes the historical Chinese family. For a sampling of works on the topic, see Baker 1977, "Extended Kinship in the Traditional City"; Freedman 1958, *Lineage Organization in Southeastern China*; Hsu 1971, *Under the Ancestors' Shadow*; Lang 1946, *Chinese Family and Society*; Levy 1949, *The Family Revolution in Modern China*; Waltner 1990, *Getting an Heir*; Watson and Ebrey 1991, *Marriage and Inequality in Chinese Society*; and Wolf and Huang 1980, *Marriage and Adoption in China, 1845–1945*. Two works based primarily on data from the Pearl River Delta region and concerned with the special circumstances of women in Chinese marriage are Jaschok 1988, *Concubines and Bondservants*; and Stockard 1989, *Daughters of the Canton Delta*. Works analyzing the family under Mao include Parish and Whyte 1978, *Village and Family in Contemporary China*, as well as chapters in Whyte and Parish 1984, *Urban Life in Contemporary China*. For the recent period see Davis and Harrell 1993, *Chinese Families in the Post-Mao Era*.

3. This woman more or less arranged her own son's marriage many years later when she was in Hong Kong and he in the United States. Her son was not particularly interested in marriage at the time (the 1960s), but all his friends were getting married, and he began to feel left out. He wrote his mother, asking whether she knew of any girls he could write to. She quickly obtained a suitable pen pal for him, and he began to write her. After several months, he returned to Hong Kong, asking his mother to set up appointments with other marriageable young women in the space of a few days. After meeting all the candidates, he decided to marry the one he had been writing. His mother and wife, both now in the United States, get along splendidly. Though they do not actually live together, the daughter-in-law regularly helps her mother-in-law set up mah-jongg parties at her home and provides a steady flow of snacks. Other women praised this daughter-in-law to me as just like a daughter.

4. The terms for siblings of parents are differentiated more in Chinese than in English, reflecting the patrilineal and hierarchical kinship system. Thus Cantonese has two primary terms for aunt, to indicate whether the aunt is on the paternal or the maternal side; and it has three terms for uncle because the terms for paternal uncles distinguish those who are older than one's father from those who are younger. When asking a stranger on the street for directions, one uses paternal kinship terms for people judged much older, and maternal kinship terms for those not much older, than oneself. The most senior kinship term used in this context is Maternal Grandmother for elderly women and Older Paternal Uncle for elderly men. Presumably the term Paternal Grandfather indicates a status too elevated to bestow casually on a stranger.

5. A contemporary manifestation of this same pattern is the predominance of infant girls available for both domestic and foreign adoption. For example, in 1988 a childless couple in the Family Study acquired directly from a hospital the fourth girl born to a rural family. The birth mother had announced in advance that if the child was a girl she would not keep it. Similarly, the babies made available for adoption abroad since 1991 have overwhelmingly been girls (Sege 1992).

6. According to Pan 1987, an analysis of the national survey conducted by the Chinese Academy of Social Sciences in 1982, known as the Five City Family Study, which was published in 1987 by the Shandong People's Publishing Company, a nuclear family consists of a married couple with or without unmarried children; a stem family consists of two generations, each including a single married couple (or the remnants thereof) with or without unmarried children; a joint family has more than one married couple in the same generation with or without unmarried children. A joint family could, of course, include members of a generation senior to that of the two (or more) married couples. These distinctions, basically the same as those made by non-Chinese social scientists, allow greater precision than the more general concept of the extended family.

7. The texts of the 1950 and 1980 marriage laws can be found in the following sources: *The Marriage Law of the People's Republic of China with Explanatory Materials* 1959; *The Marriage Law of the People's Republic of China* 1982; for the inheritance law, see Schwartz 1987, "The Inheritance Law of the People's Republic of China."

8. *The Marriage Law* 1959, p. 1.

9. Teng 1959.

10. *Nanfang Ribao*, Feb. 27, 1986. Similar cases are described in Honig and Hershatter 1988, and in Ocko 1991.

11. *Nanfang Ribao*, Apr. 3, 1986.

12. Ibid., May 16, 1987.

13. Wu 1982, pp. 21–30.

14. The regulations appear in Tien 1991, pp. 273–82.

15. See Davis-Friedmann 1991, pp. 125–27.

16. See Ikels 1993.

17. To discover what Guangzhou residents (young and old) had to say about a hypothetical case in which a son was raising objections to his widowed mother's contemplated remarriage, see Ikels 1990.

18. *Laoren Bao*, no. 3 (1991).

19. Honig and Hershatter 1988, pp. 211–15.

20. *China Statistical Yearbook 1991*, p. 725.

21. Guangzhou Shi Tongji Ju 1993, p. 47.

22. Members of the same family might be employed by the same unit for two reasons: first, because a young couple were workmates before they became spouses, and second, because work units often assume responsibility for finding employment for the children of their employees. This topic is developed further in Chapter 5.

23. See, for example, Goode 1963, *World Revolution and Family Patterns*; Lang 1946, *Chinese Family and Society*; and Levy 1949, *The Family Revolution in Modern China*.

24. See, for example, Leete 1989; and Whyte and Parish 1984.

25. Although this 1984 graduate seems to have followed the path prescribed for a university student, the practice of vacating the room to give a couple privacy was already known in 1980.

26. Similarly, Jankowiak reports that in 1987 he was told by a senior gynecologist at the Inner Mongolian Hospital in Huhhot, the capital of Inner Mongolia, that between 1985 and 1987 over half of all abortions were performed on unmarried women (Jankowiak 1989, pp. 74–75). Honig and Hershatter 1988, p. 114, cite a report in a 1986 newspaper that 28 percent of all abortions in Beijing were performed on unmarried women, 90 percent of whom were engaged.

27. *Nanfang Ribao*, Mar. 6, 1986.

28. Ibid., Apr. 10, 1986.

29. Ibid., June 19, 1986.

30. Zha and Geng 1992. Zha Bo is a lecturer in history at Sichuan University in Chengdu, and Geng Wenxiu is a lecturer in psychology at East China Normal University in Shanghai and a researcher at the Shanghai Research Center of Sex Sociology. The study was carried out in Shanghai, Lanzhou, Chengdu, Chongqing, and "several smaller cities." The sample was composed exclusively of married people with children: males between the ages of 24 and 60 and females between the ages of 20 and 55 randomly drawn from among the employees of factories, schools, companies, the service trades, and so forth. About 40 percent of the men and 30 percent of the women were professionals or cadres, or were engaged in various other white-collar occupations. The remainder were in blue-collar occupations. The data reported are from 2,000 of the most complete questionnaires.

31. Ibid., p. 10.

32. Jankowiak 1989, p. 74.

33. Zha and Geng 1992, p. 11.

34. Pan 1987, p. 65. The change represented by these figures might be exaggerated. The people interviewed in 1982 were not necessarily urban residents before 1938, when their weddings took place. We might be seeing rural-urban differences as much as longitudinal differences. This question arises whenever comparisons are made across cohorts in the study. A 1987 study carried out in the two main urban districts of Chengdu found similar reductions in the percentage of arranged marriages, but much greater self-reliance in mate selection, with 89 percent of female respondents claiming to have found their own spouse. This high rate of self-reliance goes back all the way to the mid-1950s, and the researcher attributes the change

directly to the government's campaign for the free choice of marriage partners. See Whyte 1993, pp. 189–216.

35. Pan 1987, pp. 73–76.

36. See Honig and Hershatter 1988, pp. 82–90, for a discussion of how these introduction bureaus actually operate and some examples of personal ads.

37. Pan 1987, pp. 80–82.

38. Ibid., p. 105. Again, as in note 34, the extent to which the figures reflect rural-urban differences rather than cohort differences is unclear.

39. Ibid. Whyte found similar patterning in Chengdu in 1987 (Whyte 1993).

40. There were also two divorces, both initiated by the wives.

41. S. Xue et al. 1981, "Report of Findings on Marriage in Urban Shanghai," *Shehui Kexue* (Social Sciences) 2: 77–79ff., cited in Tien 1991, p. 33.

42. See Leete 1989, p. 18.
43. Davis 1993.
44. Cited in Unger 1993.
45. Unger 1993.
46. Pan 1987, p. 145.

47. Unger 1993 also cites a number of studies that found higher rates of stem family living among the elderly (and the older the elder, the greater the likelihood of this arrangement). He relates this finding to the life course: an elderly person, after a period of nuclear family living once all the children marry and move out, eventually joins a child's household. This analysis is treating cross-sectional data as if they were longitudinal. My own Guangzhou data suggest that for the current cohort of elders, this interpretation is incorrect. Most elders living with a child in old age have always (or nearly always) lived with a child. Because of the housing shortage or the elder's (or young person's) needs, there was no period during which the child could live apart. Furthermore, most of this coresidence (at least up to 1987) was in the home of the elder, not the child.

Many studies of household structure pay little attention to internal dynamics. For example, in the case of Guangzhou, the 60 percent of elderly living as stem or joint families (almost all stem) actually includes 4 percent who "live together but eat and budget separately." In other words, while occupying a room (or even just a bed) in a shared physical space, the older and younger generations lead separate financial (and sometimes even entirely separate social) lives. Though I have chosen to count these as stem families, an argument can be made that they are actually something else. For a fuller discussion of these variant family forms (albeit in a rural context), see Goldstein, Ku, and Ikels 1990.

48. Chinese Academy of Social Sciences 1988, p. 23.

49. Chu and Ju 1993, p. 74.

50. Indeed, just as in Europe and North America, Chinese elderly seem to prefer to live separately, at least while they are healthy and able to afford the expense.

51. The most thorough history of population policy in the PRC is found in Tien 1991.

52. For example, Tien 1991, p. 40, quotes documents from Sichuan as follows: "To those who fail to register their marriage or cohabit and become pregnant or give birth, criticism, education or punishment shall be meted out according to circumstances, attitudes, and repercussions. Children born of private [unregistered] marriages will not enjoy labor and welfare rights." Furthermore, the parents must bear

all medical expenses associated with abortion or delivery, and the mother forfeits any rights to paid maternity leave. Similarly Whyte and Parish 1984, p. 161, indicate that individuals inappropriately pregnant (after already having a second child, before the completion of the four-year interval between births, or out of turn in their organization's birth quota system) were subject to incessant persuasion to obtain an abortion; if they did not succumb, they were unable to register their child and therefore could not obtain increases in their rations.

53. Tien 1991, p. 96.

54. That women were reluctant supporters of Chinese pronatalist views is the thesis of Gates 1993, who argues that when women are able to contribute financially to the household they feel entitled to reduce their childbearing and child-rearing contributions.

55. Leete 1989, p. 21.

56. For an eyewitness account of how the policy was implemented in one brigade in Guangdong in 1980, see Mosher 1983, *Broken Earth*. For another account of the same period, from a very different perspective, see Potter and Potter 1990, *China's Peasants*, especially chapter 11, "Chinese Birth Planning: A Cultural Account." Huang 1989, *The Spiral Road*, reports on implementation in a suburban village in Fujian in 1986.

57. According to Wang 1987, p. 52.

58. Guangzhou Shi Tongji Ju 1993, p. 44.

59. Ibid., p. 47.

60. Cited in Tien 1991, pp. 34–35. These figures are based on the date of marriage registration — the *official* beginning of the marriage. Some couples, however, consider themselves married whenever they hold a wedding banquet and carry out various traditional rituals independent of registration, after which they are free to begin sexual relations. And, as we have seen from the surveys on sexual practice, premarital intercourse is not unusual either. These practices must be kept in mind when interpreting the high conception rates in the first year of marriage.

61. Pan 1987, p. 255.

62. Ibid., pp. 242–43.

63. Ibid., p. 258.

64. Chinese Academy of Social Sciences 1988, pp. 260–61.

65. Ibid., p. 299.

66. More details on the Jeung and Gunn families as well as further examples of the cost of medical and personal care are available in Ikels 1993.

67. For a good introduction to the topic of death rituals in China, including Hong Kong and Taiwan, see Watson and Rawski 1988, *Death Ritual in Late Imperial and Modern China*. For general information about funeral reform in the PRC, see Whyte 1988, "Death in the People's Republic of China"; and for a particular case, see Jankowiak 1988, "The Soul of Lao Yu."

68. I obtained the data on funeral reform in Guangzhou from the director of the Guangzhou Funeral Parlor in an interview, June 12, 1991.

69. Indeed, at the entrance to the funeral parlor an announcement, dated June 1, 1991, specifically prohibited firecrackers and the burning of materials. The

director explained that the rules, though promulgated in Nov. 1990, would have been too much for the masses to absorb all at once, so they were being enforced gradually. If people want to burn things for the dead, they may do so elsewhere, e.g., at their own homes or at the cemetery.

70. If an individual belonged to no unit, no unit representative attends, except perhaps someone from the son's unit if it is making a contribution to defray the cost of the funeral.

4 | Education

1. For a broader discussion of education in China, see Bennett and Montaperto 1971, *Red Guard*; Cleverley 1991, *The Schooling of China*; Hayhoe 1984, *Contemporary Chinese Education*, and 1989, *China's Universities and the Open Door*; Hayhoe and Bastid 1987, *China's Education and the Industrialized World*; Pepper 1984, *China's Universities*, and 1990, *China's Education Reform in the 1980s*; Shirk 1982, *Competitive Comrades*; Thogersen 1990, *Secondary Education in China after Mao*, and 1991, *Vocational and Technical Secondary School Education in China*; and Unger 1982, *Education Under Mao*. The works by Bennett and Montaperto, Shirk, and Unger rely primarily on interviews with former students of middle schools in Guangzhou. For explicitly comparative works involving Chinese, Japanese, and American education, see Tobin, Wu, and Davidson 1989, *Preschool in Three Cultures*; and Stevenson and Stigler 1992, *The Learning Gap*.

2. See Miyazaki 1976 for a detailed description of the examination hall and the security measures in force during the imperial examinations. These security measures are similar to those currently in use for the citywide exams for entrance to senior middle school (see note 43, Chapter 2) and the national exams for entrance to university.

3. Not under discussion here are such well-known and legal exceptions to the rule as "yin privilege," by which the son of a high official was automatically eligible for posts a few ranks below that of his father, and the sale of ranks by the government itself in economic hard times. The extent of yin privilege was increasingly limited, and the purchaser of a rank was entitled only to the status perquisites belonging to an official of that rank; he could not actually occupy the office.

4. See also Liang and Shapiro 1983.

5. Detailed analyses of the characteristics of these Cultural Revolution–age students and of the factors contributing to their development are provided in Shirk 1982 and Unger 1982.

6. These figures, from Guangzhou Shi Tongji Ju 1991, p. 37, do not add up to 100 percent. It is unclear whether the population on which they are based has the same base age as that used for determining illiteracy (fifteen).

7. The term *xiaoxue*, designating the first six years of formal education, is translated both as "primary school" and as "elementary school." The literal translation (never used) is "little school." During the Cultural Revolution elementary schooling was reduced briefly to a four-year course. In Guangzhou the five-year course was restored in the mid-1970s and the six-year course in the early 1980s. Because of the overcrowding caused by increasing the years of schooling, some elementary schools

had to restrict the age of entry to seven rather than six and a half. The development of an extra (fourth) year of preschool is probably related to this age restriction for entry to elementary school.

Pepper (1990) describes the promulgation in 1986 of the national law making nine years of schooling compulsory "as at least a declaration of intent" because the overall timetable set for implementation was flexible. She points out that cities were expected to achieve the goal by 1990 (this is certainly the case in Guangzhou), whereas "less-developed cities, towns, and rural areas" had until 1995, and poor and backward areas may wait until conditions permit (p. 89).

8. "Within Ten Years Basic Upper [Middle School Attendance]," *Yangcheng Wanbao*, Oct. 17, 1993, p. 1.

9. Guangzhou Shi Tongji Ju 1993, p. 476. Drop-out rates for junior and senior middle school are not available, but my discussions with people and officials familiar with the middle schools in Guangzhou suggest that few students drop out of junior middle school because they are not eligible for work until they are at least sixteen. Similarly, few students drop out of ordinary middle schools because by enrolling in such schools they have essentially committed themselves to trying to get into a university. Students not interested in the university track or not qualifying for it attend vocational schools. Drop-out rates for these schools are believed to be somewhat higher than for ordinary schools but are also said to vary by type of vocational school.

10. Guangzhou Nianjian Bianzuan Weiyuanhui 1990, p. 390.

11. Descriptions of preschools (kindergartens) can be found in Kessen 1975 and in Tobin, Wu, and Davidson 1989.

12. Guangzhou Shi Tongji Ju 1993, p. 480.

13. By contrast, in a city-government-sponsored kindergarten each class has its own sleeping room separate from its classroom, and each child has a bed and a set of bedding.

14. Figures for 1980 and 1985 are from Guangzhou Shi Tongji Ju 1989; 1990 figures are from ibid., 1991.

15. "Lively News About Incoming Elementary and Secondary School Students," *Yangcheng Wanbao*, June 7, 1994, p. 1.

16. Previously, prospective entrants to a keypoint elementary school were given an oral examination to assess their comprehension and thinking power. For example, a teacher would tell the child a story and ask the child to tell it back or would show a picture and ask the child to make up a story about the people in it.

17. Guangzhou Shi Tongji Ju 1991, p. 379.

18. *Yangcheng Wanbao*, June 7, 1994, p. 1.

19. "Elementary and Middle School Student Fees Appear Everywhere," *Guangzhou Ribao*, Jan. 16, 1994, p. 1.

20. "All Living Creatures in School Have Fees; Nowadays Many Bitter Complaints About High Costs of Study," *Yangcheng Wanbao*, Oct. 20, 1993, p. 1.

21. Shirk 1982, pp. 97–104, and Unger 1982, pp. 89–91, describe in greater detail the roles of student class officers and the significance of the peer group just before and during the Cultural Revolution.

22. According to a Guangzhou elementary school principal interviewed in

1980, elementary school teachers at that time were receiving monthly incomes of between 40 and 90 yuan, with the majority of the teachers receiving under 50 yuan. Wages had not been raised for years.

23. But even under the revised rules the assignment process is not totally random. First, the best students in each elementary school are given some preferential treatment; and second, principals still have the right to select up to four students for each classroom of students on whatever grounds they see fit. These are the students who have to pay the exorbitant extra entrance fee.

24. Formal courses in politics are also given at both senior middle schools and universities. In the wake of the student demonstrations of 1989 these courses have been given a more conservative slant. Rosen 1992a summarizes Chinese efforts to determine the effectiveness of these courses (and other educational techniques) and suggests that students give lip service at most to the official values.

25. Pepper 1984, pp. 54–59.

26. Thogersen 1990, pp. 97–101.

27. A more detailed discussion of the differences among vocational schools is available in ibid., pp. 101–9, and in Thuno 1991.

28. The percentages were reported on the English-language news on Guangzhou television, Feb. 27, 1991. The camera panned classrooms full of students wearing glasses. Perhaps a caveat is in order: some of these students might not have needed to wear glasses. In Hong Kong I learned that some people wore them to enhance their intellectual credibility. It will be interesting to see which segments of the population respond favorably to the advertisements for contact lenses that were already being televised in Guangzhou in 1991.

29. There are actually three additional sets of entrance examinations specifically for students attending specialized middle schools who wish to continue in their specialty. These students early on (even in elementary school) are selected because of their special talents in athletics, the fine arts, or foreign languages.

30. "Responsibility Set for Incoming Students in Guangdong Institutions of Higher Learning," *Nanfang Ribao*, June 3, 1994, p. 1.

31. "High Fees for Hot Specializations; Excellent Students to Receive Major Awards," *Yangcheng Wanbao*, May 12, 1994, p. 2.

32. Thogersen 1990, pp. 88–89.

33. National institutions include Zhongshan University (also known as Sun Yatsen University), Jinan University, South China Engineering University, Zhongshan Medical University, Guangzhou Foreign Trade College, and Guangzhou Foreign Languages College. Provincial institutions include Guangdong Pharmaceutical College, South China Teacher Training University, Guangdong Minorities College, Guangzhou Fine Arts College, and Guangzhou Physical Education College. Among the city institutions are Guangzhou University and Guangzhou Teacher Training College.

34. *South China Morning Post*, Jan. 12, 1991.

35. Thogersen 1990, p. 89.

36. Guangzhou Nianjian Bianzuan Weiyuanhui 1990, p. 381.

37. Thogersen 1990, p. 90.

38. Guangzhou Nianjian Bianzuan Weiyuanhui 1990, p. 381.

39. "Going to University [Means] Withdrawing [One's] Own Cash," *Guangzhou Ribao*, Apr. 17, 1994, p. 2.

40. Some of these rules were abandoned during the 1980s and then resurrected following the student movement of 1989.

41. The concern about connections was not exactly a new one, but students in the 1980s were more indignant about them in the face of the official rhetoric about the importance of merit.

42. Rosen 1992b discusses the prominence of some of these theories as described by the Chinese themselves.

43. Summarized from Guangzhou Nianjian Bianzuan Weiyuanhui 1990, p. 385.

44. "Jiang: Elevate Moral Standards," *Beijing Review*, Feb. 7–20, 1994, p. 5.

5 | *Employment*

1. For an overview of youth unemployment in urban China, see Feng 1988, "Youth Unemployment in China"; Jefferson and Rawski 1992, "Unemployment, Underemployment, and Employment Policy in China's Cities"; and "A New Wave of Unemployment," *China News Analysis*, no. 1392, Sept. 1, 1989.

2. See, for example, Gold 1980.

3. Gold 1990.

4. Feng 1988, p. 285. Feng points out that not only was there an oversupply of people looking for work, but also the supply of jobs was not what it could have been. During the Cultural Revolution (and even earlier) an estimated 17 million youths had been sent to the countryside; meanwhile, urban work units had recruited workers from the countryside since they could not assign the jobs to urban youths. Feng estimates that on the order of 13 million jobs that could have gone to urban youth during this period went to villagers instead.

5. Davis 1988.

6. Youth Problem Study Group 1988.

7. Ikels 1993.

8. Youth Problem Study Group 1988, pp. 43–44.

9. The most complete discussion of the revival of the private sector can be found in Kraus 1991.

10. Ibid., p. 20. The terms "private business" and "individual business," with their explicit size characteristics, are still in use, though "private business" also frequently includes individual businesses. This double usage sometimes leads to statistical confusion.

11. Connor 1991, p. 28. Connor expresses serious reservations about the success with which these regulations are enforced, especially the one on child labor.

12. Kraus 1991, p. 17. For a sympathetic but depressing assessment of the short life of a private street trader in Beijing, see *Black Snow* (Liu 1991). This novel, available in English, about an ex-convict who opens a clothing stall was made into the movie *The Year of Bad Luck*.

13. See "The Privately-Run Enterprise," *China News Analysis*, no. 1382, Apr. 1, 1989; and Wank 1990.

14. The get-rich-quick mentality, however, was not confined to individual entre-

preneurs. Often rural collectives and anyone else relatively free of state supervision pursued gain without regard to the long-term costs to the individuals or communities concerned. Those free to make decisions apart from the state plan commonly ignored the consequences of pollution, failed to maintain equipment, neglected worker safety issues, and squandered profits on banquets or housing instead of reinvesting them. For a detailed assessment of what economic development in Guangdong means for the environment (and the population), see Neller and Lam 1994.

15. "The Privately-Run Enterprise," *China News Analysis*, Apr. 1, 1989, p. 2.

16. Kraus 1991, p. 45.

17. "Guangzhou's Private Economy Deepens," *Guangzhou Ribao*, Nov. 30, 1992, p. 1.

18. Pearson 1991a.

19. Ibid.

20. See, in particular, Davis 1988 and Howard 1991.

21. These off-plan positions are by no means restricted to the children of an enterprise's own workers. Anyone with the appropriate household registration and *daiye* identification may apply for them. In fact, however, young people already connected to the workplace through family members are normally given preference.

22. In the mid-1980s the state attempted in a minimal way to link performance with promotion. Because many people in their 30s had spotty educational backgrounds, work units began to require those already employed to demonstrate competence by taking either examinations at work or formal courses elsewhere. Poor performance would mean either no promotion or, more likely, a delay in both promotion and wage increases. In 1987 in Guangzhou these examinations clearly caused considerable anxiety, even though they were based on one's everyday work and thus every worker could have expected to pass. Exam results were publicly posted. Everyone on the particular list I saw had passed, and most had received a high pass.

23. Vogel 1989, p. 106, reports that when first introduced, bonus distribution was often determined by the workers themselves, who frequently used non-performance-related criteria for allocation—sometimes insisting on equality, sometimes favoring those who had waited longest for a wage increase or had suffered most during the Cultural Revolution.

24. Although reluctant to provide across-the-board raises to cadres, the state, reportedly to encourage scholars studying abroad to return, in 1992 was said to be working on a revised pay program for "outstanding intellectuals in research centers, universities, hospitals, [and] cultural and sports centers." The report on the program that appeared in *China Daily* said that in 1991 "more than 9,000 experts and scholars received a special monthly supplement of 100 yuan ($20)." The report was reprinted in *China Exchange News* 20 (2) (1992): 31.

25. Cai 1993.

26. "Reforms Should Close Wage Gap of State Workers," *China Daily*, May 22, 1993, p. 4, discusses the *Economic Daily* article (but gives no date, author, or title for it).

27. Around 1989 Guangdong began requiring even those entering the labor force as permanent workers to sign contracts spelling out the conditions of their

employment, i.e., their duties. According to an official of the Guangdong province Labor Department, this type of (nonterm) contract will probably be extended eventually to permanent workers who have already spent many years in the labor force. The purpose of such contracts seems to be to provide the work unit with some leverage against poor performers.

28. See, for example, Davis 1990.

29. Li 1993.

30. "Guangzhou Unemployment Insurance . . . ," *Yangcheng Wanbao*, Nov. 19, 1992, p. 1.

31. "Unemployment Insurance in Ram City," *Nanfang Ribao*, Jan. 4, 1993, p. 5.

32. Zou 1993.

33. "Seventeen Million Workers in Employment Reshuffle," *China Daily*, Mar. 6, 1993.

34. The text of the regulations is available in *Guangzhou Ribao*, Apr. 28, 1993, p. 5.

35. Jefferson and Rawski 1992.

36. Pearson 1991b, pp. 173–76.

37. "Earnestly Protect the Rights and Interests of Workers in Foreign Invested Enterprises," *Guangzhou Ribao*, Jan. 21, 1994, p. 11.

38. "Guangdong Provincial Regulations Protecting the Rights and Interests of Staff and Workers in Enterprises," *Nanfang Ribao*, Feb. 2, 1994, p. 2. Indicative of other abuses the provincial general trade union found are regulations forbidding employers to constrain workers by holding their identity cards and requiring a regular monthly payday.

39. In addition to medical coverage, workers also receive sick leave and special compensation for job-related injuries. Regulations for these operated as follows in 1991 (they may have been modified): Sick leave is normally available for six months. Time with the unit determines the percentage of the basic wage (plus all *butie*) a worker receives. Sick leave payments vary from 60 percent for a worker with less than three years in the unit to 100 percent for a worker with eight or more years. After six months of sick leave, the worker's income is reduced to 40 to 60 percent of his or her wages, depending on years of service. The worker who never recovers the ability to work is entitled to this income until death; i.e., there is no shift from sick leave payments to retirement payments when the worker reaches retirement age. A worker who loses the ability to work in middle age (45 for women and 50 for men), however, takes a form of early retirement rather than permanent sick leave.

Workers seriously injured on the job are entitled to permanent disability payments, depending on the degree of permanent disability. Those who lose all ability to work but can take care of themselves are entitled to 80 percent of their basic wage (plus *butie*), and those who need an attendant, to 90 percent, along with the equivalent of a grade three worker's wages to pay the attendant, or a relative who provides such care. (A worker's pay is determined by grade: grade one is the entry-level grade, grade eight the highest.)

40. "Major Surgery Changes Free Medical Service," *Yangcheng Wanbao*, June 17, 1994, p. 1.

41. "Gains and Losses of the Free Medical Service Reform," *Guangzhou Ribao*,

July 31, 1994, p. 2. The rate based on rank varies from 3 yuan for a low-level cadre or a worker of any kind to 10 yuan for a provincial-level cadre. The component based on age varies from 3 yuan a month for those 30 or younger to 10 yuan for those 61 or older.

42. As early as 1991 (*Yangcheng Wanbao*, Sept. 13, 1991, p. 3) Guangzhou, in an effort to extend health protection to temporary workers, introduced term medical and accident insurance programs, each with the option of supplementary hospitalization insurance. The maximum payout for medical insurance is 50,000 yuan, for accident insurance, 200,000 yuan. Premiums, paid by the individual workers, are based on age, amount of insurance, and (for accident insurance) the danger inherent in an occupation. Charges are modest; e.g., for every 1,000 yuan of medical insurance coverage, the premium is 5–10 yuan, paid twice a year; for every 1,000 yuan in supplementary hospital coverage, the fee is 30 yuan annually. Whether this insurance will be phased out as protection is extended to all workers, including temporary workers (see p. 195), is unclear.

43. Manion 1992.

44. Ibid., pp. 12–13.

45. "Liwan District Introduces Worker Contributory Pension Scheme," *Nanfang Ribao*, Oct. 4, 1991, p. 2.

46. The text of the provincial regulations is available in *Nanfang Ribao*, June 18, 1993, p. 2.

47. For an overview of life in the *danwei* prior to the reforms, see Henderson and Cohen 1984, *Chinese Hospital*; and Walder 1986, *Communist Neo-Traditionalism*. For more recent analyses of changes in the *danwei*, see Bian 1994, *Work and Inequality in Urban China*.

48. For a fuller discussion of the significance of rank, see Bian 1994.

49. There are three main types of tenure: temporary and probationary, the least secure; contract; and (truly) permanent, the most secure. Temporary or probationary workers may be discharged at any time. It is understood that temporary workers will work only so long as work is available (seasonally or for a specific short-term project) and probationary workers, only so long as their performance is satisfactory. Probationary workers usually hope for longer-term work. If they prove themselves satisfactory in the space of three to six months, they might be asked to sign a contract more or less guaranteeing them several years of steady employment. When the contract period expires, they might be asked to sign another contract or they might simply be let go.

Contract work, in one form or another, has existed for most of the duration of the PRC, but it was not the common lot of urban youth until the mid-1980s. Workers hired under the older form of contract work (which co-exists with the new) are "contracted workers outside the hiring plan," whereas those hired under the new form are "workers under the labor contract system." In the city districts of Guangzhou those "outside the hiring plan" normally have rural household registration when they sign their contracts, and those under the contract system normally have urban registration. The rights and privileges of workers hired under the older form of contract work are more or less identical with those of temporary workers, whereas those of workers hired under the new form are sometimes difficult to

distinguish from those of permanent (*guding*) workers. The positions of permanent workers are guaranteed — i.e., they have budgetary support regardless of the
danwei's financial position — thus, all the excess workers. It is these permanent positions that are (or have been) "inherited" by the children of those who retire from
them. As I have indicated, the state has been attempting to reduce the differences in
security and benefits among workers with different kinds of tenure.

50. This ceiling on living space is consistent with one described by another
young professor at a different university in Guangzhou; there the ceiling is 36–37
square meters. Administrative higher-ups, however, can obtain more space. Johnson 1991 provides data on housing characteristics for faculty of different ranks at
seven national universities elsewhere in China. Although full professors elsewhere
seem to have more space than those in Guangzhou (50–95 square meters per
family), lecturers and associate professors do not seem to do any better. In fact,
some do even worse. Johnson mentions one lecturer at Beijing University whose
family of three occupies a room of 10 square meters, has no kitchen, and must use
the public toilets, and another at People's University whose family of three occupies
a room of 14 square meters with no amenities.

51. Across Xingang Road, not far from the main entrance to the university, lay
Kangle Village, the village featured in Yang 1959.

52. The most extensive work on this topic is Whyte 1974.

53. For students the relevant *danwei* is the school, and students are subject to the
same mobilization and control as workers.

54. Walder 1986.

55. See Ikels 1990 for the responses of Guangzhou residents to a hypothetical
case of elder abuse in a neighbor's household. People thought of all manner of ways
of dealing with this problem, not the least of which was to contact the supervisors at
the suspected abuser's workplace.

56. Guangzhou Shi Tongji Ju 1993, p. 433.

57. Guangzhou Nianjian Bianzuan Weiyuanhui 1990, p. 540.

58. Guangdong Sheng Tongji Ju 1991, p. 123.

59. Since the focus in the Family Study was the elder, who exhibited puzzlement
when the questions strayed to the family as a whole, it was sometimes inconvenient to
pursue data on other household or family members. Consequently data are lacking
for 38 households. Of the remaining 162 households 96 (59 percent) had no
changes in *danwei* affiliation whereas 66 (42 percent) experienced a change. To provide some limits to the analysis, the household and not the family is the unit of analysis; i.e., sons and daughters living elsewhere who retired or changed jobs are not included in the tables. Similarly, individuals who received promotions but remained in
the same unit are not counted as changing jobs. These figures are still less precise than
one would like, but elders who were the chief suppliers of information often did not
know the ownership of the units to which members of their household belonged.

60. Contracting out (*chengbao*), or leasing, is another route to enterprise profitability. Ownership remains with the lessor while responsibility devolves to the
lessee, who within the limits of the law gains complete control over management
decisions. The manager guarantees the official owner a certain sum for each year of
the contract and retains all profits above the guaranteed amount. Some theorists

have argued that to all intents and purposes these are de facto private enterprises, but officially they remain state or collective enterprises.

61. Vogel 1989, pp. 331–32.

6 | Leisure Activities

1. "How to Put into Effect the State Council's Regulations of Staff and Workers' Working Hours," *Guangzhou Ribao*, Feb. 9, 1994, p. 3. Implementing what amounted to a five-and-a-half-day week proved confusing. The government authorized *danwei* that found this arrangement inconvenient to give workers an extra day off every two weeks rather than a half day off every week to allow them to keep half their force on site every Saturday rather than forcing them to close for half the day every week.

2. For a detailed analysis of television viewing practices in Beijing, Shanghai, Guangzhou, and Xian, see Lull 1991.

3. Guangdong Television has its own ratings system, but some Hong Kong advertisers conduct independent surveys of the provincial television audience.

4. Nickerson and Lappin 1993.

5. See Jones 1992 and Schell 1994, especially pp. 293–320.

6. Witke 1977.

7. Information for the sections that follow derives from interviews I conducted in Guangzhou in Nov. 1992 with officials of Guangdong Television, Guangzhou Television, and Guangdong Radio as well as with reporters from one of the leading daily papers. Descriptions of programming content derive from many hours of watching television in 1987 and 1991 as well as sporadic watching in other years.

8. See Su and Wang 1991 for a summary of the debate.

9. Brauchli 1993; see also Karp 1993.

10. *Far Eastern Economic Review*, June 23, 1994, p. 63.

11. These and subsequent figures are informal estimates from staff of one of the newspapers.

12. To avoid repetition no detailed presentation of *Yangcheng Wanbao* is presented here. Although it is the most popular of the three papers, it contains, in addition to the kinds of material presented in *Guangzhou Ribao*, many very short articles, tales, and trivia and is thus the least useful to scholars.

13. *Programs Catalogue Guangdong Television* 1992.

14. Ibid.

15. See Burns and Rosen 1986, pp. 148–59, 219–29, for two examples of such a dialogue.

16. Ward 1985 discusses the importance of traditional popular dramas.

17. For example, in one Shanghai-made movie shown on television in midday in 1991, a middle-aged woman was hospitalized and agonizing in the final throes of cancer. So great was her torture that she wanted, against the wishes of family members, to ask the doctor to end her life. (The issue of euthanasia has already been taken up in China.) The scenes in which family members are forced to come to terms with her decision are replete with overwrought relatives, especially males, sobbing and writhing against the hospital walls in their distress.

18. Guangzhou Nianjian Bianzuan Weiyuanhui 1992, p. 481.

19. That such practicing is also a problem in Hong Kong is clear from a letter to the editor published in the *South China Morning Post* in 1991. It complained that the racket went on at all hours of the day and night without regard for the neighbors. A few days later another writer explained how he had gotten the police to pay attention to this matter.

20. Extensive descriptions of these traditional festivals are available in Bredon and Mitrophanow 1982, *The Moon Year*; Doolittle 1966, *Social Life of the Chinese*, vol. 2; and Eberhard 1972, *Chinese Festivals*.

21. As I indicated in Chapter 3, residents with overseas Chinese connections may be buried elsewhere in sites set aside for this purpose. Christians may be buried (following cremation) in their own old graveyard, located a short walk from the Silver River graveyards.

22. In the late 1970s on this date White Cloud Mountain was the site of a major demonstration by former Red Guards.

| Conclusion

1. Jiang 1993, pp. 25–26.

2. Ibid.

3. "Statistical Communique of the State Statistical Bureau of the People's Republic of China on the 1993 National Economic and Social Development," *Beijing Review*, Mar. 14–20, 1994, pp. 19–26.

4. "24 Cities Reach 'Well-Off' Goal," *China Daily*, Nov. 27, 1993, p. 1. The cities said to have reached the target were Beijing, *Shenzhen*, Shanghai, *Zhuhai*, *Guangzhou*, Hangzhou, *Foshan*, Daqing, Xiamen, Changsha, Suzhou, *Jiangmen*, Dalian, Nanjing, Tianjin, Chengdu, Kunming, Anshan, Wuhan, Jinan, Qingdao, Liuzhou, Shenyang, and Wuxi. (The cities in italics are located in Guangdong.)

5. Li H. 1993.

6. Cao 1994.

References

Baker, H. D. R. 1977. "Extended Kinship in the Traditional City." In G. W. Skinner, ed., *The City in Late Imperial China*, pp. 499–518. Stanford, Calif.: Stanford University Press.

Benedict, R. 1946. *The Chrysanthemum and the Sword: Patterns of Japanese Culture.* Ithaca, N.Y.: Cornell University Press.

Bennett, G., and R. Montaperto. 1971. *Red Guard: The Political Biography of Dai Hsiao-ai.* Garden City, N.Y.: Doubleday.

Bian, Y. 1994. *Work and Inequality in Urban China.* Albany: State University of New York.

Blake, C. F. 1981. *Ethnic Groups and Social Change in a Chinese Market Town.* Honolulu: University of Hawaii Press.

Brauchli, M. 1993. "Star-Struck." *Wall Street Journal,* May 10.

Bredon, J., and I. Mitrophanow. 1982. *The Moon Year.* Hong Kong: Oxford University Press. (Orig. pub. 1927.)

Burns, J., and S. Rosen. 1986. *Policy Conflicts in Post-Mao China: A Documentary Survey, with Analysis.* Armonk, N.Y.: M. E. Sharpe.

Butterfield, F. 1982. *China Alive in the Bitter Sea.* New York: Times Books.

Cai Y. 1993. "'Second Job Fever' Not a Crippling Disease." *China Daily,* Mar. 8, p. 4.

Cao M. 1994. "Minimum Wage Set to Protect Labourers." *China Daily,* Jan. 7, p. 1.

Chan, A., R. Madsen, and J. Unger. 1984. *Chen Village: The Recent History of a Peasant Community in Mao's China.* Berkeley: University of California Press.

Chan, C. 1993a. *The Myth of Neighborhood Mutual Help: The Community-Based Urban Welfare System of China.* Hong Kong: Hong Kong University Press.

———. 1993b. "Urban Neighborhood Mobilization and Community Care for the Elderly in the People's Republic of China." *Journal of Cross-Cultural Gerontology* 8: 253–70.

Chan, C., and N. Chow. 1992. *More Welfare After Economic Reform? Welfare Development in the People's Republic of China.* Hong Kong: Centre of Urban Planning and Environmental Management, University of Hong Kong.

Chang, K. 1986. *The Archaeology of Ancient China.* 4th ed. New Haven, Conn.: Yale University Press.

China Statistical Yearbook 1991. 1991. Beijing: State Statistical Bureau of the People's Republic of China.

Chinese Academy of Social Sciences. 1988. *China 1987 Aged Population over 60 Years Sampling Survey Data (Computer Tabulation)* (in Chinese). Beijing.

Chu, G., and Y. Ju. 1993. *The Great Wall in Ruins: Communication and Cultural Change in China*. Albany: State University of New York.

Cleverley, J. 1991. *The Schooling of China: Tradition and Modernity in Chinese Education*. 2d ed. North Sydney, Australia: Allen and Unwin.

Connor, A. W. 1991. "To Get Rich is Precarious: Regulation of Private Enterprise in the People's Republic of China." *Journal of Chinese Law* 5 (1): 1–57.

Davis, D. 1988. "Unequal Chances, Unequal Outcomes: Pension Reform and Urban Inequality." *China Quarterly* 114: 223–42.

———. 1990. "Urban Job Mobility." In D. Davis and E. Vogel, eds., *Chinese Society on the Eve of Tiananmen*, pp. 85–108. Cambridge, Mass.: Harvard University Press.

———. 1993. "Urban Households: Supplicants to a Socialist State." In D. Davis and S. Harrell, eds., *Chinese Families in the Post-Mao Era*, pp. 50–76. Berkeley: University of California Press.

Davis, D., and S. Harrell. 1993. *Chinese Families in the Post-Mao Era*. Berkeley: University of California Press.

Davis, D., and E. Vogel, eds. 1990. *Chinese Society on the Eve of Tiananmen: The Impact of Reform*. Cambridge, Mass.: Harvard University Press.

Davis-Friedmann, D. 1991. *Long Lives: Chinese Elderly and the Communist Revolution*. 2d ed. Stanford, Calif.: Stanford University Press.

DeFrancis, J. 1984. *The Chinese Language: Fact and Fantasy*. Honolulu: University of Hawaii Press.

Deng X. 1987. *Fundamental Issues in Present-Day China*. Beijing: Foreign Languages Press.

Doolittle, J. 1966. *Social Life of the Chinese*. Vol. 2. Taipei: Cheng-wen. (Orig. pub. 1865.)

Dutton, M. 1988. Editor's introduction. *Chinese Economic Studies* 22 (1): 3–21.

Eberhard, W. 1972. *Chinese Festivals*. Taipei: Orient Cultural Service.

Ekblad, S., and F. Werne. 1990. "Housing and Health in Beijing: Implications of High-Rise Housing on Children and the Aged." *Journal of Sociology and Social Welfare* 17 (1): 51–77.

Fairbank, J. 1992. *China: A New History*. Cambridge, Mass.: Harvard University Press.

Feng L. 1988. "Youth Unemployment in China." *International Social Science Journal* 116: 285–96.

Fessler, L., ed. 1983. *Chinese in America: Stereotyped Past, Changing Present*. China Institute in America, Inc. New York: Vantage Press.

Freedman, M. 1958. *Lineage Organization in Southeastern China*. London: Athlone.

Friedman, E. 1994. "Reconstructing China's National Identity: A Southern Alternative to Mao-Era Anti-Imperialist Nationalism." *Journal of Asian Studies* 53 (1): 67–91.

Frolic, B. M. 1980. *Mao's People: Sixteen Portraits of Life in Revolutionary China*. Cambridge, Mass.: Harvard University Press.

Gates, H. 1993. "Cultural Support for Birth Limitation Among Urban Capital-Owning Women." In D. Davis and S. Harrell, eds., *Chinese Families in the Post-Mao Era*, pp. 251–74. Berkeley: University of California Press.

Gladney, D. 1994. "Representing Nationality in China: Refiguring Majority/Minority Identities." *Journal of Asian Studies* 53 (1): 92–123.

Gold, T. 1980. "Back to the City: The Return of China's Educated Youth." *China Quarterly* 84: 755–70.

———. 1990. "Urban Private Business and Social Change." In D. Davis and E. Vogel, eds., *Chinese Society on the Eve of Tiananmen*, pp. 157–78. Cambridge, Mass.: Harvard University Press.

Goldstein, M., Y. Ku, and C. Ikels. 1990. "Household Composition in Two Rural Villages in the People's Republic of China." *Journal of Cross-Cultural Gerontology* 5: 119–30.

Goode, W. 1963. *World Revolution and Family Patterns*. London: Free Press.

Guangdong Sheng Tongji Ju [Guangdong Province Statistics Bureau]. 1991. *Guangdong tongji nianjian 1991* (Guangdong statistical yearbook 1991). China: Zhongguo Tongji Chubanshe.

Guangzhou Nianjian Bianzuan Weiyuanhui [Guangzhou Yearbook Compilation Committee]. 1990. *Guangzhou nianjian 1990* (Guangzhou yearbook 1990). Guangzhou: Guangdong Renmin Chubanshe.

———. 1992. *Guangzhou nianjian 1992* (Guangzhou yearbook 1992). Guangzhou: Guangdong Renmin Chubanshe.

Guangzhou Shi Tongji Ju [Guangzhou Municipality Statistics Bureau]. 1989. *Guangzhou sishinian 1949–1988* (Guangzhou 40 years 1949–1988). China: Zhongguo Tongji Chubanshe.

———. 1991. *Guangzhou tongji nianjian 1991* (Statistical yearbook of Guangzhou 1991). China: Zhongguo Tongji Chubanshe.

———. 1992. *Guangzhou tongji nianjian 1992* (Statistical yearbook of Guangzhou 1992). China: Zhongguo Tongji Chubanshe.

———. 1993. *Guangzhou tongji nianjian 1993* (Statistical yearbook of Guangzhou 1993). China: Zhongguo Tongji Chubanshe.

———. 1994. *Guangzhou tongji zhaiyao 1994* (Guangzhou statistical summary 1994). Guangzhou.

Guangzhou Social Sciences Research Institute. 1986. *Handbook of Investment and Tourism in Guangzhou*. Beijing: Beijing Review.

Guldin, G. E., ed. 1992. *Urbanizing China*. New York: Greenwood Press.

Hayhoe, R. 1989. *China's Universities and the Open Door*. Armonk, N.Y.: M. E. Sharpe.

———, ed. 1984. *Contemporary Chinese Education*. Armonk, N.Y.: M. E. Sharpe.

Hayhoe, R., and M. Bastid, eds. 1987. *China's Education and the Industrialized World: Studies in Culture Transfer*. Armonk, N.Y.: M. E. Sharpe.

Henderson, G., and M. Cohen. 1984. *The Chinese Hospital: A Socialist Work Unit*. New Haven, Conn.: Yale University Press.

Honig, E., and G. Hershatter. 1988. *Personal Voices: Chinese Women in the 1980's*. Stanford, Calif.: Stanford University Press.

Howard, P. 1991. "Rice Bowls and Job Security: The Urban Contract Labour System." *Australian Journal of Chinese Affairs* 25: 93–114.

Hsu, F. L. K. 1952. *Americans and Chinese: Two Ways of Life*. New York: H. Schuman.

———. 1973. *Under the Ancestors' Shadow*. Stanford, Calif.: Stanford University Press. (Orig. pub. 1948.)

Huang S. 1989. *The Spiral Road: Change in a Chinese Village Through the Eyes of a Communist Party Leader*. Boulder, Colo.: Westview Press.

Ikels, C. 1990. "The Resolution of Intergenerational Conflict: Perspectives of Elders and Their Family Members." *Modern China* 16 (4): 379–406.

———. 1991. "Aging and Disability in China: Cultural Issues in Measurement and Interpretation." *Social Science and Medicine* 32 (6): 649–65.

———. 1993. "Settling Accounts: The Intergenerational Contract in an Age of Reform." In D. Davis and S. Harrell, eds., *Chinese Families in the Post-Mao Era*, pp. 307–33. Berkeley: University of California Press.

Jankowiak, W. R. 1988. "The Soul of Lao Yu." *Natural History* 12: 4–11.

———. 1989. "Sex Differences in Mate Selection and Sexuality in the People's Republic of China." *Australian Journal of Chinese Affairs* 22: 63–83.

———. 1993. *Sex, Death, and Hierarchy in a Chinese City: An Anthropological Account*. New York: Columbia University Press.

Jaschok, M. 1988. *Concubines and Bondservants: The Social History of a Chinese Custom*. London: Zed Books.

Jefferson, G., and T. Rawski. 1992. "Unemployment, Underemployment, and Employment Policy in China's Cities." *Modern China* 18: 42–71.

Jiang M. 1993. "Living Standards Climb in Urban Areas." *Beijing Review*, Dec. 20–26, pp. 25–26.

Johnson, T. 1991. "Wages, Benefits, and the Promotion Process for Chinese University Faculty." *China Quarterly* 125: 137–55.

Joint Economic Committee, Congress of the United States. 1991. *China's Economic Dilemmas in the 1990s: The Problems of Reforms, Modernization, and Interdependence*. Armonk, N.Y.: M. E. Sharpe.

Jones, A. F. 1992. *Like a Knife: Ideology and Genre in Contemporary Chinese Popular Music*. Cornell East Asia Series 57. Ithaca, N.Y.: East Asia Program, Cornell University.

Karp, J. 1993. "Stay Tuned." *Far Eastern Economic Review*, Aug. 12, 1993.

Kessen, W., ed. 1975. *Childhood in China*. New Haven, Conn.: Yale University Press.

Kohut, J. 1992. "China's 'Canton Ripper' at Large." *Boston Globe*, June 27.

Kojima, R. 1987. *Urbanization and Urban Problems in China*. Tokyo: Institute of Developing Economies.

Kraus, W. 1991. *Private Business in China: Revival Between Ideology and Pragmatism*. Trans. E. Holz. London: Hurst and Company.

Kwok, R. Y., W. L. Parish, A. G. Yeh, and X. Xu, eds. 1990. *Chinese Urban Reform: What Model Now?* Armonk, N.Y.: M. E. Sharpe.

Lang, O. 1946. *Chinese Family and Society*. New Haven, Conn.: Yale University Press.

Leete, R. 1989. "Overseas Chinese: Towards a One-Child Family Norm?" In A. Loquian, ed., *Megacities in China*, pp. 15–27. New Delhi: International Union for the Scientific Study of Population.

Levy, M. 1949. *The Family Revolution in Modern China*. Cambridge, Mass.: Harvard University Press.

Li D. 1986–87. "One Hundred Cases to Be Resolved." *Nanfang Ribao*, Feb. 27, Mar. 6, Apr. 3, Apr. 10, June 19, May 16.

Li H. 1993. "All Urban Employees to Get Job Insurance." *China Daily*, Aug. 14, p. 1.

Li Z. 1993. "Guangzhou Lures Top Talent with Labour Fair." *China Daily*, Mar. 4, p. 3.

Liang H. and J. Shapiro. 1983. *Son of the Revolution*. New York: Random House.

Liu H. 1991. *Black Snow*. Beijing: Chinese Literature Press.

Lull, J. 1991. *China Turned On: Television, Reform, and Resistance*. New York: Routledge.

Manion, M. 1992. "Politics and Policy in Post-Mao Cadre Retirement." *China Quarterly* 129: 1–25.

The Marriage Law of the People's Republic of China with Explanatory Materials [1950]. 1959. Beijing: Foreign Languages Press.

The Marriage Law of the People's Republic of China [1980]. 1982. Beijing: Foreign Languages Press.

Miller, S. 1969. *The Unwelcome Immigrant: The American Image of the Chinese, 1785–1882*. Berkeley: University of California Press.

Miyazaki, I. 1976. *China's Examination Hell: The Civil Service Examinations of Imperial China*. New York: Weatherfield.

Mosher, S. 1983. *Broken Earth: The Rural Chinese*. New York: Free Press.

Neller, R., and K. Lam. 1994. "The Environment." In Y. M. Yeung and D. K. Y. Chan, eds., *Guangdong: Survey of a Province Undergoing Rapid Change*, pp. 401–28. Hong Kong: Chinese University Press.

Nickerson, D. L., and T. Lappin. 1993. "Frustration in Peking." *Far Eastern Economic Review*, Aug. 12.

Nolan, P., and F. Dong, eds. 1990. *Market Forces in China: Competition and Small Business — the Wenzhou Debate*. London: Zed Books.

Ocko, J. 1991. "Women, Property, and Law in the People's Republic of China." In R. S. Watson and P. B. Ebrey, eds., *Marriage and Inequality in Chinese Society*, pp. 313–46. Berkeley: University of California Press.

Pan Y., ed. 1987. *Zhongguo chengshi hunyin yu jiating* (Chinese urban marriage and family, a report on the CASS Five City Family Study). Jinan: Shandong Renmin Chubanshe.

Parish, W. L., and M. K. Whyte. 1978. *Village and Family in Contemporary China*. Chicago: University of Chicago Press.

Pearson, M. 1991a. "The Ideology of Managers in China's Foreign Sector." Talk presented at the New England China Seminar, Harvard University, Dec. 12.

——. 1991b. *Joint Ventures in the People's Republic of China: The Control of Foreign Direct Investment Under Socialism*. Princeton, N.J.: Princeton University Press.

Pepper, S. 1984. *China's Universities*. Ann Arbor: Center for Chinese Studies, University of Michigan.

——. 1990. *China's Education Reform in the 1980s: Policies, Issues, and Historical Perspectives*. San Francisco: Institute of East Asian Studies, University of California.

Phillips, M. R., V. Pearson, and R. Wang, eds. 1994. *Psychiatric Rehabilitation in*

China: Models for Change in a Changing Society. Special issue of the *British Journal of Psychiatry* 165, supplement 24.

Potter, S. H., and J. M. Potter. 1990. *China's Peasants: The Anthropology of a Revolution*. Cambridge, Eng.: Cambridge University Press.

Ramsey, S. R. 1987. *The Languages of China*. Princeton, N.J.: Princeton University Press.

Rosen, S. 1982. *Red Guard Factionalism and the Cultural Revolution in Guangzhou*. Boulder, Colo.: Westview Press.

———. 1992a. "The Effect of Post–June 4 Reeducation Campaigns on Chinese Students." Paper presented at 44th annual meeting of the Association for Asian Studies, Washington, D.C.

———. 1992b. "The Role of Chinese Students at Home and Abroad as a Factor in Sino-American Relations." *In Depth* 1: 115–53.

Schell, D. 1994. *Mandate of Heaven*. New York: Simon and Schuster.

Schwartz, L. B. 1987. "The Inheritance Law of the People's Republic of China." *Harvard International Law Journal* 28: 433–64.

Sege, I. 1992. "Families Made in China." *Boston Globe*, Oct. 8.

Shirk, S. 1982. *Competitive Comrades: Career Incentives and Student Strategies in China*. Berkeley: University of California Press.

Skinner, W., ed. 1977. *The City in Late Imperial China*. Stanford, Calif.: Stanford University Press.

State Council Leading Group for Reforming the Housing System. 1988. *The Plan for Phasing in Reform of the Housing System in Urban Areas Throughout the Country*. Feb. 15. Xinhua Domestic Service, Mar. 9, 1988. Trans. in *FBIS-CHI-88-057* (*Foreign Broadcast Information Service–China*), Mar. 24, 1988, pp. 41–46.

State Statistical Bureau. 1990. *The 1987 Survey of Income and Expenditure of Urban Households in China*. Honolulu: China Statistical Information and Consultancy Service Centre and East-West Center.

Stevenson, H., and J. Stigler. 1992. *The Learning Gap*. New York: Summit Books.

Stockard, J. 1989. *Daughters of the Canton Delta: Marriage Patterns and Economic Strategies in South China, 1860–1930*. Stanford, Calif.: Stanford University Press.

Su X., and Wang L. 1991. *Deathsong of the River: A Reader's Guide to the Chinese TV Series Heshang*. Trans. R. Bodman and P. Wang. Cornell East Asia Series 54. Ithaca, N.Y.: East Asia Program, Cornell University.

Sung, B. 1967. *The Story of the Chinese in America*. New York: Macmillan, Collier Books.

Teng Y. 1959. "Breaking the Yoke of the Feudal Marriage System." In *The Marriage Law of the People's Republic of China with Explanatory Materials*, pp. 35–47. Beijing: Foreign Languages Press.

Thogersen, S. 1990. *Secondary Education in China After Mao: Reform and Social Conflict*. Aarhus, Denmark: Aarhus University Press.

———. 1991. *Vocational and Technical Secondary School Education in China*. Special issue of *Chinese Education* 24 (3).

Thuno, M. 1991. "Secondary Vocational Schools in Post-Mao China." *China Information* 6 (3): 44–56.

Tien, H. Y. 1991. *China's Strategic Demographic Initiative*. New York: Praeger.

Tobin, J., D. Wu, and D. Davidson. 1989. *Preschool in Three Cultures*. New Haven, Conn.: Yale University Press.

Tu J. 1988. "A Brief Analysis of China's Consumption Pattern at the Present Stage." *Guangming Ribao*, Feb. 13. Trans. in *FBIS-CHI-88-052 (Foreign Broadcast Information Service–China)*, Mar. 17, 1988, pp. 30–31.

Unger, J. 1982. *Education Under Mao: Class and Competition in Canton Schools, 1960–1980*. New York: Columbia University Press.

———. 1993. "Urban Families in the Eighties: An Analysis of Chinese Surveys." In D. Davis and S. Harrell, eds., *Chinese Families in the Post-Mao Era*, pp. 25–49. Berkeley: University of California Press.

Vogel, E. F. 1969. *Canton Under Communism: Programs and Politics in a Provincial Capital, 1949–1968*. Cambridge, Mass.: Harvard University Press.

———. 1989. *One Step Ahead in China: Guangdong Under Reform*. Cambridge, Mass.: Harvard University Press.

Walder, A. 1986. *Communist Neo-traditionalism: Work and Authority in Chinese Industry*. Berkeley: University of California Press.

Waltner, A. 1990. *Getting an Heir: Adoption and the Construction of Kinship in Late Imperial China*. Honolulu: University of Hawaii Press.

Wang, G. 1987. *Jiehun fa jiaocheng* (Marriage law course of study). China: Falu Chubanshe.

Wank, D. 1990. "Private Commerce as a Vocation: Social Mobility and the Wholesale Trade in Urban China." *China News Analysis*, no. 1424, Dec. 15.

Ward, B. E. 1985. "Regional Operas and Their Audiences: Evidence from Hong Kong." In D. Johnson, A. Nathan, and E. Rawski, eds., *Popular Culture in Late Imperial China*, pp. 161–87. Berkeley: University of California Press.

Watson, A., ed. 1992. *Economic Reform and Social Change in China*. London: Routledge.

Watson, J. L., and E. S. Rawski, eds. 1988. *Death Ritual in Late Imperial and Modern China*. Berkeley: University of California Press.

Watson, R. S., and P. B. Ebrey, eds. 1991. *Marriage and Inequality in Chinese Society*. Berkeley: University of California Press.

Whyte, M. K. 1974. *Small Groups and Political Rituals in China*. Berkeley: University of California Press.

———. 1988. "Death in the People's Republic of China." In J. L. Watson and E. S. Rawski, eds., *Death Ritual in Late Imperial and Modern China*, pp. 289–316. Berkeley: University of California Press.

———. 1993. "Wedding Behavior and Family Strategies in Chengdu." In D. Davis and S. Harrell, eds., *Chinese Families in the Post-Mao Era*, pp. 189–216. Berkeley: University of California Press.

Whyte, M. K., and W. L. Parish. 1984. *Urban Life in Contemporary China*. Chicago: University of Chicago Press.

Witke, R. 1977. *Comrade Chiang Ching*. Boston: Little, Brown.

Wolf, A., and C. Huang. 1980. *Marriage and Adoption in China, 1845–1945*. Stanford, Calif.: Stanford University Press.

World Bank. 1992. *China: Implementation Options for Urban Housing Reform*. Washington, D.C.: World Bank.

Wu X. 1982. "Explanations on the Marriage Law (revised draft) and the Nationality Law (draft) of the People's Republic of China." In *The Marriage Law of the People's Republic of China*, pp 21–30. Beijing: Foreign Languages Press.

Yang, C. K. 1959. *The Family and the Village in Communist Transition*. Cambridge, Mass.: MIT Press.

Youth Problem Study Group. 1988. "The Policy of Stand-in Employment and Its Impact: A Survey of Enterprises in Beijing Municipality." *Chinese Economic Studies* 21 (4): 29–44. (Orig. pub. in *Qingnian Yanjiu* [Youth studies] 10: 23–27, 1982.)

Zha, B., and W. Geng. 1992. "Sexuality in Urban China." *Australian Journal of Chinese Affairs* 28: 1–20.

Zhang H. 1987. "Composite Report on the Symposium on Problems of Contracted Youth." *Chinese Economic Studies* 21 (4): 92–100. (Orig. pub. in *Qingnian Yanjiu* [Youth studies] 6: 46–48, 1987.)

Zhu Y. 1987. "Resolutely Reform the Housing System in Cities and Towns." *Jingji Guanli* 12: 12–24. Trans. in *FBIS-CHI-88-019* (*Foreign Broadcast Information Service–China*), Jan. 29, 1988, pp. 10–13.

Zou J. 1993. "Report on National Economic and Social Development for 1992 and the Draft 1993 Plan." *Beijing Review*, Apr. 19–25, pp. 12–19.

Index

In this index "f" after a number indicates a separate reference on the next page, and "ff" indicates separate references on the next two pages. A continuous discussion over two or more pages is indicated by a span of numbers. *Passim* is used for a cluster of references in close but not consecutive sequence.

Abortions, 44–45, 111–12, 125f
Adoption practices, 282n5
Advertising, 64–66, 223–36 *passim*
Agricultural (*nongye*) population, 26
Agricultural production, 10, 12; decollectivization of, 58–61
Air pollution, 73, 92
Ancestor worship, 132–37 *passim*, 249, 255–58
Arab traders, 12–13

Baiyun Airport, 24, 71, 186
Baiyun district, 24, 93, 214
Baiyun (White Cloud) Hotel, 31–32, 70
Baiyun (White Cloud) Mountain, 8, 259
Baomu (domestic servant), 94, 130, 212
Beijing University, military training at, 173
Bicycles, 29, 76–77; theft of, 36, 44
Birth control, 44–45, 106, 123–25, 126f, 137–38, 209
Boat People population, 22–23
Butie (standard of living subsidies), 196, 215

Canton, *see* Guangzhou (Canton)
Cantonese (provincial language), 5, 18–20, 22f, 64, 227, 233, 235f
Cantonese cuisine, 9–11, 254–55
Canton Trade Fair, 16
Capitalism, Chinese, 2, 174
Capital punishment, 3, 39–41
Central planning, demise of, 2f, 177, 263
Chaotian Road Elementary School, 158–61

Chaozhou population, 22
Child labor laws, 181
China, *see* Imperial China; People's Republic of China; Republican China
China Central Television (CCTV), 16, 234f
Chinese Academy of Social Sciences (CASS), 110, 264
Chinese Communist Party, 2, 34, 52, 55–56, 97, 133, 136, 203, 249; Central Committee, 207
Chinese Export Commodities Fair (Canton Trade Fair), 16, 61
Chinese Muslims, 13
Christianity, 14f, 142
Cohong (trade guild), 14
Committee for Scholarly Communication with the People's Republic of China (CSCPRC), 5
Communist Party, *see* Chinese Communist Party
Communist Party congresses: Thirteenth (1987), 2, 39–40, 175, 181; Fourteenth (Provincial) (1992), 229; Fourteenth (1992), 231
Communist takeover (1949), 15; impact in Guangzhou, 18, 52; as anti-urban, 55–56
Communist Youth League, 188
Community property, in marriage, 107–8
Confucianism, 98–103, 137, 141–44, 181
Confucius, 174
Consumer goods: availability of, 54, 56, 62, 94–95; types of, 64–66; ownership of, 76–78

Correspondence (*jidu*) school students, 155
Corruption, 3, 188, 213–14
Courtship, modern, 110–18
Cremation, 132–36 *passim*, 257
Crime and crime rate, 3, 27, 37–38, 43, 182–83
Crimes, definition of, 33–40
Cultural Revolution, 2, 4, 15–16, 38, 43, 52, 57, 86, 145–48, 149, 207, 223f, 237, 246; and religion, 87, 132, 135, 149, 258; and employment, 178, 185, 199, 204
Customs officials, 63–64

Danwei, see Work units
Day care, 127, 150, 205
Daylight saving time, 72
Death: official reporting of, 44; and filial obligations and rituals, 132–36, 250; and euthanasia issues, 294n17
Death penalty, *see* Capital punishment
Decollectivization, 58–61
Definitive Cantonese population, 21–22
Democratization, 268
Deng Xiaoping, 3–4, 39, 55, 163, 175, 208, 235, 264
Disabilities, *see* Handicapped population
Dispute mediation: public, 30–33, 53; among family members and neighbors, 45, 121–23, 210; in marriages, 103f
Divorce, 45, 102–5, 109
Dongshan district, 23, 70, 84
"Double Nine" holiday, 259–60
Dragon Boat Festival, 143, 249, 258–59
Dramas, on television, 239–48
Drivers' licenses, 68–69
Durable goods, *see* Consumer goods

Eastern Network (cable), 227, 235
Eating practices, 28–29. *See also* Cantonese cuisine
Education, 15, 110; of children of illegal residents, 27; goals and curriculum for, 140f, 156, 161–62, 164–65, 169, 175f; funding and fees for, 141, 150–56 *passim*; 167–72 *passim*; in preschool (*you'eryuan*), 141, 149–54, 206; history of, 141–48; higher, 146, 166–67, 168–75, 204–5, 265; in middle school (*zhongxue*), 146f, 148–49, 161–68,

281n43; contemporary, 148–49; in key-point (*zhongdian*) schools, 148–49, 159, 161, 165; in elementary schools, 154–61; correspondence schools, 155
Education Department, 150, 153, 159
Elderly population: author's study of, 5; social welfare for, 49–52, 210, 267; impact of 1980 Marriage Law on, 106–9; remarriage among, 109, 131; adult children of, 128–36; and gambling, 225. *See also* Pensions; Retirement
Electrical power, 72–73
Elementary school education, 154–61
Employment: and job security, 177; of youth, 178–83, 220; substitution policy (*dingti*) in, 179–80, 185; labor contract system of, 180, 190, 191–92, 201, 220; in the private sector, 180–83; legislation and reforms, 181, 185–94; current patterns of, 214–20. *See also* Labor force; Sick leave; Worker productivity
Enterprise reforms, 61–67
Entrepreneurship: and wealth, 20–21; in agriculture, 60, 180; among excess laborers, 62–63; and population control, 126; and employment opportunities, 180–83
Evictions, of tenants, 87
Examinations, for government service, 143–44
Exchange marriages, 104
Executions, *see* Capital punishment
Expenditure patterns, by household, 74–78
Exports, 14, 16
Extramarital affairs, 105–6

Family: disputes in, 45, 121–23, 139, 210; Confucian norms of, 98–103, 137; Communist regulation of, 103–9, 136–39; urban versus rural, 109–10
Family planning, *see* Birth control; One-child family policy
Family Planning Regulations of Guangdong province (1980), 106
Fangcun district, 24
Fengshui, 132
Festivals and official holidays: traditional festivals, 143, 249, 258–60; Qingming, 249, 255–58; Spring Festival, 249, 250–55; state control of, 249–50; official holidays, 260–61

Five City Family Study (CASS), 110, 116, 118–21, 127f, 282n6
Five Guarantees (rural welfare plan), 276n45
Food, *see* Cantonese cuisine
Food subsidies, 59, 74
Foreign currency, 15, 214
Foreigners, 9, 16: as investors, 2f, 16f, 20, 183, 263, 267; in Pearl River Delta, 4; historical contact with, 12–14; restrictions on, 14f, 207–8; diplomatic relations with PRC, 16; impact in entertainment industries, 223–24, 235, 238, 261–62
Fourteenth Party Congress (1992), 231
Fourteenth (Provincial) Party Congress (1992), 229
Friendship Store, 15, 70
Funerals, 132–33, 134, 250

Gambling, 225
Gang of Four, 147. *See also* Cultural Revolution
Gangs (*heishe*), and crime, 38–39
Garbage and littering, 28, 31–32, 55
Garden Hotel, 70
Gender hierarchy, 101–2, 136
Geti hu (individual household or entrepreneur), 182
Ghosts, 132
Government service, education for, 142–43
Grain rations, 26f, 77
Great Leap Forward, 185
Guangdong Academy of Social Sciences (GASS), 5
Guangdong province: economic reform movement in, 4
Guangdong Radio, 233
Guangdong Television (GDTV), 11–12, 69, 227, 234–36, 238, 243, 245, 262. *See also* Television
Guangzhou (Canton): description and history of, 4, 7–17; trade and industry in, 17, 20, 52; population of, 17–23; administrative divisions of (*Guangzhou Shi*), 23–27; urban life in, 23–41; neighborhood organization of, 27, 42–52; housing lottery in, 85; 1995 survey of residents in, 95–96; quality of life in, 264

Guangzhou City Construction Development General Corporation (GCCDGC), 83f
Guangzhou Civil Affairs Bureau, 46, 49–50, 132
Guangzhou Daily (*Guangzhou Ribao*), 229, 231–33
Guangzhou Economic and Technological Development Zone, 24
Guangzhou Family Study, 5, 13, 15, 20; residents committees in, 42; residence patterns, 86–87, 90f, 93, 223; inheritance disputes in, 108; urban family life in, 110, 122–23, 223; modern marriage practices in, 119–22; care of elderly in, 129–31; funeral practices in, 133–35; retirement in, 179; employment patterns in, 215–20, 221
Guangzhou Housing Management Bureau (HMB): control of housing by, 57, 80, 86, 91, 93, 207; rent schedule of, 80, 86f; statistics on housing from, 88
Guangzhou municipality (*Guangzhou Shi*), 23–27
Guangzhou Suihua House Property Development Company, 279n33
Guangzhou Television (GZTV), 16, 234, 236, 239
Guangzhou Trade Fair, *see* Chinese Export Commodities Fair (Canton Trade Fair)
Guangzhou University, 167–68
Guanxi, 20, 189
Guoying (state-operated) enterprises, 3
Guoyou (national) enterprises, 3

Haizhu district, 24, 68, 125, 206
Hakka population, 22
Han Chinese, 7, 12, 17–18, 21–23
Handicapped population, 46–49, 125
Health insurance, 129, 177, 194, 197–99, 210f, 265
Hepatitis, 29
Heshang (television documentary), 227–28
Hobbies, 225
Hokkien dialect, 101
Hong (official trade agents), 14
Hong Kong, 4, 17, 20, 39, 58, 64, 119, 124, 133, 195, 227, 233, 235, 238, 270
"Hong Kong 1982/1983/1984" (television program), 245–46

"Hong Kong in Turmoil" (television drama), 236
Hongmian flowers, 11–12
Household expenditure patterns, 74–78
Household (*hukou*) registration system, 4, 7, 25–27, 44, 209
Housing, 16, 25, 79–83, 232; restoration of home ownership rights, 27, 54, 78, 85–88; changes in average living space, 55, 78–79; under Communist control, 57–58; and real estate development, 83–85, 266; public housing reform, 88–90; and migration, 90–94; impact on marriage, 119–21; *danwei* control of, 206
Huaisheng Mosque, 12–13
Huanghuagang Park, 273n2
Huangpu district, 24
Hui (Muslims), 13, 17
Hui Nationality Elementary School, 13
"Hungry Ghosts" Festival, 249, 259

Ideology: role in reform movement, 2f; and traditional values, 97; and education, 176
Immorality, 33–34
Imperial China, education in, 141–44
Income: growing gap in, 3, 268–69; increases in, 54, 59, 74, 185, 263–64; and wage reforms, 185–88, 220; subsidies of, 195–97, 215. *See also* Minimum wage
Indecent assault, 34
Infanticide, 101
Infrastructure, impact of reform on, 67–73
Inheritance Law of 1985, 103, 107–9, 136
Intestate property settlements, 107

Jankowiak, William, 30, 33f
Jiating (Family; magazine), 138
Jiedao Kindergarten, 152–54, 158
Jinan University, 170
Jintie (work-related subsidies), 196, 215
Joint economic ventures, Chinese-foreign, 17, 20, 183, 188, 195, 203, 209–10, 267

Kapok flowers (*hongmian*), 11–12
Karaoke bars, 246–47

Keypoint (*zhongdian*) schools, 148–49, 159, 161, 165
Kowloon Walled City (Hong Kong), 280n42

Labor company facilitation, 190–91
Labor Department, 159
Labor force, 16–17, 56, 101; migrant workers in, 24–25, 60–61; urban versus rural, 26–27; and handicapped workers, 46f, 267, 291n39; childless members of, 49–50, 51–52; mobility of, 110, 192–94, 204–5, 213, 217–18, 266; unions, 181; and worker motivation, 185–87; "second-job fever" in, 187, 222, 264; recruitment and retention of, 188–92; redundancy in, 194, 204. *See also* Employment; Income; Worker productivity
Labor protection legislation, 181, 266
Languages: Cantonese, 5, 18–20, 22f, 64, 227, 233, 235f; *putonghua*, 18–20, 64, 227f, 233–36, 243; dialects, 18f, 21f, 101
Law on Safeguarding the Legal Rights of the Disabled (1991), 46–47
Leisure time, 222f, 261
Li Dongdong, 104–13 *passim*, 137
Lingnan (television channel), 234f
Li Peng, 238–39
Li population, 12
Literacy, 148
Liwan district, 22f, 70, 201
Lixiu cadres, privileging of, 93, 146, 198, 201

Macao, 14, 17, 39, 133
Malaysia, 119, 124
Mandarin dialect, 18f
Mao Zedong, 1, 97, 145–47, 223. *See also* Cultural Revolution
Marriage: Confucian norms of, 99–100; minimum age at, 103, 106, 119, 137; Communist regulation of, 103–9; and modern courtship, 110–18; modern practices in, 118–28
Marriage Law of 1950, 103, 136
Marriage Law of 1980, 103–7, 109, 136
Martial arts dramas, on television, 239–43
Marxism, 174, 176
Mass media: television, 3, 16, 19, 77, 158, 222, 234–48; newspapers, 222, 228–

33; radio, 222, 233–34; impact of reforms on, 222–23, 226–28
Maternity leave, 127, 194
Mediation, *see* Dispute mediation
Medical care: and health insurance, 129, 177, 194, 197–99, 265; free (*gungfei yiliao*), 197–98, 265
Medical insurance, *see* Health insurance
Meritocracy, 143, 145, 172
Miao population, 12
Mid-Autumn Festival, 249
Migrant workers, 24–25, 60–61
Migration: rural to urban, 26–27, 58; and housing, 90–94; and family life, 110, 118–19
Min dialect, 22
Minimum wage, 266f
Moonlighting, 187
"Morning Show, The" (GZTV), 69, 173, 235
"Mother" (television drama), 243–45
Motorcycles, regulation of, 69
Movies, 223–24
MTV (Music Television) Asia, 228
Municipal Education Bureau, 13
Municipal Planning Bureau, 12, 24

Nanfang Department Store, 55, 62, 218
Nanfang Ribao (*Southern Daily*), 104, 228–31, 232, 262
Nanhai prefecture, 12
National character, 97
National Day, 260
National Day for Aiding the Disabled, 47
Neighborhood patrols, 43–44
Newspapers, 222, 228–33
News programs, on television, 238–39
Nonagricultural (*feinongye*) population, 26
North America, Chinese laborers in, 14–15
Nurseries (*tuo'ersuo*), 150

Official holidays, 260–61
Olympics School, 157
One-child family policy, 5, 44–45, 49, 124–25, 127–28, 137–38, 209
"One Hundred Life Events" (television drama), 114–16, 117–18, 245–48, 262
Overseas Chinese New Village, 15, 86

Overseas Chinese Property Development Company (OCPDC), 83–84

Patrilineal descent, 98–99, 132
Patrilocal residence, 98–99, 101–2, 119–21, 137
Peach blossoms, symbolism of, 252
Pearl (television channel), 234f, 243
Pearl River: silting of, 8
Pearl River Delta, 4, 17, 60, 227
Pensions, 129, 177, 194–95, 199–202, 210, 220, 265ff. *See also* Retirement
People's Republic of China (PRC), 4, 16, 18, 199, 260
Personal hygiene: and human waste, 28; and eating practices, 28–29, 48
Planned birth certificates, 126
Population: regional differentiation of, 18–21; intraprovincial differentiation of, 21–23; agricultural, 26. *See also* Elderly population; Handicapped population; *and individual ethnic groups by name*
Population control, 106, 123–24. *See also* Birth control; One-child family policy
Pornography, 3, 33
Premarital sex, 110–12
Preschool (*you'eryuan*) education, 141, 149–54, 206
Privacy, 123, 206
Private markets, reestablishment of, 58–59
Private property rights, 16, 102, 107–9, 231
Property crimes, 36–37
Prostitution, 34, 35–36, 41, 101, 111, 113–16
Provisional Regulations of the People's Republic of China Concerning Private Enterprises (1988), 181
Public encounters: ordinary (daily), 28–33; extraordinary (immoral and criminal), 33–41
Public housing, 85, 88–90
Public Security Bureau: population statistics from, 23f; focus on public safety, 34, 61; traffic accident tallies by, 69
Public transportation, 29f, 70; impact of reform on, 68, 70
Puizheng Middle School, 232
Putonghua (official national language), 18–20, 64, 227f, 233–36, 243

Qianlong Emperor, 14
Qin Dynasty (221–206 B.C.), 12
Qing Dynasty (1644–1911), 12, 133, 141f, 144, 150
Qingming, 249, 255–58
Qingping Road market, 10

Radio, 222, 233–34
Ram, symbolism of, 11
Ram City Evening News (Yangcheng Wanbao), 11, 90, 217, 229, 294n12
Ram City Traffic (radio), 234
Rape, 34f, 41
Rationing, 56–57, 59, 205, 209, 222
Real estate development, 83–85
Red Guards, 15–16, 38, 178, 198, 249
Reform movement, 1–3, 264; in Guangdong, 4; impact of, 16–17, 54–58; influence on residents committees, 43; and changes in financing, 184–85; and changes in labor practices, 185–94; and changes in welfare policy, 194–202
Religious worship, 249–50
Renmin Road, 70
Republican China (1912–49), education in, 141
Residents committees, 4, 42–52, 155
Retirement, 179, 194, 199–202, 210–17 *passim*, 225, 267. *See also* Pensions

Sanitation, *see* Garbage and littering; Personal hygiene
Satellite Television Asia Region (Star TV), 228, 238
Scams and swindles, 37, 182–83
Self-employment, *see* Entrepreneurship
Sexual harassment, 34–35, 251–52
Sexual offenses, 34–35
Shamian Island, 14
Shenzhen Special Economic Zone, 20, 66, 193, 215, 267
Shenzhen University, 167–68
Shiqu (city districts), 23
Short subject television shows, 237–38
Sibling hierarchy, 100–101, 137
Sick leave, 177, 194, 291n39
Silk Road of the Sea, 12
Silver River Revolutionary Public Graveyard, 256
Singapore, 119, 124

Sixth National Games (1987), 11, 61, 205, 227
Smuggling, 63–64, 216
Snake Food Restaurant, 9
Social control, 207–10. *See also* Dispute mediation: public
Socialism, Chinese, 1–3, 18, 78, 145, 174, 263
Socialist market economy, 3, 6, 140f, 177, 263
Social welfare, 2, 46–52, 177, 194–202, 210
Song Dynasty, 234
South China Construction College, 168, 170
South China Engineering University, 170
South China Teacher Training University, 157, 167, 170
Southern Daily (Nanfang Ribao), 104, 228–31, 232, 262
Soviet Union, 25, 268
Special Economic Zones (SEZs), 20, 218
Spiritual pollution, 3, 37, 174
Spring Festival, 249, 250–55
Star Plus (entertainment), 228
State Council: and housing reform, 89f; and entrepreneurship, 180; and labor reform, 194; and pension reform, 201
Sterilization, 44–45, 117–18
Street (*jiedao*) committees ("wards"), 4, 7, 42, 126, 150, 152, 181, 189
Subway line, 70
Sun Yatsen, 273n2
Surname exogamy, 102

Taiji (shadowboxing), 225
Taiping Rebellion, 273n2
Taishan county, 14–15
Taishanese subdialect, 21
Taiwan, 17, 119, 124, 133, 238, 270
Tanka population, 22–23
Tax incentives, 47, 194
Teachers, 142–47 *passim*, 175, 187; in preschools, 153–54; in elementary school, 157, 159–60; in middle school, 165; in higher education, 170
Tebie kunnan ("exceptional hardship") households, 85, 267–68
Telephone service, 71–72
Television: access to, 5, 16, 77, 227–28;

language use on, 19, 227f, 234–35, 236, 243; exposure to information via, 158; impact of reforms on, 222, 234–48; short subject and variety shows, 237–38; news on, 238–39; dramas on, 239–48. *See also individual television programs by title*
10,000-Yuan Households, 60
Thirteenth Party Congress (1987), 2, 39–40, 175, 181
Tiananmen Massacre (June 4 Incident), 174–75, 208, 227f, 268
Tianhe district, 24, 84
Tianhe Stadium, 24
Toilets: public, 28; in houses, 79, 81, 83
Traffic accidents, resolution of, 30–31

Unemployment, *see* Employment
Unemployment compensation, 193–94, 266
Urban anthropology, 4
Urbanization, Chinese, 23–41, 109–10

"Valiant Woman, The" (television drama), 239–42
Variety shows, on television, 237
Vocational technical (*zhiye jishu*) education, 140, 142, 163–64, 166, 175, 190
Vogel, Ezra F., 5, 14, 16, 21, 221
Volunteerism, 43, 146

Wages, *see* Income
"*Wan, xi, shao*" policy, 124
Weddings, 250
Welfare, *see* Social welfare
West River, 8
White Swan Hotel, 70

Widows, 131
Women: sexual harassment of, 34–35, 251–52; employment discrimination against, 191
Women's Day, 260–61
Women's Federation, 103, 135, 138, 260
Worker productivity, 177, 184, 220
Work information stations, for handicapped workers, 47
Work units (*danwei*), 177, 202–14, 224
World Bank, 58, 79, 83, 89
Wu dialect, 19

Xiamen Special Economic Zone, 20
Xian (counties), 23
Xiang dialect, 19

Yangcheng (City of Rams), 11
Yangcheng Wanbao (*Ram City Evening News*), 11, 90, 217, 229, 294n12
Yao population, 12
Yuan Dynasty (1279–1368), 13
Yue dialect, 19
Yuexiu district, 23, 70, 84, 253
Yuexiu Park, 8, 11f, 35

Zhongshan Medical College, 206
Zhongshan University, 5, 71, 171, 224; impact of Cultural Revolution at, 147–48; admission and fees for, 167–68, 170; Soviet reorganization of, 169; as a *danwei*, 202, 206
Zhou Dynasty, 11
Zhuang population, 12
Zhuhai Special Economic Zone, 20, 193, 267

Library of Congress Cataloging-in-Publication Data

Ikels, Charlotte.
The return of the god of wealth : the transition to a market
economy in urban China / Charlotte Ikels.
   p. cm.
Includes bibliographical references and index.
ISBN 0-8047-2580-2 (alk. paper). — ISBN 0-8047-2581-0 (pbk. :
alk. paper)
1. Canton (China) — Economic policy. 2. Canton (China) — Economic
conditions. 3. Mixed economy — China — Canton. I. Title.
HC428.C34I38 1996   95-34237   CIP

⊗ This book is printed on acid-free, recycled paper.

Original printing 1996

Last figure below indicates year of this printing

05 04 03 02 01 00 99 98 97 96